Penelope Farmer was born in Kent. She read history at Oxford University, followed by a postgraduate diploma in social studies at London University. Apart from spells as a teacher and a brief period of doing sociological research, she has spent most of her working life writing fiction for children and adults. Her books include *Charlotte Sometimes* (1969) – inspiration for the song of the same name by the rock group, The Cure; *Eve Her Story* (1985); *Glasshouses* (1988); *Snakes and Ladders* (1994) and two previous anthologies: *The Virago Book of Twins and Doubles* (1996) and *Sisters* (1999). She has two grown-up children and lives sometimes reluctantly, but mostly happily, in London.

Also by Penelope Farmer

THE VIRAGO BOOK OF TWINS AND DOUBLES

THE VIRAGO BOOK OF

Grandmothers

An Autobiographical Anthology

Written and edited by
PENELOPE FARMER

Virago

A *Virago* Book

Published by Virago Press 2000

First published in Great Britain by Virago 2002

This collection and introduction copyright © Penelope Farmer 2000

Acknowledgements on pp. 405-11 constitute an extension of this copyright page

The moral right of the author has been asserted

A CIP catalogue record for this book
is available from the British Library.

ISBN 1 86049 848 5

Typeset in Berkeley by M Rules
Printed and bound in Great Britain by
Bookmarque Ltd, Croydon, Surrey

Virago
An imprint of
Time Warner Books UK
Brettenham House
Lancaster Place
London WC2E 7EN

www.virago.co.uk

CONTENTS

ACKNOWLEDGEMENTS

As usual with anthologies, I picked the brains of everyone in sight, quite shamelessly, from the moment I embarked on this one. It is impossible to acknowledge all my informants therefore; not least I can't always remember where some suggestions came from. Apologies and many thanks to those I cannot name here. To some, however, I owe more particular thanks. First and foremost to my father, Hugh Farmer, whom I pestered over many long lunches for memories of his mother, my grandmother, and also to my cousin, Roger Parker Jervis, who lent me my grandmother's diary and wrote me a long and instructive letter about his memories of her. I turned to Colin Tudge, as usual, for zoological material. David Rhodes told me about his grandmother. Ann Thwaite reminded me of Tennyson's poem and sent me the piece by Jill Paton Walsh first printed in her anthology, *Allsorts*. Judith Keenlyside suggested Frances Partridge. I owe huge thanks to Shelagh Duckham Cox and Lauris Edmonds for their wonderful contributions, freely offered and made. I am equally grateful to Phyllida Law and Shirley Hughes in London; to Nelly, Beryle, Pat, Florrie, Doris, Jean and Erica, of Bishop's Court in Northfield, Birmingham; to the two Mrs Lees, Mrs Wong and Mrs Chen, of Connaught Gardens, also in Birmingham, for letting me interview them at length for their experience of grandmotherhood. Erica Clarkson not only contributed to the Birmingham discussion, but got her group of grandmothers together. Wai-Ling Bickerton organised the Chinese group and together with her colleague, Raymond Wong, acted as interpreter during their sessions. Many thanks to them, as to Nick Moreton, who set up the Birmingham interviews – and in particular suggested the Chinese group. Thanks to him, also, more personally, for his reading of the early drafts of the introductions. His comments helped sharpen my ideas considerably. Thanks, too, to my daughter, Clare Mockridge, for an insight which led to the writing of the Afterword.

I thank, as usual, my wonderful agent, Deborah Owen, and my editor at Virago, Lennie Goodings, for their support and help throughout. One final and much sadder acknowledgement: Lauris Edmonds died suddenly in February of this year, for which reason I dedicate this anthology to her memory, as well as to the memory of the many lost grandmothers in my own family.

THE VIRAGO BOOK OF

Grandmothers

EPIGRAPHS

What everyone needs in the millennium is access to the Internet and a grandmother.

Quoted to P. Farmer, source unknown

———————

The survival of so many men and women into old age has led one observer to suggest that grandparents were invented in New England. Few ordinary Englishmen of that period ever lived to see their grandchildren . . . By comparison, it seems likely that grandparent–grandchild relationships were relatively widespread and at least potentially close in New England.

THOMAS COLE, The Journey of Life, 1992

———————

The grandmother's tenderness towards the grandchild and that of the grandchild towards the grandmother must be regarded not as a product of civilisation but a general trait of the human soul . . .

H. PLOSS AND M. BUTELS, *Das Weib*, 1827

I love love love being a grandmother. Children are all about love and innocence . . . Being with them is incredibly creative . . .

DONNA KARAN, *Observer Life*, 1996

This is the first time in history the average married couple has more parents than children . . . Active involvement in child rearing is likely to be over by the time women are grandparents. The extent to which this has made grandmotherhood a more distinct role has not been fully explored.

G. HAGESTEAD, 'Women and Grandparents as Kin-keepers', 1986

If old parents become objects of scorn and pity, all generations suffer.

Source unknown

Your children are your principal; your grandchildren are your interest . . .

Quoted in A. J. CHERLIN AND F. F. FURSTENBERG,
The New American Grandparent, 1992

_____

My mother-in-law said to me, 'You are a tree without fruit. I want profits. Children come with labour pains, but grandchildren are pure profit.'

Source unknown

_____

A mother never stops battling – even for grandchildren.

ISOBEL WHITE, DIANE BARWICK AND BETTY MEEHAM,
Fighters and Singers, 1985

_____

I learned from my grandmother how to be loved, and therefore how to be loving.

JILL PATON WALSH, personal communication

_____

There's no one quite like Grandma, and I know you will agree
She always is a friend to you, and she's a friend to me.

GORDON LORENZ, 'There's No One Quite Like Grandma', 1980

_____

Ye cannae shove your granny off a bus.
Ye cannae shove your granny off a bus.
Ye cannae shove your granny for she's your mammy's
  mammy,
Ye cannae shove your granny off a bus . . .

Anon., Scots Traditional, c. 1920

INTRODUCTION

The phone rang at around four a.m., in May 1996. It was unexpected only in one way: I'd awaited this for the seven months since I'd been told, and agitated over it for sixteen hours and more. 'We've had a beautiful little girl,' cried my daughter's partner. And I'd been assuming from the day my daughter announced her pregnancy that it would be a beautiful little boy. I suspect the reverse of wishful thinking; if you expect what you don't want, then you might get what you do. And I wanted a granddaughter above all.

The arrival of any grandchild with all its appendages and faculties intact would have overwhelmed me, gender no matter. But the idea of, let alone the actuality of, three extant generations of females had – has – a particular resonance and poignancy in my family. Indeed grandmotherhood has a resonance and poignancy all on its own for us. Let me explain. On my mother's side of the family I am the first natural grandmother in four generations; the step-grandmothers who took their places were not at all the same thing. My great-grandmother died young of some unspecified ailment. My grandmother fell downstairs when my mother was three. Though my children's grandmother, my mother, did live long enough to see my brother's son, she died aged fifty-three of what we now know to be inherited breast cancer, a year before the arrival of my own first child, my daughter. In my generation, my twin sister succumbed aged fifty-one to the same inheritance, eighteen months after writing in her diary of her longing to see her grandchildren. It has left me on my own, starting from nothing, with no tradition to follow, avoid, live up to, improve on. With no idea really what a grandmother is – let alone how to be one. Part of the impetus for putting together this book has been, undoubtedly, the need to invent grandmotherhood for myself by one means or another.

I did know my other grandmother, my father's mother. But father's mothers aren't always as significant as mother's mothers. Moreover, our paternal grandmother was eighty-eight when my twin and I were born, and died when we were eight, which gave us little chance of developing a relationship. Even to my father she had been more like a grandmother than a mother. He was born when she was already fifty and my grandfather sixty years old, his arrival a surprise to everyone, not least his parents. Since my grandmother had spent most of her pregnancy sitting on a sofa wrapped in discreet shawls, as one could in 1907, the first most people knew of it was a telegram announcing that Emmy had given birth to a red-headed son. (I never saw any trace of red in my adult father's hair. But since these things go down through the generations I could not help remembering the story when my grand-daughter's hair turned out auburn – I hoped that this inheritance, and not just that from *her* father's family, had some bearing.)

Thus my grandmother was more like a great-grandmother to my twin sister and me, neatly fitting many of the stereotypes we younger grandmothers object to. I remember her clad in black from head to foot, a black choker round her neck, silver hair piled up on her head, and sitting very upright on a sofa in our sitting-room holding a cane. I can't remember her knitting, but she must have done, because I do remember the sweaters she knitted for us, pink-striped and in very scratchy wool, the discomfort of which remains much more vivid to me than my grandmother. Disguised as Tweedledum and Tweedledee in those very sweaters and two cricketing caps of my father's, my twin and I won first prize for fancy dress at the local Whitsun gala.

Everything else I know of my grandmother comes from stories. My mother's story, for instance, of being asked by my grandmother not to wear shorts because 'Dad' (my grandfather) didn't like it. Only to be asked by 'Dad' next day why she wasn't wearing her nice shorts. (Granny's insistence on 'Dad's' embarrassment when he met my mother on her way to the lavatory – couldn't she pretend she was going somewhere else? – was probably nearer the truth.) Then there were the stories round my grandmother's loathing for what she called 'Abroad' – that is, anything across the English Channel. According to my father she crossed it twice. The first time – a disaster – was on her honeymoon; the second, fifty years later, in her seventies. Having for no obvious reason rented a house in Normandy for a family holiday, she spent the overnight Channel crossing sitting upright, fully dressed in hat and coat, in case the boat sank. The clothes were to help her float.

But then my grandmother, born in 1857, was quintessentially both English and Victorian – more stereotypes. I've only learned recently from much older cousins how lively and energetic she also was; a prodigious hostess who expected everyone she entertained to overeat. The provisioning grandmother – as in the yiddisher '*Ess, mein kind*' variety – is one that we will encounter frequently. That my own grandmother was just such a one I only found out by embarking on this book. As indeed I learned – with some delight, given its hint of the faintly disreputable absent in all other accounts of her – of the flask of whisky my grandmother kept secreted in her handbag, and with which she doctored her frequent cups of milkless tea. Preferring our tea black is something my father and I have in common with her. This grandmother, on the other hand, prefers to take her whisky neat.

Something else came into my hands in the course of researching; my grandmother's diary for the year she was nineteen. It is a document alarmingly innocent and tedious, centred round church, garden and kitchen; 'Today is the fifth anniversary of my confirmation' is as dramatic as it gets. Such confessions are interspersed with accounts of choir practice, occasional picnics in the company of local worthies and some of her many brothers and sisters (the menus, given in full, are consistent with her image as provider later) and visits to the dentist in York who replaced all her front teeth with false ones before she was twenty. A life more different from my nineteen-year-old one, let alone my daughter's, can hardly be imagined.

Of course I only knew my other grandmother as youthful. A portrait of her painted when she was in her very early twenties, which used to hang above the sitting-room in my parents' house, disappeared to Australia for twenty years with my younger sister but now stares down on me in bed. These days, to me, she looks absurdly young. The mistake of the freight company official asked to trace her at the start of her visit to Australia, who reported that there was no portrait of a grandmother, only one of a young woman, was excusable; who doesn't forget that grandmothers used to be young?

Until I read her diary I never thought of my aged, black-clad paternal grandmother as anything but old, either. This is why, at a time when I was still getting to grips with the idea of myself as grandmother, when I was still feeling, in some respects, more connected to my own nineteen- or twenty-year-old self than to such an image, her diary felt so significant. It fitted with the reflections I had on observing that newborn scrap in the arms of a woman I had given birth to, and held as an equally newborn scrap myself, no time ago at all. Oh, the heart-breaking brevity of it! *Sic transit*. Like my once nineteen-year-old grandmother, so early gone; like my silver-haired other granny; like my almost as long dead mother; like myself in time to come and in due course like this same tiny, mewling thing, my granddaughter.

That matter of mortality is something I imagine grandmothers through all ages have encountered most poignantly at the birth of their first grandchild. But it's possible that it's only more recently that they have had to rethink, even invent the role of grandmother, the way my generation has had to. Given my lack of role models, my problem may be particularly acute. But all of us find it bemusing to some extent, judging by the flood of books on grandparenting that have appeared over the past few years. Stereotypes there may be still; but they are, thank god, no longer prescriptive. Nor indeed, for reasons I shall discuss later, can we depend on enjoying the advantages of achieving such a status. The term 'grandmother' suggests redundancy rather than respect. Even those of us who look grandmotherly in the stereotypical sense don't expect to have seats given up for us on tube trains, let alone to be respected for our wisdom and experience.

But there are other factors at work here. First and foremost, demography; we live longer, obviously. Unless they have some genetic misfortune as in our family, women now are more likely than in the past to live to see their grandchildren and even their great-grandchildren. Children in their turn are more likely to have grandparents throughout their childhood and on into adult life, and even to see both sets of them. A child born in 1900 would have had a one-in-four chance of having two sets of grandparents at birth. By 1976, that figure was two out of three. And the numbers whose grandmothers survive their childhood has risen at a comparable rate. Something like half of all those over sixty-five belong to families spanning four generations. My own family spans four generations – my grandchildren have a great-grandfather; one a great-grandmother, also.

There have always been, of course, some grandmothers around. Homer and Euripides' Hecuba, mother of Hector, wife of Priam, doomed king of Troy, may have had some factual basis. Livia, wife of the Emperor Augustus, grandmother of Claudius, certainly did. And so on, throughout history. These were powerful women; a higher standard of living helped them survive. Yet even among lesser mortals, there would always have been a few such. In the seventeenth century, John Locke's Alice George, whom he 'never heard speak one idle or impertinent word', claimed to be 108, and with an eldest son of seventy-seven couldn't have been much less.

I doubt that many of us in less patriarchal, less stratified societies regret the respect we no longer merit. The increase in our numbers makes us powerful in other ways. These days the marketing men are more inclined to woo us. If we get together, as in the American Grey Panthers, we may have political clout. At the same time, our traditional knowledge and experience is of little obvious use in a society where technology moves so fast that our grandchildren may have to teach us how to use it. 'My granddaughter showed me how to work the video. And she's only three,' said one of a group of grandmothers I interviewed in Birmingham.

And then there's this. I sit writing during the last three months of a century and a millennium in which I will have spent the greater part of my life. Our grandchildren's lives, on the other hand, particularly those of us relatively new grandparents, will be spent almost wholly in the new century and the new millennium. For them, their grandparents *are* the twentieth century; a fact at the heart of this book. In our century, war became, in Europe, the experience of the masses, at home and in conscripted armies. We grew up, often without fully realising, with the grief it generated in our parents and grandparents, as well as with the profound and ever more rapid social and technological change that resulted. We also grew up with the fear of nuclear weapons – the word 'H-bomb' that screamed from a newspaper headline when I was fourteen has haunted most of my adult life, at least. Our immediate fears of disease were driven away by antibiotics, only to be driven back these days, at least in anticipation, by antibiotic resistance. The sexual repression that made our fathers lock us up, relatively speaking, went out with the advent of the pill; even the fear of AIDS has not brought it back. All this, and the merits and demerits – the dis-eases – resulting, will form our grandchildren's new century. To say we grandparents are history is no insult. It is reality.

One thing in particular doesn't change. We may live longer, but in the end, we die the same as ever. No matter how young we may feel, becoming a grandparent is a significant waystation on that road; ageing and death are inevitable subtexts.

Which brings me to the content and form of the anthology that has resulted. The rather random oral material is one important thread; there are interviews with Phyllida Law and Shirley Hughes, with a group of grandmothers from a sheltered housing project in Birmingham (in no particular order, Nelly, Beryle, Pat, Florrie, Doris, Jean, Erica, Sheila) and with a Chinese group (Two Mrs Lees, Mrs Wong and Mrs Chen) from another sheltered housing project, also in Birmingham. There are also many comments from friends and contemporaries whose brains I picked. Two New Zealand writers, Lauris Edmonds and Shelagh Duckham Cox, interviewed each other on my behalf and mailed me the essays that resulted. The printed material comes from every possible source, not just literary and biographical, but anthropological, sociological, zoological – not all of my grandmothers are human. There's journalism, biography, children's fiction; there's even the odd academic abstract. Where I found more than one piece making the same point, I opted for the better written. But literary merit was far from the sole criterion. What mattered more was illumination of the subject; and that the material should range widely, geographically, chronologically and intellectually.

It is arranged in rough chronological order; beginning with the new grandmother, ending with the aged and dying one. In between, making no attempt to separate fact from fiction, science from literature, sociology from mythology, I've found useful and good grandmothers, traditional, unconventional amorous, powerful, and of course hellish or at least ambiguous ones, from Sleeping Beauty's mother-in-law to the Hopi Indian Spider Grandmother.

Though some of what I'm saying applies to grandfathers as well, there's little directly about grandfathers, I'm afraid. I'm not one, I've never had one, I don't know anything about grandfathers. What you see here is what I've got. All that remains to say, in good grandmotherly fashion, is: *Ess, meine kinder.* Enjoy. Enjoy.

PROLOGUE

from Blackberry Winter

In the presence of grandparent and grandchild, past and future merge in the present. Looking at a loved child, one cannot say, 'We must sacrifice this generation for the next. Many must die now so that later others may live.' This is the argument that generations of old men, cut off from children, have used in sending young men out to die in war. Nor can one say, 'I want this child to live well no matter how we despoil the earth for later generations.' For seeing a child as one's grandchild, one can visualize that same child as a grandparent, and with the eyes of another generation one can see other children, just as light-footed and vivid, as eager to learn and know and embrace the world, who must be taken into account – now. My friend Ralph Blum has defined the human unit of time as the space between a grandfather's memory of his own childhood and a grandson's knowledge of those memories as he heard about them. We speak a great deal about a human scale; we need also a human unit in which to think about time.

MARGARET MEAD, 1973

I

BECOMING A
GRANDMOTHER

The years before I became a grandmother had not been good for me. I'd experienced all three of what are considered the most stressful traumas in anyone's life. First, bereavement: my twin sister died. Second, divorce: my second marriage broke up. Third, a month before my grandchild was due, in direct consequence of trauma number two, I moved house. The prospect of new life emerging on, I hoped, a little overoptimistically, the far side of agony was total joy.

And it was joy. That had been predictable. As, perhaps, was the closeness of understanding that the physical reality of her pregnancy seemed to bring, if only temporarily, to the profound, precious but, as between all mothers and daughters, inevitably prickly friendship that my daughter and I contrive to sustain. I also expected the tricky redefining of relationships that the arrival of the child would mean not only between her and me but between her partner and me. What I had not predicted was the pain of these realignments. Nor how particularly volatile and painful my feelings would be. It was a relief to encounter Frances Partridge's wonderful account of the emotional roller-coaster she found herself on at the birth of her first grandchild; an account the more poignant because she, too, was emerging from a miasma of loss.

Birth may be commonplace; it remains extraordinary, ask any midwife. Birth of one's own children ought to be and is still more extraordinary than that of grandchildren. But when it is your own child you are so physically engaged in the process that the intensity experienced is a different kind of intensity to the one from which the space of a generation both removes and yet doubly binds you. The emotional binding is fraught with memory. Even the physical binding is far more powerful than you'd expect, though the stirring in your body is more diffuse, the event experienced in the head as much as the loins and breast. You experience the event rather as you observe joy and tragedy in books, plays, films, where the trivia of daily life can't mediate emotion in the comforting way it does in reality.

For what *is* our role here? This show belongs to our sons and daughters. We've had our show; life in its usual ruthless way moves on. I suppose it was the stark reality of that which was hitting me, not just lack of sleep, as I drove down to Bristol around 8 a.m. after my four-o'clock wake-up call. My first sight of the new generation moved me beyond words. As I gazed at the crumpled face of Eleanor Roser in my daughter's arms through the glass door of the maternity ward, I was filled with an ecstasy of an exhausting and bewildering kind. At the same time, the locked door, the notices forbidding me entrance, drove the other messages home still harder. They are messages I suspect I would have had to absorb the hard way, even had I, like Sheila Kitzinger, been allowed to cradle my labouring daughter in the birthing pool. (Any leanings I might have had in that direction had been swiftly suppressed, not just because of my daughter's views on such matters. With experience of new grandmothers and new fathers fighting – literally – in the labour ward, the Bristol maternity unit permits either but not both to attend the birth.)

The messages are right and have to be listened to. But knowing that in advance did not stop the next few days being simultaneously the most joyful and most painful of my life. The more painful, I think, precisely because the grandparents' lack of obvious status and function is as much a feature of life after the birth as during it. This present – an unimagined future for us in the days of our own childbearing – is another country; they do things differently here. The technology is different not least; no one needed my skill at wrestling with safety-pins and terry-towelling nappies (not that it was ever great).

Once, it was daughters-in-law who were minefields in matters of childcare; now when, as most of my interviewees told me, parents have become interchangeable, fathers as much part of infant care as mothers, the tensions apply equally to those once temporarily ousted figures, the sons-in-law. Of which the fights on the Bristol labour ward are, presumably, one manifestation. An abiding memory of the ten days I spent around the newly made family was the sight of the health visitor, my daughter and her partner engaged in an animated discussion of the colour of my granddaughter's shit.

I am not a domestic animal. Nor by nature am I meek and retiring. But since I'd decided from the beginning that my only function was to enable the new family to put itself together, I spent those ten days cooking, cleaning, washing up. When asked, but only when asked, thanking them meekly for the privilege, I cuddled the baby and indulged my as yet one-sided love affair with her. In between I retired to my room. All this I'd planned. I'd also expected to feel bemused, and ecstatically in love with the baby – and through her, her parents. But I had not expected to feel so lonely. My newly single status had something to do with it; but it was by no means just that. I found myself wondering, often, if my mother would have felt the same thing at the birth of my daughter. I suspect she might. That she hadn't been there to find out for herself was another part of my pain, which also made me weep, in this case not for the first time.

Things have levelled out since. Now her parents are only too delighted to hand Ellie over to me. She is still the love of my life. But another love has been added, my son's daughter, whose birth, for me, was quite a different experience, and not just because it wasn't my daughter giving birth. The comments of almost all the grandmothers quoted here confirm that it is only with the arrival of the first grandchild that the conflicting emotions around grandmotherhood appear in full force, and that the first grandchild remains special, even when, over the years, another grandchild has grown closer. What was new to me in the arrival of the second child was the emotion I felt at the sight of my son's tenderness with the truly tiny creature he'd engendered. My daughter-in-law having had a Caesarean, he had to take on the major part of baby care at first. To see his hands, ridiculously out of proportion to Emily's midget limbs, changing her nappies so deftly and tenderly made me tearful, yet again. To be moved watching my daughter care for her child was expected. But I hadn't expected this.

Delight then; a delight shared, along with the bemusement very often, by all those whose words I use in this section of the book. Gushing over her new status as grandmother was all poor Queen Victoria could do; her daughter immured in Prussia, it was over a year before she even got to see her grandchild. Not much over forty at the time, she could well say 'that no one could believe she was a grandmother', unlike that usually stern literary figure, George Sand, who came to grandmotherhood much later in her life, and who, also unlike the poor Queen, was allowed, as a grandmother, to be thoroughly hands on. Her pleasure seemed in no way abated by her particularly rough experience of one of the less touted delights of grandchildren, namely grandparental susceptibility to their frequent ailments. She suffered not just from the head colds inflicted on most of us, but also, in her late sixties, from a bout of whooping cough.

None of these nineteenth-century figures, of course, discuss how they are to conduct themselves as grandmothers. That is a twentieth-century affair, still more so, I dare say, in this new millennium. Profound social change is one reason, particularly in the status of women and their relations with men. Even in the 1940s, long before the majority of women went out to work and many men expected to share childcare, there were comments that women didn't need their mothers as much because their relations with their husbands were so much closer. Often, they had to need them less, because, due to increased mobility, parents no longer lived close by. With reduced contact, relationships with grandchildren had to be reinvented somewhat. Add changes in diet, notions of discipline and structure of family life, even the intrusion of the media into every home, and what used to be invaluable knowledge held by the older women was no longer of value; the younger women had rather, or thought they had, far more to teach *them*.

This doubt and uncertainty, felt by everyone I interviewed, is reflected in all the written sources. Feminism has led to a huge increase in self-consciousness, particularly among what you might call the Virago generation, for whom every female waystation, formerly the private knowledge of women, experienced rather than articulated, became the source of discussion, analysis, newspaper articles, fiction. Menstruation; our sex lives; childbirth; relations with spouses; child rearing; the angst parents feel around teenagers; as we aged, even that particularly sticky subject, the menopause, ceased to be taboo. And now arrived at grandmotherhood, we not only find ourselves anatomising every feeling we have about it, we also feel obliged to find a way of inventing, containing our grandparental role.

We should be grateful to Margaret Mead for pointing out what a strain on us it is not to be able to take ourselves for granted in any way; having to 'edit ourselves', as Phyllida Law, one of my interviewees, put it. I'm grateful, too, to another woman, much less known and now forgotten, the Quaker leader Hannah Whitall Smith, whose advice from a more self-effacing view of women is so unassuming, so loving, so sane – and so realistic – that one can forgive her for it. One can even forgive its implication that all that is left for the older woman is to be a good grandmother. This grandmother directed much energy at her other life as a well-known religious teacher, and nothing she says leaves one feeling as exhausted as Sheila Kitzinger's robust suggestions, in her grandmother book, of jolly activities for grandmothers and granchildren (set out under headings like 'Kitchen Magic', 'Make-Believe', 'Growing Things', 'Making Things'; granny as alternative kindergarten, no less). We'll hear more of Mrs Whitall Smith. Together with her earlier co-religionist Elizabeth Fry, she leaves me with the feeling that the perfect grandmother to *have* if not to *be* would be a Quaker one.

Should I apologise, then, for ending this section on a sourer note? Probably not. Even if Thomas Hardy does seem like a spoilsport here, his ghost of a grandmother cutting the optimism of birth by reminding us of what we are all too well aware of but don't want to be reminded of now, that the optimism will most likely turn out misplaced. Queen Victoria herself provides the awful warning. The sweet little grandson she gushes about, her 'dear darling little Willie', laid the foundation of us grandmothers' twentieth-century blues. He grew up to be the warmonger Kaiser Wilhelm, instigator of the First World War.

Every time a baby is born a grandmother is born too . . .
A. KORNHABER AND K. WOODWARD, *Grandparents, Grandchildren, the Vital Connection*, 1981

I'll never forget. My husband and I were in the hospital when my granddaughter was delivered, and the doctor knew me. So the first thing, he said to the nurse, 'Before you bathe the baby, take it out to the grandparents.' And you know, with me, I still swear when the nurse brought Barbara, Barbara looked at us: they say a new-born baby doesn't see, but I swear that she looked at us. That was a wonderful feeling.

RUTH KATZ in Sydelle Krammer and Jenny Masur (eds.), *Jewish Grandmothers*, 1976

MRS HENDERSON: Your inside just seems to churn up when you see them . . . part o' ours really. Not like another baby when you go in and see them. Part o' ours really.

MRS SINCLAIR: Well, when I saw her it just took me back, you know, flash back memories. It could ha' been her father lying there, and all those years. Then I just couldna' *believe* that David was a father. I had visions of him with his school cap on, running into the kitchen.

SARAH CUNNINGHAM BURLEY, *Ageing and Society*, 1987

'We are a grandmother.' Congrats to . . . Shirley Williams, who is now a granny. 'The hardest part of the birth was keeping her out of the delivery room,' quipped the feisty baroness's son-in-law about the arrival of the sweet-natured baby, Samuel . . .

Pandora column, *Independent*, April 1999

---

from Hanging On

August 8th, Thursday

Very perturbed by calling the hospital and being told 'no change'. Last night Burgo [her son] thought the child should have been there already. He had been with Henrietta during the afternoon when 'contractions were coming every five minutes', but I feel he has no real conception of how much more tremendous the whole process had to become. I spent most of yesterday, and am today, in the middle of a familiar frantic attempt to wait calmly.

3 p.m. I'm seriously worried. Rang Henrietta's doctor at lunchtime and he broached the possibility of a Caesarian if nothing has happened by tomorrow morning. 'I don't understand it,' he said, 'she's so young, everything's normal, and she does everything she's told.' Yet she is having contractions, but no more. My heart bleeds for her, and I don't know how to get through the time.

9.30 p.m. I had E.Q. to supper but it was a *supplice*. Would it have been more so to be alone? I don't know. Burgo came in for a drink; he had been told about the possible Caesarian and was dreadfully shaken. Duncan [Grant] rang up and it was some small consolation to talk to someone who also really cared about that sweet girl. I feel like someone caught in the wreck of a railway accident.

August 14th

The gap is the measure of how long it took me to recover from catapulting so hopelessly into agitation. Henrietta and Burgo's dear little baby, Sophie Vanessa, is now five days old and Henrietta is recovering from the operation. Their delight in their child is marvellous to see and they express it with refreshing abandon. I have been twice to see Henrietta and had Burgo here a good many times – hoping not to seem interfering or

fussing, but now sure that attentions and interest are appreciated. I have been much moved – obsessed is really the word –
by the whole thing. Each night as I close my eyes to the darkness this obsession returns, even if it has been quiescent all day.
The baby looks very like Henrietta, with a wide mouth and
perfect little hands.

August 16th

I've been all day on the run – to see Craig in the morning – to
visit Henrietta in the afternoon – a drink with Isobel in the
evening. I feel like one of the silver balls in machines in fairs,
which gets shot up by the insertion of a penny, bounces wildly
from metal peg to metal peg, rattles here, slides along there,
jingles and jolts until it drops into the last hole of all from
which there is no return. Henrietta comes out of hospital on
Friday, and after buying her a pram with Burgo and driving
her home – what then? It's difficult to strike a happy balance
between doing all one can, and longs to do for those one
loves, and backing gracefully off the stage. I see clearly the
warning Ralph would have been the first to give me: don't
interfere in their lives. But I'm aware of one thing at least:
here at last, in flesh and blood, is a motive for going on far
stronger than any I have encountered during nearly three
years of struggle.

FRANCES PARTRIDGE, 1963

[NB. Henrietta, Frances Partridge's daughter-in-law and
mother of her grandchild, was herself the granddaughter of
Vanessa Bell (see pp. 107–8, 122–4).]

---

from Dearest Child

Windsor Castle, January 19, 1859

God be praised for all his mercies, and for bringing you safely through this awful time! Our joy, our gratitude knows no bounds.

My precious darling, you suffered much more than I ever did – and how I wish I could have lightened them for you! Poor dear Fritz – how he will have suffered for you! I think and feel much for him; the dear little boy if I could but see him for one minute, give you one kiss. It is hard, very hard. But we are so happy, so grateful! And people here are all in ecstasies – such pleasure, such delight – as if it was their own prince and so it is too! All the children so delighted! You will and must feel so thankful all is over! But don't be alarmed for the future, it never can be so bad again! Your's and baby's healths were drunk on Thursday evening and the Sydneys were here!

We are starting for Wellington College and so I must stop. God bless and protect you.

Dear Papa is so happy too.

[. . .] How I do long to see my little grandson! I own it seems very funny to me to be a grandmama, and so many people tell me they can't believe it! That dear, dear locket gives me such pleasure! Not only because it was the dear little darling's hair, but because it shows me that you thought directly of poor absent Mama, who quite pines at times to be with you.

I send you today a little cushion for your back when you are on your sofa, every stitch of which I have worked myself with the English colours which I trust you will like.

Windsor Castle, February 5, 1859

Countess Blücher says you are very good and tractable – which I am delighted to hear.

I think you and your child must look like two babies together as you have such a child's face still. There were such quantities of people out on Thursday when we went to open parliament: and so enthusiastic, – all to see Grandpapa and Grandmama.

QUEEN VICTORIA

---

from Interview

Being a grandmother for the first time, it's like it was with your first child, it brings up all sorts of things. It brings up your hopes and fears and your lack of confidence – you find yourself reviewing your virtues – and your faults. And you think, I do want to see you grow up. I want to take you to Slava the Clown. I want you to . . . But I felt so unsure about what my role should comfortably be. Not to behave as if it was my baby. I think that they were so strongly sure of what they wanted it made things easier for me, right at the beginning. Because what they wanted then was that week. For themselves, with the baby. If I was rung up I went. I brought up the hot food. I thought I'd be doing that for about ten days. I'd ring them up, and say tonight it will be . . . for dinner, or is there anything else you'd like? And then I was rung up and told it's beginning to get normal now. So we'll cook tonight. That was within a week. I think, possibly, I found it a bit painful. It's all painful, isn't it? You give your daughter away. And you realise that you have to step back. And I remember bowing to my ancestors. To my mother. And thinking you must have felt this as well.

PHYLLIDA LAW, 1998

from Blackberry Winter

When the news came that Sevanne Margaret was born, I suddenly realized that through no act of my own I had become biologically related to a new human being. This was one thing that had never come up in discussions of grandparenthood and had never before occurred to me [. . .]

I always have been acutely aware of the way one life touches another – of the ties between myself and those whom I have never met, but who read *Coming of Age in Samoa* and decided to become anthropologists. From the time of my childhood I was able to conceive of my relationship to all my forebears, some of whose genes I carry, both those I did not know even by name and those who helped to bring me up, particularly my paternal grandmother. But the idea that as a grandparent one was dealing with action at a distance – that somewhere, miles away, a series of events occurred that changed one's own status forever – I had not thought of that and I found it very odd.

I felt something like the shock that must be felt by those who have lived all their lives secure in their citizenship in the nation of their birth and who then, suddenly, by the arbitrary act of some tyrannical government, find that they are disenfranchised – as happened to the old aristocracy in Russia after the revolution, to the Jews in Germany in the 1930's, and to the Turkish Armenians in Turkey. But of course what happened to me was not an arbitrary denial of something I had regarded as irreversibly given, but rather an arbitrary confirmation of a state which I felt that I myself had done nothing to bring about. Scientists and philosophers have speculated at length about the sources of man's belief that he is a creature with a future life or, somewhat less commonly, with a life that preceded his life on earth. Speculation may be the only kind of answer that is possible, but I would now add to the speculations that are more familiar another of my own: the extraordinary sense of having been transformed not by any act of one's own but by the act of one's child.

Then, as a new grandmother, I began both to relive my own daughter's infancy and to observe the manifestations of temperament in the tiny creature who was called Vanni – to note how she learned to ignore the noisy carpentry as the house was finished around her but was so sensitive to changes in the human voice that her mother had to keep low background music playing to mask the change in tone of voice that took place when someone who had been speaking then answered the telephone. I remarked how she responded to pattern in the brightly colored chintzes and the mobiles that had been prepared for her. I showed the movies of Cathy's birth and early childhood, to which my daughter commented, 'I think my baby is brighter' – or prettier, or livelier – 'than your baby!'

However, I felt none of the much trumpeted freedom from responsibility that grandparents are supposed to feel. Actually, it seems to me that the obligation to be a resource but not an interference is just as preoccupying as the attention one gives to one's own children. I think we do not allow sufficiently for the obligation we lay on grandparents to keep themselves out of the picture – not to interfere, not to spoil, not to insist, not to intrude – and, if they are old and frail, to go and live apart in an old people's home (by whatever name it may be called) and to say that they are happy when, once in a great while, their children bring their grandchildren to visit them.

MARGARET MEAD, 1973

---

from The Family Life of Old People

[A] grandmother attached special significance to the first grandchild, particularly the eldest child of the eldest daughter.

The child embodied her right to the status of grandmother. From its birth she seemed to feel a special affection for it and their relationship was close, particularly when the child was aged from 10 to 15. The grandmother took pride in preparing him or her for adult life, being able to give the adolescent child many attentions a mother tied to work and smaller children, could not give.

Mrs Sheldon said she paid a shilling a week endowment policy for her eldest granddaughter. '[. . .] You know with your first grandchild you give them more than you should give them. You spoil them.'

Mrs Dominion's eldest grandson was with her at the time of the interview. 'He didn't go home last night. I thought [the weather] looked too bad. I told him to stay here in the warm . . .' The boy butted in to say, 'I'm the one who's up here most. I'm the only one that's slept here lately.'

On average a woman was 53 when she became a grandmother.

PETER TOWNSEND, 1959

Shelagh

My eldest grandson was born in 1993. With his birth I summoned up Granny Roley as my guide – so-called because her children agreed, presumably affectionately, that she looked like a roly-poly pudding. She was unquestionably the grandmother I hoped I would in my turn become, though – two generations and twelve thousand miles later – without a moniker that invited comparison to a suet pudding . . .

The trouble was I couldn't do what I knew a proper grandmother was supposed to do. I didn't have the strength to change nappies, look after an infant for an hour or two or take over the cooking and the washing at busy times. [Shelagh has been disabled by chronic ME.] I couldn't even hold the baby for more than a few minutes at a stretch. Instead of being the rock-like support I wanted to be, I felt I added to my daughter's burden when we were together to the extent that I, as well as the new child, had to be looked after. I minded my helplessness very much.

I was obsessed by the new baby. I dreamed about him, thought about him, knitted for him. I think now that at the beginning of his life I saw him as a fourth child of my own. There was a compelling visceral connection. His flesh was my flesh; I saw myself when I looked into his eyes. I was separated from him by an intervening generation and by not having borne him, of course, but in every way that counted I was, if not his mother, one of his mothers. Perhaps I underestimated the prolonged inner effort becoming a grandmother involved. A sense of passionate internal muddle came, it may be, from failing to make in one clean leap the transition from one bio-logical stage of life to the next. Certainly my thoughts, at that time, ran along the following lines: I was an experienced mother, so when there was a problem it was my place to help my inexperienced daughter learn how mothering was done. Though I hadn't told her what to do for years, with a new life at stake that's what I must now do. The way I'd brought her and her siblings up must have been basically right even if I often got things wrong. After all, I wouldn't have stuck with the methods I adopted if they didn't more or less work.

It was a shock to realise that sometimes my daughter wanted my advice but more often she didn't. And it was even more of a shock to understand as the months went by that she intended to raise the baby her own way, not mine. The inten-sity of my feelings – predictable and corny and the basis of every mother-in-law joke that had ever found its way onto a seaside postcard – were not to be reasoned away. My strong opinions on the baby and what should be done with him, my conviction I knew better than my daughter, simply wouldn't be argued out of existence. But I had to learn to keep my mouth shut. I mustn't voice my views. Here I was, a feminist – a former teacher of women's studies, for goodness' sake – who believed in a woman's individual autonomy as well as in openness and honesty. Not only did I value being able to 'say anything' to my daughter, I felt that in her adult life she and I together had developed a freedom of exchange we'd both come to rely on. I'd spent the last two decades learning to cast off the shackles of hypocrisy and subterfuge in my relations with women who were close to me, and now – with her of all people – I was dissembling again.

The baby spent time on my bed. I gained strength by simply lying beside him and learning him – his straightening legs, hands that began to hold, a face that opened up more each day like a flower in sun. I liked to think he bloomed in the steadfastness of my attention; he watched me watching him and that helped him grow. My muddle became less, my passion more directed. Perhaps I was being a 'proper grandmother' after all, but not in the conventional way. He got older, and toys and books joined us on the bed. Words came, and his invention of curiously antiquated games. *I'm the uncle, you're the woodcutter, and I'll go shopping while you look after the fire.* There'd be bouncing on the bed, of course, and getting bored, and needing things I couldn't provide, but at the heart of things there was us.

Then came two more babies, one in Auckland and one in Christchurch. Each lay on my bed to be learned like another mysterious language. Yet I knew each one deeply, as if a Chomskyan deep structure of genetic familiarity underpinned the unfamiliar dialect embodied in each new baby. Three boys, two families with their own distinctive ways of doing things. Very slowly, I began to gain physical strength. I could lift the babies now and even play with them a little when I was out of bed. Equally slowly, I began to dissemble less. I still need to pretend at times; I think I always shall. In the company of my children and their children I remember the way I did things at their stage of my own life. So there are occasions when I still long to stick in my oar, put debating parents right, suggest, take over. But they are fewer and less frequent than when I first became a grandmother in 1993.

My Auckland and Christchurch families have two loving parents who have nearly interchangeable roles in relation to the children. The mothers are breadwinners and the fathers change nappies and cook meals. Anyone who's around reads aloud, fills the drinking cup, deals with bumps and bruises and opens loving arms. The division of labour that was absolute in the world of my childhood no longer applies in the way it did [. . .]

One of my fancies, theories, half-supported discoveries, is that women's lives have changed more in the last two generations in the Western world than at any time in history. The sexual division of labour that once ruled destinies has largely broken down in the educated middle class, though not so much in the working class. The lives of many older women have changed and are changing at the end of the millennium as much as the lives of younger women did in the sixties and seventies, mainly because today's feminist grandmothers were often second-wave feminists a generation ago. I believe I'm living the kind of life old women have not lived before. Not in every way, of course, and I wouldn't want to jettison the past. But I want to be able to separate in myself what is cyclic, the recurring history, the myth, from what is new or I feel might be new.

Having an occupation of my own at the present stage of my life is new. Few women lived long enough to work for themselves in old age before. And if they did live to be over ninety like Granny Roley, they seldom had the money needed for independence. If they lived to their mid-eighties like Granny Guy, my other grandmother, and had money to support themselves, they had no psychological precedent, no inner permission-granting mechanism, that allowed them to live as they pleased and do what they wanted. As a result, or so it seems to me, the grandmother role consumed the lives of both my grandmothers.

It doesn't consume mine. Instead there are opposing tugs between my own carefully guarded life as an independent woman, and spending the time I want to spend with my grandchildren. The small amount of energy I have for doing anything at all, with my still-impaired health, compounds the problem. I never seem to find a once-and-for-all solution to it. But in an odd kind of compensation I have gradually discovered that the illness helps me simplify my sense of the sort of grandmother I am when I am with the children. I can't cook and wash and baby-sit, play exciting physical games or plan special outings. And of course there are still times when I very much wish I could. But I can stay still and simply be around.

I've also had to relinquish the directly educative role I once thought I might have. I don't seem to pass on much knowledge in a momentous manner. So far anyway, there are no stories from my past begged for by wide-eyed little people, and if I read aloud I tend to be the nearest available lap and eyes and voice rather than the person in the household whose special task this is.

What do I do, then, distinctively as a grandmother? I feel my grandsons through the entire surface of my skin, whether I touch and hold them or simply watch and listen. They exhaust me at the same time as they give me life when my own life-force feels as if it's ebbing. They connect me to the future in the very moment they remind me of the past. I need them. But do they need me? I believe they do.

They need me in the visceral way I need them, so that, through me, they can make a largely unconscious physical connection to their genetic heritage. They also need me in the way they need fairy stories. Or that's how the youngest two will need me in the future. The oldest already does. The games he likes to play with me, where woodcutters and uncles figure more than Action Man and the Spice Girls, take us both into an imaginative world we tend not to inhabit when we're apart. It's the meeting-place of a grandson with a grandmother who has largely moved out of the active world. My illness makes me one of its natural occupants, and he likes to come to my bed and join me there. It's beyond time. Fairytales belong there, and so do we.

SHELAGH DUCKHAM COX, 1999

---

from A Quaker Grandmother

October 16, 1888

The baby is devoted to me, and trots over to my table the moment she enters the drawing-room and calls out 'Up! up!' in the most bewitching little voice. Of course I take her up, no matter what I am doing, and then I let her play with *everything* I possess, pen and ink, paste pot, watch, specs, scissors, glue bottles, letter-receiver, Concordance, Bible and all! . . . I waste hours over her, if it *is* waste.

HANNAH WHITALL SMITH

Sulaiman is an outdoor child and everything in the garden enchants him. A leaf will excite him or a blade of grass: I get enormous pleasure from just watching his reactions. It is not just sentiment. It is a satisfying feeling of connection with another generation that will live on after I die. It is also the sense that life cannot be bleak when a child finds the world so breathtaking. I see everything through fresh eyes.

ANNABEL GOLDSMITH, *Electronic Telegraph*, 9 May 1998

Mlle Aurore shouts 'Wait, wait, wait!' That's all she can say, and she says it laughing like anything. When she laughs at all, that is, because she's really very serious and attentive, as clever as a monkey with her hands, and more amused with the games she invents for herself that with any suggested by other people. I think *she*'ll have a phiz all her own.

From *Flaubert–Sand: The Correspondence*, 15 January 1867

Aurore is the sweetest and most waggish creature imaginable. When her father gives her a drink he says, '*Dominus vobiscumi*,' and she drinks and answers '*Amen*.' And here she is, walking already. How wonderful it is, the way a child develops! And it's never been done. It would be valuable from every point of view to follow the process day by day. It's one of those things we all see without really seeing them.

From *Flaubert–Sand: The Correspondence*, 30 May 1867

Aurore is very flirtatious with her arms, which she holds out to be kissed; her hands are wonderful and incredibly nimble for her age . . .

From *Flaubert–Sand: The Correspondence*, 21 or 22 August 1867

What a blessing they exist . . . and what an incredible difference such small creatures make to life. They're so full of it, it
seems to spill over all around.

> VANESSA BELL, letter to Angelica Garnett, 1946

———————

Knowing how to be a grandmother does not come instinc-
tively.

> SHEILA KITZINGER, *Becoming a Grandmother*, 1997

———————

What is our role? We have to make it up as we go along. You
find out different things from anyone you talk to.

> SHIRLEY HUGHES, author's interview

———————

Grandparents are walking through a minefield. The first mine
is the temptation to give advice.

> JOAN GOMEZ, *Sixty Something*, 1993

———————

Grandparents have to carve out a role for themselves within
limits of expectation and custom. This is a sensitive task.

> PAUL THOMPSON ET AL., *I Don't Feel Old*, 1990

———————

Meaningful grandparenthood, in short, is not automatic, but has to be achieved.

PAUL THOMPSON ET AL., *I Don't Feel Old*, 1990

I remember when my babies were small, I didn't want my mother to go out to work. I wanted her there laughing and talking to me, lifting the babies out of my arms. It feels like you don't have any arms – well, you do, but not enough – just to have someone else there, holding the baby, it's bliss. Sophie and her husband are extending their flat by a couple of rooms, so they ring sometimes and say, 'Mum, could you come and play with Ernie for a bit while we pack up the glasses?' That's it, isn't it? Play. You can put them in a cot, or you can put them on the floor with toys, but you still need another eye and another hand. Grandmas do have that.

[. . .] You have to edit it yourself, though; have to rethink yourself. I wouldn't like it if someone started to tell me what to do with my child. How do I edit myself? Well, in work and play I'm inclined to say, Please don't let me help, because I'm overenthusiastic. I've got a wart . . .

PHYLLIDA LAW, author's interview

What do the rest of you do with your grandchildren? (*A great chorus*) 'Read, read, read!' (*Individual voices*) 'Take them to the park.' 'Take them to McDonald's.'

Birmingham grandmothers, author's interview, 1999

What Is a Grandmother?

A grandmother is a lady with no children of her own. She likes other people's little girls and boys.

Grandmothers don't have to do anything except to be there. They're old, so they shouldn't play hard or run. It is enough that they drive us to the market where the pretend horse is, and to have lots of dimes ready.

Or if they take us for walks, they should slow down past pretty things like pretty leaves and caterpillars, and they should never say, 'Hurry up.'

Usually, grandmothers are fat, but not too fat to tie your shoes. They wear glasses and funny underwear. They can take their teeth and gums off.

Grandmothers don't have to be smart, only answer questions like 'Why isn't God married?' and 'How come dogs chase cats?'

Everybody should try to have a grandmother, especially if you don't have television, because they are the only grownups who have time.

Internet, 1998

---

from Interviews

"She came one Saturday afternoon, her father was doing something for me in the kitchen. And she wanted to go in the bedroom. And I went in the bedroom with her. And then she got under the duvet and she was getting really excited. 'Now you come under, Nanny.' And there we were with it right over our heads. And I don't know what I was doing. But she was really screaming. And her father came in and he said, 'Hmm. You've got her all right, haven't you?' And I thought, How much longer . . .? Then she wasn't three. But I thought, I can't stand much more of it. Get her Frank and go. But my mother used to say about her great-grandchildren, 'I love to see you. But I'm glad when you go.'"

"You've got much more time for them than you have for your own children. Because they only come to visit. You haven't got the responsibility of looking after them all the time. Washing them. Bathing them. Feeding them and all that. With grandchildren you can enjoy the company and hand them back."

"Amy calls me Granny Whizz. Because you like to do with your grandchildren the things you did with your own children. So I put a towel down on the floor and give her a whizz."

(What about discipline and so forth?) "When they were little and you were responsible yourself, then you went by your own standards. But you have to be careful they don't play one off against the other – you always tell their mother what you've done – I used to."

Birmingham grandmothers, 1999

---

from Aging and Adaption

When they first moved in together, Mrs Chin had tried to help her daughter-in-law in cleaning up after meals, but learned quickly that her cleaning standards were not the same as those of the younger woman, so she had retreated. While she believed in intergenerational living, Mrs Chin was also aware that it could present delicate problems in human relations. For example, she knew that she and her daughter-in-law had different opinions about child-rearing, particularly on issues of discipline, and Mrs Chin hesitated to express her opinions or to act on them. In her Toisan village, it had been customary to yell at children, to call them names such as *sei jai* ('dead boy' – the implication is one of wishing the child dead) or *neih mouh yuhngge* ('you good-for-nothing'), to threaten them, to isolate them (locking them in a storage closet or out of the house), and to strike them with little regard to possible negative consequences. These punishments were seldom graded by the nature of the child's offense, but tended more to reflect: the state of mind of the parent, how quickly he or she wanted to make the point that the offending behavior was unacceptable; the accessibility of the child, whether within reach of hand or voice; and the presence or absence of witnesses from outside the family, witnesses being a stimulus to parental action. Mrs Chin did not dare to strike her grandchildren. She would yell at them and threaten them with punishment from her daughter-in-law, but her daughter-in-law does not strike them. She believes in talking with them or punishing them by restrictions on their freedom of movement.

CHARLOTTE IKEB, 1983

Lauris

My first grandchild was a miracle, an amazing phenomenon, an endless surprise. I wrote poems about her, played with her, sometimes looked after her. As she grew, I found I slipped into my mother's habits, played the same hand games, singing games, animal mimicry games, all of which surfaced again when needed . . .

But I made my mother's mistakes too. While this young family lived in my house, Ruth began coming upstairs to my part of the house for breakfast. It was always the same, grilled cheese on toast, and we developed some pleasurable little routines around these occasions; but I failed to notice that as she came more and more often, her mother became increasingly restive and eventually a row blew up between us. It was my first lesson in learning that the claims (and inducements) of grandparents must be carefully balanced against the greater claims of the parents. In the grandmotherly profession, knowing how to stand back is just as important as knowing how and when to step forward. For someone with my temperament, probably more so.

Many more grandchildren were born into the family – I now have fourteen, which among my friends is a rare and remarkable total – but I think I began with the very first to realise that there is, or can be, a special affinity between the very young and those beyond active parenthood. Parents have conscience-building as part of their responsibility to their children; grandparents have left this duty behind, and can enjoy being as open to experience – as amoral? – as children themselves. My inclination is often to say 'Why not?' when children want to experiment, where as a mother I far more often said 'Not just now' or 'Think of the effect on . . .' or 'It's not your turn'.

However, there is another side to this too. I have learnt to be wary of being seen to 'know better' than the parents of any grandchild, even if only by implication. There is a strict, if invisible, hierarchy of authority in the cross-generational structure, and there are swift punishments for breaking its rules. A couple of years ago Tess, my granddaughter aged twelve, came to stay with me for part of her school holidays; we embarked on many activities involving other children (two other of my families live in Wellington, both quite near me), but whenever possible she would escape to her room, sometimes in the middle of conversations, and stay there for hours together, if I didn't manage to persuade her to come out. I was concerned about the extent of these withdrawals, and decided to say to the parents that I thought she needed a bit more 'social experience'. Well, the heavens broke open and a

storm of emotional thunder and lightning came down upon
me.

I know now . . . that a cardinal rule in peaceful grandpar-
ently involvement is: never give advice unless asked for it, and
even then with great caution. What these young parents wish
to hear from me is that they and their children are uniformly
wonderful . . .

Was I aware of the 'climate of the times' when I first
embarked on this new role, this unexpectedly different relationship? Probably, but quite unconsciously; one does not,
cannot, recognise such conditioning influences at the time. I
see now that having my own children in the years after the
war meant, as sociologists have now pointed out to us, that
child-rearing, often of families of four or more, by mothers
dedicated to it as their full-time occupation, was a norm. For
young mothers now, it's not. Now that I too have moved into
the post-sixties awareness that women should be able to claim
more of their time for their own purposes, I realise that 'putting families first' has in many ways stayed with me, and not
always comfortably.

I find for instance that I can make myself available for my
grandchildren more often than suits my own present professional needs – to have them to stay, take them out, spend time
with them when their parents are busy. It is somehow what I
was trained for, and I don't easily see how to change it.

LAURIS EDMOND, 1999

---

from The Nine Lives of Minnie Winder

Mary came to stay with us when John was born. I could
manage quite well since we had a girl living in at the time.
Frank and I found Mary delightful company. Not that she

said much. 'Tado,' she demanded one lunch time, which I interpreted as potato. 'Please,' I said. 'Please,' she copied me. At least, I thought, I can teach her some new words, and some manners. Frank played cooking with her, just as he had done with Mollie when she was small. Frank loved small children, he was so good with them. He had a magic lantern, with pictures of Egypt and Greece, he had a real interest in history. 'Magic, magic,' Mary said, delightedly, staring at the pictures with big eyes.

'I've a surprise for you,' I said to Mary one day, 'you just wait until teatime.' I had managed to have Nancy [Mary's sister] come and visit us just for a few hours. It would give Mollie a rest in any case. How she managed to cope with all those children, with only a daily help I can't imagine. However I could see by Mary's expression that the presence of Nancy was not a nice surprise at all. She scowled, and her face fell. It was stupid of me perhaps, I think Mary had come to regard Frank and me as her personal property, not to be shared by any other member of her family. One has to be so careful of a small child's feelings.

MARY HOPE WILLIAMS, c.1920

---

from Duties of the Decline of Life

Affectionate tendencies in the bosoms of the old proceed, in some instances, to an extreme; and require, though not to be checked, yet to be regulated. Fondness attaches itself with pernicious eagerness to one of the children of the family; rests not without the preference of the favourite object; destroys its health by pampering it with dainties; and stimulates and strengthens its passions by immoderate and indiscriminate gratification. Many a child, whom parental discipline would have trained in the paths of knowledge and virtue, has been nursed up in ignorance and prepared for vice by the blind indulgence of the grandmother and the aunt. Unwillingness to thwart the wishes of old age, curtailed of many enjoyments, and impatient of contradiction, frequently restrains the parent from timely and effectual interference. Were this obvious circumstance considered beforehand, and with due seriousness, by women advanced in years, they would less frequently reduce those with whom they live to the embarrassing dilemma of performing a very irksome duty, or of acquiescing in the danger and detriment, perhaps in the ruin, of their offspring.

ANON., 1796

from A Quaker Grandmother

My grandmother's creed, about grandmothers, was very complete. They must love their grandchildren, in the first place. I do not think she would say that this was their duty, but rather that it was their nature [. . .]

The second part of a grandmother's duty was to devote herself to her grandchildren. Mothers, she would say, were busy. They naturally had other interests, other friends, and their own life still to live, and their work to do. They might, and in fact must, be excused if they sometimes attended to other things. But grandmothers are old: their life is past, their friends are dead, they have grown tired of their interests, and the new generation is carrying on their work. They, therefore, are free to devote themselves to the children, and they are foolish and troublesome if they don't seize this last opportunity. But although they must devote themselves to their grandchildren, they must be very careful not to interfere unnecessarily with them [. . .]

[The] third aspect of a grandmother's duties, that of providing fun and preventing trouble, was the one most noticed by the children . . .

RAY STRACHEY, 1914

———————

One thing is, though you mustn't have a favourite child – or at least admit you do – you can have a favourite grandchild . . .

Personal communication to P. Farmer, 1999

———————

from Interview

Time is different for a grandparent than it is for a mother, when you don't notice from day to day much. I don't draw them. But I do remember what they look like. And they tell me things. And of course that's great. They make me realise more and more the great technological explosion that's in every part of our lives, more than it was between myself and my children. With grandchildren that's an enormous thing. It means they're riveted by the things I do manually. I've a Singer sewing machine I still use. And we got out John's portable gramophone the other day because they came round and had nothing much to do – it's so heavy you can hardly lift it. And you're talking about seventy years of records. Which he took around right through soldiering. And that amazed them. We've got a lot of Fred Astaire. And that gets on to conversations about what it was like and what sort of dancing we did, and having all the things which seem so archaic to them. Because everything's so fast-moving. To me memory's pinpointed by what were the hits of the year. What sort of clothes I was wearing. I've got terrific recall. I remember exactly when Billie Holiday singing 'Time on My Hand' began; I was trying to let down the hem on my dresses in order to have long skirts. The problems of these little children is that every period of music, the Beatles, the Stones, the sort of music I had, is all there in Virgin Records, it's around the whole time, the whole century merges into one blob and you can pull out whatever record you want, and they find it terribly hard to sort it out.

They have points of reference, they have the war. They started to ask about it when they first heard about it at school. But they are terribly vague about it, because the past is always being dished up to them in a way that it was never being dished up to me. It was much more linear in my childhood. You didn't keep whizzing about in it. Because it wasn't being recreated for you all the time on discs. Theme-park history. Which I simply can't stand. I think it's vital to have a sense of history to see your way through life – I think perhaps a grandparent can help you with that. The melancholy of the first war pervaded my childhood, the memory of the trenches – we never had pictures of it, but it was there. I've not got grandchildren old enough yet to understand the emotion of it, the feelings. They're interested in the hardware. But I think in time, we can help. And of course they love to hear all the daft things you did. They like the stories of your youth. Not just the war. They want to know about their parents. Last Christmas we got a slide projector and we showed them a whole lot of slides of their parents at the same age. And they thought it was amazing.

But all this change! You do have to adapt. Inevitably bringing up children is different. They're more in with the family. They go to bed later. They're more in with the adults. We weren't. If my mother had been in a crisis, I wouldn't have known much about it. I'm not a wise woman grandmother. I'm asking them how to do it all the time. I'm asking their mothers and their fathers. They're interchangeable these days.

Small babies I always did find rather alarming – so small and vulnerable. I don't have this Mother Earth thing. I'd rather somebody else looked after them, somebody competent, I couldn't compete. I've always got on well with toddlers. We've got all the old toys still, we didn't throw them out, and now it's absolutely brilliant. It's very odd that in spite of all electronic things, and toys structured round telly, etc. – junk is fine – every child needs junk. We hung on to a Noah's ark and old cars and a Hornby train set – basic toys – and they come out over and over again. We had a doll with clothes. A little girl doll. And again, we spend hours at a time, taking its clothes on and off, putting its shoes on, it's so basic the things they will do. I suddenly realise that this is an important part of life. You have to look around now to avoid the oversophisticated toy. We do watch videos sometimes, but not often – most of the time they're playing about. They're even interested in my work, much more than my children ever were – for them my work was just part of life. I show my grandchildren my book dummies – they get a certain amount of kudos at school by saying, 'Granny did that.' I draw with them too – there's so much stuff. The best times we have are playing consequences. And playing really daft games. And coming on dressed up in something. But consequences are just bliss – and heads, bodies and legs.

There's all those old-hat images of grandparents still. And now there's another stereotype, a whole lot of books about trendy grandparents. And that's grotesque. Or it can be. I think children have an instinctive respect for age. And one doesn't want to destroy that. The older grandchildren do now realise we are quite old. And they are quite protective if they think we're doing too much. They realise we can't rush about. And I think that's good. And it would be awful if they didn't realise that age is something you protect as well as respect – not respect because you're made to. All the stereotyping, you see, is bound to be wrong. It's clear the family is going through a tremendous reappraisal, traumatic change, but I do think you have to relate back as well as forward. And perhaps this is our role.

SHIRLEY HUGHES, 1998

----

from Age Concern survey

- Almost half of today's grandparents, 45%, feel that the stress of modern life on parents and children is a factor in changing the grandparent/grandchild relationship
- Two thirds of today's grandparents say they are more involved in the lives of their grandchildren than their parents were with their grandchildren
- A quarter of grandparents in our in-depth survey felt that their main role was to look after grandchildren when parents were busy
- 40% of grandparents felt their main role was to provide love for their grandchildren
- Only 10% of children thought their grandparents' main function was to 'give things'
- According to the interviewees in our survey, today's generation of grandparents are more than twice as likely to act as childminders to their grandchildren than the previous generation were
- Two thirds of grandparents on the mother's side see their grandchildren every week, whereas only one third of paternal grandparents see their grandchildren so frequently
- The first thing grandparents and grandchildren are likely to talk about when they meet is what the grandchildren have been doing. 70% said this was the first topic of discussion.

- Nearly two thirds of grandchildren described the love they felt for their grandparents as 'more than words can say'.

1998

———

In Childbed

In the middle of the night
Mother's spirit came and spoke to me,
Looking weariful and white –
As 'twere untimely news she broke to me.

'O my daughter, joyed are you
To own the weetless child you mother there;
"Men may search the wide world through,"
You think, "nor find so fair another there!"

'Dear, this midnight time unwombs
Thousands just as rare and beautiful;
Thousands whom High Heaven foredooms
To be as bright, as good, as dutiful.

'Source of ecstatic hopes and fears
And innocent maternal vanity,
Your fond exploit but shapes for tears
New thoroughfares in sad humanity.

'Yet as you dream, so dreamt I
When Life stretched forth its morning ray to me;
Other views for by and by!' . . .
Such strange things did mother say to me.

THOMAS HARDY, 1928

———

II

USEFUL GRANDMOTHERS

I claimed I did not know how to be a grandmother. Silly me! Seeing how quickly the role sought me out. Or rather, how quickly its functions did.

My granddaughter Ellie and I have our private rituals. When I stay the night at her house, first thing in the morning we pretend to be bears in my bed. Later we inspect the pigs and other animals at St Werberg's City Farm. Then we have drinks at the café in the Bristol Climbing Centre – a converted church. We tell each other stories, all the time.

Now this is entirely my own choice. It is not demanded of me by my daughter and her partner. Given how fond of one another we all are, they might be slightly upset if I took no interest in Ellie. But my granddaughter would survive perfectly well. What I do is not expected, needed, let alone demanded of me by society.

Just the same, when I break these activities down into their component parts, I find them pretty similar, on an informal level, to activities formally assigned to grandmothers in many traditional societies, and assumed to be redundant in our world. And why should that surprise me? The lives and expectations of their parents may have changed across time and place; the needs of small children don't. And it is these needs that I, like the traditional grandmothers, find myself addressing, as provider (orange juice in the climbing café), as childminder (as I am throughout these excursions, so freeing her mother for other activities) and as educator and entertainer (storyteller, namer of pigs).

Although the balance between these functions shifted from group to group in more traditional societies, nevertheless they are seen with a consistency that has led researchers to suggest an evolutionary function in the menopause. According to the anthropologist Karen Hawkes's work on hardworking Hadza grandmothers, summarized here by Jared Diamond, the success of *Homo sapiens* could be due in part to the existence of a pool of competent women no longer subject to the physical burdens of childbirth and the rearing of their own children. This was particularly so in hunter-gatherer societies. Here, either by gathering an increased amount of food for their kin, or by taking over the care of their grandchildren, leaving their daughters free to gather food, grandmothers helped ensure the survival of their genes, down through the generations. The odd animal society where some kind of menopause functions – those of pilot whales and elephants, for instance – seems to demonstrate the same thing. But even without such evolutionary necessity, provision, child care, education, remain an important part, if no longer the basis of grandmotherly input.

Take Grandma as provider. '*Ess, mein kind*' – 'Eat, my child' – connects the Yiddisher grandmother directly to those indefatigable Hadza foragers, and no less to many mythological grandmothers; the piece from Sarawak is the ultimate example, I think. As it connects them to the tradition of grandmothers spoiling grandchildren, plying them with sweets, sticky drinks and other goodies frowned on by responsible parents. My own grandmother, according to my cousins, expected her grandsons, especially, to overeat. This is not an aspect of grandmotherhood I undertake, much. I've no more desire to wreck my grandchildren's teeth and figures than I had to wreck those of their parents. A naughty shared flapjack in the climbing café is about as far as I go, and even that is more connected to a mutual greed for such things that I seem to have passed on down to my granddaughter, along, no doubt, with other traits not yet apparent. But provision of other kinds is different. I can barely keep out of bookshops and children's clothes shops these days. (Though I can't see myself attempting to fulfil a request for an elephant, like that exemplary grandmother Hannah Whitall Smith.)

The second traditional function of grandparents, childcare, may still *in extremis* have a certain evolutionary function; that is, when natural parents die or defect. In principle, orphaned or abandoned grandchildren from deprived and affluent families alike are better off adopted by grandparents, like the orphaned Fenella in Katherine Mansfield's tender account, rather than dispatched to boarding schools at an early age or left to the mercies of the state, according to social status. The most heroic examples, perhaps, of grandparents stepping into the breach are the mostly African-American and Puerto Rican grandmothers single-handedly rearing grandchildren because their sons and daughters have succumbed to the related epidemics of crack cocaine and AIDS.

Since both my working daughter and daughter-in-law are not only alive and healthy but can pay for childcare, my own self-inflicted bouts of childcare, though welcome, serve no such essential function. The nearest I came to that may have been my excursions with my second granddaughter during the first few months of her life, when she rarely stopped screaming from colic. To give her exhausted parents a break, I once spent two dreadful hours marching her around Kew Gardens, while she startled every water bird in sight.

Finally, grandmothers as educators. My grandchildren are too young for me to influence, let alone teach them, the way Bertrand Russell was influenced and taught by his grandmother or the chef Peter Gordon by his. The influence of

Penelope Betjeman was not wholly appreciated by her grand-daughter until she was in her late teens. But I can undertake that essential role summed up for me by an Israeli friend appalled at my lack of grandmothers, who asked, 'But who was there to tell the stories?' Grandmothers are keepers of history, both family and national; of mythology; of the dialect of the tribe, as well as of the rituals, of which more in a later section. These days, videos, tapes, CD-ROMs, the printed word, take care of the stories, up to a point. But there's still room for grandmotherly retelling. I sing, too, the songs my mother sang to me, many of which I've never heard elsewhere. As I also begin to tell my elder granddaughter stories of her mother's childhood, and of mine. She's not yet quite ready for history. But I note Susan Sibbald's grandmother recounting her memories of the second Jacobite rebellion, as I note my interviewees telling their grandchildren about living through the Second World War.

The difference between grandmothers like me and more evolutionary grandmothers is that I am given the choice. Perhaps just a little, like Lauris Edmond, I am still of a generation conditioned to believe that I should put my family first. More importantly, I undertake what I do because, to my total but, I suspect, not uncommon surprise, I find being around small children again, my grandchildren, pure privilege; a rechecking into life at a very fundamental level.

But just because I am not strictly necessary, I don't have to stick around any longer than I want to. Fascinating as it is watching small children develop, doing so has made me recall that it can, unrelieved, be as boring as watching grass grow and much more exhausting. I am no endlessly patient Hannah Whitall Smith; let alone a willing resource, as our government would have it. Yet in our brave new millennium world, would you believe it, the old usefulness of grandmothers is once more being noticed. Neither state nor private provision for childcare is adequate. So Granny sets to again. Her readiness to mind toddlers or pick up older children from school can free their mothers for productive work. How about Grandma as classroom auxiliary? How about her being helped to find sheltered housing near the family home as a means to such ends? Nothing changes. Except the grandmothers. For the luckiest of whom these days grandchildren are a bonus rather than a duty.

In a later section we'll encounter grandmothers with better things to do than tend their grandchildren. For now I'll just point out that across Europe in general and the United Kingdom in particular, many grandmothers have made themselves a willing resource anyway, without government instruction. Despite the break-up of close-knit communities, of increased social mobility, dividing generations both socially and geographically, despite the much higher incidence of marital breakdown – and sometimes because of it – the grandmother has survived. As Shirley Hughes points out, among divorced or divorcing couples it may sometimes be the grandmother who holds a family together.

The USA is, or was, another matter. It is no coincidence that the recent flood of books and articles about grandparenting originated there. Grandparenthood may have been, according to a writer, Thomas Cole, quoted on my opening page, invented in nineteenth-century New England, following earlier marriage and increased longevity there, as compared to in Europe. But the immigrant society which succeeded it across the USA regarded Granny as expendable, very often – we can see similar tendencies among recent Chinese immigrants to Britain, in the interviews with a group of Hakka-speaking grandmothers from Hong Kong quoted in a later section of this book. Many grandparents, of course, remained in the old country, while even those who did make the move were unable to speak the same language as their grandchildren – '*Ess, mein kind,*' the limit of conversation. (A friend from another immigrant society, Israel, remarked that the first thing she noticed in England was that grandparents and grandchildren were able to talk to each other.) Finally, the traumas so many immigrants were escaping from – poverty and discrimination at best; persecution, pogrom, famine, holocaust at worst – made the past something to be shunned, not clung to, let alone celebrated.

In nineteenth- and early twentieth-century America, the hardships of pioneer life, of course, militated against the presence of an older generation, while poor communications made it difficult, if not impossible, to communicate with those left behind. But as society developed, the intense mobility of middle-class America, setting families to move from one side of the continent to the other in the interests of work, continued to prevent significant contact between the generations. Even where contact was maintained, not only was there no obvious role for the grandmothers, but their influence on their grandchildren was seen by some psychologists in the 1930s and forties as positively pernicious. No surprise that the USA saw the first ghettoisation of the old, with 'sunset' communities appearing in places with good climates like Florida and southern Arizona. Or that the more lively pensioners, responsibilities behind them, took to the roads in recreation vehicles. No room for grandchildren in them.

The irony, of course, is that outside such affluence the USA has also seen the highest incidence of grandparents rearing their children, following the related epidemics of crack cocaine and AIDS, especially among the African-American and Puerto Rican communities. Out of the Afro-American community, too, came, in the seventies, the new passion for exploring family and tribal roots which I sense was and is one of the contexts in which the upsurge of interest in grandparents and grandparenting should be seen, alongside changing demography. The flood of books and papers – and more recently websites – increases yearly and has done so since the seventies. In Britain, there are now grandparenting courses. Yet English books about grandparents are often nostalgic and anecdotal, called things like *I Don't Feel Old*. American titles are more portentous: *The Changing American Grandparent*, *The Significance of Grandparenthood* and so forth. The fact that Sheila Kitzinger's *Becoming a Grandmother* was commissioned and first published in the USA rather than her native England is probably significant. I am not alone, it seems, in having to learn grandmotherhood from scratch.

Providers

Many of these old houses are former silkworm depositories . . . Early photographs show old women hatchers. Grandmothers, being rather inactive, were rather good egghatchers, incubating silkworms in the warmth of their corsets. At night they wore little egg-boxes in bed.

MARION BULL, 3 October 1998

The progress of technology and the introduction of laborsaving devices into the home have limited the former activities performed by the grandmother for her children and grandchildren. In the past, if the stocking had a hole, the grandmother would darn it; now, with nylon, this cannot be done . . .

In ERNEST BURGESS (ed.), *Ageing in Western Societies*, 1960

Retirement is a word unknown to the peasant of the Andes. Healthy people continue to labour, though in reduced form, just as long as they are physically able to do so. Appropriate to the older members of the household are such tasks as weeding the fields near the house, scaring the birds away from the fields when the crops are maturing, minding the house when the younger members of the household are away, tending distant fields or herding animals or going away on a trading expedition. Elders also play an important part in the care and supervision of children. They are in large measure responsible for the transfer of much of the myth and folklore of the society to their grandchildren.

ALLAN R. HOLMBURG, 'Cultural Differences and the Concept of Time', 1961

Old women would cultivate their garden patch till very feeble and 'carried wood and water as long as they were able to move their legs'. They prepared milling stones, wove baskets and plaques out of rabbit weed, made pots and bowls from clay, ground corn, darned old clothes, cared for children and guarded the house; and when there was nothing else to do, they would sit and watch the fruit drying in the sun. The old frequently expressed the desire to keep on working till they died.

LEO SIMMONS, *Role of the Aged in Primitive Societies*, 1945

During the winter my grandmother made lots of fish-nets of nettle-stalks fibre. As winter came on, grandmother had a supply of thorn-apple thorns and she got these up and pinned up the children's coats so that they could be warm, and we started off in the snowstorm and went to the sugar-bush.

Grandmother had charge of storing the fish and made the young girls do the work . . .

> Quoted in LEO SIMMONS, *Role of the Aged in Primitive Societies*, 1945

Women find it easier than men to grow old in a becoming way . . . With old men it is different. They do not belong so much indoors as women do. They have no pretty little manual occupations. The old lady knits her stitches as long as her eye and finger will let her.

> OLIVER WENDELL HOLMES, *Over the Teacups*, 1891

It always astonished me that I could make my grandmother go into raptures of joy just by being hungry.

> JEAN-PAUL SARTRE, *The Words*

Always she would prepare one of my favorite dishes – hot oatmeal with cream and brown sugar, apple cobbler, brownies, fudge, lemon custard tart – and I sat and ate as she watched, and, eating, I felt hunger: the hunger was in my mouth. To remember those foods brings the hunger back now, the sudden rush of it, the pain. In my mouth.

> JOYCE CAROL OATES, 'Why Don't You Come Live with Me It's Time', 1992

from Importance of Grandparents in Family Life

An older sibling was brought to a clinic physician for a facial hemangioma. As that child left with its parent the clever doctor noticed the mother took a plump 7 year old with her. At the next visit the physician inquired about that child's obesity and prevailed on the mother to permit an examination. Physical tests and laboratory, including endocrinological, studies were normal. Inquiry of the mother about the child's past as well as her own was fruitless. The mother and father were of normal size and weight. A psychiatric interview was scheduled and repeat inquiry, especially in regards unusual eating patterns, was negative. When the mother and siblings left the psychiatrist noticed they walked over to a tremendously obese woman who sat in the rear of the clinic waiting room. Further inquiry revealed she was the maternal grandmother and that she was so obese she couldn't walk. Questioning of her brought out her encouragement of the child to visit her house between meals and her use of food as an enticement. She apparently desired companionship and bought it with food to the child's harm.

MARVIN HADER, 1965

---

from Why Is Sex Fun?

That extended role of postmenopausal women has been explored by Kristen Hawkes, the anthropologist . . . Hawkes and her colleagues studied foraging by women of different ages among the Hadza hunter-gatherers of Tanzania. The women who devoted the most time to gathering food (especially roots, honey, and fruit) were postmenopausal women. Those hardworking Hadza grandmothers put in an impressive seven hours per day, compared to a mere three hours for teenagers and new brides and four and a half hours for married women with young children. As one might expect, foraging returns (measured in pounds of food gathered per hour) increased with age and experience, so that mature women achieved higher returns than teenagers, but, interestingly, the grandmothers' returns were still as high as those of women in their prime. The combination of more foraging hours and an unchanged foraging efficiency meant that the postmenopausal grandmothers brought in more food per day than any of the younger groups of women, even though their large harvests were greatly in excess of what was required to meet their own personal needs and they no longer had dependent young children to feed.

Hawkes and her colleagues observed that the Hadza grandmothers were sharing their excess food harvest with close relatives, such as their grandchildren and grown children. As a strategy for transforming food calories into pounds of baby, it would be more efficient for an older woman to donate the calories to grandchildren and grown children rather than to infants of her own (even if she still could give birth) because the older mother's fertility would be decreasing with age anyway, whereas her own children would be young adults at peak fertility. Naturally, this food-sharing argument does not constitute the sole reproductive contribution of postmenopausal women in traditional societies. A grandmother also baby-sits her grandchildren, thereby helping her adult children churn out more babies bearing the grandmother's genes. In addition, grandmothers lend their social status to their grandchildren, as to their children.

If one were playing God or Darwin and trying to decide whether to make older women undergo menopause or remain fertile, one would draw up a balance sheet, contrasting the benefits of menopause in one column with its costs in the other column. The costs of menopause are the potential children that a woman forgoes by undergoing menopause. The potential benefits include avoiding the increased risk of death due to childbirth and parenting at an advanced age, and gaining the benefit of improved survival for one's grandchildren and prior children.

JARED DIAMOND, 1998

Annie, my mother-in-law, lived with us for seventeen years and was picture-book perfect. She washed Monday, ironed Tuesday, Wednesday was bedrooms, Thursday baking, Friday fish and floors, Saturday polishing, Sunday God and sewing . . .

She had *The Light of the World* on her bedroom wall and her drawers were full of knitting needles. She made rock cakes and breast of lamb with barley, she cooked pig's livers and stuffed hearts, only stopping short of tripe for my sake. If things weren't going smoothly in our world, she would open a tin of condensed milk and hide it in the fridge with a spoon in it.

PHYLLIDA LAW, author's interview

You see, on Saturday they will come and Robert will say, 'Tweet gran!' He means sweet. Well I can't give him one because they only allow . . . You see I buy them sweets and then they pocket them and they don't give 'em them. Well if I was me he'd have the packet immediately . . . You're a bit restricted aren't you with your grandchildren?

PAUL THOMPSON ET AL., *I Don't Feel Old*, 1990

But of course you do feed them. They always come saying, 'Nan, I'm starving.' You try to give them what you couldn't give your own. Like we pay for music lessons for one of ours.

Birmingham grandmother, 1999

My grandmother I did meet, she used to wear a white apron and a long black skirt. And whenever we went to visit, she said, 'Come on, kneel down,' and she'd get the tooth comb out, and tooth-comb our hair onto her white apron, in case we'd picked up anything at school. I always remember that. And then she'd say, 'Give me the tin off of the chest of drawers. Here's a sweet for you. Only one.' And then we'd have to put it back.

Birmingham grandmother, 1999

The Cupboard

I know a little cupboard,
With a teeny tiny key,
And there's a jar of Lollypops
    For me, me, me.

It has a little shelf, my dear,
As dark as dark can be,
And there's a dish of Banbury Cakes
    For me, me, me.

I have a small fat grandmamma,
With a very slippery knee,

And she's Keeper of the Cupboard
  With the key, key, key.

And when I'm very good, my dear,
As good as good can be,
There's Banbury Cakes and Lollypops
  For me, me, me.

WALTER DE LA MARE, 1904

---

from The Natives of Sarawak

I. Manang – Come up, grandson, this my house is large
  enough for you all.

Up they went, and not before the army was all inside was
  the house filled.

And the army rested there.

'Let us of the army fetch wood and seek for meat:' so said
  they.

I. Manang – No, no, grandchildren; at all costs, I will give you
  a meal.

And she filled with rice a pot the size of a chestnut;

And a pot of meat the size of a bird's egg.

Said Sampurei: 'I will go in, and see grandmother cooking.'

Sampurei – Where is the rice which has been cooked, grandmother?

I. Manang – That is it, grandson, only that.

Sampurei – Let me swallow it all up and no man know it.

I. Manang – Not so, grandson, let each one fairly have his
  share: do you go and get leaves.

Away went Sampurei and fetched some blades of *lalang* grass.

I. Manang – Why bring that – for a pig's litter?

Sampurei – No, friend, to eat rice with.

I. Manang – How can a man eat with *lalang* leaves?

Sampurei – Don't you know how much a grain of rice is?

I. Manang – Go again and fetch some plantain leaves.

Sampurei – I will not weary myself to no purpose:

   Were they required I know how to get *ataps*:

   As for rice there is none to be put into the leaves.

   And grandmother Manang arose, and took rice and meat;

   She served it out sitting, piling it in heaps as high as herself
      was sitting.

   She served it out standing, piling it in heaps as high as her-
      self was standing.

I. Manang – Sampurei, you divide the food; long have men
      praised your skill in dividing portions.

Sampurei – Yes, grandmother. Get ready, all ye of the army.

   And he took the rice and meat, and tossed it to the left;

   He tossed it to the right and behind, and sprinkled it about:

   And yet not a grain was lost.

   Astonished was grandmother Manang.

I. Manang – In truth you are clever, grandson, skilful with the
      tips of your fingers.

   But why do you not eat, Sampurei?

Sampurei – Full is the bag made by my mother, the pouch
      made by my grandmother.

   And the remainder of the rice left by the army was a matful;

   The fragments of meat five plates full.

   But it was all devoured by Lualimban:

   Yet still he wanted to eat, wide open was his mouth.

   They fetched ten *pasus* of rice, and upset them into his
      mouth; yet still he wanted more.

   They got a chest of paddy, and poured it into his mouth,
      rammed it down with a rod; but yet he was not satisfied.

   And he proceeded to eat the gongs big and small and the
      jars.

   And all the goods of grandmother Manang were consumed,
      and the old lady wept.

Klieng – You have also shown your power, grandmother: so
    have we:
  But do not be vexed at heart;
  Your things shall all be restored as before.
  After their jokes were ended, grandmother Manang
    departed.

Collected and translated by H. Ling Roth, 1896

---

from Lactation in Grandmothers

I have recently had the privilege of witnessing what can only be
considered a most unusual physiological phenomenon – a lactating grandmother. A 55-year-old Black woman who lives in
Johannesburg had 2 daughters; the youngest, born in
December 1942, had 4 children, born respectively in 1958,
1963, 1965 and the last on 9 August 1973. Three days after this
baby's birth, the mother died. Ten days later the grandmother
fetched her granddaughter from the hospital, and was determined to breast-feed, in spite of being postmenopausal, and of
the lapse of 32 years since last lactating. She knew that the 'old
people' had done so under similar circumstances. Although she
was instructed on feeding with a commercial formula, she
began sucking immediately. After a month of patient and persistent suckling, her efforts were rewarded. She was again
lactating, 32 years after her last child and without having had
an intervening pregnancy. At no time was she concerned or
worried that she might not be able to feed. Black children are
commonly suckled for 12–24 months or longer, and this baby
was no exception.

  The health visitor who looked after their welfare was thrilled
with the baby, her progress and her *Gogo*'s (affectionate term
for grandmother) ability to breast-feed. Only two visits to the

clinic, for minor illnesses, were necessary during this period. Her weight chart (based on Harvard standards) showed her weight to be well above the third percentile, not reaching the 50th, but running satisfactorily parallel. Three months before her second birthday, her weight was 11 kg and her height 76.9 cm, well within the normal range for her age.

In the eastern Transvaal lives another *Gogo*, about 50 years of age. Her 24-year-old daughter-in-law came to live at the paternal kraal. She bore a son on 3 March 1973. For 4 months the mother fed him, but then had to return to work. The paternal grandmother took over the feeding. Her youngest son, now 12 years of age, was the last of 8 children. The baby was temporarily put onto the bottle, but continued to prefer the breast – *Gogo* suckled frequently and waited. Her milk came, again after a period of 1 month. She had enough milk for the baby, and the bottle was thankfully discarded.

Yet another grandmother, who died some 15 years ago, lived at Tlaseng, in the Rustenburg area, north-western Transvaal. After raising her own family (all breast-fed) she is reported to have, after an interval of 27 years, successfully breast-fed her granddaughter (born 1909), whose mother died when she was 6 months of age. Once again a month elapsed before lactation was induced by frequent suckling, and continued until the child was 2 years of age.

We hope to be able to carry out far more detailed investigations on the breast milk, its amount, concentration, etc., of non-puerperal lactators.

If only present-day mothers could be encouraged to take a chapter out of the grandmothers' book and establish successful lactation by frequent and persistent suckling immediately after pregnancy, they too would be able to produce a plentiful supply of breast milk, which is the baby's right. Come on, mothers!

BARBARA D. RICHARDSON, 1975

from A Quaker Grandmother

That Gram should ever fail to provide sweets when we wanted them did not enter our heads, and I cannot now remember a single instance, save one, when she disappointed our expectations. That was a time – I suppose I was seven or eight – when we had set our hearts on having a pet elephant, and went, as was our custom, to ask Gram for one. The next day we were sent off to the country, where she was to follow in a few days. We went, fully expecting her to arrive with the animal, and she was left to find it. She knew we expected one, and, in her desire not to disappoint us, she actually drove to Whiteley's (who advertised then to provide anything on earth) to ask them if she could hire one for us. She would have done it, and brought us the creature, had she not discovered that it had to be fed daily on a ton or so of hay. The difficulty and expense of procuring hay in such quantities was finally too much for her, and she brought down only toy elephants, with which we, heartless wretches, were far from satisfied!

RAY STRACHEY, 1914

from Folk Tales of Israel

My grandmother, may she rest in peace, was a midwife. She carried on her work for the love of it, without seeking any reward. She was sure that her payment would be to go straight to Heaven. As there were neither doctors nor qualified midwives in Zakho, Kurdistan, at that time, my grandmother had her hands full.

One day she sat outside her house embroidering. She was very tired after a hard day's work. Suddenly she saw a beautiful cat creeping stealthily into the house, so that she could not be heard, and sniffing in all the corners as if she were searching for food.

The cat found favor with my grandmother, who fed her, noticing as she did so that the cat was pregnant! My grandmother said to herself, 'If only I were this cat's midwife!'

Days passed, and one dark and stormy night my grandmother was awakened from sleep by the sound of steps. There was a rap at the door. She got up hurriedly, dressed, and opened the door. On the threshold someone stood, tired and sweating. He spoke hurriedly, '*Sotte* (Grandma), come with me, and you will earn a lot of money. My wife is with child and the pangs of birth are already with her. There is no one to help her.'

Grandmother listened to the request, rejoicing with delight. This was simply a windfall at such an hour and on such a night. It would be like doing all the six hundred and thirteen commands at once.

Zakho is a small town, and Grandma strode up the main street behind the man. She could not understand why she did not hear his footsteps. Suddenly she noticed that they had gone beyond the last house in the town and were now walking in an open field. She trembled all over, knowing that no one lived there. She understood that the man, leading her, was no other than a *shed*.

'Lord, have mercy on me,' she muttered to herself, but she did not utter a sound. They reached a stone bridge, with each stone ten meters square. They entered a huge cave, and therein Grandma heard a man's voice, 'Grandmother, come in. It is here.'

My grandmother became scared. Inside there were many *shedim* and *shedot*, with little horns on their heads, singing and mewing like cats.

'What a pleasant company in which to find myself,' she thought to herself, but she did not say a word. The *shed* with the longest horns took her aside and said to her, 'If the newborn is a son, you will get everything you want, but if it is a daughter, God forbid.'

Pale with fear, Grandma did not answer a word. She entered the confinement room, and whom did she see? The cat that had visited her a little while ago was lying there. The cat opened her mouth and whispered, 'Dear grandmother, do not eat here or you will be turned into a *shed.*'

My grandmother kept in mind the cat's warning and did not eat anything in the cave during the whole night, although she was offered the best and most delicious foods and drinks. When the time of birth came, she rolled up her sleeves and set to work. A male cat was born. What rejoicing broke out in the cave! It reached the heavens! The chief of the *shedim* called my grandmother and said to her, 'Whatever you ask even up to half of my kingdom, I will give you.'

'No,' said my grandmother, 'I do not want anything. The price for a good deed is the deed itself.'

'That is impossible! You must take something! She saw a bunch of garlic in the corner of the room and asked for a little bit, just to get rid of the obligation. They stuffed her dress with garlic and then escorted her home.

Tired and broken, Grandma threw the garlic by the door and sank into her bed. The next morning her grandchild woke her up: 'From where did you bring so much gold, Grandma?' She looked toward the door and saw that the garlic was nothing else than pure gold. She distributed the gold among her children, grandchildren, and all the family.

Collected and translated by Dov Noy, 1963

---

from The Pilgrim's Progress

By this river side in the meadow, there were cotes and folds for sheep, an house built for the nourishing and bringing up of those lambs, the babes of those women that go on pilgrimage.

Also there was here one that was entrusted with them, who could have compassion, and that could gather these lambs with his arm, and carry them in his bosom, and that could gently lead those that were with young. Now to the care of this man, Christiana admonished her four daughters to commit their little ones; that by these waters they might be housed, harboured, succoured and nourished, and that none of them might be lacking in time to come. This man, if any of them go astray, or be lost, he will bring them again; he will also bind up that which was broken, and will strengthen them that are sick. Here they will never want meat, and drink and clothing, here they will be kept from thieves and robbers, for this man will die before one of those committed to his trust shall be lost. Besides, here they shall be sure to have good nurture and admonition, and shall be taught to walk in right paths, and that you know is a favour of no small account. Also here, as you see, are delicate waters, pleasant meadows, dainty flowers, variety of trees, and such as bear wholesome fruit. Fruit, not like that that Matthew eat of, that fell over the wall out of Beelzebub's Garden, but fruit that procureth health where there is none, and that continueth and increaseth it where it is.

So they were content to commit their little ones to him; and that which was also an encouragement to them so to do, was, for that all this was to be at the charge of the King, and so was an hospital to young children and orphans.

JOHN BUNYAN, 1630

---

from Grandmother's Child

But it was not only at school that a little girl could learn lessons. There were such lots of things going on in Grandmother's house, especially in the big kitchen in the ell. There was no sink in the kitchen and the dishes were washed at the table, in a round dishpan, and drained in a large black pan, similar to the pan that was used for baking five loaves of bread. On the farm at Turtle Creek, Grandmother had had a built-in oven, but Hillsborough kitchen contained a high oven stove, with an apron front, where a little girl could warm her cold feet when she came in from playing in the snow.

For supper, Grandmother made buckwheat pancakes, poured from the jug in which a little batter had been left the night before. She had added yeast to the batter, then, just before supper, she put in sour milk and saleratus and buck-wheat meal, and beat the mixture briskly with a wooden spoon. For small cakes, the butter might be spooned on the griddle, but for large ones, it was poured from the jug. Very deftly, Grandmother would keep two griddles going, spoon-ing or pouring, turning, removing the cooked pancakes to two plates on the apron of the stove, buttering, turning the plates to keep the cakes evenly warmed, flipping the pan-cakes on the griddle. Lastly, she would quarter the pile of cakes, all hot and dripping with butter. Usually there was molasses to put on the cakes, but sometimes the last of a bottle of strawberries or raspberries might be produced as a special treat.

Harriet learned to cut out paper rounds and dip them in paraffin to put on the tops of the preserves. Then she would put paper caps over the bottles and tie them with string. There were no self sealers in those days. She learned to peel apples for drying, to string beans for drying, to cut up cabbage for sauer kraut, to chop fruit for mincemeat and vegetables for pickles and relishes.

All the pots in Grandmother's kitchen were heavy iron pots, very black. The little girl used to marvel that such white things could come out of such black pots. When the family came for a visit, Grandmother used to make boiled apple dumplings, three pots of apple dumplings for the big crowd. She would swirl the dumplings around in the boiling water, then take them out, all fluffy white, and big. How did she know the precise moment when they were done and would collapse if left in a moment longer?

ESTHER CLARK WRIGHT, 1959

---

from Old Age Among the Chipewyan

The situation of an old woman in Chipewyan society [of Canada] is quite different. Where a man has a single paramount activity – obtaining food from the bush – a woman has three: reproduction, handicrafts, and processing food . . .

Women's role in reproduction is extended after menopause by the common Chipewyan practice of adopting children . . . Grandparents have the right to adopt a child from each of their children's marriages, and almost any woman can obtain a small child to care for without any trouble. This allows a woman to fulfill most of the duties of motherhood and be called mother, 'enna', by a child independently of her actual ability to reproduce. Moreover, small children are of great service in the minor tasks of running a household (hauling water, wood, etc.) and are eagerly sought. Since many of the duties of child rearing are assumed by older children, the mother or grandmother who has or adopts several children may find her work load lessened.

The second major aspect of women's work is handicrafts, primarily sewing and beadwork, but also such other tasks as the preparation of hides for leather. This work is demanding and requires both strength and good hand-eye coordination. Even though talent varies greatly among women, a lifetime of experience gives a competent older woman a real advantage over women many years her junior. And if a woman's strength and eyesight fail with age, she can still teach her skills to younger women and supervise their work – an option that men do not have when their strength fails them.

The third aspect of women's work is processing food. Cooking is only a minor part of food processing, a task that can be entrusted to young girls under minimal supervision. Processing food means primarily cutting dry meat and splitting and deboning fish for drying. These tasks are hard, requiring considerable skill and expertise. They must generally be done outside the dwelling under uncomfortable conditions. Fortunately, the demand for food is proportional to the size of the household, and as demand increases, so does the female labor pool available to supply it. Like sewing, food preparation can be done by several women working together, and old women can supervise when they cannot perform much of the actual work themselves.

Because women's work is considered to involve the use of skills acquired through instruction and practice rather than the use of magic, women are able to remain competent adults much longer than men. Since no special powers are involved, women can cooperate in their work without any loss of face. And old women whose physical strength is waning are valued for the advice and expertise they can contribute. If being able to do it all by herself does not confer the same prestige on a young woman as hunting confers on a man, neither does needing some help destroy an old woman's self-respect and reputation as it does an old man's.

HENRY S. SHARP, 1981

Minders

from Old Mrs Harris

Grandmother's own lot could improve only with the family fortunes – any comfort for herself, aside from that of the family, was inconceivable to her; and on the other hand she could have no real unhappiness while the children were well, and good, and fond of her and their mother [Victoria]. That was why it was worth while to get up early in the morning and make her bed neat and draw the bed-spread smooth. The little boys loved to lie on her lounge and her pillows when they were tired. When they were sick, Ronald and Hughie wanted to be in her lap. They had no physical shrinking from her because she was old. And Victoria was never jealous of the children's wanting to be with her so much; that was a mercy!

Sometimes, in the morning, if her feet ached more than usual, Mrs Harris felt a little low. (Nobody did anything about broken arches in those days, and the common endurance test of old age was to keep going after every step cost something.) She would hang up her towel with a sigh and go into the kitchen, feeling that it was hard to make a start. But the moment she heard the children running down the uncarpeted back stairs, she forget to be low. Indeed, she ceased to be an individual, an old woman with aching feet; she became part of a group, became a relationship. She was drunk up into their freshness when they burst in upon her, telling her about their dreams, explaining their troubles with buttons and shoe-laces and underwear shrunk too small. The tired, solitary old woman Grandmother had been at daybreak vanished; suddenly the morning seemed as important to her as it did to the children, and the mornings ahead stretched out sunshiny, important.

WILLA CATHER, 1932

from The People of Ship Street

The granny in Ship Street plays a very important part, nearly as important as the Jamaican granny. She is, therefore, being given a section to herself, although she is obviously a Mum at the same time. Children show some of the Jamaican child's mobility in regard to the granny, or 'nin', or 'nanny', or 'nanna' or 'gran', as she is often called. Sometimes a child differentiates between its maternal and paternal grandmother by reserving a different name for each. No constant rule has been found about which name is given to which grandmother. A child will go and sleep in its granny's house without previous arrangement with the parents. For example, I asked Tim, aged 14, if he likes his new flat. He replied, 'I would rather be here.' He misses granny. It was 10.25 p.m. when we left. I glanced at Tim and said to granny, 'I think someone intends to spend the night here.' Tim looked at granny and asked, 'Might as well? It's too late to go back now.' Granny nodded her head, Tim smiled. I asked if his parents wouldn't be worried. Both granny and Tim said together that they would know where he is. As recorded, Bill, aged 12, still sleeps in granny's household. The only reason I could gather for this is because Mrs J. does not want to be without any grandchild. (She has two bachelor sons living with her.) Bill hadn't come in before we left.

[. . .] In a crisis the granny will take charge.

Joe was brought up by his mother's mother. When he was about two he got pneumonia very badly. Granny took charge and took Joe over to her place. When he got well he remained with granny. 'Granny was a woman with a will of her own. Perhaps that is why she had three husbands.' Granny was strict but kind. There were always children about in her household. When they needed beating 'Granny didn't hesitate to beat us'. She never used a stick. 'Granny was always boss.' She died quite recently. Joe continues to live with his stepgrandfather. Joe is now 23.

Besides helping in a crisis a granny gives a lot of help in everyday affairs, such as minding the children, cooking the midday dinner when the mother is out at work, and looking after little children when the mother has gone into hospital to have a new baby.

When Mrs E.'s husband died and she had to go out to work again to keep her children, it was her mother who came and did the cooking and looked after her children. Mrs E. would go out to work in the morning locking the young children in the bedroom. 'I had to and me mother would come as soon as she could.'

Another woman said: 'Me mother does all the cooking for me and me children. She's a very good cook although she's 78. I do all the washing.'

In some cases, although this occurs only among the older people, there is a trace of the granny acting as midwife, or being called in to lay out a neighbour. Mrs G. said that in the olden days, many a time women in labour sent for her when the nurse hadn't arrived. She had attended many births in this street of theirs and brought many a baby safely into this world. Sometimes she went to help the midwife. Of course now it is a different matter, she is getting old and she doesn't go out much. She was present in the room at the births of all her grandchildren.

MADELINE KERR, 1958

---

from Baha of Karo

Two years after the child's birth, one of the child's grand-mothers, usually his father's mother who often lives in the same compound, comes at dawn and knocks on the mother's hut door; she goes in and picks up the child and takes him or her off to her own hut. The child's mother runs off to her own mother's home. In the morning the child bursts out crying, he cries bitterly . . . He keeps running to his mother's hut, but he doesn't see her there and he bursts out crying. After three or four days he forgets about the breast. His grandmother has him in her hut and she looks after him.

MARY SMITH, 1954

———————

from State Could Pay Grannies to Mind Baby

Parents of single mothers could be offered incentives to help their daughters to raise their children as part of a sustained new attempt to tackle the growing problem of teenage pregnancies.

Tony Blair has made the issue of teenage mothers the new priority of his social exclusion unit, established to look into and suggest remedies for the problems caused by poverty and deprivation. The issue is particularly pressing not only because of the dramatic rise in the number of teenage pregnancies but also because the resulting children are more likely to have health problems and even to die in infancy.

Ministers are studying proposals to encourage or cajole grandparents actively to help their young children to raise their offspring. This could be done either through financial incentives or penalties. Other suggestions include establishing hostels, with training centres and creches, for young mothers to help them off benefit and into work.

One problem with mobilising grandmothers is that offering incentives would mean paying money to those who are already helping their daughters. Critics complain that these are the

very people who raised their own children to become teenage
mothers.

ROBERT SHRIMSLEY, *Electronic Telegraph*, 1999

---

from The Voyage

What a very small cabin it was! It was like being shut up in a
box with grandma. The dark round eye above the wash-stand
gleamed at them dully. Fenella felt shy. She stood against the
door, still clasping her luggage and the umbrella. Were they
going to get undressed in here? Already her grandma had
taken off her bonnet, and, rolling up the strings, she fixed each
with a pin to the lining before she hung the bonnet up. Her
white hair shone like silk; the little bun at the back was covered
with a black net. Fenella hardly ever saw her grandma with her
head uncovered; she looked strange.

'I shall put on the woollen fascinator your deal mother crocheted for me,' said grandma, and, unstrapping the sausage,
she took it out and wound it round her head; the fringe of grey
bobbles danced at her eyebrows as she smiled tenderly and
mournfully at Fenella. Then she undid her bodice, and something under that, and something else underneath that. Then
there seemed a short, sharp tussle, and grandma flushed faintly.
Snip! Snap! She had undone her stays. She breathed a sigh of
relief and, sitting on the plush couch, she slowly and carefully
pulled off her elastic-sided boots and stood them side by side.

By the time Fenella had taken off her coat and skirt and put
on her flannel dressing-gown grandma was quite ready.

'Must I take off my boots, grandma? They're lace.'

Grandma gave them a moment's deep consideration. 'You'd
feel a great deal more comfortable if you did, child,' said she.
She kissed Fenella. 'Don't forget to say your prayers. Our dear

Lord is with us when we are at sea even more than when we are on dry land. And because I am an experienced traveller,' said grandma briskly, 'I shall take the upper berth.'

'But, grandma, how ever will you get up there?'

Three little spider-like steps were all Fenella saw. The old woman gave a small silent laugh before she mounted them nimbly, and she peered over the high bunk at the astonished Fenella.

'You didn't think your grandma could do that, did you?' said she. And as she sank back Fenella heard her light laugh again.

The hard square of brown soap would not lather and the water in the bottle was like a kind of blue jelly. How hard it was, too, to turn down those stiff sheets; you simply had to tear your way in. If everything had been different, Fenella might have got the giggles . . . At last she was inside, and while she lay there panting, there sounded from above a long, soft whispering, as though someone was gently, gently rustling among tissue paper to find something. It was grandma saying her prayers . . .

A long time passed. Then the stewardess came in; she trod softly and leaned her hand on grandma's bunk.

'We're just entering the Straits,' she said.

'Oh!'

'It's a fine night, but we're rather empty. We may pitch a little.'

And indeed at that moment the Picton boat rose and rose and hung in the air just long enough to give a shiver before she swung down again, and there was the sound of heavy water slapping against her sides. Fenella remembered she had left that swan-necked umbrella standing up on the little couch. If it fell over, would it break? But grandma remembered too, at the same time.

'I wonder if you'd mind, stewardess, laying down my umbrella,' she whispered.

'Not at all, Mrs Crane.' And the stewardess, coming back to grandma, breathed, 'Your little granddaughter's in such a beautiful sleep.'

'God be praised for that!' said grandma.

'Poor little motherless mite!' said the stewardess. And grandma was still telling the stewardess all about what happened when Fenella fell asleep.

KATHERINE MANSFIELD, 1922

---

from Hehe Grandmothers

Young children may be said to have a very carefree time at the homes of their grandmothers, and they learn to expect much harsher criticism and occasional beatings from their parents for failings which would pass unremarked at the homes of their grandparents. One thing of value they gain from association with their grandmothers. In the evenings the grandmother is free to teach them folk-tales, songs and riddles. The tribe [a Bantu people of east Africa] is fairly rich in this kind of lore, and all old women are practised raconteurs. Women are far more interested in such tales than the men. Men spend long hours discussing events of the day, or alternatively talking of hunting or wars of the past. The mothers of the children are usually too busy or preoccupied to tell them stories, so the children have a much-appreciated opportunity of listening to tales and songs at the hut of the grandmother. One young girl, who possesses a marvellous fund of tales, spontaneously said to me that she did not know where children would ever learn tales if they had no grandmothers.

ELIZABETH FISHER BROWN, 1935

from The Hidden Patient

Case # 1. Ms H is a thin, tired-looking, 57-year-old African-American woman employed as a nutritionist for a Head Start program. Divorced, with some college education, she lives with her seven grandchildren, ages 5 to 13, in a relatively spacious, low-rise public housing project in the center of one of New Jersey's poorest cities. The family has a household income of less than $17,000 a year.

None of the children are HIV infected. Ms H is proud of her grandchildren, the oldest girl is 'an A and B student and very active in church'. She is raising the five granddaughters and two grandsons alone and has been the surrogate parent for 11 years. Her two daughters, the children's mothers, are both drug users, one of whom is infected with HIV. Ms H's concerns as a custodial grandparent speak directly to the stress she faces. 'I'm afraid to let them out to play. I worry about the neighborhood with the drugs and police activity. Police race through the walk way, endangering the children who play there. I won't let the children, especially the girls, go out alone.'

Raising her grandchildren has meant reducing her hours of work. 'I'm supposed to work from 8 to 4 and I have to take time off from work to get [the youngest] to school. I'm afraid to keep taking time off because the job may be laying people off. I almost got fired because of the children. If they're sick or not in school, what am I to do? When they're out of school I have to take them to work with me. My boss is not sympathetic. But I'm not going to leave them to run around by themselves.'

Financial needs, discipline concerns, and coping with children's emotional reactions to their mothers' addiction and illness are compounding pressures. 'I have no time for myself. I am pooped. By the time I get home, do dinner, help with homework, get them from [sports] practice. There's no time left for me. I had planned to travel but I can't now. I miss doing things I used to do, like going to plays, visiting other churches. I was really into a lot of things. Like tomorrow, there's a trip to a church in Pennsylvania. I was supposed to go but I told them no. I want to get my ironing out of the way. I have to be where I am needed. My grandkids come first.'

Ms H described her health as 'fair', although worse than before she began raising her grandchildren. 'I had no problems then.' Her health has deteriorated over the past year. She has lot weight, gets less exercise, experiences greater fatigue, and has greater difficulty sleeping. A tobacco user, Ms H is smoking less than one year ago. As she described these health problems she noted, 'I have two asthmatic [grand]children. The doctor says [sleep problems] happen as you get older.' Ms H wears a neck brace for pain, which she attributes to stress and to an accident several years ago.

Self-reported chronic health problems include vision problems, diabetes, arthritis, high blood pressure, and an undiagnosed lung problem. 'There is a milky substance on my lungs. The doctor says it could be cancerous. I gotta go for tests.' Ms H has medical insurance for herself through her job, but it does not extend to any of the grandchildren, including the two who have asthma.

Several months following the interview, the HIV-infected daughter died on the street, of hypothermia.

Case # 2. Mrs F is a 62-year-old Euro-American widow living in her own home in a working class suburb with her 37-year-old daughter and 2½-year-old granddaughter, both of whom have AIDS. She completed some high school and was employed as an office worker until she was laid off when her daughter was pregnant. Once they both became ill, she could not go back to work as she maintains their home – providing meals, housekeeping, transportation, and other basic tasks. 'I've used up lots of money to care for them. Social Security doesn't make it. My charge card is maxed out. Even though the family receives financial assistance through Social Security

Disability for both the daughter and granddaughter, Mrs F is having difficulty paying their bills. She is especially worried about paying the mortgage once her daughter and granddaughter die and disability payments are terminated.

Mrs F's daughter, weakened by AIDS, still cares for her daughter, but relies on her mother's daily help with the child's medication regimen and other needs. The granddaughter is physically disabled, unable to walk or speak, and stands only with assistance. Medical appointments and hospitalizations for both the daughter and granddaughter organize Mrs F's life. 'I learned that Janna, my granddaughter, was HIV positive on her first birthday. She was born with a lot of problems. I didn't think she'd live. Finally, she was diagnosed at Babies Hospital. That is how my daughter learned that she [also] was infected.'

Family conflict over the HIV diagnosis also burdens Mrs F. One daughter-in-law has been very unsupportive. 'She thinks I didn't tell them right away, that I lied. And I don't know what she told her kids because they don't come around as often.'

The sense of social isolation is profound, as it was in the case of Ms H. 'I went to a group for other mothers of women with AIDS, but they were ready to fight. I was ready to sob, so I never went back. I don't go out much anymore. I'm only relating to doctors, nurses, and family so I don't see other people. I don't have the money to go out, and I don't have many people I trust.' Her confidant is a sister who lives across the country in Texas. her enjoyment of social events with other HIV-affected families with children is evident as she shows photos from a Christmas party for HIV-infected children.

Mrs F showed little emotion of any kind during the interview, but when asked how her own health compared to the time before she assumed care for her daughter and granddaughter, she became tearful. 'I get very emotional talking about them.' Her outlet is gardening. 'When I get upset, or it gets too much, I go outside and dig.' One area of the garden is named for her granddaughter.

She assessed her health as 'fair' and as having deteriorated over the past year. Chronic problems include glaucoma, hearing deficits, arthritis, and osteoporosis. She also complained of dental pain, indigestion, sleep difficulties, chest and back pain. Nervousness and tension may occur at times and may last for a few hours or persist for several days. Mrs F lost medical insurance when she stopped working to care for her daughter and granddaughter. Despite her chronic conditions and symptoms, she has no regular source of medical care. 'I can't afford to be hospitalized and I can't go for a checkup.' At age 62, she is too young for Medicare, but her income exceeds Medicaid eligibility. Her last physical exam was more than four years ago.

Her daughter died 11 months and her granddaughter 13 months after the interview.

JOSLIN HARRISON, 1998

Educators

from My Childhood

To see her wipe the dust from the icons and clean the chasubles was both an interesting and a pleasant experience. The icons were very rich, with pearls, silver and coloured stones along their edges. She would nimbly pick an icon up, smile at it and say with great feeling:

'What a lovely little face!'

Then she would cross herself and kiss the icon.

'It's all dusty and covered in soot. Ah, Holy Mother, light of my life! Look, Lenya, the writing's so fine and the figures so tiny, but everything stands out clearly. It's called "The Twelve

Holy Days" and there in the middle is the saintly Fyodorovna. And this one's "Don't mourn me in the grave, Holy Virgin".'

Often, it seemed, she played at icons like my crippled cousin Katerina played with her dolls, seriously and with deep emotion.

Many times she claimed to see devils in large numbers or one at a time:

'One night in Lent I was passing the Rudolfs' house. Everything was bathed in moonlight. Suddenly in front of me I saw something black sitting astride the roof, near the chimney. It was bending its horned head over the chimney and sniffing and snorting. So big and hairy it was, lashing away with its tail against the roof and scraping its feet over the tiles. I crossed myself and said: "Christ will rise again and his enemies will be scattered." At this he gave a little squeak and somersaulted down from the roof into the yard. – That got rid of him! The Rudolfs must have been cooking meat and of course he caught wind of it and came to enjoy the smell, so pleased he was that it was Lent and they were eating meat.'

The thought of the devil rolling head over heels down from the roof made me burst out laughing. Grandmother laughed too and said:

'They love getting up to mischief, like little children! I remember once I was doing the washing in the bath round about midnight. Suddenly the oven door blew open, and out they poured, smaller and smaller, red ones, green, black, just like cockroaches. I made for the door but couldn't reach it: I got stuck in the middle of thousands of devils. They filled the whole bathroom so tight that you couldn't move, crawling under my feet, tugging at me and pressing up against me so I couldn't even cross myself! Just like kittens they were, all furry-soft and warm, but they stood on their hind legs the whole time. They whirled and strutted about, showing their little teeth like mice. Their tiny eyes were green and their horns were just coming through and stuck out like small knobs. They had piglet's tails. Oh, Good Lord! I fainted clean away and when I came to, the candle had almost burnt out, the water in the tub had gone cold, and there was washing all over the floor. "You devils!" I thought, "Go back to hell!"'

When I closed my eyes I could see a dense stream of hairy creatures, all different colours, come pouring out of the mouth of the stove and from the little pebbles round it, filling the bathroom, blowing on the candle and cheekily sticking out their pinkish tongues.

It was both funny and horrifying. Grandmother shook her head and said nothing for a moment. Then she made another passionate outburst.

'I've seen lost souls as well. At night-time, too, in winter, when a storm was raging. I was crossing the ravine at Diukov where Yakov and Mikhail wanted to drown your father in one of the ice-holes in the pond – remember? Well, I was going my way and was just slithering down the path to the bottom of the gully when I heard such a whistling and whooping! There, in front of me, was a troika of black horses bearing right down on me with a fat devil in a red nightcap standing out like a piece of wood on the driving-seat and driving them on with reins made from steel chains in his outstretched hands. There wasn't any path round the gully and the troika, hidden in a cloud of snow, went straight over the pond. All the passengers were devils, and they whistled and shouted and waved their caps. I counted seven troikas that flew past like fire engines. The horses were black as crows and all of them were people who'd at one time been cursed by their parents. They provide good sport for devils, who ride them and drive them through the night to their different celebrations. It must have been a devil's wedding I saw . . .'

It was impossible not to believe Grandmother – she spoke so simply and convincingly.

MAXIM GORKY, 1913–14, translated by Ronald Wilks

from The Grandmother's Tale

I was brought up by my grandmother in Madras from my third year while my mother lived in Bangalore with a fourth child on hand after me. My grandmother took me away to Madras in order to give relief to an over-burdened daughter.

My grandmother Ammani was a busy person. She performed a variety of tasks all through the day, cooking and running the house for her two sons, gardening, counselling neighbours and the tenants living in the rear portion of the vast house stretching away in several segments, settling disputes, studying horoscopes and arranging matrimonial alliances. At the end of the day she settled down on a swing – a broad plank suspended by chains from the ceiling; lightly propelling it with her feet back and forth, chewing betel, she was completely relaxed at that hour. She held me at her side and taught me songs, prayers, numbers and the alphabet till suppertime.

I mention 'suppertime', but there was no fixed suppertime. My uncles returned home late in the evening. The senior uncle conducted a night school for slum children . . . The junior uncle worked in the harbour as a stevedore's assistant and came home at uncertain hours. Suppertime could not be based on their home-coming but on my performance. My grandmother fed me only when I completed my lessons to her satisfaction. I had to repeat the multiplication table up to twenty but I always fumbled and stuttered after twelve and needed prodding and goading to attain the peak; I had to recite Sanskrit verse and slokas in praise of Goddess Saraswathi and a couple of other gods, and hymns in Tamil; identify six ragas when granny hummed the tunes or, conversely, mention the songs when she named the ragas; and then solve arithmetic problems such as, 'If a boy wants four mangoes costing one anna per mango, how much money will he have to take?' I wanted to blurt out, 'Boys don't have to buy, they can obtain a fruit with a well-aimed stone at a mango

tree.' I brooded, blinked without a word, afraid I might offend
her if I mentioned the stone technique for obtaining a fruit.
She watched me and then, tapping my skull, gently remarked,
'Never seen a bigger dunce . . .' It was all very taxing, I felt
hungry and sleepy. To keep me awake, she kept handy a bowl
of cold water and sprinkled it on my eyelids from time to time.

R. K. NARAYAN, 1993

from Reflections of Ambrosine

Grandmamma has given me most of my education herself
since we came to England, and she has been especially particular about deportment. I have never been allowed to lean back
in my chair or loll on a sofa, and she has taught me how to go
in and out of a room and how to enter a carriage. We had not
a carriage, so we had to arrange with footstools for the steps
and a chair on top of a box for the seat. That used to make me
laugh – but I had to do it – into myself! As for walking, I can
carry any sized bundle on my head, and Grandmamma says
she has nothing further to teach me in that respect, and that I
have mastered the fact that a gentlewoman should give the
impression that the ground is hardly good enough to tread
on. She has also made me go through all kinds of exercises to
insure suppleness, and to move from the hips. And the day
she told me she was pleased I shall never forget.

There are three things she says a woman ought to look;
straight as a dart, supple as a snake, and proud as a tiger-lily.

ELINOR GLYN, 1903

from Autobiography of an Indian Fox Woman

And my grandmother would keep on giving me instructions there, telling me how to lead a good life. She really was a very old woman. Surely she must have spoken the truth in what she had been saying to me. 'My grandchild,' she would say to me, 'soon I shall tell you how to live an upright life. To-day you see how old I am. I did exactly what I was told. I tried and thought how to live an upright life. Surely I have reached an old age,' she told me. 'That is the way you should do, if you listen to me as I instruct you. Now as for your mother, I began giving her instructions before she was grown up, every time I saw her. Because she was my relative is why I gave her instructions, although she was well treated by her father's sister by whom she was reared. That is why she knows how to make things which belong to the work of us women. If you observe the way your mother makes anything, you would do well, my grandchild. And this. As many of us as entered young womanhood, fasted. It was very many days: some fasted ten days, some four, five, every kind of way. To-day, to be sure, things are changing. When I was a young woman I fasted eight days. We always fasted until we were grown up,' my grandmother told me.

[. . .] 'Do not touch your hair: it might all come off. And do not eat sweet things. And if what tastes sour is eaten, one's teeth will come out. It is owing to that saying that we are afraid to eat sweet things,' my grandmother told me. She always gave me good advice from time to time. 'Well, there is another thing. Now the men will think you are mature as you have become a young woman, and they will be desirous of courting you. If you do not go around bashfully, for a long time they will not have the audacity to court you. When there is a dance, when there are many boys saying all sorts of funny things, if you do not notice it, they will be afraid of you for a very long time. If you laugh over their words, they will consider you as naught. They will begin bothering you right away. If you are immoral your brothers will be ashamed, and your mother's brothers. If you live quietly they will be proud . . . When one lives quietly the men folks love one. And there is another thing. Some of the girls of our generations are immoral. If one goes around all the time with those who are immoral, they would get one in the habit of doing so, as long as one has not much intelligence. Do not go around with the immoral ones, my grandchild,' my grandmother told me. 'And this. You are to treat any aged person well. He (she) is thought of by the manitou; because he (she) has conducted his (her) life carefully is why he (she) has reached an old age. Do not talk about anyone. Do not lie. Do not steal. If you practice stealing, you will be wretched. Do not (be stingy) with a possession of which you are fond. (If you are stingy) you will not get anything. If you are generous you will (always) get something. Moreover, do not go around and speak crossly toward anyone. You must be equally kind to (every) old person. That, my grandchild, is a good way to do,' my grandmother said to me. She was indeed always instructing me what to do.

ANON., 1918

When you go out with gentlemen never take wine. It's quite exciting enough without.

ALICE DOWSON, quoted in Alix Meynell,
What Grandmother Said, 1998

If you meet a man who smells like your grandmother – don't marry him!

Source unknown

Many years ago, when I was a child, my grandmother explained to me the difference between Jews and Christians, in simple terms: 'You see,' she said, 'Christians believe that the Messiah was here once and will return one day. The Jews maintain that the Messiah is yet to come. Over this,' said my grandmother, 'there has been a lot of anger, persecution and bloodshed. Why?' she said, 'why can't everyone just wait and see? If the Messiah came saying, "Hello, it's nice to see you again," the Jews would have to concede. If, on the other hand, the Messiah came saying, "How do you?" the entire Christian world would have to apologise to the Jews. Between now and then, just live and let live.' Said my grandmother.

AMOS OZ, 'How to Cure a Fanatic', 1999

———

Try to remember to accept fate without noise.

At fifty, creature comforts begin to matter more – each age has its pleasures.

It is very fatiguing to be long in the company of people who pass their lives morally eating suet pudding.

One should have fine perceptions and be able to see with one's eyelashes.

In a public place – unless the exigences of politeness require one to come into personal contact with people – one ought never to be aware that there are anything but tables and chairs about.

ELINOR GLYN, *The Sayings of Grandmothers and Others*, 1908

———

Guinea Hen

In Granny's eyes, our foremost barnyard warrior is not
    after all our fierce Rooster or surly Turkey Gobbler
but mild Guinea Hen, her badge of office her spotted
    feathers. She stands on guard at that barrier they call
Reputation. For Granny explicating the difference
    between Good Girls and Bad always ends her homily
with warning as fact: *Seven year not enough*
    to wash speckle off Guinea Hen back.

When Granny holds up Guinea Hen as the symbol
    of girls' ruin, we study her pattern and interpret
Granny's warning to mean: *Not that you can't do so.*
        Just don't let the world know.
        Never let the spots show.

OLIVE SENIOR, 1998

Grand-mothers are to be encouraged to go into schools and
become mentors to children as part of the Government's drive
to promote the family.

[. . .] The Government is going to urge schools to invite
grandparents to become voluntary classroom assistants and
involve them in helping children with homework. A nation-
wide scheme will be set up to promote 'grandparent mentors'.

RACHEL SYLVESTER, Independent, 2 November 1998

Over the course of 6 years of evaluating patients, who had
complaints of gender dysphoria, we were impressed by the

number who spontaneously reported that their maternal grandmother had played a significant role in raising them during their early childhood. The following report is a review of 21 cases of transsexualism in which early reporting involved a grandmother . . .

ELLEN HALLE ET AL., 'The Role of Grandmothers in
Transsexualism', 1980

———

from The Memoirs of Susan Sibbald

[N]ot long after we were settled, my Father asked my grandmother to come and reside with us, which I believe she did not dislike the idea of doing, as she had let her own house soon after my grandfather's death, and since lived at Benrig, which might have been very well at first, but as the children increased and were much spoilt, the two boys in particular, the continual noise must have been irksome to her. With us she had a quiet, comfortable apartment, from whence, if she liked she could go up and down by a separate stair. She generally remained in her own room between meal-times, and I loved often to go and sit with her, the expression on her countenance was so mild and she appeared so contented.

She had a spinning wheel, which was the employment of most females, old or young, rich or poor, in that Age, and she taught me to spin, and no slight assistance did she give me in spinning thread enough for a dozen pocket handkerchiefs, which I was vain to wear and to show, not for their fineness by any means, but because I helped to spin the thread of which they were made. Much amused was my grandmother when I brought into her room the spinning wheel which I used after having learnt on hers. She could not use mine, which was a highly finished Tunbridge ware one that had belonged to Mrs Elliot (Governor E.'s wife) and been left in the house with several other articles. My grandmother's was much larger, and she said she liked to hear the burring noise it made.

A small round table stood by her side on which was a large Bible that appeared to have been long and much used. It always lay open and her spectacles laid on it, if I did not find her reading when I entered her room. One day when wondering I did not see any other book there, I asked her if I should bring her one. 'Na, na,' she answered, 'there's na other Buke can do ane the gude this can.' 'But then Grandmamma, you must have often read it through.' 'Aye, 'deed ha' I, mony's the time, an' yet I ha'na got a' the gude out o' it, that I hope still to get, for this I ken the oftener ane reads it the muir ane learns, an' you Shusan whan ye ha' your share o' this World's troubles, which ye maun ha' if ye live, maun gang to that Buke in your time o' sorrow, an' ye'll fend it will be the first thing that can comfort ye an' gie ye peace of mind.' Yes, dear Hugh, and well can I testify that she was right.

[. . .] She was very fond of music and in the evening when I heard her door shut and knew she was coming to the Drawing room, I would rush to the Piano, which being a grand one I could make very loud, and as she opened the door she would hear a reel or some other lively tune, and then she would laugh and say, 'Ah! Shusan, ye're a blythe lassie,' and sit down by my side, and as I sang to my Father every evening, she would remain till I had finished.

[. . .] But nothing delighted me more than to hear my dear old Grandmother speak of 'the year '45' and 'the young Pretender, or Prince Charlie, as some ca'ed him'. 'Aye they were unco times then, the hale country was astir; sic riding and rinnings aboot; we had horses ta'en oot o' oure stables i' the night and unco anes left, which was na sae bad as it showed it maun be other folk concerned an' no us, for the puir beasts that war left were half deed wi' riding an' then

after seeking we wou'd fend oure ane at some distant farm in
na better condition, an' folk i' some other gate wad come an'
claim there's.'

SUSAN SIBBALD, 1783–1812

'When they were younger, they were great, they loved to ask
about the old days.' (*Echo from all present,* 'That's right!') 'And
they used to be fascinated to think we had no washing
machines, to think we used an old boiler and a wringer. What's
a wringer, they'd ask? And we had to explain. It was like a different age. But they always wanted to hear about it. And I
could keep them quiet for hours. It was "tell me about the
olden times".' (*Much laughter!*)

'The dark ages, my son used to call them. Oh, the dark ages!
When you come from a big family it's "How did you sleep?"
"Oh, top to tail!" "Didn't you have a bed of your own?" Oh
no. And it was so cold, putting your clothes on. I used to sleep
with my sister. Till I was married actually. When one of you
wets the bed, it's dreadful, isn't it, all sleeping in the same bed.
No lino on the floor, just bare boards. My big sister used to
lean out of bed to catch the mice.'

(*Voice of eighty-year-old great-grandmother*) 'I remember
back to the First World War. No covering on the stairs. A pot
under the bed. Plus the toilet was across the yard.' (*Another
voice*) '*And* that was shared sometimes. Of course the children
don't believe it. When I moved here from my old home, I was
clearing out and I had these bills all clipped together. And my
younger son was going through the prices and he said, "I can't
believe the prices for all these various things." Such as my
sewing machine. I never had a washing machine, I always said
I never wanted one, but really I couldn't afford one. He said,
"You must have set up home with less than a hundred

pounds." But a hundred pounds was a lot of money then. And of course it was linked to the wages.'

'When my grandmother was doing a project about the war, she asked me all sorts of questions about it, even though I was only a child during the war, and I could only tell her about my childhood experience. They do come and ask about the war. I felt important to her then.'

Birmingham grandmothers, 1999

———————

I'd like to be a rich vein . . .

PHYLLIDA LAW, author's interview

———————

from The Autobiography of Bertrand Russell

My grandmother . . . was the most important person to me throughout my childhood. She was a Scotch Presbyterian, Liberal in politics and religion (she became a Unitarian at the age of seventy), but extremely strict in all matters of morality . . .

As a mother and a grandmother she was deeply, but not always wisely, solicitous. I do not think that she ever understood the claims of animal spirits and exuberant vitality. She demanded that everything should be viewed through a mist of Victorian sentiment. I remember trying to make her see that it was inconsistent to demand at one and the same time that everybody should be well housed, and yet that no new houses should be built because they were an eye-sore. To her each sentiment had its separate rights, and must not be asked to give place to another sentiment on account of anything so cold as mere logic. She was cultivated according to the standards of her time; she could speak French, German and Italian faultlessly, without the slightest trace of accent. She knew Shakespeare, Milton, and the eighteenth-century poets intimately. She could repeat the signs of the Zodiac and the names of the Nine Muses. She had a minute knowledge of English history according to the Whig tradition. French, German, and Italian classics were familiar to her. Of politics since 1830 she had a close personal knowledge. But everything that involved reasoning had been totally omitted from her education, and was absent from her mental life. She never could understand how locks on rivers worked, although I heard any number of people try to explain it to her. Her morality was that of a Victorian Puritan, and nothing would have persuaded her that a man who swore on occasion might nevertheless have some good qualities. To this, however, there were exceptions. She knew the Miss Berrys who were Horace Walpole's friends, and she told me once without any censure that 'they were old-fashioned, they used to swear a little'. Like many of her type she made an inconsistent exception of Byron, whom she regarded as an unfortunate victim of an unrequited youthful love. She extended no such tolerance to Shelley, whose life she considered wicked and whose poetry she considered mawkish. Of Keats I do not think she had ever heard . . .

After I reached the age of fourteen, my grandmother's intellectual limitations became trying to me, and her Puritan morality began to seem to me to be excessive; but while I was a child her great affection for me, and her intense care for my welfare, made me love her and gave me that feeling of safety that children need. I remember when I was about four or five years old lying awake thinking how dreadful it would be when my grandmother was dead. When she did in fact die, which was after I was married, I did not mind at all. But in retrospect, as I have grown older, I have realized more and more the importance she had in moulding my outlook on life. Her fearlessness, her public spirit, her contempt for convention, and her indifference to the opinion of the majority have always seemed good to me and have impressed themselves upon me as worthy of imitation. She gave me a Bible with her favourite texts written on the fly-leaf. Among these was 'Thou shalt not follow a multitude to do evil'. Her emphasis upon this text led me in later life to be not afraid of belonging to small minorities.

BERTRAND RUSSELL, 1961

---

from Stone Soup and Seaweed

Molly Gordon, my paternal grandmother, had a profound effect on my life and my views on food . . .

Dad tells a much loved story about Molly's famous Stone Soup. I've never been able to corroborate it entirely, as his love of tall stories is well known. He claims that when things were tough she'd boil up a river stone in water for dinner. I've heard similar stories about gold miners in the early New Zealand settlements. As Molly's father had died falling down the family mine, maybe that's where she got the idea from . . . or maybe that's where Dad got his.

Gran [lived in] a large house on a hill in Wellington [New Zealand]. She had a fantastic garden and time on her hands to relish . . . and bottle and preserve. But what always struck me was Gran's ingenious way with leftovers. The roast mutton from the night before would be turned into a delicious soup next day. Magically transformed by her hand, it was hard to tell that the main ingredients had been around twice!

Gran used lots of different types of herbs in her cooking, many of them unusual for New Zealand. She grew all sorts of delicious mints, variegated pineapple thyme, lemon verbena and comfrey. These often lent an unrecognisable flavour to the meals she prepared and there were regular guessing games around the table to figure out what exactly had got into the fish stew this time.

[. . .] I remember going to the beach at Seatoun to collect seaweed. We'd tie it with rope to the back bumper of her Wolseley and drive back to her house, the journey dislodging all the stones and driftwood. Most of it was put in big barrels above the terraced garden. With rainwater, it would slowly ferment and turn into the best liquid garden fertiliser available. The rest would be dried for use later on – with some usually ending up in the stew pot.

My parents divorced when I was almost five, so my youngest sister and I spent several months with Gran and Grandpa, while my two older sisters stayed with Mum. We played up whenever we could, but once we were seated at the dining table, things were different. We were encouraged to behave ourselves and to talk. This was sometimes a little scary and usually it was a relief to get down and escape back to the garden to run riot again.

As I grew older, lunch or dinner became the highlight of any visit to Gran's house. She encouraged me to help her with the cooking, and wheeling the finished meal into the dining room on one of her trolleys made me feel as if I was her closest confidant.

PETER GORDON, 1997

from Grandmother's Footsteps

In her brown gaberdine jodhpurs (jodhpurs with a long O as she always pronounced them correctly because they came from Jodhpur in India) and an Aertex short-sleeved shirt under her mauve and white cotton apron, my grandmother stood at the end of her garden at The Mead, in Wantage, when I first took her in properly.

It is likely she was feeding her ducks or perhaps she was about to wring the necks of some of her chickens. Once, an old school friend took her husband to meet Penelope: 'Come and see my fowl!' commanded my grandmother as she led the timid couple down the garden. 'Oh!' she said, 'they don't seem to be laying well at all!' And she promptly began to kill the chickens, one by one, cracking their necks as she carried on talking, until there were ten hens lined up at the feet of her visitors, ready for the pot. Without reference to the slaughter, she then led them on to see her horses.

She had big squashy shoes in brown leather which were mis-shapen by her bunions, and calves like strong trunks which grew from her shoes without the help of ankles. When she walked she appeared to rock from squashy shoe to squashy shoe, and the shoes seemed to squelch as if she was always stepping in mud (which she was quite often anyway).

She must have been sixty or thereabouts when I saw her at the end of the garden, and her hair was a silver grey helmet, fringed and bobbed around her wrinkly face. It seemed wrinkly at the time, although later I found out that it was smoother than other people's – which may have had something to do with her smearing Pond's cold cream on her face each night (her only concession to a beauty regime). Also, she never smoked cigarettes. The silver hair was cut in a straight line at least an inch above her dark currant eyes, and before she went out she would comb it firmly down.

Her voice was loud and high-pitched and slightly nasal and she said words that I had not heard before, like 'gawn' for gone and 'gel' for girl, but she had this laugh which came with a res-onant boom from right deep inside her, and when she really roared, the laughter would send her rocking backwards, silver-helmet head in the air. She had an authentic giggle as well, and often she got so carried away that tears used to run down her cheeks, and then she'd plead, 'Stop! Stop, I can't *bear* it!'

Her bosom came down to her waist and when I first saw her in the bath, I thought her skin was like an elephant's, except softer and paler. But her hands were smooth and shiny and brown and speckled with freckles. Her fingers spanned out like flattened sausages, and you noticed them especially, because she held them up a lot. She used to flick her fourth finger nail or her little finger nail from underneath with her thumb nail, which was fairly annoying. Her only other annoying physical habit was her elephant's trumpet-call nose blowing, which she did quite often into the handkerchief which she kept either up her left sleeve or in her bloomers if she was wearing a skirt (which was rare).

[. . .] We called her first GrandmamaElope, and then GramElope, a shortened version which was shortened even further to GramElps by my brothers, and finally GrElope. She taught us to sit on a horse and how to jump fences, and then she took us hunting and on long-distance rides through forests. She taught us how to make brandy snaps and lemonade, and how to cook sausages over a fire when we camped in a tent in her garden. She read us the ancient Hindu epic, *The Ramayana*, before we went to bed and she taught us how to say Hail Marys and the Lord's Prayer.

Often she got cross. It was more likely to be a form of exasperation than true anger, though, and she would throw her bunch of sausage hands in the air when we had let a pony loose on the road by mistake and cry, 'Oh, what am I to do?'

She was bossy too, by all accounts, and sent my mother letters about how to bring us up:

you MUST NOT feed the kiddiwinks with those
coloured biscuits with icing . . . How will they ever grow
if you fill them WITH RUBBISH??? They MUST have
wholemeal bread, preferably homemade . . .

[. . .] It had been our grandmother's intention to take all of us, individually, to India, for what she called an 'educational tour'. She had taken Lucy when she left school, and in the spring of 1985 it was my turn. I did want to go, but I was nervous of travelling alone with my grandmother. I thought it was fairly uncool to travel around India with a seventy-five-year-old, when all my friends were joining up together to go 'travelling'. Secondly, I was still sulky, podgy and perhaps even slothful, and I was terrified that I would disappoint her and that we would not get on together at all.

She sent me a packing list which included 'petticoat (if required?)', something I had never owned nor was likely to, 'bosom busters', 'inflatable cushion', 'linen sun hat' and 'two rolls W.C. paper'. I packed up my rucksack ('It is CORRECT to say ROOKsack, because it comes from the German RUCK,' she would say) and set off with her on an aeroplane to Bombay. I was eighteen, at the same age as she had been when she first arrived in India in 1928.

Three months later I had decided that my grandmother was definitely cool. The education I had received was richer than a whole MA's worth of learning; the people I had met had opened my eyes to their culture, their forms of worship, their ideas of family life; we had ridden, taken trains, gone on buses, bicycled, walked, in fact, we had positively danced around India, covering the length from the Himalayas to the southern city of Madurai, and I, for one, had been dazzled.

It was a relief to return to England, though, for after three months in India, one is often overwhelmed and certainly in need of a breather. I didn't say I'd never go back on my return, but I think I said that it would be a while before I hit Bombay again.

IMOGEN LYCETT GREEN, 1994

III

ACROSS THE GENERATIONS

A friendship is developing between my elder granddaughter
and me. Two days ago I spent the night with her family in
Bristol. As usual she woke me in the morning, and we spent
our half hour or so telling stories and playing silly games. But
afterwards, for the first time, I took her to breakfast in a café
down the road, where, surrounded by people reading their
Sunday papers, we ate eggs and toast and told each other more
stories. Having given her parents an hour and a half to themselves on a Sunday morning, I could have taken her home then
and sat down to my own paper. In her more wearing toddler
days I would have done just that; no indefatigable granny I.
But she is not a toddler any longer. I found I was enjoying her
company so much that we went straight on to the City Farm.
And to the climbing church. To her orange juice and my herb
tea, and our illicit flapjack, to a discussion on the climbers
and, subsequently, on the usefulness of dock leaves for easing
nettle stings as we avoided the nettles on the narrow path
which took us home; while I tried and failed to remember
more words of 'Mad Dog and Englishman Go Out in the
Midday Sun', which is one of our mantras just now.

Now most of these things we'd done before. Just as everything else I do and have done with my grandchildren is a more

intermittent version of what I did for and with my own children when they were babies. All the same, the level of sheer mutual enjoyment in this expedition moved us into new territory. I'd never been friends with a grandmother myself. But Ellie's and my developing friendship, it seems to me, shows the beginning of the more particular, more informal connection between grandparent and grandchild that may transcend the purely useful functions of grandmothers in all cultures. And which this section is trying to address.

It figures, perhaps, that the most generally fraught relationships between grandparents and grandchildren are in societies where the obligations of grandchildren towards their grandparents are so heavy that they lead to the kind of resentments more common in other societies between parents and children. (This used to occur among the Navaho people of northern Arizona, for instance, according to an account I don't quote here.) Where this is not the case, much more relaxed relations between these generations than between parents and children appear common across the globe. There can even be an element of mutual naughtiness. I am, after all, relieved of the responsibility her parents have of bringing Ellie up, and Ellie is relieved of having to rebel against that. 'Let's not tell Clare and Steve about this,' we giggle. I am planning to buy her an outright party dress, although her mother would never have allowed me to indulge such leanings on her own behalf. Now, it seems, on mere whim, I am allowed to subvert things.

It may not last, of course. The love affair between grandmother and grandchild often fails to survive pre-adolescence, let alone adolescence. It can reanimate itself when the child grows up, but not always. I fear grandmotherhood involves accepting such things without complaint, unless you want to slide into family memory as the grandmama from hell, crying 'nobody loves me'. But what matters is that you exist; living evidence of a family reaching back into the past. Not only were my siblings and I denied such evidence, we were also denied an adult friendship with my mother. Experiencing my relationships with my adult children makes me understand better the significance of this aspect of the generation game. My mother, too, was denied such a friendship with her mother and I was denied the opportunity of observing that.

Cross-generational friendships are always important perhaps; something people with living parents and grandparents take more for granted than I could. Only now do I realise what I missed by not having them. I make up for it now, partly, not only through my friendships with my children, but also through friendships with other much younger people. Except in passing, however, for a month or two here and there, I have not made up for the lack of friends old enough to be my mother, let alone my grandmother. I wish I could.

What luck! some people might think, whose relationships with their mother and their mother's relationship with hers are so unsatisfactory that they prefer to stick around their own generation entirely; aren't you lucky to have been spared all that? And yes, maybe. But I loved my mother and cannot imagine things being altogether bad. And even the bad elements would have been part of that rich sense of being part of generations past and generations to come. I had stories; good stories. My mother's capacity to tell them made up in part for that unavailable grandmotherly role. But stories are not the same as flesh and blood.

To be quite literal, it was not that we didn't have grandparents. It was just that in our case they happened to be dead grandparents. And it's not that they had no influence on us. But it was a different, more painful influence.

My grandfather, for instance, never got over the death of his wife, my grandmother, and the death of the son she was carrying who died with her when she fell downstairs. He committed suicide twenty-three yeas later, just after my brother was born. That was the final blow to my mother and her sister, from whom he had wrested everything else when they were three and six. Grief-struck, their father sold anything that could remind him of his wife, up to his daughter's clothes, their dolls, their teddy bears. On her deathbed I heard my mother say, in the voice and with the perfect faith of a little child, 'Now I'm going to see Mummy again.' Her longing has haunted me consciously ever since. I dare say it haunted all our lives before, but without our understanding so clearly the nature of the ghost.

The grief emanating from that grandmother was private grief; that from my other grandmother was more public, of the kind that has seeped through the consciousness of almost all European families in a century now dead, and dying as I write. My grandmother has four sons. One died young. Two others were killed during the First World War. She was spared seeing her fourth son, my father, swept up into the Second, only by his being in a reserved occupation, much to his disgust, but not hers, I imagine. Her experience was all too common. As was the preoccupation with war, the histories, the analyses, which filled the bookshelves in my parents' home. As was the grief; there are still tears in my ninety-year-old father's eyes when he talks of his brothers killed in the First World War and of his friends killed in the second. Shirley Hughes observed in her family, too, the way such grief permeated the seemingly more carefree life of children without their knowing it. Setting a book during the First World War, I only gradually appreciated where the gloom came from which pervaded the story and me throughout the time I was writing. And now it seems important that I tell the stories, transmit this felt if not always experienced history to my grandchildren in turn.

I start this section with letters between grandparents and grandchildren. Most of them are letters between grandparents and younger children. But letters to older grandchildren can be at least as significant. One friend of mine said that the letters from his grandmother were like letters between friends; for instance, 'Your grandfather just went to the butcher, and I'm worried about him because he can't see so well any more.'

The friendship between this grandson and his grandmother was more essential than most. He was an only child of non-communicative parents who showed him little if any affection, and his grandmother's total belief in him connected him emotionally to life. 'In your grandmother's eyes you can do no wrong,' his mother would snarl.

The superiority of Quaker grandmothers is demonstrated yet again: by Elizabeth Fry, whose gift to her grandson of money so that he could buy anything he wanted would shame more recent grandmothers, who send their grandchildren presents of what they think their grandchildren ought to like; and by Hannah Whitall Smith, who also wrote to one absent granddaughter, 'I miss you, but if you are enjoying yourself, I *like* missing you.' Of letters from grandchildren, I can only quote Tommy Bangs. What his grandmother would have made of his letter is another matter. But friendly it certainly was.

Most of the other material, both on friendship and generational overlap, can speak for itself. The material on friendship in particular catches the leap of mutual understanding between grandparent and grandchild, bypassing the parents, which I am beginning to experience with Ellie. The ¡Kung legend is a neat expression of some wider implications of what I am trying to say. Extracts showing the concern of children for their grandmothers – as in Proust's alter ego's concern for his – demonstrates what grandchildren learn of humanity through relationships with an older generation. The significance of such relationships for both sides is summed up by the recruitment of surrogate grandparents in Bolinas, northern California, to give children whose grandparents lived far away the chance of relating to a generation beyond that of their parents. That the 'grandparents' themselves queued up for the privilege testifies that they got something from it; something akin, presumably, to what my time around my grandchildren does for me.

And finally, more ambivalently, as time passes there is the realisation, not only by the grandmothers now but by their children and grandchildren, of what the presence of new generations has to say about mortality as well as birth; understandings all the more poignant because it is too late to share them with grandmothers already gone.

Letters Between Grandparents and Grandchildren

from a letter to Amaryllis and Henrietta Garnett

Monday [December 8, 1947]   *Charleston*

My darling Amaryllis and Henrietta,

What a lovely letter I got from you today. I went into the kitchen to make tea and I looked to see if the postman had been but I didn't much expect him to have left a letter for me, and then I saw there *was* one with your names outside and you can't think how excited I was. A real letter from those two clever creatures, I thought. I showed it to Grace and she read it too. The kitchen table has 5 Christmas puddings sitting on it which she has made. I wish you were going to help to eat them, but you will have lots of your own at Hilton I am sure. Now I must think what news I have for you. It has been raining cats and dogs here. Has it been at your home? It has rained so hard that a lot of water which should have run in a drain underground from the farm has burst out and made a pond near my bee hive – quite a large pond. I expect you would try to get into it if you were here. The ducks and the geese are very happy and swim about quacking and cackling and enjoying themselves so much that they won't come home to bed, naughty creatures.

When it gets fine I do some gardening and I wish I had you to help me. Do you remember how you took all the dead plants away for me and how useful you were? That is just what I want doing now. But I daresay you have lots to do in your own garden. I wonder how much French you can talk. *Bonjour* and *petite fille* and *petit garçon* and I expect a lot more by now.

When you write me another letter I think you must send me a drawing too . . .

Goodbye my darling creatures.

Your
Nessa
VANESSA BELL

---

from The Autobiography of Bertrand Russell

When he and your mother, in the bloom of youth and health, asked me to look upon you as my own child in case of their death, I little thought that I should be called upon to fulfil the promise I gave them. But ere long the day came and your home was left empty. You came to us as an innocent, unconscious little comforter in our darkened home, and have been to us all three as our very own child. You were intertwined with our very being, our life was shaped and ordered with a view to your good; and as you grew in heart and mind you became our companion as well as our child. How thankfully I remember that all through your childhood and boyhood you would always cheerfully give up your own wishes for those of others, never attempt an excuse when you had done wrong, and never fail to receive warning or reproof as gratefully as praise. We trusted you, and you justified our trust, and all was happiness and affection.

Manhood came and brought with it fresh cause for thankfulness in your blameless and honourable University career. But manhood brings also severance and change. You are leaving us now for a new life, a new home, new ties and new affections. But your happiness and welfare must still be ours and our God will still be yours. May you take with you only that which has been best, and ask His forgiveness for what has been wrong, in the irrevocable past. May He inspire you to cherish holy thoughts and noble aims. May you remember that humble, loving hearts alone are dear to Him. May such a heart ever be yours, and hers who is to travel life's journey by your side.

God bless you both, and grant you light to find and to follow the heavenward path.

Ever, my dear, dear Child
Your most living
Granny

---

from A Quaker Grandmother

May 12, 1907

My darling Ray:

Such a strenuous day deserves the enclosed box of peanut chocolates. They have just reached me from A. He sent two boxes, so thee shall have one.

I enclose a letter from mother, detailing unheard-of tom-foolery. Do tell me, as a psychological problem, whether *thee* would have enjoyed them. Tell me the honest truth.

What about thy toothache? Thee must tell me in every letter. Some one says the sole business of every Englishwoman is to belong to committees, so thee is fulfilling thy mission!

Most lovingly thy
Grandma.

While I think of it, I want to say thee need never be at a loss what to say in thy letters, for what thy mother and I like are just the little commonplace happenings of the days – what thee does, who thee talks to, how thee passes thy time, and what thee has to eat. Nothing is too trivial for us.

HANNAH WHITALL SMITH, 1907

My dear Eudora Alice, I do wish I could go on the choo choo train and see you and be at your little party, I would bring you two pretty little pigeons, for I know both you and your friends would enjoy having them, but as I cannot go nor send the little pigeons, I am going to the Court House this morning and see if I can send you a little cup of sugar you can eat and think of Grandma. I hope you will have a nice time and be well. With lots of love from Grandma. P.S. Tell your Ma I will write to her next time.

Eudora Welty's grandmother, quoted in *One Writer's Beginnings*, 1985

[Elizabeth Fry] sent our son Frank this letter, in allusion to his approaching birth-day.

Lynn, 10 Month 28, 1841

My dearest Frank,

Accept this very small token of love from thy grandmother, I wish thee to buy any thing thou likest for my sake. I thought it better to leave it to thy taste – not to mine. My desires for thee are very strong; my love for thee very great, and my prayers are earnest for thy blessing, peace, prosperity, and to crown all, thy salvation by Christ. Write me one of thy kind notes to Earlham, and believe me thy most loving grand-mother, E.F.

Memories of Her Mother, by R.E.C., 1845

---

from Little Men

My dear Grandma, – I hope you are well. Uncle James sent me a pocket rifle. It is a beautiful little instrument of killing, shaped like this – [Here Tommy displayed a remarkable sketch of what looked like an intricate pump, or the inside of a small steam-engine] – 44 are the sights; 6 is a false stock that fits in at A; 3 is the trigger, and 2 is the cock. It loads at the breech, and fires with great force and straightness. I am going out shooting squirrels soon. I shot several fine birds for the museum. They had speck-led breasts, and Dan liked them very much. He stuffed them tip-top, and they sit on the tree quite natural, only one looks a little tipsy. We had a Frenchman working here the other day, and Asia called his name so funnily that I will tell you about it. His name was Germain: first she called him Jerry, but we laughed at her, and she changed it to Jeremiah; but ridicule was the result, so it became Mr Germany; but ridicule having been again resumed, it became Garrymon, which it has remained ever since. I do not write often, I am so busy; but I think of you often, and sympa-thize with you, and sincerely hope you get on as well as can be expected without me. – Your affectionate grandson,

Thomas Buckminster Bangs.

P.S. – If you come across any postage-stamps, remember me.

N.B. – Love to all, and a great deal to Aunt Almira. Does she make any nice plum-cakes now?

P.S. – Mrs Bhaer sends her respects.

P.S. – And so would Mr B. if he knew I was in act to write.

N.B. – Father is going to give me a watch on my birthday. I am glad, as at present I have no means of telling time, and am often late at school.

P.S. – I hope to see you soon. Don't you wish to send for me?

T.B.B.

LOUISA M. ALCOTT, 1871

Friendships

For old people the affection of the grandchildren is a revenge upon the generation in between.

SIMONE DE BEAUVOIR, Old Age, 1971

Why do grandparents and grandchildren get along so well together? Because they have an enemy in common.

Source unknown

In some tribes relations are particularly easy, and grandparents and grandchildren joke together. Radcliffe Brown suggests that this freedom and ease between alternative generations is due to the marginal position of each; the old people have relinquished some of the burdens and responsibilities of life, the children have not yet assumed them. The result is that there is a feeling of identity between them.

ELIZABETH FISHER BROWN, 'Hehe Grandmothers', 1935

[Among the Kikuyu] there are close links between grandparents and grandchildren, and symbolically they belong to the same age group. The grandmother calls her grandson husband . . .

SIMONE DE BEAUVOIR, *Old Age*, 1971

Mother said, 'In your grandmother's eyes you can do no wrong.' She spoke as if amused but I understood the accusation.

JOYCE CAROL OATES, 'Why Don't You Come Live with Me It's Time', 1992

Grandparents . . . are remembered much more favourably. Alternate generations are recognised as having a special relationship, especially when the child is the grandparent's 'namesake'. Personal and intimate details not discussed with parents are often taken up freely with grandparents, and grandparents often represent a child's interests at the expense of those of the parent. Also, since older people contribute less to subsistence than do younger adults, they have more time to play with their grandchildren. It is not surprising that children are willing to live with them . . . especially during times of conflict with parents.

M. SHOSTAK, *Nisa: The Life and Words of a ¡Kung Woman*, 1981

When the car stopped in front of her daughter's house, Moon Orchid asked, 'May I get out to meet my grandchildren?'

'I told you no,' said Brave Orchid. 'If you do that you'll stay here, and it'll take us weeks to get up our courage again. Let's save your grandchildren as a reward. You take care of this other business, and you can play with your grandchildren without worry. Besides, you have some children to meet.'

'Grandchildren are more wonderful than children.'

MAXINE HONG KINGSTON, *The Woman Warrior*, 1977

'Grandchildren just accept us, don't they? Mum's mum and they take it in their stride and accept us.' (*Other voice*) 'And they treat us like friends now. Mine are like friends. My Brian was amazed they were having an argument outside and one was saying something about what his grandmother could do, and the little one said, "But my nanny rides a racing-bike!"'

'The things my grandchildren say; three particular things stick in my mind. I was sat on the settee, and my youngest granddaughter said, "Ooh, Nanny you're going bald." Because I'm losing my hair on the top. And she said, "But don't worry. You're tall. When you stand up nobody can see." They're more open now. It's not cheeky.'

Birmingham grandmothers, 1999

from Grandma Rolled Her Own

Grandma was a perfect companion for a small boy. At home I was considered a faulty cog in the family machine, in need of constant repair. It seemed that I was always about to do something to bring a stain on the family honor, that at any minute some seemingly harmless act would bring that 'disappointed-in-you' look to Dad's or Mother's face. Somehow, whatever I did at home would turn out to be unworthy of my heritage.

With Grandma everything was different. To her I was not a worry. She accepted me as I was, and I had the feeling that to her there was something other than nuisance value in my company. With her natural tact and constant good cheer, she bolstered up my self-confidence by treating me as an adult, except when I didn't deserve it.

She was a born teacher, and she transmitted to me, with great gusto, a compendium of miscellaneous but important information about life. By the time I was six I knew, among other things, how to tell a lead quarter from a silver one, to shake hands firmly, that brown eggs are stronger than white ones, that honest people look you straight in the eye, that only chippies wear a lot of make-up. She initiated me into the secrets of life by a six-month joint project of preserving frog spawn through the winter and watching it turn into tadpoles in the spring. She could skip stones wonderfully, with a sidearm sweep that made passersby stop and stare. Together we made kites and, sprinting down the park green with her full skirt flying, she taught me the art of keeping them out of the tree-tops. We made long tails out of colored cloth, and sent messages of paper singing up the cord to the dipping, dancing kite, so far away it could hardly be seen.

TED PECKHAM, 1954

---

from Nisa: The Life and Words of a ¡Kung Woman

'We can see. She says she didn't steal the klaru. Well then, what did eat them? Who else was here?'

I started to cry. Mother broke off a branch and hit me, 'Don't steal! Can't you understand! I tell you, but you don't listen. Don't your ears hear when I talk to you?' I said, 'Uhn, uhn. Mommy's been making me feel bad for too long now. I'm going to go stay with Grandma. Mommy keeps saying I steal things and hits me so that my skin hurts. I'm going to go stay with Grandma. I'll go where she goes and sleep beside her wherever she sleeps. And when she goes out digging klaru, I'll eat what she brings back.'

But when I went to my grandmother, she said, 'No, I can't take care of you this time. If you stay with me, you'll be hungry. I'm old and only go gathering one day in many. Most mornings I just stay around. We'll sit together and hunger will kill you. Now, go back and sit beside your mother and father.' I said, 'No, Daddy will hit me. Mommy will hit me. My skin hurts from being hit. I want to stay with you.'

I lived with her for a while. But I was still full of tears. I just cried and cried and cried. I sat with her and no matter if the sun was setting or was high in the sky, I just cried. One month, when the nearly full moon rose just after sunset, I went back to my mother's hut. I said, 'Mommy, you hate me. You always hit me. I'm going to stay on with Grandma. You hate me and hit me until I can't stand it any more. I'm tired.'

Another time when I went to my grandmother, we lived in another village, nearby. While I was there, my father said to my mother, 'Go, go bring Nisa back. Get her so she can be with me. What did she do that you chased her away from here?' When I was told they wanted me to come back I said, 'No, I won't go back. I'm not going to do what he said. I don't want to live with Mother. I want to stay with Grandma; my skin still hurts. Today, yes, this very day here, I'm going to just continue to sleep beside Grandma.'

So, I stayed with her. Then, one day she said, 'I'm going to take you back to your mother and father.' She took me to them, saying, 'Today, I'm giving Nisa back to you. But isn't there someone here who will take good care of her? You don't just hit and hit a child like this one. She likes food and likes to eat. All of you are lazy. You've just left her so she hasn't grown well. If there were still plenty of food around, I'd continue to take care of her. She'd just continue to grow up beside me. Only after she had grown up, would she leave. Because all of you have killed this child with hunger. With your own fingers you've beaten her, beaten her as though she weren't a Zhun/twa. She was always crying. Look at her now, how small she still is.' But my mother said, 'No, listen to me. Your little granddaughter . . . whenever she saw food with her eyes, she'd just start crying.'

Oh, but my heart was happy! Grandmother was scolding Mother! I held so much happiness in my heart that I laughed and laughed. But when Grandmother went home and left me there I cried and cried. My father yelled at me, but he didn't hit me. His anger usually came out only from his mouth. 'You're so senseless! Don't you realize that after you left, everything felt less important? We wanted you to be with us. Yes, even your mother wanted you and missed you. Today, everything will be all right when you stay with us. Your mother will take you where she goes; the two of you will do things together and go gathering together. Why do you refuse to leave your grandmother now?'

But I cried and cried. I didn't want to leave her. 'Mommy, let me go back and stay with Grandma, let me follow after her.' But my father said, 'That's enough. No more talk like that. There's nothing here that will hit you. Now, be quiet.' And I was quiet. After that, when my father dug klaru bulbs, I ate them, and when he dug chon bulbs, I ate them. I ate everything they gave me, and I wasn't yelled at any more.

As told to Majorie Shostak, 1981

from Grandmothers, Mothers, Daughters

Mum has miscarried with twins and was very sick. I got packed off to my grandmother in the country . . . Living with my grandparents was the period in which I learned to read and became more self-conscious of who I was and what I was in the world. [When] I arrived back . . . obviously Mum would have been pretty shattered by all the things . . . happening to her, and then she was confronted with this very . . . sullen and withdrawn five-year-old. What it felt like from my side was that I'd gone from being spoken to as an adult to as a child again . . .

My grandmother had been born in the late 1880s and my grandfather in the 1890s. They viewed children as imperfect adults, and all you needed to do was treat them with discipline and respect . . . I was terrified of their displeasure, but at the same time, I really enjoyed their company and would do anything to be allowed to sit up and listen to them talking . . . Back at home it was a matter of being put to bed with the baby . . .

Apparently my grandmother missed me a good deal and wrote to Mum asking if I could stay. She said I could go to the local school, but Mum panicked and brought me home. I suppose she thought she wasn't being a good mother . . . She didn't have a good relationship with her mother. And I think . . . may have been a bit jealous. Somehow, I was going to get the time with her mother that she had never had . . . It's been of great concern to her to have a good relationship with me. In a sense, she's come to grips with her mother, through our relationship as mother and daughter.

[. . .] Grandma . . . years later . . . said how much she'd loved her husband. The thing she regretted was that she'd let passion get away with her one time, and that resulted in a child they could ill afford to raise. Fear of pregnancy created such awful tensions. Mum was horrified after I reported this conversation back to her. She said Grandma had no business having such conversations with me.

As told to Diane Bell, 1987

My mother was divine. I used to long for my children to go and talk to her, because I would sneak outside the door to listen. They would ask her wonderful questions which I never could ask and which she would produce these long and interesting answers about sex and that which I would be completely glued to, sitting outside the door. They loved her and they used to ask her things when she was very old. They disapproved, I think rightly, of old people not being asked rude questions; what happens is you're sidelining them. But they poked about in her past in a very excellent manner. My mother had divorced and remarried, you see, and she was very funny about it, they really loved that. So I'd love my daughter to be able to say to Ernie, 'You can go and ask your granny questions which you can't ask me.'

PHYLLIDA LAW, 1998

from The Granny Project

But then Ivan said:

'It wasn't that, you know . . . About there being no one around after the Great War for Granny to marry . . . It was a personal thing. A mistake. And what with both her parents being so strict, and living on that farm away from Art Galleries and things, and there not being anyone around to talk to, she just didn't realise for years and years.'

'She didn't realise *what*?'

'Her mistake. You see, she thought she was the only woman in the world who had thick curly hairs in her arms and down –' Seeing his father's eyes on him in the mirror and quite misunderstanding the appalled expression, he changed what he was going to say to: 'Well, you know . . .'

Natasha . . . quelled Tanya's nervous giggle with one short look. She searched her elder son's face for one relieving sign that he might be lying.

'You made that up! Ivan!'

Ivan was pale but firm. He shook his head.

'Who told you?'

'Sophie.'

Sophie never lied. The family sat in total silence, knowing that Sophie, back at the house with grandmother, never lied.

Henry stopped drumming, gripped the steering wheel . . . Through the small mirror Ivan watched the tears roll down his father's face . . .

ANNE FINE, 1983

———

None of the Huas recall [the grandmother] as a family burden. Her grandchildren recall her fondly as not bothering anyone, and staying much of the time in her own bedroom where the children would go to chat with her. They were impressed by her bound feet and her ability to open Pepsi bottles with her bare hands.

CHARLOTTE IKEB, *Aging and Adaption*, 1983

———

from Melanie Klein

Between 1953 and 1959 Melanie Klein worked intermittently on her autobiography, a document marked by an elderly person's repetitiveness and blocking out of painful memories. Ultimately the autobiography trails off, as though she were preoccupied with her impending death.

That change from strong personal ambition to the devotion to something which is above my own prestige is characteristic of a great deal of change that went on in the course of my psycho-analytic life and work . . . I have never been hopeless, nor am I now. It is a mixture of resignation and some hope that my work will perhaps after all survive and be a great help to mankind. There are, of course, my grandchildren who contribute to this feeling that the world will go on, and when I speak of my having been completely dedicated to my work, this does not exclude my also being completely dedicated to my grandchildren. Even now, when they have become much less close to me, I know that I have been a very important figure in the first few years of their lives and that this must have been of great benefit to them. All three loved me deeply until 6 or 7 years old, and Hazell even up to 9 or 10, and I believe that they have kept some affection for me, though unfortunately they are far less in contact with me; except Michael, who has in recent years become much closer to me again and who I know has at least unconsciously, and perhaps partly consciously, the feeling that I am of great value and also that he can speak freely to me.

Klein and Judy experienced the inevitable tensions between a mother-in-law and her son's wife. Judy recalls that she was terrified whenever her mother-in-law held one of the babies, because she seemed tense and unnatural with infants. Every Sunday Mrs Klein came to lunch. Judy Clyne complained that this ritual prevented the family from doing anything else that day; and on one occasion she expostulated: 'If you would wait for once to be invited!' Her complaint fell on deaf ears, and Klein continued stolidly to occupy her accustomed place. Not that her grandchildren objected. Diana and Hazel say that she was 'a very good kind of gran, always there to listen to whatever we wanted to tell her'.

PHYLLIS GROSSKURTH, 1987

From Vanessa Bell

When the morning service came on the air, she [Vanessa Bell] was unusually brisk in her move to switch off the wireless. 'God is not allowed in the studio,' she firmly told her grandchildren who nevertheless did their best to reintroduce religion into the house by singing hymns in their bedroom at the top of their voices. Her granddaughter, Henrietta, has recalled:

> When we stayed at Charleston, Amaryllis and I were always made to sit as models. Breakfast over, we walked down the length of the passages to get to Duncan's studio. We were not altogether willing models and both of us charged our grandparents sixpence for each hour that we endured. We were seldom painted in our ordinary clothes. In her bedroom, next to Duncan's studio, Nessa kept a huge painted cupboard which was filled with a fantastic assortment of coloured silks, discarded dresses and

moth-eaten tapestries in which we were variously draped. I remember there was a vermilion hat, like the head-dress of a Venetian Doge, which was excruciatingly itchy for me to wear. Generally, Nessa sat down to paint. Her easel was infinitely more spindly, more rickety than Duncan's. She sat behind it, mixing the colours on her palette, glancing first at one and then at the portrait, gently stabbing the canvas so that, posing somewhat uneasily and swathed in remnants on the models' throne, one could see the back of her canvas quiver from the impressions she made on it. The glances she sent to one across the room were extraordinarily intimate and reassuring; an observant nod, an amused smile in order to encourage one to keep still.

While they painted Vanessa and Duncan told stories about the figures in their past. The children became familiar with intimate details concerning such semi-mythical creatures as George Duckworth, Julia Stephen and Virginia. Often they listened to music on the radio, in particular to Beethoven, Mozart, Debussy and Ravel. Sometimes Amaryllis read aloud while they posed. They were all addicted to the novels of Charlotte M. Yonge, relishing the death scenes which made them both cry and laugh. 'Nessa would laugh too,' Henrietta recollected; 'a strangely mellow cackle; the amused hoot of a barn owl.' When these sessions ended the children would stretch out on the rug on the studio floor, in front of the pither stove and would munch digestive biscuits as they all listened to Mrs Dale's Diary. 'After each episode ended to the twinkling tones of its signature tune we would all speculate and elaborate wildly upon the curious lives of Mrs Maggs, Mrs Dale and her scandalous sister Sally, dwelling as they did in Virginia Water.'

Vanessa's granddaughter goes on to describe how the

midday meal usually consisted of ham, baked potatoes, pick-led walnuts and dressed salad, followed by pudding.

> Whilst Nessa and Duncan and Clive sipped their coffee, Nessa gave us *canards*. The duck, a lump of white sugar, would be sent for a sail in a silver teaspoon boat across the dark waters of the black coffee within her painted blue cup. And then, very gently, the silver boat capsized. The snow-white duck became stained with the brown liquid and then Vanessa would lift the spoon as far as she could reach to our gaping mouths and we swiftly gobbled up the ducks.
>
> FRANCES SPALDING, 1983

Formal relationships with grandparents on both sides are allowed to be considerably freer than with parents. This is particularly the case in the sphere of conversation, when the proscription of lewd joking and the mention of sexual matters does not hold with the same force. The avoidance of personal names and of bodily contact is also lighter, though some decorum still has to be observed. It may be suggested that the freedom between grandparent and child is to some extent a reflex of the constraint between parent and child. The latter is to be correlated with the authoritarian position of the parent and his or her capacity for active control of affairs. With the waning energies of the grandparent there is a tendency for authority in practical affairs to be resigned, and so there is no hindrance to the growth of an easy familiar relationship with the grandchildren. The difference in age and status does still play a part in putting the social weight on the side of the grandparent. In the ordinary Tikopia household a phrase continually addressed to young children is 'A mata tou puna', 'Mind your grandparent' . . .

Grandparents usually take some share in regulating the conduct of children in the house, giving advice in ordinary affairs. For instance, two youngsters were proposing to go out on a stormy day. Their grandmother said to them sarcastically, 'Where are you two going? The sky is bad. Are you going to look for a house for the two of you?'

RAYMOND FIRTH, *We the Tikopia*, 1930

————

Because Grandmother loved me best of all the grandchildren, yes, and she loved me best of all the family. I basked in her love as in the warmth of a private sun. Grandmother loved me without qualification and without criticism, which angered my parents since they understood that so fierce a love made me impervious but indifferent to the threat of its being withdrawn . . . which is the only true power parents have over their children, isn't it?

JOYCE CAROL OATES, 'Why Don't You Come Live with Me It's Time', 1992

————

The grandparents were notably lenient towards grandchildren. The relationship of privileged disrespect between alternate generations has been reported from many other societies and is a feature of anthropological literature. Something of the same kind existed in Bethnal Green. The grandchildren were expected to show greater respect for the authority of parents than that of grandparents and the parents were expected to maintain authority in a way not expected of grandparents. Several old people said they had noticed changes in their attitude to young children as they got older. One woman said,

'I used to slosh my children. But I don't like to see my grand-children walloped.' . . . Others referred more directly to the difference between parents and grandparents.

Mrs Aylesbury was lenient with her grandsons. 'The grand-mother can be free and easy. She [her daughter] has to be fairly strict with them.'

Mrs George was talking about her mother. 'I paid her rent, and I paid my mother for doing things for my children. She was different to my children from what she was to us.'

PETER TOWNSEND, The Family Life of Old People, 1959

---

from Truth, Dare or Promise

It was my Granny who most fed these dreams. My maternal grandmother, who lived with us, had her own fantasies and dreams of grandeur. The arch conservative of the working class, who hated everything to do with proletarianism, she spent at least part of most evenings as the centrepiece of the local pub, drinking Double Diamond like an early version of Ena Sharples at the Rovers Return. But while she might have looked like Ena, her aspirations were more in line with those of Annie Walker.

The Midland Drapery was the largest department store in Derby. I loved it when she took me there for tea. They had waitresses, music, and mannequins swirling around between the tables. Granny and I played this little game together. We had sandwiches in little triangles with the crusts cut off, toasted teacakes and tea in heavy, pewter pots. Then we would look around the shop and fantasise about what we might have bought. Granny seemed a funny old lady, but she had class!

VALERIE WALKERDINE, 1985

from Tales of a Grandmother

With the children she was in her element, for in spirit she was still and always a child. She brought out of her treasures 'things new and old' for their delectation and, as long as she could, and far longer than she ought, she joined in their outdoor fun. 'Beechie' recalls how once when Ernest and Ronan were quite tiny boys 'she spent a whole afternoon tobogganing with them on the slope above the lime avenue, enjoying it as much as they did because of her spirit of adventure that always incited her to risks – and then her pride and fun afterwards about tobogganing at that age (probably the late sixties).' She adds, 'Perhaps, though, for the grandchildren, it will be the Christmasses they will keep among their first memories – "going to Dawyck for Christmas with Grannie," and that welcoming figure on the steps to hug them all in turn as they tumbled out of the motor; she was so wholly their friend, enjoying it all every bit as much as they did.'

JESSIE BALFOUR, 1923

Every generation thinks that the kids have much more leeway, much more licence. The other day [my son] Tom was saying, 'Discipline, you've got to have it. You're not your children's friend. You're their parents. What you say has to go.' John [my husband] said I was easy-going and Tom said, 'No, you were terrifying sometimes.' It's heaps easier for grandparents. You can be – the big family row going on, your children trying to make their children go to bed, or children having a row between themselves – you can be the friend of everyone. You're not the one saying, 'For God's sake, break it up, go to bed. Get out of the bath' – I remember that being a terrible problem with my own children. Now when they say, 'No, I won't,' you just leave it. Of course you do back their parents up – but you're not there with a terrible sense of failure.

When they're adolescent I still imagine you would be around. A calling-off place. But you're not a thrill the way you are when they're little. A bit more of a duty maybe. And of course if you get really deaf and infirm, then you're a real duty. A real chore. And then you've got to bribe them, I suppose. Just keep on handing out the cash. Of course being a grandparent is just as hairy as being a parent at one or two moments. There was a moment when one of my grandchildren was really ill. And it was . . . God – it was the most terrible time. And you're right there on the line – in fact I think you're more worried. You're worried about the parents and how tired they are. But you are also worried about the child – you're so aware of the fragility of the child. The telly endlessly pours out stuff about abuse etc., and I feel I can't take this. So you have far more worries about their safety and their health than about how well they're going to do at school. If they end up as part-time deckchair attendants, does it matter? Clara says it's still the same between parents – *Schadenfreude*, my kid is better than yours – deep down people are deeply competitive about their children. But with grandchildren it isn't such an agony. When you get older you don't care what people think about you any more.

SHIRLEY HUGHES, author's interview

---

from Raw Material

Mary-Ann never turned a beggar away from the door, and solemnly told me never to do so, either.

If there wasn't a penny to give she'd make a cup of tea, or fetch some bread and fat bacon from the pantry . . .

Any civilising influence in my life could only have come from Mary-Ann Tokin. It was she alone who suggested I do my best to get into a grammar school instead of slogging off to work at fourteen. I think that since her grandson Howard had already died – and the same track had been broached for him – I was the next one suitable.

So on a wet autumn morning I sat in a room of Nottingham High School to do the tests. The atmosphere seemed quite outside me, though I was there with a couple of friends and didn't feel particularly uneasy. The problems were like pages of Chinese ideographs, and I could make nothing of them at first because I had gone through no preparation beforehand. I can't say that I expected to pass, though after puzzling out some of the answers I hoped that by a miracle I would do so.

The rain was stultifying during the hour it took. My feet were saturated because I wore plimsols, though I soon ignored the discomfort and got stuck in. Nothing could have put me into that school, for even if I'd had a vague chance of getting through this troubling initiation, my spirit wasn't ripe for it . . .

But I took the test again a year later, and failed that too, proving to me for the last time that I wasn't the right material for higher education. My grandmother may have been disappointed, though I never saw any sign of it.

[. . .] She was a kind, hardworking woman, and thought more about other people than herself. Because of this she was seen as a simple person – a deceptively simple judgement which isn't worth much comment.

She used to collect the coloured cards from Burton's cigarettes and store them in the spice cupboard. They lay there for weeks and months until she had enough to make it worth while presenting them to me in an empty Robin packet. They were impregnated with the smell of curry and pepper, aloes and cloves, sage and thyme. A few years before she died she gave the same cupboard to me and I kept my first collection of books in it.

With a touching and solemn expression she also gave me a stick of oak about six inches long, no more than a piece of kindling, assuring me that it had been part of the ship in which the Good Lord Nelson died. She had paid the exorbitant sum of sixpence for it to some cunning old robber who had once come to her door. I don't remember what happened to it. No doubt I treasured it for a while, then lost it on the long road my itching feet have since travelled.

It is good for the self-confidence of a child to be spoiled when young. The awful word 'spoil' only means love and care, and freedom from unreasonable restrictions so that any good qualities can develop. To do good is the only way to teach others to do good, and to spoil is not to ruin, for it gives a child a sense of his own significance that will strengthen him to face the world and survive.

The reason people don't know what they want, and therefore do not know what to do at certain vital moments of their lives, is because they were told too often as children exactly what they could have and do, and not left enough to their own usually innocent choices. One sees it all the time, even on the streets.

Parents may spoil a child yet not ruin it, though many are too frightened or ignorant to try what is new or relaxed. It is usually left to the grandparents, who need to love a child in order to go on living themselves, and who often spoil grandchildren to make up for having been too harsh with their own. They can also spoil a grandchild so as to make life hard for its parents when that child grows up and begins to assert itself, but that is another matter, and nothing to do with the relatively uncomplicated Burton morality.

Grandmother Burton used to make her own rugs, sat by the fire on winter evenings with a large piece of sacking pulled over her knees. Near her chair were two or three baskets of rug clippings, cut into pieces by herself and her daughters from rags and cast-offs. They were sorted into a few basic colours, from which she planned out the rough patterns.

The result was crude and of a primitive spectrum, but there was always something warm underfoot to stand on in the kitchen – though as rugs they were never considered fine enough for the parlour, in which was laid a large piece of coconut matting. These rugs were her only art form, if they can be called such, and I suppose the designs she concocted from these mounds of vari-coloured clippings gave as fair a picture of her inner mind as one was ever likely to get.

On a summer's afternoon (when her rugs would hang on an outside line to air) I can smell newly-baked bread coming from the heated oven. In a state of grace I get that warm and floury whiff as my grandmother laid the tins on the table. I shall always be able to smell it, as if no one else can, and as if I am the last person in the world to recall it.

Mary-Ann, in saying goodbye, used a refrain that came over from Ireland with her mother: 'God between ye and all harm,' she said – and meant it.

ALAN SILLITOE, 1978

---

from Desolation

For her six-year-old grandson Alie had a deep but inarticulate tenderness. All the little warmth that life still held for her came to her through Stephan's Koos. It was she who had saved him when Anna died. It was she who had stood between him and the fury of his father when Stephan, in his illness, turned against his own son. All that Stephan's son had known of love had come to him through her, yet for that love she had found no words and to it she could give no expression beyond a rare and awkward gesture, too harsh or too restrained to be called a caress. Yet the boy – a slim small child with eyes as dark as her own, and long thin fingers like the claws of a bird – was conscious of no shortcomings in his grandmother. His father had always been strange to him, and death had but added another mystery to the many which had surrounded him in life. But with his grandmother nothing was strange or mysterious. With his grandmother he knew where he was going, he knew what he was doing. She was his tower of strength, his shadow of a great rock in a dry and thirsty land. By her side he was safe. Wherever she went, whatever she did, by her side he was safe . . .

When they reached the house Alie sat down, as was her custom, upon the high stone step in front of the door, and the boy, pressing close to her side to deepen his sense of security there, sat down beside her. For a time they were silent, the child content, his grandmother brooding on the past. She was a woman of little imagination. Her mind, moving slowly among familiar things, was heavy always with the melancholy of the Verlatenheid, and from it she had but one escape – to the village of Hermansdorp where once as a girl she had lived with her mother's cousin, Tan' Betje, and worked with her at mattress-making at one of the stores. Beyond this her thoughts never ventured. And it was to Hermansdorp that her thoughts travelled slowly now with their dawning hope.

[. . .] She saw again the long wide straight Kerk Straat, with its running furrows of clear water and its double row of pear-trees in blossom. Behind the pear-trees were whitewashed dwelling-houses set back in gardens or green lands, and stores with *stoeps* built out on to the street under the trees . . .

Tan' Betje's little house, she remembered, had been up a narrow lane. Three rooms it had had, with green wooden shutters, and a pear-tree in the yard . . . Tan' Betje had been kind to her, and at the store too they had been kind. Her master's son had himself come several times to speak to her when she went for the coir. The old master would be dead now, perhaps. But the young master would be there. And he would remember. He would give her work . . .

As if following her thoughts her fingers, stiff with labour and old age, fell awkwardly into the once familiar movements of teasing the coir in the sunlit yard. The boy, wearied at last of her long silence, pressed closer to her side. She looked down upon him sombrely and drew his thin, claw-like hand into hers. Slowly, halting often in her speech, she began to talk to him of Hermansdorp where together they would go. And into the child's sense of security there came a new sense of romance and adventure, deepening his confidence in the wisdom and rightness of all that his grandmother said and did.

PAULINE SMITH, 1925

---

from Through a Window

A truly wonderful relationship developed between Getty and his grandmother. Melissa first set eyes on Getty when he was one day old – she had not been present during the birth, for Gremlin like most females had gone off on her own. When Melissa approached, that first time, Gremlin backed away nervously fearing, perhaps, that her domineering mother would try to appropriate this new and precious possession just as she took everything else. But Melissa sat quietly nearby and merely glanced at the new infant from time to time, and soon Gremlin relaxed. Not until Getty was ten months old did we see Melissa touch her grandson at all – and then it was merely to groom him for a few moments during a session with Gremlin.

Soon after that I watched a fascinating incident. It began as Melissa was grooming Gremlin's back and Getty pushed his way between them. Melissa looked down at him, then lifted him into her lap and began to groom him – just as though he were her own infant. Gremlin glanced round, then seemed to stiffen. Very slowly she turned; very cautiously, glancing into her mother's face, she reached towards Getty with a soft pleading whimper. He responded at once and climbed into her arms. Quickly Gremlin moved away, settling to rest some five yards distant. Clearly, once again, she had feared that Melissa might try to steal her beloved son.

As the days went by, Melissa seemed to become more and more enchanted by Getty and the bond between them grew. When Melissa and Gremlin were grooming together Getty repeatedly interrupted, leaping down onto his grandmother from some overhanging branch – and Melissa, who had never played much with any of her own offspring, would stop grooming and start to tickle him. During these games, which sometimes lasted for fifteen minutes, Gremlin usually sat watching. Melissa actually initiated some of the play herself – sometimes she even followed Getty when he was romping with another youngster and pulled him away so that she could play with him herself. This was not always to his liking, for he was a self-willed little fellow, and then he would struggle until he had escaped from Granny and could run back to his chosen playmates.

JANE GOODALL, 1992

---

from Swann's Way

My grandmother, in all weathers, even when the rain was coming down in torrents and Françoise had rushed the precious wicker armchairs indoors so that they should not get soaked, was to be seen pacing the deserted rain-lashed garden, pushing back her disordered grey locks so that her forehead might be freer to absorb the health-giving draughts of wind and rain. She would say, 'At last one can breathe!'

and would trot up and down the sodden paths – too straight
and symmetrical for her liking, owing to the want of any
feeling for nature in the new gardener, whom my father had
been asking all morning if the weather were going to
improve – her keen, jerky little step regulated by the various
effects wrought upon her soul by the intoxication of the
storm, the power of hygiene, the stupidity of my upbringing
and the symmetry of gardens, rather than by any anxiety (for
that was quite unknown to her) to save her plum-coloured
skirt from the mudstains beneath which it would gradually
disappear to a height that was the constant bane and despair
of her maid.

When these walks of my grandmother's took place after
dinner there was one thing which never failed to bring her
back to the house: this was if (at one of those points when her
circular itinerary brought her back, moth-like, in sight of the
lamp in the little parlour where the liqueurs were set out on the
card-table) my great-aunt called out to her: 'Bathilde! Come in
and stop your husband drinking brandy!' For, simply to tease
her (she had brought so different a type of mind into my
father's family that everyone made fun of her), my great-aunt
used to make my grandfather, who was forbidden liqueurs,
take just a few drops. My poor grandmother would come in
and beg and implore her husband not to taste the brandy; and
he would get angry and gulp it down all the same, and she
would go out again sad and discouraged, but still smiling, for
she was so humble of heart and so gentle that her tenderness
for others and her disregard for herself and her own troubles
blended in a smile which, unlike those seen on the majority of
human faces, bore no trace of irony save for herself, while for
all of us kisses seemed to spring from her eyes, which could
not look upon those she loved without seeming to bestow
upon them passionate caresses. This torture inflicted on her by
my great-aunt, the sight of my grandmother's vain entreaties,
of her feeble attempts, doomed in advance, to remove the

liqueur-glass from my grandfather's hands – all these were things of the sort to which, in later years, one can grow so accustomed as to smile at them and to take the persecutor's side resolutely and cheerfully enough to persuade oneself that it is not really persecution; but in those days they filled me with such horror that I longed to strike my great-aunt. And yet, as soon as I heard her 'Bathilde! Come in and stop your husband drinking brandy,' in my cowardice I became at once a man, and did what all we grown men do when face to face with suffering and injustice: I preferred not to see them; I ran up to the top of the house to cry by myself.

MARCEL PROUST, 1913, translated by C.K. Scott Moncrieff and
T. Kilmartin

---

from My Childhood

I could see as well that Grandfather was cooking up things to scare Grandmother and Mother. Often he would shut himself in Mother's room and start screeching like that horrible wooden pipe used by the lame shepherd Nikanor. On one of these occasions Mother shouted fit to wake the whole house:

'No, never, never!'

The door slammed shut and Grandfather started howling.

That was in the evening. Grandmother, who was sitting at the kitchen table, was making a shirt for Grandfather and whispering to herself. When the door slammed she pricked up her ears and said:

'She's gone to the lodgers!'

Suddenly Grandfather leaped into the kitchen, ran up to Grandmother, hit her on the head and hissed, waving his bruised hand:

'When are you going to stop your prattling, you old witch!'

'You old fool,' Grandmother said calmly, putting her hair straight. 'You won't make me shut up. I'm going to tell her everything I know about your little tricks, you see!'

He flung himself on her and started raining blows on her enormous head. Grandmother put up no resistance and said:

'Beat me, beat me if you like! Go on!'

From my bunk I started hurling pillows, blankets, shoes at them, but my infuriated grandfather didn't notice. Grandmother fell on to the floor, where Grandfather kicked her on the head as she lay there. Finally he tripped and fell, upsetting a bucket of water. He jumped up, spitting and snorting, gave one wild look round the room and fled to his attic. Grandmother got to her feet, groaning terribly, sat on the bench and began tidying her hair. I jumped down from the bunk to be greeted with an angry: 'Pick the pillow up and put everything back by the stove! What got into *you*, flinging pillows around! You keep out of it in future! And that old devil, he's gone right out of his mind, the fool . . .'

Suddenly she groaned and her face set in a deep frown. Then she lowered her head and called me over.

'Have a look here, where it hurts.'

I parted her thick hair and found a hairpin had gone deep into the skin. I pulled it out, found another, and my fingers went numb.

'I'd better call Mother. I'm frightened!'

She waved her hand.

'What's the matter with you? I'll give you call Mother! Thank God she didn't hear or see anything . . . and you want to call her? Get out, quick!' And with her nimble lace-maker's fingers she started ferreting around in her thick black mane. Summoning up my courage, I helped her pull out another two, thick bent hairpins.

'Does it hurt?'

'Not much, I'll have a hot bath tomorrow to ease the pain and wash the blood away.'

Then she asked me gently:

'And you, dear, don't breathe a word to your mother about your grandfather beating me. They've got their claws into each other as it is. Promise you won't tell.'

MAXIM GORKY, 1913–14, translated by Ronald Wilks

As she had been a dutiful and loving daughter, a faithful affectionate and attached wife, so, in her old age, she became an indulgent but wise grandmother. 'To her grandsons,' says her daughter, 'she could not deny anything, and was fain they should appear in the world with distinction, and omitted nothing she could devise to further them this way; but yet, whenever she spoke about them, the great thing she expressed herself with most concern about was that they might become virtuous and religious men.' That they were not insensible to the beauty of their grandmother's character is manifest from the fact, that when the troubles in Scotland cut off for a time the transmission of her usual supplies, she was sometimes reduced to severe straits. [. . .] one of her grandsons hearing this, and possessing a horse of which he was exceeding fond, sold it unknown to anyone, for £18, and carried her the money.

LADY BAILLIE, *The Book of Noble Englishwomen*, 1875

Vespasian, the emperor, . . . was brought up under the care of Tertulla, his grandmother by the father's side . . . When he became emperor, he used frequently to visit the house where he had spent his infancy, the house being kept just as it had been in former times, that his eyes might miss nothing of what they were wont to see there. And he so loved the memory of his grandmother that on all solemn occasions and festival days, he constantly drank out of a silver cup she had been accustomed to use.

SUETONIUS, c. 70–c. 122, *Lives of the Twelve Caesars*

'When grandma went away, it seemed as if the blinds were all pulled down, and all the daylight was shut out at once.' Bless the dear boy! How grateful to the old woman's heart was that tribute of affection.

ANON ., *The Jottings of an Old Woman of Eighty*, 1794

'Now, Grandmother,' cried Gregory, 'say you'll go and I'll promise to show you a larger school of "practical industry" than your own.' Their mother smiled. 'My dears,' she said, 'Grandma is not so well able to run about London for your amusement as she used to be.' 'She is just as well able to please the boys as ever she was, I know,' cried Gregory again, kissing my wrinkled cheek. 'If I didn't love her I would rather go without her a precious deal! But I do love her dearly and I want her to go, so come now old lady!' he continued, twitching my shawl as he stood beside me; – 'come, say yes! just because of the school.' And thus flattered into submission, while one rings for her bonnet and another pulls on her cloak, the old goose is perfectly obedient and goes just where they like to carry her.

ANON., *The Jottings of an Old Woman of Eighty*, 1794

When the Hopi girl, Cactus Flower, is being tested by the Kachina, one of the tests is not to weep at a song they sing about her unhappy experiences in leaving home. She does weep, but Spider Grandmother is sitting on her cheek in her familiar role of ear prompter or monitor, and this time swallows the tears as they fall.

ELSIE PARSONS, *Pueblo Indian Religions*, 1939

_____

Lauris

From my perspective, the young are a marvellous source of information about the way the world is going. One of my families is made up of three teenagers – one now out of his teens and turned twenty-one – and over the last five or six years they have spent a good deal of time here. I live closer to town than their parents, and it is easy to walk here after a late night at a dance party or a rave (I don't have a very clear idea of what these occasions are actually like, though I have been given many descriptions) and 'crash' in my spare bedroom or on my living-room floor, if there are two or three of them.

This puts me in a kind of vicarious front line in the war that most adolescents need to have with their parents. I have suffered, again, the dreadful small-hours anxieties of parents and all other teenage guardians, when, for example, a young lad who has said he'll be 'home about one' has not arrived by three. I have had some painful reckonings with these casual guests; very occasionally I have had to ring the boys' mother (two boys, two years apart, have given me the most poignant of these experiences) and say I don't know where they are.

The response has been another surprise in the history of unexpected twists and turns that I have found grandmothering to be. She has been much less frantic than I; she is sure he'll be at So-and-So's, and here's the number. I have now learnt of course to collect phone numbers, names and details myself, and I have made some telephone friendships with mothers and other grandmothers suffering similar torments, I have met a number of the boys' friends, and have a much stronger and more vivid impression of their generation, their nineties attitudes, than I could possible get from any of the public information channels. I find them delightful company, and as they grow older, my old anxieties about overstepping the line or challenging parental authority gradually disappear; we are simply friends.

LAURIS EDMOND, 1999

The Meaning of Generations

from The Old People Give You Life

Now the Elephant Girl had already warned her grandmother that something might happen to her. She had said 'Watch well: a little wind will come to you. The little wind will come to you with something in it. It will bring you some droplets of blood. The blood will come to lodge inside your groin. Take that bit of blood and put it into a container. Don't let on what you're doing – just take it and put it into something. Something like a little dish or a little bottle.' It happened just as the girl had said. A little wind came back to her grandmother. The bit of blood came to lodge in her groin. The grandmother saw it and said 'Didn't the child tell me something like this would happen?' She didn't speak aloud, she just said this in her heart. She took the drops of blood and put them in a bottle. Then she sat and thought, and asked herself 'Should I go to see what has happened to my granddaughter? No, it has already happened just as she said it would, so he must have killed her already and there's no help for it.' She turned it over and over in her mind; meanwhile the bit of blood was growing. It grew and grew until it was too big for the bottle. Then the grandmother took it out and put it in a skin bag. It grew again and burst the bag, so the grandmother put it into something bigger. Then it grew some more and broke that. Only the grandmother knew about it. No one else knew that she had the Elephant Girl and was restoring her to life. She kept it a secret. She had the bit of blood and it grew, and she fixed it, and it grew some more and she fixed it. When it had grown completely it was a woman again! She looked just like she had before.

One morning when the camp awoke, the women decided to go gathering *n/n*. They got up and went off picking *n/n*. The Elephant Girl's little daughter went with them, saying 'Today I'll accompany my aunts and eat *n/n*.' The old grandmother said 'Go ahead, go with them.' So the Elephant Girl's mother and all the other women went gathering. The old woman stayed home alone. She spent the day quietly. In the afternoon she took a skin and spread it in the shade, spread it in the late afternoon shadows. Then she took out the Elephant Girl and sat her upon the skin. She ground ocher and spread it upon the young woman's face. She replaced her old rags with soft new skin clothing and hung her all over the ornaments. Then the old woman tied copper rings in her granddaughter's hair the way people used to tie them long ago. She fixed her up so that she was the beautiful Elephant Girl again.

Later the women came back from gathering. Toward sunset they returned. The old woman was telling funny stories and the Elephant Girl was laughing '/eh-/eh-/eh-/-eh-o!' As the women came near the village, the Elephant Girl's little daughter said to the others 'Who's that laughing just like my mother in the village?'

Her aunt said 'How can you be so crazy? My older sister died a long time ago. Don't go saying you hear her laughing someplace.'

Another girl said 'My aunt is certainly dead: this child is crazy.'

So they came closer, listening. The Elephant Girl laughed again. This time they said 'Can it be? Whose laughter is this? When we left there was nobody but the old woman in the camp; we had all gone gathering. What young girl can that be whose laughter sounds just like our sister's?' When they came into the camp they saw the Elephant Girl sitting there with her grandmother. Her daughter cried 'Mother, mother, mother!' and ran to her, flopped down, and began to nurse. The others cried out and said 'Yo! Who has accomplished this?'

The Elephant Girl answered softly 'Granny, of course, Granny lifted me up. Granny spoke the word and I sat up and was alive. If it had been up to you others alone, I wouldn't be here. Long ago Granny took me and sheltered me in a skin pouch and now I am alive again. That's how it was. The old people give you life.'

Collected and translated by Megan Biesele and Nancy Howell,
1981

---

from Look the Demon in the Eye

Many of the schemes described here have evolved at least in part as a substitute for life in an extended family or among a mix of generations in the neighbourhood. Howard, a forty-year-old American sometime actor and taxi driver who lives and works in the hilly Marin County region of California, talks of how the community where he lives has come to recognize the loss of a generation of elders who have an interest and emotional investment in the younger generations.

He lives in a group which set out to be self-sufficient and did not pay enough attention to family roots in its youthful, ideological quest for a place where members could build an alternative lifestyle. He explains: 'People came from different parts of the world – Europe, Australia, the big American cities – and that gave us a kind of unity, a sense of being very self-sufficient. But there was almost a complete loss of family. There were some older people but virtually nobody had their parents around. It was when the younger people began coupling up and having children that they became very aware of what a loss it is not to have parents and grandparents around.'

They saw very clearly how their children needed someone who knew more than they do about the world. There was quite a lot of sadness and Howard explains: 'Out of that grew the idea that we could ask the older people who are here to become surrogate grandparents and in some cases they have moved into the homes where families live. They are given free accommodation and food and in return they take the role of a grandparent involving themselves with the children, helping care for them, and being there as a source of knowledge and experience.

'The older people know that when they become frail and need help their 'family' will be there. In Bolinas old people are at a premium and families have to compete to "win" one!'

ANGELA NEUSTATTER, 1996

---

from The Significance of Grandparenthood

Bekker and Taylor (1966) have explored what influence the number of generations in a young person's own family will have on his perceptions of old people. Their findings suggest that young people with grandparents and great-grandparents have fewer age prejudices than those who do not. Specifically, they found that young subjects who had living great-grandparents perceived their grandparents as having fewer characteristics of old age than did young people who had no living great-grand-parents. There was no significant difference in the ages of the grandparents of the two groups.

VIVIAN WOOD AND JOAN F. ROBERTSON, 1976

from Una Anciana

The body has its seasons. I am in the last one; winter is never without pain and breakdown . . . I have already lived over twice as long as our Savior. How greedy ought one to be for life? God has his purposes. I wake up and feel those aches and I notice how wrinkled my skin is, and I wonder what I'm still doing alive. I believe that it is wrong to ask a question like that. One lives. One dies . . . I am here to care for my husband, to care for this house, to be here when my sons and my grand-children come. The young have to see ahead. They have to know there's youth and middle age and old age. My grandson, Domingo, asked me a while ago what it is like to be one hun-dred. He is ten. I told him to be one hundred is to live ten of his life times. He seemed puzzled, so I knew I had been thoughtless. I took him around. I put my hand besides his and we compared skins. I said it is good to be young and it is good to be old. He didn't need any more explanations. He said when you're young you have lots of years before you, but when you're old you have your children and grandchildren and you love them and you're proud of them. I took him round again and hugged him tightly, and in a second he was out there with his father and his grandfather, looking at the cows.

ROBERT COLES, 1970

I know there are some persons who, at sixty, think it right to put on the old woman. 'My children are grown up,' they will tell you, 'My duties are done; there is nothing left for me to do now . . . I shall rest upon my oars and pass smoothly down the stream of time . . . they forget that still they form part of the great mosaic picture of society; they may not be 'polished corners of the temple', they may not decorate its Corinthian columns, nor inscribe their names upon its walls, yet the place they hold in the composition of the piece, will, if inadequately filled, injure the general effect.

ANON., *The Jottings of an Old Woman of Eighty*, 1794

Today, most people not only take long-term family bonds for granted, and invest accordingly in them, but because of reduced fertility rates, there are also fewer individuals within each generation to invest in.

G. O. HAGESTEAD, 'Women and Grandparents as Kin-keepers', 1986

MRS COOKSON: I mean it's a part of you continuing all the time. I mean your family when you marry and there's grand children.

In Sarah Cunningham-Burley, 'Becoming a Grandparent', 1987

MRS ANDERSON: Well for me I would say it's something . . . It's something I'll leave, still here on earth when I'm not you see,

that's how I feel, if I hadn't had any grandchildren that
would have been me finished, when I was dead and gone
there would be nothing left on this earth of me, that's how I
look at it . . .

In Sarah Cunningham-Burley, 'Becoming a Grandparent', 1987

———————

Larissa looks skeptical, and then she says, 'When I went for my
Harvard interview I told them my grandmother was a com-
munist.'

'Are you kidding. You're lucky you got in.'

'They asked if I was interested in politics,' she says, with a
knowing smile. 'I started talking about Grandma. I felt proud
of her.' She pauses here to think it over. 'It's hard to believe my
own grandmother has lived that kind of life. When I was little
I used to want the kind of grandmother who bakes things.
But not now.'

Larissa goes on talking . . .

My mother gestures to me and takes my elbow and pulls me
down so that she can whisper in my ear. 'Think of it,' she says,
'a mother and a daughter together like this.'

Larissa says, 'And a granddaughter.'

KIM CHERNIN, *In My Mother's House*, 1985

———————

So Boaz took Ruth, and she was his wife: and when he went in
unto her, the Lord gave her conception and she bore a son.

And the women said unto Naomi, 'Blessed be the Lord,
which hath not left thee a day without a kinsman, that his
name may be famous in Israel. And he shall be unto thee a
restorer of thy life, and a nourisher of thine old age: for thy

daughter-in-law which loveth thee, which is better to thee than seven sons, hath born him.'

And Naomi took the child, and laid it in her bosom, and became nurse unto it. And the women her neighbours gave it a name, saying, 'There is a son born to Naomi: and they called his name Obed: he is the father of Jesse, the father of David.'

The Book of Ruth, the Bible, 1610 version

[A] grandmother must ever be loved and venerated, particularly one's mother's mother I always think.

QUEEN VICTORIA, letter to her daughter, the Princess Royal, 27 June 1859

----

from The Three-Generation Rural Family in Italy

In the twelve rural villages in Abruzzia the three-generation family is the rule. The old people never live alone in the house. Usually the oldest son, his wife, and his children live with them. Sometimes the old parents prefer to live with a daughter and her husband.

The living-together of the generations is economical. The old women in one of the twelve villages make the ancient *ricamo* and *merletto*, which is very fine embroidery work. In wintertime this work of the grandmother is almost the only economic resource of the family. This fact is very important, since it gives the grandmother a significant economic role in the family.

When the young couple is working in the fields, the grandmother keeps house. The grandparents take care of the children. They are more strict with them than the parents. Obedience and reverence for the grandparents are general. One of their roles is that of educators of the grandchildren. The grandmother is accustomed to help the grandchildren with their homework.

It is natural to have the old people at home. They do not constitute a problem. Sometimes we find only old people and their grandchildren in the household. The mother and father will be elsewhere in Italy or in other countries.

[. . .] In case of sickness the old people are well attended. The community is likely to criticize a daughter-in-law who does not take good care of her father-in-law and mother-in-law.

When old people are sick, the relatives do not call the doctor, because they are convinced that the doctor can do nothing for old people. The old people are always kept in the home of one of the children – sometimes one of the daughters if they feel that they are better looked after by daughters than by daughters-in-law.

The old women are counselors in matters of maternity, cooking, medicine, and clothes. People are often afraid of the power of their chatter. For many hours of the day they sit in front of the houses on the village square commenting on and controlling every event.

The old people are very influential even if they are poor and propertyless. People go to them to find a mediator in case of fights. Old people are deeply respected.

ERNEST BURGESS, 1960

———

[T]he quality of the mother-grandmother relationship had its strongest effects *when mother and grandmother were not living together* . . . Counter to our expectation that co-residence would heighten modeling effects, it may be that such effects occur most readily 'from a distance' . . . For example grandmother involvement in the parenting role may result from or contribute to tensions between mothers and grandmothers who live together and share child-rearing.

WAKESCHLAG ET AL., 'Not Just Ghosts in the Nursery', 1996

----

from The Mental Health of Muslim Mothers in Extended Families Living in Britain: The Impact of Intergenerational Disagreement on Anxiety and Depression

OBJECTIVES: The study assessed the impact of intergenerational differences of opinion over child rearing on the mental health of Muslim mothers living in extended families. DESIGN: The study adopted a correlational design in an attempt to identify factors that accounted for mental health problems. METHODS: The child-rearing attitudes of mothers and grandmothers, mothers' mental health, levels of family acculturation and a range of other background and demographic information was collected from 54 extended families living in two Muslim communities in London using Urdu versions of standard questionnaires. RESULTS: Rates of depression and anxiety among the mothers in the study were high. Grandmothers had more traditional attitudes to child rearing than did mothers. Intergenerational discrepancy over child rearing was more marked in more acculturated families. Discrepancy was associated with higher levels of mothers' anxiety and depression. CONCLUSIONS: The unusually high levels of depression and anxiety displayed by Muslim mothers living in extended families can in part be accounted for by patterns of intergenerational discrepancy. These possibly reflect discordant world views within those families that have been assimilated into the dominant British culture.

E. J. SONUGA-BARKE ET AL., 1998

---

from Parents and Children

Lady Sullivan appeared unconcerned by this limit placed to her usefulness. She was sitting in the chair on the hearth, where she sat throughout the year, as though her comfort depended alternately on a full grate and an empty one. She was a portly, almost cumbrous woman of seventy-six, with a broad, exposed brow, features resembling her son's under their covering of flesh, pale, protruding eyes that recalled her second grandson's, large, heavy, sensitive hands, and an expression that varied from fond benevolence to a sort of fierce emotion . . . Regan was a woman who only loved her family. She loved her husband deeply, her children fiercely, her grandchildren fondly, and loved no one else, resenting other people's lack of the qualities and endearing failings of these. And it meant that she had loved thirteen people, which may be above the average number.

She looked at Eleanor with a guarded, neutral expression. She could not see her with affection, as they were not bound by blood; and the motives of her son's choice of her were as obscure to her as such motives to other mothers; but she respected her for her hold on him, and was grateful to her for her children. And she had a strong appreciation of her living beneath her roof. If Eleanor saw it as a hard choice, her husband's mother saw it as an heroic one, and bowed to her as able for things above herself. The two women lived in a formal accord, which had never come to dependence; and while each saw the other as a fellow and an equal, neither would have grieved at the other's death.

Luce sat down on the floor and laid her head on her grandmother's lap. Regan put a hand on the head. Eleanor took her
usual seat and her skilled needlework. She was a woman who did
not make or mend for her family. Her daughter broke the silence
by throwing her arms across Regan's knees and giving a sigh.

'Grandma,' she said, putting back her head to regard the
latter's knitting, 'your needles flying in and out remind me of
the things that work in and out of our lives. Each stitch a little
happening, a little step forward or back. I daresay there are as
many backward steps as forward. But that is not like your
knitting, is it?'

She continued to survey the needles with a steadiness that
was natural, in view of what she derived from them; and
Regan smiled and continued to knot, as if she did not take so
much account of the employment.

'We have not much chance of going back,' said Eleanor.

'Not in your sense, Mother,' said Luce, not moving her eyes.
'But there is a certain progression in our lives, which we do not
always maintain. It so often comes to a swinging to and fro.'

'You mean in ourselves, don't you?'

'Yes, Mother, I do mean that,' said Luce, looking at her
mother as if struck by the acuteness of her thought.

'My days for progress are past,' said Regan.

'I wonder why people say that in such a contented tone,' said
Eleanor.

'They may as well put a good face on it.'

'No, Grandma, I do not think it is that,' said Luce, tilting
back her head to look into Regan's face. 'I think it is just that
many things still stretch in front of them, though some may be
behind. I think we all go on advancing in ways of our own,
until some sort of climax comes, that we all look towards as a
goal.' She said the last words lightly, as if not quite sure if she
had made or avoided a reference to her grandmother's death,
and settled herself in a better position on the floor, to indicate
that her thoughts were on trivial, material things.

Regan kept her eyes on her needles, which she seldom did if her thoughts were on them. She was thinking for a moment of her own end. It engaged her mind no oftener as it drew nearer, and it did this so lightly at the moment that it failed to keep its hold.

'Where is Grandpa, dear?' she said . . .

IVY COMPTON-BURNETT, 1947

---

from Great-Grandma's Swing

I had ridden with my grandmother up to my great-grandmother's farm to spend some time. I always enjoyed visiting this farmhouse because it was very special to me. The large, wrap-around porch provided ample room for the old wooden swing that rocked with every breeze.

[. . .] My grandma accompanied me into the living room where my great-grandma was lying on her bed, pale and feeble. She sat up and a smile appeared on her wrinkled face as she saw that her great-grandson had come to visit her. Her vision was very poor so she couldn't make me out very well. She just recognized the bright red hair that gleamed as the morning sun shone through the windows.

My great-grandmother, some 94 years old, was not in the best health. Every summer, when I would come to visit, she seemed to get worse and worse. Her frail body was smaller than the last visit and she could barely sit up in her bed, which had been moved to the living room because of her declining condition. I came close enough to hold her hand and say a polite hello. As I walked away, my great-grandma spoke to my grandmother about how good I was to give a greeting. Each year, during my annual excursion to my great-grandma's house, she would remark on how I had grown in appearance and maturity. I, in turn, would reply, 'You haven't changed a bit.' But inside, I acknowledged the evidence of her aging.

I opened the front door and walked out onto the porch, which was angled just so that the breeze of the hollow could enter . . .

There before me was the porch swing made of thin, white wooden slats. It was not bright or fashionable, but old. I recalled the many times I had approached this swing before and the many memories it held. From that swing, you could see almost every part of the farmland. Sometimes I would swing with my cousins. Other times I would sit and listen to the conversations between my parents, aunts, and uncles. But mostly, I enjoyed swinging alone.

I took a seat and began to swing . . .

Hearing the creaking on the porch, my great-grandma asked, 'What is that?' My grandmother told her of my fascination with her porch swing. It had been a few years since my great-grandmother had had the strength to sit on the swing. Unknown to me, she had a love for that porch swing just as I. My grandma was extremely surprised when my great-grandmother said, 'I think I would like to join him out on the swing.'

It took several minutes for my great-grandma to prepare for the feat of going outside. My grandmother stood her up and wrapped her in a shawl to keep warm in the breeze. After she was bundled up in blankets, my great-grandma was helped out the door and to the porch swing by my grandma. I was amazed at her strength and determination for I had never seen her up and about. In her sweet, soft voice, my great-grandmother said, 'May I sit and swing with you?' I replied by saying, 'Sure, great-grandmother, I would love you to.' So, she eased herself down onto a few cushions for support.

I began to rock the swing slowly. My great-grandmother's legs did not reach the floor so she could not push. She grasped the rail with one hand for balance and I took the other hand. My great-grandmother's face brightened as she sighed with happiness. Very few words were exchanged because they weren't needed. Several glances passed between us and a connection was made. A feeling came over me like I knew all about my great-grandmother without even speaking. A few minutes seemed like hours as we smoothly glided back and forth on that porch swing. I could sense that my great-grandmother held many memories involving that swing, as did I.

My grandma walked out on the porch to help my great-grandmother back inside. My great-grandmother was definitely more peaceful now than she was when she asked to swing with me. It was not much longer when I had to say good-bye and my grandma and I departed. As we drove down the gravel path, I could see the porch swing swaying in the breeze. That day was my most meaningful visit to my great-grandmother's house. As I left her house that cool August morning, I had no idea that I would never see her again. That fall, my great-grandmother passed away in her sleep.

TIM VALENTINE, *The Internet*, 1997

Grandmother let me look over the drawers where she kept her beautiful scraps of silk and velvet, ever so many of which she gave me . . . She let me 'tidy' her best work-box, a *wonderful* box full of every conceivable treasure and curiosity – and then, when I was a little tired with all my exertions, she made me sit down on a footstool at her feet and talked to me so nicely – fancy that, Molly, your great-great-grandmother ever having been a little girl! – and about the queer legends and fairy tales that in those days were firmly believed in the far-away Scotch country place where her childhood was spent!

MRS MOLESWORTH, *Grandmother Dear*, 1878

Persimmons and Hermit Crabs

Disconcerting how smells change as one grows older.
My grandmother smelled of persimmons. I smell
  of seafood
A bit past the feeding stage. And the best perfumes.
Even one's smell acquires reminiscence.
It is no longer the urgent smell of sweat,
Pungency of sex, or periodical
Smell of blood. One's smell seeps into the noses
Of the very smallest nieces, grandniece,
  granddaughter,
Wherein it fades and fades, not quite forever.

GRACE GOLDIN, 1981

Thus Mrs Harris slipped out of the Templetons' story; but Victoria and Vickie had still to go on, to follow the long road that leads through things unguessed at and unforeseeable. When they are old, they will come closer and closer to Grandma Harris. They will think a great deal about her, and remember things they never noticed; and their lot will seem more or less like hers. They will regret that they heeded her so little; but they, too, will look into the eager, unseeing eyes of young people and feel themselves alone. They will say to themselves: 'I was heartless, because I was young and strong and wanted things so much. But now I know.'

WILLA CATHER, Old Mrs Harris, 1932

A Mother's Eyes

My mother's frightened eyes
What did she expect?
I never wondered,
In most of the family photos
she is younger than I am –
but seemed an old woman,
already out of the picture.

A picture of my mother.
She wears a fur round her neck
a felt cloche hat with a metal clip
yet isn't elegant.

Maybe it is her posture, hunched,
and the way that handbag is clutched
against her chest,
her frightened eyes.

Every picture of my mother
Whether alone or with others,
as a young girl or
just before she died,
shows the same wide gaze
desolate and stoic as a punished child.

When she first saw my baby
and later, during visits
grudgingly accepted,
her eyes did not alter.

A grandmother's eyes
are meant to show delight,
but the sight of the child

who makes her child a parent
can be another sign of how little time is left,
of death, not life –

Or so I interpret
my mother's expression
in answer to the question
the rankling problem the unsolved
puzzle of what she feared
and expected, as I gaze into
my new-born grandson's eyes.

RUTH FAINLIGHT, 1999

IV

TRADITIONAL GRANDMOTHERS

Recently I spent some time in the basement of a well-known children's publisher, looking for books for my grandchildren. I was astonished to discover how, even now, the stereotype of a grandmother in many picture books for the young is still some dumpy, preternaturally patient creature with grey hair and spectacles, forever knitting and cooking. And the more surprised, in some cases, to find this image promulgated by artists who, as very far from traditional grandmothers themselves, ought to know better.

Now there's nothing wrong with the stereotype in itself. Such comfortable grandmothers are by no means dream stuff. My elder granddaughter's other grandmother, for instance, though no stereotype in any other way, is a traditional grandmother in such respects and Ellie loves her. So do I, not least because she lets me off that hook.

Elsewhere I quote Sue Limb's account of her daughter insisting that by the time she has a baby her mother must develop white hair and 'appley cheeks'. While Sheila Kitzinger has an example of a very youthful grandmother astonished to find herself described in a school essay written by her grand-daughter as 'a white-haired old lady, walking with a stick'. Of course this could partly be because children, too, have been fed

by the stereotype in the picture books. Confused by grandmothers who don't fit, they are trying to make order for
themselves. But I think it is as much because children at all
times need the security of such comfortable figures around
them. Shirley Hughes sees the stereotype of the trendy, young,
roller-blading, bungee-jumping grandmother that is developing alongside the old stereotype in children's books as equally
grotesque, because 'children have an instinctive respect for age.
And one doesn't want to destroy that.' To which I would add
that such respect for age also helps give children a sense of
generations, of past feeding into present, which might be lost
where grandmothers are seen as indistinguishable from mothers.

Some children, of course, make such boasts as 'My grandmother rides a racing bike', indicating that they see the joke
perfectly well and have no difficulty in distinguishing the generations. All the same, the need for such distinctions, in some
form, could be an added instinctive motive for those women
seeking grandmother figures for their children, to make up for
their own mother's refusal to adopt any such role; of this we
will hear more in the next section. It is, of course, too, a question of convenience. Traditional grandmothers, as we've seen,
are useful; especially for working mothers.

As for myself, I was always quite happy with the image
presented by my briefly known paternal grandmother; that
was how I imagined grandmothers in general. Not realising
that my grandmother's great age made her quite untypical, it
never occurred to me to question Katherine Mansfield's
invariable labelling of the grandmothers in her stories as 'old
woman' – presumably her death at the age of thirty-two had
something to do with it. I only began to do so when confronting the possibility of being a grandmother myself; I
could not see myself as an old woman in any way; and with
difficulty imagined myself as what is undeniably more true, an
ageing one.

The stereotype, of course, was never absolute. An eighteenth-century instruction book on how women should behave throughout their lives inveighed against overexuberance in, not to say pursuit of eternal youth by, older women, suggesting that some grannies had no desire to behave like ones, even then. In the 1850s the English prime minister Lord Palmerston married a very merry widow in her fifties, a lively dancer, far from being a sedate figure in black sitting at the side of the ballroom as tradition would have had a female of such an age. A novel written in the 1880s, *The Baby's Grandmother*, recounts the romantic entanglements of an admittedly exceptionally young grandmother who confounded the conventional expectations held by all before meeting her. Writing of the period before the First World War, Lady St Helier too, in a later section of his book, suggests that grandmothers were no longer the retiring figures of earlier days. All this makes me remember more vividly the glee with which my mother reported the comment of an old man she met as she was wheeling out in his pram the only grandchild she ever saw, my brother's son: 'I do think you young mothers are so wonderful these days.' Her glee was comparable to my own when my granddaughter gets mistaken for my child, as has happened.

How would *her* mother have been, I wonder? She would have been less than fifty when my brother, her first grandchild, was born. The only story I know about her offers the smallest of clues. She was walking down Piccadilly one day, it goes, when the elastic broke on her knickers – not the skimpy things we have, either; they were bloomers, more like. She did not pause, did not even stop talking; as they fell to the pavement she simply bent down and scooped them up, and went on as if nothing had happened. The spirit in this makes me suspect that she would not have abandoned her youth that easily either.

But these days, it is not simply a matter of hanging on to our youth that makes us reject the stereotype so fiercely. It is also the absolutely self-conscious, thoroughly articulated resistance of my generation to the stereotypes which have been imposed on every age of women; shy virgin; repentant or golden-hearted whore; earth mother; old woman/crone/wise woman/witch.

In some ways, of course, the image of old women, as we'll explore in the section on lively grandmothers, could be liberating, at least in some more traditional societies. I'll simply point out now that if you look at medieval or Renaissance pictures, even some portraits, where the women all come out as oval-faced Madonnas or ripe Venuses, only the older women, like the men in the same pictures, are depicted as individuals, if you can forget the stress laid on the wrinkles of the oldest.

This is not to say we can or should reject all traditional aspects of grandmotherhood. Why should we? Myself, I'll make one bow towards Germaine Greer's suggestion that we embrace cronedom gladly, by saying that I think dignity matters at any age; and that some ways of going on or dressing that I might have undertaken in my twenties are not for me. (And not, I hope, just because I've taken too much to heart my mother's adage that mutton shouldn't be dressed as lamb.)

An old woman I knew, now dead, who insisted on wearing bright tights and sweaters, came back weeping from the park once after being mocked by a group of youths on the grounds that 'she wasn't wearing old-woman clothes'. That upsets me, then as now. Whatever care I might take myself, I would defend to the death the right of any women of any age to dress as old or young as she chooses; young women, after all, are adopting granny accessories, according to one piece here. And I am grateful that I can pick and mix my granny role; be traditional where I want to be, and not where I don't. And even more grateful that I don't suffer the still not wholly unknown fate of the traditional middle-class Bengali materfamilias of the kind we see here. Never allowed a proper education, let alone a job outside the home, she is deprived of all her practical functions by her younger daughters-in-law, denied, conventionally, her sexuality even before menopause, and her sole duty is to devote herself to religion and the teachings of her guru. No, thanks.

The irony of all this, of course, is that it is so often the very same put-upon grandmothers who insist on upholding the traditions that bind them and their families. If mothers and grandmothers hadn't marched their daughters off to the footbinders, I've been told, this Chinese torture wouldn't have survived as long as it did. We have examples here of a Moroccan grandmother defending the harem; an Indian grandmother sabotaging her granddaughters' education; a Sabbatarian Scottish one enforcing a dismal Sabbath; a Jewish grandmother hijacking her grandson to get him circumcised against the will of his nonreligious parents.

I observed for myself once the influence wielded by grandmothers, in Africa in this case, but also elsewhere, on the maintenance of female circumcision. I was sitting in a psychiatric clinic in Nairobi, when there shuffled in a girl of twelve or so, plainly out of her head on Largactil. She'd had a breakdown; *grand mal* epileptic seizures one symptom, self-mutilation another, all dating from the night her grandmother came home and said she'd fixed for the girl's circumcision, despite her long-standing resistance; she could not, according to her grandmother, be a proper woman without it. The psychiatrist turned to the gaunt old man who'd followed her in: her father. What had he been thinking of to allow such a situation? The old man shrugged and replied that the grandmother and the mother did what they wanted; what made the psychiatrist think that *he* could stop them?

Grandmothers as inhibitors of social change are one thing. Reversing the spectrum, grandmothers as keepers of social order, of the wisdom of the tribe, are another, and much less negative. There's the example here of the old woman whose otherwise lost knowledge saved her people after a tidal wave; of the elephant matriarchs whose knowledge of migrating routes meant the disintegration of their herds if they were shot. In our electronic world, many grandmotherly skills may be of little practical use to our grandchildren. Why should she bother to learn skills offered by her grandmother which she'd no intention of using? said Oprah Winfrey in a recent interview. Nevertheless, as Shirley Hughes has found, redundant technology can fascinate children and help them grasp some chronology and context. Those of us who no longer possess wind-up gramophones and clockwork trains have still got our experience of history to offer; assuming history matters.

Even a knowledge of tradition may matter in the end. Some sadder examples here; the Japanese grandmother, for instance, banished to the basement while her children and grandchildren play at being Americans upstairs may seem to deny that tradition has any future. Yet such an example is contradicted elsewhere by the seeking-out of roots and traditions seen in both exiled and still indigenous communities round the world, Native American and Australian Aboriginal communities, for instance. Here the grandmother's knowledge is vital.

Do I expect mine to be vital? Who knows? Grandmothers and grandchildren these days are already exchanging emails. And what I hope, a little, is that for twenty-first-century grandmothers and their grandchildren alike, access to the Internet might mean, sometimes, filling a few websites with what the one has to give the other. Tradition need not be maintained in traditional ways.

———

Dear Granny! I think I see her now, sitting almost upright in her high-back chair, a kerchief of snowy muslin folded over her bosom, her hands . . . employed, or seemingly employed, with her knitting needles on socks for great-grandchildren. But it was not of her appearance I meant to write, but tell you of many little bits of wisdom she had collected during her long life which I profited by . . .

C. H. PAISH in *Work and Leisure*, February 1893

———

I should remind readers, that to dress in accordance with one's age and position is necessary . . . A young-looking woman may dress in youthful garments, in which a contemporary who looks her age appears ridiculous.

It is better to err on the side of being dressed too old than too young. To do the latter is to expose oneself to the ridicule of others . . . There is something very undignified about it too . . . To see a woman who is a grandmother in a juvenile hat, a *passé* lady in girlish clothes, an elderly woman in youthful garb, is to provoke a smile and occasion mirth . . .

'LOUISA EMILY' DOBRÉE, *The Housewife*, 1889

———

Who has not known some wonderfully young grandmama? Someone whose heart is not grown old, nor ever will do so; who in speed and act is younger than many a mamma? Such an one I have before my eye. A bright, beautiful old lady, full of energy, yet not inconveniently bustling. The family she lives with love and honour her as they ought. She is full of thought as if she had made thinking her chief business . . . There she sits, busy with her needle, her young granddaughter, a girl of thirteen, looking at her with an affectionate glance as she comes into the pleasant parlour from the garden.

The Monthly Packet, July–December 1859

———

from Grandmother Dear

'Ye-es,' said Ralph, 'I don't think she's bad for a grandmother.'

'For a grandmother,' cried Molly, indignantly. 'What do you mean, Ralph? What can be nicer than a nice grandmother?'

'But suppose she wasn't nice? She needn't be, you know. There are grandmothers and grandmothers,' persisted Ralph.

'Of course I know *that*,' said Molly. You don't suppose that I thought our grandmother was everybody's grandmother, you silly boy. What I say is she's just like a real grandmother – not like Nora Leslie's, who is always scolding Nora's mother for scolding her children, and wears such grand, quite *young lady* dresses, and has *black* hair,' with an accent of profound disgust, 'not nice, beautiful, soft, silver hair, like *our* grandmother's. Now, isn't it true, Sylvia, isn't our grandmother just like a *real* one?'

Sylvia smiled. 'Yes, exactly,' she replied. 'She could almost do for a fairy godmother, if she only had a stick with a gold knob.'

MRS MOLESWORTH, 1878

The woman who chooses to wear black and live in perpetual *lutto* is eschewing the life of the spouse and embracing the role of grandmother.

GERMAINE GREER, *The Change*, 1991

Everyone in New York has a grandmother with an apartment on Park Avenue,' Mamie had said in wonder, and he had laughed. 'At home, grandmothers collect ferns. They don't wear diamonds and go out to lunch, I might as well be on Mars.'

'You might as well be,' he had said.

SUSANNA MOORE, *The Whiteness of Bones*, 1981

---

from Bengali Women

[A young girl] may also accompany her grandmother to religious meetings or temples in the early evening, where many women of grandmother's age gather to listen to recitations from the holy books . . . The grandmother may also visit the temple for a short while to meditate or see her guru, while the little girl watches others or goes browsing through the toys and sweets in shops nearby. From these visits she learns to respect the temple, feeling drawn by the smell of flowers, sandalwood and incense.

[. . .] If a woman lives beyond sixty and is not totally satisfied with her guru she may try to find some solace in her close companionship with her grandchildren.

The ideal. Ideally the relationship is very cordial and sweet. The grandmother's only obligation is to enjoy the frolic of the grandchildren and offer emotional support to them when they (especially the male ones) need protection from the discipline of their father and their uncles. They must treat her with respect and cordiality.

The reality. The real situation corresponds fairly well with the ideal because other factors do not interfere with this relationship which is marginal anyway. There are no unfulfilled obligations to create tension. The above analysis shows that the developmental process of a woman's interaction with members of her family results in accelerated frustration unless she accepts the last compensatory role with her guru which appears to offer most satisfaction.

MANISHA ROY, 1975

[In Japan] a woman must behave decorously at any age, but it is particularly important that she should conduct herself suitably at this time of her life. She must not try to appear younger than she is, she must not beautify herself with cosmetics, elaborate hairstyles or jewellery. She should not wear 'unsuitable colours', that is the soft and tender colours (pastels) and 'bold or bright colours'.

Source unknown

Her quiet eyes are mild and clear,
   her faded cheek is fair;
the snows of many a yester year
   have settled on her hair;

She shakes her head at modern ways,
   or smiles in gentle scorn:
Has she not known far better days,
   long, long ere we were born?

Hers was a fresher youth than ours,
   a time of sun and dew;
her path was sweet with homely flowers,
   her sky was always blue;

The maidens had a modest grace,
   the men were true of tongue
And no one wore a double fair
   when grandmother was
young.

SARAH DOUDNEY, *The Girl's
Own Paper*, 22 December 1883

---

from The Grandmother

Every few moments the children ran out to the road to see if Wenzel was coming; and every passer by heard the wondrous news that Grandma was coming. The children kept asking each other, 'How do you suppose Grandma will look?'

They knew several grandmas, whose images were curiously confounded in their little heads, and they could not decide to which of them their own could be compared.

At last the long expected team arrived. 'Grandma's come!' shouted the children in a chorus. Mr and Mrs Proshek rushed out to meet her; Betty, the maid, followed carrying the youngest child, and behind her came the three children accompanied by the two dogs, Sultan and Tyrol.

The wagon stopped at the gate, and Wenzel helped a little old woman to alight. She was dressed in the garb of a peasant, having her head wrapped up in a large white kerchief. This was something the children had never seen before, and they stood still, their eyes fixed upon their grandmother. Mr Proshek welcomed her cordially, her daughter embraced and kissed her, and Betty presented the dimpled cheeks of Adelka to be kissed. Grandmother smiled, called the child 'her own sweet fledgling', and signed her with the cross. Then she turned to the other children and said: 'O my darlings, my little ones, how I have longed to see you!' But the children, with downcast eyes, stood as if frozen to the spot, and uttered never a word; and not until they were ordered by their mother would they step forward to be kissed, and even then they could not recover from their amazement. They had known many grandmothers in their life, but never one like this; they could not turn their eyes from her; they walked round and round and examined her from head to foot.

They wondered at the curious little coat, with its full pleating, like organ pipes, behind; the green linsey-wolsey petticoat, bordered with a wide ribbon was an object of great admiration; they were pleased with the flowered kerchief that was tied beneath the large, white head shawl. They sat down upon the ground that they might examine better the red wedge-shaped insertion in her white stockings, and also her black slippers. Willie touched the pretty patchwork on her handbag, and the fouryearold Johnny, the older of the two, slyly raised her white apron; he had felt something hard beneath it, something hidden away in her large outside pocket, and he wanted to know what it was. Barunka, the oldest of the children, pushed him away, whispering: 'Wait, I'll tell on you! you want to feel in Grandma's pocket!'

That whisper was a little too loud, it would have been heard behind the ninth wall; Grandmother noticed it, and turning from her daughter she put her hand in her pocket and said: 'Well, look at what I have here!' She placed upon her lap a rosary, a jack-knife, several bits of crust, a piece of twine, two horses and two dolls made of gingerbread; these were for the children. As she distributed them she said: 'Grandma brought you something more.' Thus speaking she took from her handbag some apples and Easter eggs, and set the kittens and chickens at liberty. The children shouted with delight. Grandma was the best of all grandmas! 'These kittens were born in May, are four colored, and will make excellent mousers. These chickens are so tame that if Barunka teaches them, they will follow her about like puppies.'

The children then began to inquire about this and that, and soon were on the best of terms with Grandmother. Their mother rebuked their endless questioning; but Grandmother said: 'Never mind, Theresa, we are happy in each other's love,' and so they had it their own way. One sat in her lap, another stood upon a bench behind her, and Barunka stood before her, intently gazing into her face. One wondered at her snow-white hair, another at her wrinkled forehead, and the third cried: 'Why Grandma, you have but four teeth!' She smiled, smoothed down Barunka's dark brown hair, and said: 'My child, I am old; when you grow old, you, too, will look different.' But they could not comprehend how their smooth, soft hands could ever become wrinkled like hers.

[. . . One] thing that did not quite suit her was the appearance of her daughter. She had expected to find her as she was when she left home, a bright, cheerful peasant girl; and now she saw before her a stately lady, in city garments, of stiff manners and few words. This was not her Theresa! She observed, too, that their domestic life was quite different from that to which she had been accustomed; and although, for the first few days, she was surprised and delighted, she soon grew tired of the new ways, and had it not been for the grandchildren, she would have packed up and returned to her own little cottage.

[. . .] Grandmother never sat in the parlor unless she was obliged to do so. She liked best her own little room, which was next to the kitchen and the servants' apartments. Her room was furnished according to her own taste. By the side of the large stove that stood in the corner was a long bench. Next to the wall stood her bed, at whose foot was the large flowered chest. On the other side was a small bed, where Barunka slept; she had obtained this privilege as a special favor from her mother. In the middle of the room stood the large bass-wood

table, the legs of which were bound together by braces that
served as foot-rests. Above the table hung a dove made of an
egg-shell and pleated paper; – this was to remind one of the
Holy Ghost. In the corner stood the spinning wheel and
distaff. The walls were decorated with several pictures of
saints, and above Grandmother's bed was a crucifix adorned
with garlands. Inside of the double window were some flower
pots with sweet balsams and musk, and on the sides there
hung little linen bags of medicinal herbs, such as linden blossoms, elder blossoms, and the like.

The table drawer contained Grandmother's sewing, a
bundle of sacred hymns, the prayers of the Holy Passion, some
spinning-wheel cords, and a blessed candle which was always
lighted when a thunder storm was coming up.

What the children liked the best in her room was the large
flowered chest . . .

At the bottom of the chest were her clothing and linen. All
those linen petticoats, aprons, coats, corsets, and kerchiefs lay
there in the best of order, and on the top of all were two stiffly
starched caps, with large bows behind, that were called 'doves'.
These things the children were not allowed to touch. Still,
when Grandmother was so disposed, she raised one article
after another saying: 'See, children, this petticoat I have had
for fifty years; this coat was worn by your grandmother; this
apron is as old as your mother; – and all as good as new; and
you spoil your clothes in no time. That all comes because you
do not know the value of money. Do you see this silk coat? it
cost a hundred Rhine dollars; but in those days they paid with
bank-notes.' Thus she went on, and the children listened as
though they understood it all.

Mrs Proshek wished her mother to wear city garments,
because she thought they would be more suitable; but to this
Grandmother would not listen. She said: 'The Lord would
surely punish me, if I, an old woman, should begin to grow
worldly. Such changes of fashion are not for me; they would

not suit my old age.' Thus she remained faithful to the 'good old ways'; and soon every thing in the house went according to her will, and no one thought of disputing her word.

BOZENA NEMEC, 1881

from Hehe Grandmothers

When a girl approaches the age of puberty, but before her first menstruation, she passes through an initiation ceremony. Her grandmothers, both paternal and maternal, together conduct the ceremony; other old women being present. The ceremony is long and complicated, and it is only necessary to say here that the grandmothers prepare all the medicines used, pray to the ancestors for assistance, conduct the girl to a secluded spot near a river, and there perform a slight operation on the vulva (I believe the hymen is removed). The membrane removed is thrown under a flowering tree to insure her fertility. At the same ceremony the *misimu* are sung to her by young married women and newly initiated girls, the grandmothers remaining in the background but continuing to direct the ceremony. The *misimu* are a collection of dramatic songs with accompanying dances dealing with facts of sex, things to do or to avoid doing during pregnancy and menstruation and the rules which should guide girls in their marital relations, their relations with co-wives, mothers-in-law, etc. Ridicule is freely employed in the songs, and in the explanations which follow each song. The wife jealous of her co-wife, the woman who makes a fuss when bearing a child, the woman who is attentive to her mother but who neglects her mother-in-law are all held up to scorn. The girl or girls (sometimes two or three are initiated together) return from the river in the midst of rejoicing; beer is drunk by members of the family. A period of relative seclusion for the girl then follows which is terminated by a large public feast. From the ceremony at the river the mother of the girl is excluded; she may join only in the rejoicings at the end of it.

There is no doubt that at this ceremony the grandmother appears to the girl in a new light. Not only is she closely associated with all the new knowledge which the girl must assimilate, but the grandmother has displayed in no uncertain fashion her knowledge of medicines, her ability to deal with unknown forces in moments of crisis. From this time on the girl is prepared to appeal to her grandmother for help in times of illness and distress, and to accept her word as to the course of action to be followed or avoided in times of perplexity. Hehe life is permeated with a belief in the efficacy of material medicines for use not only in times of illness but in times of crisis. Old women can hardly avoid having a large knowledge of medicines even if they are not skilled practitioners of the craft. The knowledge of the old women is put freely at the disposal of their granddaughters, and at child-birth, during illnesses of the child and mother, etc., they are always called upon. The girl may have vaguely realized before this time that her grandmother possessed this knowledge, but the initiation ceremony brings it forcefully before her.

ELIZABETH FISHER BROWN, 1935

---

from The Sisters

We were seven years old, when Grandma announced it was time to prepare us for the *navjote* – a ceremony of initiation into the Zoroastrian religion which every Parsi child must go through, whether boy or girl, wearing for ever after, the symbols of his religion – a *sudra* or thin muslin shirt and a *kusti* –

the sacred thread woven from lamb's wool. To Sophie the whole thing came as a complete surprise.

We never knew very clearly why father had married her. She had once told us that her mother on hearing of their engagement had remarked flatly, 'I'd rather see you dead than married to an Indian.' In England, wearing his beautifully tailored clothes, speaking his impeccably accented English, father must have appeared to Sophie, hardly different from anyone else, except perhaps for the suavity of his manner, the exotic nature of his background.

She was astonished and angry by the chill welcome given to her by Grandma. She was aware, of course, that father was not a Christian, but Zoroastrianism is a religion that is accommodating and not necessarily connected with any sort of ritual. Sophie had never seen father pray, go to the fire temple, or attend any religious ceremonies. The *navjote* therefore, was sprung on her as a wholly unexpected, and even unpleasant surprise. It was only after this that she first learnt about the vultures.

Nina and I [. . .] shared a large play-room built on the side of the garage. It was fitted with shelves, cupboards and large tables, an enormous rocking horse whose head reached much higher than ours and all the paraphernalia that children seem to collect. There was my shell collection and Nina's dolls from different lands, and jars and bottles of anything we were interested in at that moment. We were, as I said, seven years old and Sophie was still violently protesting about her children going through any such ceremony as the *navjote*. Grandma, of course, was adamant and Sophie's protests were no more than waves, dashing futilely on stone. I still remember this particular morning . . . Nina sat at a table, carefully drawing and colouring what looked like eagles, with wings outspread, supporting themselves on a Picasso-blue tree. Her tongue was caught lightly between her teeth, curling at the tip as she bent over the thick creamy paper. A pale beam of sunlight slanting through the open window, lit up the orange tinted water like a lamp, into which Nina, from time to time would dip the brush.

Passing to retrieve something from the other side of the room, I glanced over her shoulder and said, 'Vultures! They are going to eat you up when you are dead.'

Nina spun round on her chair at once, the wet brush held as though it were a dart, ready to fling at me. 'They are not vultures. And they will eat *you*, because you are a bad bad girl.'

I smiled smugly, secure in my superior knowledge. 'You're just silly. You don't know anything. Don't you know what happens to Parsis when they die? They are taken up to high towers and made naked and ripped up with steel hooks and then, the vultures tear their eyes out and then their hearts and then . . .'

I had no idea where or how I had acquired this knowledge but Nina's pallor deepened till she turned as white as the paper on which she had been painting. 'It's not true,' her voice quavered. She flew at me, pulling my hair and screaming, 'It's not true, it's not true. Sophie won't let them.'

I pushed her away easily. I was always so much heavier and stronger. 'It is true, it is true,' I said dancing around the table and keeping out of reach. I took an imaginary hook and lunged at her. 'Rrr . . . ip!' Her screams were so loud that everyone in the house could hear, although the purpose of the room was that we might make as much noise as we liked, without disrupting the more orderly lives of the adults.

Sophie was the first to come tearing in, followed by a couple of servants and Grandma, who had made one of her rare visits downstairs. Nina flew to Sophie who held her, rocking her up and down in her arms. 'There, there. Quiet now, quiet.' She glared across at me. 'What on earth did you do to her?'

Nina's voice rose again hysterically. 'She said, – she said, that when I die, they will put me in a tower for the vultures to eat.'

Sophie looked at me with disgust. 'What a revolting thing to say. What you need is a jolly good spanking. How dare you make up such vicious stories to frighten your little sister.'

Grandma, small, round, but commanding, moved slowly into the centre of the room.

'Wait a minute Sophie. I know it is very naughty of Rita to tell Nina this, but it's true you know. Didn't you know? I sometimes wonder whether Firoze ever tells you anything. Parsis don't bury their dead. They are taken up to what are known as *Towers of Silence* and exposed, so that the vultures can dispose of the flesh quickly. It is all very clean and hygienic. The bones roll into a special place and are dissolved in lime.' This was all said in the most matter-of-fact manner possible, but Sophie's face was a mask of horror. Her every nerve, already rubbed raw by Nina's screams, was now laid open. 'It's not true,' she gasped echoing Nina's words. 'You are civilized people, how can you do anything so barbaric?'

Grandma bridled. 'I don't see what's barbaric about it. Instead of burying the body under the ground where worms eat the flesh slowly, bit by bit, this is done quickly, within hours.'

Sophie's reply to this was to snatch Nina up in her arms and run to her room, where they remained locked in for the rest of the day. Grandma looked at me severely. 'You are a very naughty child. You shall have no pudding for three days.' She crossed over to the drawing. 'Even you should know the difference between eagles and vultures!' When father came home there was a tremendous row with father wanting to give me a good spanking as well. I could hear him saying 'Yes, but dash it all, there was no need to spring it on the child like that. I really think there is something unpleasantly morbid about Rita. You spoil her, mother.'

Grandma said 'This is what comes of marrying a *pardesi*. I warned you. The children are neither one thing nor the other. That is why I say it is time to prepare them for the *navjote*.'

Sophie, of course, disliked the idea of the *navjote* from the beginning. Long prayers, intoned in a dead language, had to be learnt, and it was decided that every evening after supper, we should be sent up to Grandma's room for instruction. Even Nina knew that when Grandma decided on something, there was no sense in throwing tantrums.

NERGIS DALAL, 1973

------

from Karl-Yankel

Simon's children moved about with his division. The old woman needed a grandson whom she might tell about Baal-Shem, and she expected a grandson from her youngest daughter Polina. Alone of all the family, the girl had taken after little old Jonah. She was easy to scare, short of sight, tender of skin, and she had lots of suitors. Polina chose Ovsey Belotserkovsky – we could never understand why. Even more amazing was the news that the young people were leading a very happy married life. A woman's household is her own affair; outsiders don't see how the pots get broken. In this case the breaker of pots was Ovsey Belotserkovsky. A year after the wedding he sued his mother-in-law, Brana Brutman. Taking advantage of Ovsey's absence on an official mission somewhere, and of the fact that Polina had gone to hospital with mastitis, the old woman kidnapped her newborn grandson, carried him off to the little foreskin-clipper Naftula Gerchik, and there, in the presence of ten ruins, ten ancient and poverty-stricken old men, assiduous attenders at the Hasidic synagogue, the ceremony of circumcision was performed upon the infant.

ISAAC BABEL, 1930, translated by Walter Morison

------

from Thatched with Gold

Sundays were observed on strict Sabbatarian lines; no cooking was done, no games were played. In the morning, between breakfast and church, our governess read to us from the Bible or *The Pilgrim's Progress* while we painted texts – dreadfully printed and embellished with stiff floral sprays – to be taken back to London and wrapped round the pennies which we were encouraged to distribute to beggars. Then came three hours of church, with interminable psalms, and a sermon lasting at least forty-five minutes. The big family pew was like a square room, open on one side, with seats all round it and a fireplace. Its chief merit in our eyes was that discipline was difficult to enforce. My brother Arthur generally managed to enliven the tedium of the service by mounting a hassock when the collection was made and dropping his penny from his mouth into the plate.

On Sunday afternoons we were permitted books with a religious bias, such as lives of missionaries or descriptions of the Holy Land, and after tea Grandmother read a sermon to us, a privilege received with anything but gratitude. As an alternative to the Sunday reading the Biblical Scrap Book was passed round. This was a book into which scraps of all kinds were pasted, with a text applicable to each one written underneath it in my grandmother's beautiful handwriting. Some of them were very strange. My sister Alice and I were never sure whether a picture – cut out from a catalogue – of a little black satin shoe, with a high Louis XV heel, under which were the words . . . 'withdraw thy foot from thy neighbour's house lest he be weary of thee and so hate thee' . . . proved Granny's sense of humour or her lack of it.

MABELL AIRLIE, 1962

from The Old Order

They talked about the past, really – always about the past. Even the future seemed like something gone and done with when they spoke of it. It did not seem an extension of their past, but a repetition of it. They would agree that nothing remained of life as they had known it, the world was changing swiftly, but by the mysterious logic of hope they insisted that each change was probably the last; or if not, a series of changes might bring them, blessedly, back full-circle to the old ways they had known. Who knows why they loved their past? It had been bitter for them both, they had questioned the burdensome rule they lived by every day of their lives, but without rebellion and without expecting an answer. This unbroken thread of inquiry in their minds contained no doubt as to the utter rightness and justice of the basic laws of human existence, founded as they were on God's plan; but they wondered perpetually, with only a hint now and then to each other of the uneasiness of their hearts, how so much suffering and confusion could have been built up and maintained on such a foundation. The grandmother's role was authority, she knew that; it was her duty to portion out activities, to urge or restrain where necessary, to teach morals, manners and religion, to punish and reward her own household according to a fixed code. Her own doubts and hesitations she concealed, also, she reminded herself, as a matter of duty. Old Nannie had no ideas at all as to her place in the world. It had been assigned to her before birth, and for her daily rule she had all her life obeyed the authority nearest to her.

[. . .] They talked about religion, and the slack way the world was going nowadays, the decay of behaviour, and about the younger children, whom these topics always brought at once to mind. On these subjects they were firm, critical, and unbewildered. They had received educations which furnished them an assured habit of mind about all the important appearances of

life, and especially about the rearing of young. They relied
with perfect acquiescence on the dogma that children were
conceived in sin and brought forth in iniquity. Childhood was
a long state of instruction and probation for adult life, which
was in turn a long, severe, undeviating devotion to duty, the
largest part of which consisted in bringing up children. The
young were difficult, disobedient, and tireless in wrongdoing,
apt to turn unkind and undutiful when they grew up, in spite
of all one had done for them, or had tried to do: for small
painful doubts rose in them now and again when they looked
at their completed works. Nannie couldn't abide her new-fan-
gled grandchildren. 'Wuthless, shiftless lot, jes plain scum,
Miss Sophia Jane; I cain't undahstand it aftah all the raisin'
dey had.'

KATHERINE ANNE PORTER, 1944

----

from Obasan in Suburbia

When my grandmother was eighty years old, she got kicked
out of her house for leaving her nighttime *kimono* in the bathroom one time too many. I remember the day she moved; I was
ten. I sat in the backseat of my parents' station wagon while
my father loaded her things – they fit easily into three or four
cartons. He wrapped her little black and white television in a
white chenille bedspread and laid it on the floor by my feet.
She sat next to me, looking out the window, with a Kleenex in
her fist.

She was living with my uncle Taro, her youngest son, his
wife and my little cousin Jenney, in the big pink house she and
my grandfather had bought after the war. When Uncle Taro
brought his bride, Michiko, down from Canada, my grandparents invited them to stay until their savings grew. They

never got any savings. They bought a car, a big one with automatic windows. They bought a fur coat. They bought television sets for every room in the pink house, and when my grandfather died ten years later, it was clear that Uncle Taro and his family weren't going anywhere.

That was all right. Nana would have been sad if they'd left her alone in all that space. But by that time the house had filled up with their things, pushing my grandmother to the outer perimeters of the house. She slept in the attic, in a small room with a slanted ceiling. Even though she was tiny, not even five feet tall, she could only stand up in the center of the room. She took her meals in the basement, back behind the laundry room where my grandfather had built a small, second kitchen, a one-burner stove next to an industrial size freezer. Sometimes she rested her plate on the ping-pong table and watched the Lawrence Welk Show while she ate.

The rest of them ate above her, Jenney spilling her Spaghetti-O's on the linoleum floor. It was like a split screen television, America above, and Japan below. Upstairs, they called themselves Ray and Lillian. Lil. I think Michiko chose that name intentionally, knowing that my grandmother would never be able to pronounce it. 'Lil-lian,' she tried to say, but it always came out sounding like 'Re-run' . . .

In the downstairs kitchen, my grandmother shuffled on the cement floor in her rubber-soled *zoris*. She washed the rice in the sink where Lil's nylons hung, dripping. There was a pantry down there, next to the enormous refrigerator. One shelf was designated for her food, the cans she carried in a canvas bag on the subway from Manhattan. *Kamaboko*, and the stinky yellow *daikon*. White fish cakes with the hot pink coating. I stacked the cans and cellophane packages, neatly, on her shelf, playing Japanese grocer with my play money. '*Ikura?*' I asked my grandmother. 'How much?' 'Two hundred dollar, please,' she laughed. Her teeth clicked in her mouth, and she covered her face with the back of her hand.

After a while they stopped letting her talk to Jenney. 'She won't be able to learn English,' said Aunt Michi. 'When she goes to school, people will think she talks funny.'

Ray and Lil gave barbecues in the backyard, my uncle wearing a red butcher's apron. They couldn't keep Nana locked in the attic, not on weekends with everyone around, so she sat in the cool basement, rolling logs of *sushi* on little bamboo mats. I helped her with the *nori*, thin sheets of green-black seaweed. You had to toast it first, holding it carefully over a gas flame or a candle. Nana didn't mind when I burned holes in it. 'Don't worry. It's a window for the *gohan* to look out.' We arranged the *sushi* pieces on a big round platter, and brought them out to the picnic table. Nana put it down right next to whatever Aunt Michi had made, green Jell-O or fruit cocktail with little marshmallows in it. Michi would make a face when she saw the *sushi*, like it was something strange and disgusting, so none of her friends would eat it either. She didn't tell them it was the same thing she loved to eat when she was a little girl. But sometimes I'd see her, after everyone went home, and she'd be standing next to the refrigerator, popping the little *norimaki* in her mouth when she thought no one was looking.

SUSAN ITO, 1994

―――――――

Lazio

It is a desperate grandmother, twice a mother, who invokes your aid for her little grandson, the only comfort of a heart saddened by misfortune. Destiny, which has persecuted me for many years, is now persecuting this little one, always to torment my heart. Up to now I believed it was fate, but now I have proof for believing what I have always sought to drive out of my mind: the child is possessed by an evil spirit. I had him blessed twice, by two good priests, but it was all in vain. Therefore I beseech you to alleviate the suffering of this innocent soul by indicating the person who can save him or at least guard him against these devils who live in the world to do harm to mankind.

GABRIELLA PARCA (ed.), *Italian Women Confess*, 1963

From the point of view of education in arts and crafts and education in developing aptitudes for acquiring and using fresh information easily, the influence of grandmothers, and to a less extent grandfathers, may be considered a mixed blessing. There is no doubt that the indulgence of grandparents slows down the process of education in the case of young children, and in the case of some older girls. As the tribal life as a whole does not offer a very stimulating mental environment to children, and the things they must learn to master are relatively simple, this is not an unduly serious matter, although it may become more important as the effects of contact with Western civilization increase. In ordinary tribal life to-day girls over puberty who live much with their grandmothers suffer more ill-effects from this indulgence than younger children do; they may become permanently lazy and unadaptable. The common observation of Europeans that native women are, as a rule, more conservative and less adaptable to change may be partly due to the immense influence of old women in preserving old tribal traditions: this influence is exerted directly upon their granddaughters.

ELIZABETH FISHER BROWN, 'Hehe Grandmothers', 1935

One grownup camp said that the harem was a good thing, while the other said that it was bad. Grandmother Lalla Mani and Chama's mother, Lalla Radia, belonged to the pro-harem camp; Mother, Chama, and Aunt Habiba, to the anti-harem one. Grandmother Lalla Mani often got the discussion started by saying that if the women were not separated from the men, society would come to a halt and work would not get done. 'If women were free to run about in the streets,' she said, 'men would stop working because they would want to have fun.' And unfortunately, she went on, fun did not help a society produce the food and goods it needed to survive. So, if famine were to be avoided, women had to stay in their place at home.

FATIMA MERNISSI, *The Harem Within*, 1995

When a little girl is born, when they cut the cord, the grand-mother will say 'That's going to be his wife' (and she would name someone). 'I want them two to get married.' That's what happened to me, I didn't have any say in it.

ISOBEL WHITE ET AL., *Fighters and Singers*, 1985

This is the case of two sisters who are 20 . . . and 18 years old respectively. They belong to a well to do family and have only finished their school. Their major problem is with their grandmother who is not letting them study further. She is looking after them as their parents are dead. The grandmother is very orthodox and keeps on doubting and suspecting them without any basis. There is a very strict code of conduct and the sisters feel entrapped. The sisters often tease and quarrel with their grandmother and their aunts because they think that they are being spied upon. One of the sisters wants to marry a boy of her choice but is not being allowed to. Not only this, the grandmother is spoiling their prestige and image in front of various people. The sisters are very angry and want to leave the family as their own grandmother is insulting them.

RENUKA SINGH, *The Oppression of Women by Women*, 1980

'Little boys say can I,' my grandmother said. 'Little girls are more polite. They say may I.'

MARGARET ATWOOD, *Bodily Harm*, 1981

They did not know the purpose of the ritual itself. They knew only that it was something that their grandmothers had done, and that they must also do. In turn their granddaughters would do it in exactly the same way, as would their grandchildren. This was one's purpose as a woman – to live out life as one's grandmother had lived it, and to ensure that's one granddaughters also lived that life. Going to that place and enduring whatever it was necessary for one to endure there, whether one lived or died, was all part of being a woman.

MARK HUDSON, *Our Grandmothers' Drums*, 1989

My grandmother always used to say you're a modern girl in every way. Now I realise what she means – you're not married. It was always meant as a slight in one way or another.

MELISSA BANKS, *Guardian*, 19 July 1999

---

from Breastfeeding in Rural Yoruba Communities

[The article discusses the influence of grandmothers on breast-feeding among the Yoruba. Some traditions – e.g. the forbidding of colostrum – have a harmful effect on the infants. Any attempt to alter received views has to begin by changing the perceptions of these older women, whose influence, as mothers, grandmothers, midwives, permeates all aspects of childbirth and the care of the newborn.]

[T]he old women insisted that the mother must have had a bath, washed her nipples thoroughly to remove dirt, and expressed and discarded colostrum before breastfeeding could begin. If a mother who has not cleaned her nipples breastfeeds, her child can have diarrhoea. The mother and baby would also have rested since the time of delivery and would have regained strength sufficiently before breastfeeding is initiated. Prayers and other rituals would have been performed before the baby is given to the mother to put to her breast. One of the old women informed that breastfeeding should not start before the third day after birth. Water is fed to the baby in the meantime, together with herbs which will purge the baby and clean its stomach. Water and herbal teas can be so fed for three days.

Most of the women . . . did not think that colostrum should be used – it should be expressed and discarded – and advised that breastfeeding cannot begin till white milk began to flow. This is because colostrum is bad milk that has stayed in the breast for nine months of pregnancy; 'it is pus'; 'it contains germs and can harm the child'; 'it is dirty and can cause the baby to contract disease'. Some of the women who attended the clinic had been informed by the health workers that colostrum was good for the baby. Even so, most of them thought that colostrum should not be given to the infant.

ANITA A. DAVIES-ADETUGBO, 1997

from Hidden Lives

I had my second baby, Jake, at home. I thought my mother would approve but she didn't. She said surely hospitals were safer and what was I doing, putting the clock back. But I hated hospitals and was sure I'd get on much better giving birth at home. It was an easy birth, with Hunter practically delivering his own son, which shocked my mother. It made her feel queasy thinking of husbands even watching a birth. It wasn't decent somehow. Even less decent was what she thought of as the appalling habit of taking photographs of the birth. A friend who had her baby a few days before I had mine turned up at our house while my mother was with us (down, traditional style, to look after me, though I didn't want to be looked after) and asked if we would like to see some photographs taken when Jason was born. My mother, expecting shots of a baby in its mother's arms, all creased from birth and looking adorable, peered eagerly at the snaps and then gasped. The pictures shown of the baby emerging from between its mother's legs seemed to her pornographic, the legs apart, the bloody vagina gaping, the head a black blot bulging obscenely, and all in glorious Technicolor. She was speechless, couldn't hide her revulsion. Had women really come to this?

Some things, she felt, should remain private. Modesty was being lost sight of. Since she'd said often enough that in her day giving birth was shrouded in mystery, and the shock of the reality was profound, I tried to persuade her that surely films and photographs of births were ways of properly informing both men and women. No. She didn't think so. It was going too far, no need for it. She wasn't entirely approving of my breast-feeding my babies either. She was never comfortable with the sight of my doing this and thought I should always do it in my bedroom 'where it's quiet'. She'd bottle-fed all of us. Breast-feeding was associated in her mind with poverty and she couldn't understand how any educated woman could do it.

It was another backward step, further proof she didn't understand the modern generation.

Feeding on demand made no kind of sense to her either. She'd never heard of Truby King, but she had always believed in and followed a rigid routine. She'd watch me breast-feeding for the second time in three hours and say she'd always waited the 'proper' four hours between feeds and seen I got the 'proper' amount of milk. Only my babies thriving and putting on weight, even if they did cry a lot and Jake hardly slept, consoled her. But there was no growing closer between my mother and me because I now had two children. Becoming a mother myself had forged no new bond. Rather the reverse. How, when I realized the passion with which I cherished my babies, could I ever get to that state of polite affection which my own mother and I enjoyed?

Motherhood had become more mysterious, not less so.

MARGARET FORSTER, 1996

––––––––––

Mexican-American grandmothers as health-care advisers . . . were interviewed to learn how they took care of specific diseases by domestic rather than professional management . . . They were asked about women's conditions such as suppressed menstruation, menstrual cramps, menopause, enhancement of fertility, contraception, assistance at labor, delivery and lying in, promotion or suppression of lactation. They were also questioned about ailments that the informants themselves brought up, including childhood illness, cough, cold, earache, eye problems, stomachache, sleeplessness, toothache, burns, rheumatism, joint pain, sore throat, fever, urinary problems, nerves, wounds and skin infections. Over 50 herbal remedies and 25 over-the-counter medicines were recorded . . .

The grandmothers relied heavily on plants that had been

introduced from Europe during the colonial period of New Spain. Thus hot and dry European plants (anise, cinnamon, camomile, garlic and oregano) were used to treat colds as well as coughs . . . Pain such as earache was treated by the hot herb rue, either prepared by the grandmother herself or obtained from the drugstore, for in Mexico, the most common herbal ingredient of over-the-counter ear drops is rue. Stomachache was treated with hot spearmint, peppermint or camomile . . .

MARGARITA KAY AND MARIANNE YODER, 'Hot and Cold in
Women's Therapeutics', 1987

---

from Why, Grandma, What Big Heels You've Got!

See that little old lady at the bus stop? She's the height of fashion, she is. Well, maybe that's a slight exaggeration. Still, while housecoats and varicose veins aren't quite *de rigueur*, all things quaint, old-fashioned and nostalgia-ridden have slowly sneaked back into style like a bunion into a slipper.

In fashion, crocheted shawls, beaded handbags, tweed and Liberty prints – once the preserve of your grandmother's wardrobe – have found their place in the hearts of the nation. At home, Gucci has revived the ultimate granny cooking accessory, the oven glove, while patchwork quilts have come out for an airing. Names like Emily, Grace and Amy are more popular than ever, even sherry and shopping trolleys are making a comeback. It's enough to make you dash out and buy a rain hat.

[. . .] It's a heady world of cardies, thermal vests and floral toilet bags. Anna Sui's latest face powder smells of parma violets, comes in a black plastic casket and looks like a postwar Avon classic. So why has fashion gone AWOL over OAP?

'Granny Chic is about the comfort factor,' says Ian Glenville, fashion historian and co-writer of *The Cutting Edge*. 'Grandmothers have that war spirit we find so comforting. They say things like "put the kettle on, darling" during disasters.' It's that *fin de siècle* thing again, but now with added angst. If the millennium bug bites us bad, we'll just get out the Tetley's and wrap up warm.

Glenville also reckons it's very English to look like a gran. 'No other country has charity shops like us,' he explains. 'It's very English to do the thrift shops. It's still inherent in this country to think those who obviously invest in new clothing are "common". If we spend £4,000 on something we like to pretend it costs next to nothing. We love Fendi patchwork baguette bags because, after two outings, they look like they've been around for years. We love anything that reminds us of what our grannies used to make for nothing.'

[. . .] As women are seen as sex-mad sirens in lad mags and ads, perhaps our way of reacting is to look demure. 'I hate that Ibiza babe stuff,' says Jane Evans, a graphic designer. 'That tarty look has been overdone. Wanting to look pretty can be just as sexy but it's not so obvious.' Nicola White, a lecturer and writer in fashion history, agrees. 'I love that embroidered cardie over the frock look. My boyfriend says I look like his granny, but I think it's pretty and comfortable.'

CAYTE WILLIAMS, *Independent on Sunday*, 1 August 1999

---

from Why Is Sex Fun?

When I began pestering my middle-aged Rennellese informants with my questions about fruit edibility, I was brought into a hut. There, in the back of the hut, once my eyes had become accustomed to the dim light, was the inevitable, frail, very old woman, unable to walk without support. She was the last living person with direct experience of the plants found safe and nutritious to eat after the hungi kengi, until people's gardens began producing again. The old woman explained to me that she had been a child not quite of marriageable age at the time of the hungi kengi. Since my visit to Rennell was in 1976, and since the cyclone had struck sixty-six years before, around 1910, the woman was probably in her early eighties. Her survival after the 1910 cyclone had depended on information remembered by aged survivors of the last big cyclone before the hungi kengi. Now, the ability of her people to survive another cyclone would depend on her own memories, which fortunately were very detailed.

Such anecdotes could be multiplied indefinitely. Traditional human societies face frequent minor risks that threaten a few individuals, and they also face rare natural catastrophes or intertribal wars that threaten the lives of everybody in the society. But virtually everyone in a small traditional society is related to each other. Hence it is not only the case that old people in a traditional society are essential to the survival of their own children and grandchildren. They are also essential to the survival of the hundreds of people who share their genes.

JARED DIAMOND, 1998

———

Then the poachers began to turn to the females – the mothers and grandmothers with the longest ivory. The matriarchs are very often the first to fall anyway, for they are among the first to defend their families from attack, and a matriarch's death makes it easier to bring down the others. 'Bang!' exclaimed Iain. 'There goes the reproducing part of the population – and its learned traditions involving migratory routes, dry-season water sources, salt licks and so on. The whole society begins to collapse.' There goes the culture, the accumulated wisdom of generations about how to use the land and its resources. Boom!

DOUGLAS CHADWICK, *The Fate of the Elephant*, 1992

'Some things are easier for kids now than for our children; they think money grows on tree. They've got videos, televisions, Walkmans, all that. But they've also got a lot more stress. The pressures are greater. Educationwise they have to work so much harder than we did or our children did. When we left school there was always jobs for us. Never any question of it. And you couldn't lose your job or anything. But it's not like that for my grandchildren. I worry about them.'

'Of course drugs are the biggest worry. That's not something I ever had to think about when my children went to school. They might have got into smoking. But not actual drugs. Now when they go to university there's always the temptation. You think no, they'd never do it. You trust them. But there's always that little bit of worry . . . They can be introduced . . . you know, you see it on television.'

'When I see people drinking out of bottles, I think that's absolutely awful. There was a programme on television the other day. And I said that looks terrible – and my husband who works with young people, training, said that's because of drugs, so that nobody can spice the drinks. And another thing my daughter said is that with the young children, you've got to be careful of stamps, transfers, because the drug dealers, they give them, they've got some kind of drug in them; and that was something I didn't have to worry about. I mean we used to tell the children, "Don't talk to strangers, don't take sweets off anybody," but now it's "Don't take anything, don't even take a stamp." I never heard of such a thing before.'

'They're intelligent. And you feel sometimes you can't keep pace with them. No, we didn't feel that with their parents. The grandchildren seem to be in another world. So many of them are going to university now, they've got far more chances than we had. With us it was leave school Friday, start work Monday. But even the little ones are much more outgoing. Harriet, she's only four and a half, but she's like a kiddy of about six.'

'They try to teach us things about computers. I was looking after my niece's little daughter and she's three. And she wanted to put a video in. And I said, "I haven't got a clue." And she showed me how to do it. They can do all sorts of things we can't. And she was only three on Tuesday.'

Birmingham grandmothers, 1999

V

LIVELY GRANDMOTHERS

The comment that a young man may fall in love with his mother, but never with his grandmother, makes it clear: a grandmother isn't, by definition cannot be, an erotic object. As for the grandmothers themselves, glamorous they may be – just – but sexy, never. Yet tell that to the grandmothers and their lovers if you dare. Not for all grandmothers the wistful confession of Diana Holman Hunt that she has forgotten the mechanics because 'It is so long ago'.

This is, of course, about categories again, rites of passage, ordering of generations; none of it in itself such a bad thing, provided it is not overly prescriptive. Some societies, like the African Hehe, specifically forbid grandmothers to cohabit with their husbands from the moment a daughter's pregnancy is announced until her child is a year old. A woman with a number of fertile daughters is effectively debarred from marital pleasure from the moment her eldest starts to breed. The logic isn't the unseemliness of congress among the ageing, but the evolutionary pressures of survival: if she cannot get pregnant herself – and the pregnancies of older women grow ever more chancy – a grandmother can devote herself to the more viable progeny of her daughters. Yet the seemliness, or lack of it, originally a byproduct, becomes the only clear rationale in societies no longer driven by necessity. The expectation that middle-class Indian women with married or grown-up children should withdraw from sexual activity (there's no space, alas, to quote this source here) or, among the Gwembe people of Zambia and others, the disapproval inhibiting elderly couples from sharing a house, let alone a room or bed, are two such manifestations of this.

In Western societies, the issue has always been complicated, of course, by Christian – especially Catholic – suspicion of sexual activity, except for the business of procreation. Ironically, the parallel insistence on monogamy meant that since men were not free to take second, younger wives or use prostitutes to satisfy their sexual needs – always more acceptable, whatever the age of the man, than the needs of women – sex within marriage was more likely to continue, discreetly, to a greater age. Pregnancy, of course, not being discreet, might appear faintly indecent; hence my grandmother's reticence during her late pregnancy with my father – and hence the racy reputation of the Lark Rise grandmother with her assorted brood of children and grandchildren. What a pleasure it is, by contrast, to encounter Elizabeth Fry's unabashed delight at having her last child and first grandchild born on the same day.

Given the moral norms that used to prevail in Western – certainly English – society, the impossibility of pregnancy after menopause meant that, for women, the justification for sexual activity was then gone. Any advantage to the continued sex life of women previously burdened with constant pregnancies was not likely to be advertised before this last century. If the notion of pleasure for pre-menopausal women went unacknowledged, how much less so for those expected to take up their knitting, smile benignly on the no longer available pleasures of the young, on the one hand, and comfort themselves with memories of their own days of love, on the other. In the past the exhortation on the merits of masturbation for women over sixty without other means of sexual outlet would have been as unthinkable as, up to a point, the uninhibited delight of Bessie Head's ancient in pulling younger men still is in more ageist societies. Where the sexuality of older women is acknowledged, it's done with a disgust demonstrated by Aristophanes, among classical writers, and in eighteenth-century perorations on marriage between young men and old women, works not sufficiently grandmotherly to be quoted here, but significant just the same.

It's stereotype time, yet again. Many women may willingly or unwillingly have conformed to such stereotypes; worse, they have absorbed them so thoroughly that they view themselves with as much disgust as everyone else – Brantôme's comment, quoted by Simone de Beauvoir, is significant. But the fact is that there is no such thing as 'the grandmother'. There is just a legion of women who happen to be grandmothers and every one of them quite different. The youngest grandmother I've come across was round twenty-seven, which, since both mothers would have been fourteen at the time they gave birth, is hardly to be recommended. But it makes the point. Grandmothers aren't necessarily old; period. And even when, fifty-odd, let alone sixty- or seventy-odd, they might admittedly be described as ageing, chronological, mental and physical age are by no means always the same thing. There have always been some far from elderly grandmothers, in every sense. But increasingly, because of the changing status of women, because of hormone-replacement therapy, some women in middle age are too busy working or having a good time to want to play cosy granny, let alone to start abnegating themselves yet again on behalf of their progeny – hence those irritated younger women seeking proxy grandmothers, as in the newspaper article here.

But it has always been the case that some women are older at fifty than others at seventy. Some sixty-year-old women have the energy of twenty-year-olds. Some women are sexier, and in some cases more desirable, at fifty than at thirty. One splendid friend of mine was fifty and already a grandmother when her marriage broke up and she discovered sex. At which point, far from being disgusted by her aged lineaments, the men were queuing up. She is now well over seventy and not past it yet. She is also, of course, devoted to her grandchildren.

As someone of sixty myself who's not given up on anything, least of all sex, I admit there's an element in all this of 'she would, wouldn't she?' in the way I look at this. I also admit that there are ways of going about it and ways of not, for me at least. We're talking dignity again here, which matters in this area more than most. But I'd have looked silly playing sexy at any age. And still not Elizabeth Taylor, let alone Joan Collins, I don't go for toy boys; these days I prefer my men grown-up – if without prostate problems. (Now who's being ageist?) All I'm saying really, in this as in everything else, is that I was a woman long before I was a grandmother – and remain that woman. Like all women. The headlining of the word 'grandmother' in accounts of any exploit, heroic or disreputable, past or present, by elderly women, denies all that, and uses the label to excuse or downgrade her actions. Witness the stress recently laid on the status as not only grandmother but even great-grandmother of a British woman in her eighties uncovered as a long-term spy. On the other hand, the supposed harmlessness of an old woman can have its uses: if you suffer from the cliché why not use it, after all. A Mafia grandmother used it for years to get away with drug smuggling.

But grandmothers are also, or can be – to take a random sample from this section and elsewhere – war workers, actors, authors, musicians, dancers, murderers, gamblers, aviators, drinkers; all activities common to both genders and most ages. The word 'grandmother' adds a frisson, for most of those seen here as lively, eccentric or subversive always were so. Like my mother's outrageous best friend, heard to say aged eighty, of a conversation with her granddaughter, 'I told her I lost my virginity at fifteen, so why shouldn't she, if she wanted.' While staid, conventional grandmothers, more often than not, were conventional all along.

I will make one proviso: that just as the menopause relieving a woman from the fear of pregnancy can release her sexuality, so age may free other women from the bonds of property and convention which bound them in earlier years. Anthropologically, in some cultures, women old enough to have lost their sexual threat, and to have ceased, not least, to produce such unclean substances as menstrual fluids, are given licence to be outrageous. They become honorary men in a way, making up for the constraints they've suffered in earlier years. Some aspects of this will be discussed further in the section on powerful grandmothers. It's enough here to point quickly at how having small grandchildren does give one licence – if one needs it – to get down on the floor again and be generally silly.

I also note, to myself as much as anyone else, that I, too, feel less inhibited than I used to be in all aspects of my life. Not least I feel no obligation whatever to take men seriously, which makes life, not just sexually, much easier and much more fun. But this is a factor of experience maybe as much as age. It also relates to the sense, as time rushes on, that life is short and getting shorter, not to say at times nastier and more brutish, so let's enjoy ourselves while we can, before age and infirmity get us.

But when they do get us? Ah, then – and this is true of men and women, grandfathers and grandmothers – even if our bodies cease to let us be physically outrageous, our tongues can take up the cause with more and more licence. One writer recently described his or her grandmother as feeling free to say precisely what she felt, no matter how rude; since she wasn't going to be around much longer, what did it matter? In conversation once with a ninety-year-old who'd just written her first book, I praised it highly before moving on to other matters. This she put up with for a sentence or two; then she interrupted me: 'And now,' she said, 'tell me more about my book.' A kind of immodest longing that as a writer I recognised, gleefully. But one that I am still not quite crone enough to admit.

Grandmothers and Love

'I know how babies come out, I want to know how they get in. Grandfather says he's forgotten but he thinks you may remember.'

She gazed at me.

'Is that what he said?'

She picked a little mirror off the desk: 'Look at that!' she pointed at her jaw, just above the lace. 'Old age is a disaster. Who would believe I once was a beauty?'

'Yes, but what about the baby?'

Of course she was old but what did it matter?

'My love,' she sighed, gently drawing me to her, 'I have forgotten too. It is so long ago.'

DIANA HOLMAN HUNT, *My Grandmothers and I*, 1960

---

from Lark Rise

When her husband was asleep, or lying, washed and tended, gazing at his picture, Laura's grandmother would sit among her feather cushions downstairs reading *Bow Bells* or the *Princess Novelettes* or the *Family Herald*. Except when engaged in housework, she was never seen without a book in her hand. It was always a novelette, and she had a large assortment of these which she kept tied up in flat parcels, ready to exchange with other novelette readers.

She had been very pretty when she was young. 'The Belle of Hornton', they had called her in her native village, and she often told Laura of the time when her hair had reached down to her knees, like a great yellow cape, she said, which covered her. Another of her favourite stories was of the day when she had danced with a real lord. It was at his coming-of-age celebrations, and a great honour, for he had passed over his own friends and the daughters of his tenants in favour of one who was but a gamekeeper's daughter. Before the evening was over he had whispered in her ear that she was the prettiest girl in the country, and she had cherished the compliment all her life. There were no further developments. My Lord was My Lord, and Hannah Pollard was Hannah Pollard, a poor girl, but the daughter of decent parents. No further developments were possible in real life, though such affairs ended differently in her novelettes. Perhaps that was why she enjoyed them.

It was difficult for Laura to connect the long, yellow hair and the white frock with blue ribbons worn at the coming-of-age fête with her grandmother, for she saw her only as a thin, frail old woman who wore her grey hair parted like curtains and looped at the ears with little combs. Still, there was something which made her worth looking at. Laura's mother said it was because her features were good. 'My mother,' she would say, 'will look handsome in her coffin. Colour goes and the hair turns grey, but the framework lasts.'

[. . .] Laura's grandmother had never tramped ten miles on a Sunday night to hear her husband preach in a village chapel. She had gone to church once every Sunday, unless it rained or was too hot, or she had a cold, or some article of her attire was too shabby. She was particular about her clothes and liked to have everything handsome about her. In her bedroom there were pictures and ornaments, as well as the feather cushions and silk patchwork quilt.

When she came to the end house, the best chair was placed by the fire for her and the best possible tea put on the table, and Laura's mother did not whisper her troubles to her as she did to her father. If some little thing did leak out, she would only say, 'All men need a bit of humouring.'

Some women, too, thought Laura, for she could see that her grandmother had always been the one to be indulged and spared all trouble and unpleasantness. If the fiddle had belonged to her, it would never have been sold; the whole family would have combined to buy a handsome new case for it.

After her husband died, she went away to live with her eldest son, and the round house shared the fate of Sally's. Where it stood is now a ploughed field. The husband's sacrifices, the wife's romance, are as though they had never been – 'melted into air, into thin air'.

FLORA THOMPSON, 1939

---

from Hehe Grandmothers

From the time a woman's daughter becomes pregnant, Hehe society imposes certain avoidances upon the elder woman which forcefully impress upon her the fact of her changed status. The most important rule to be observed is that for certain periods she must not cohabit with her husband; if she does so her grandchild will be injured . . . The first year of life is considered a period of danger for the child, and rightly so, considering the high infant mortality rate. By imposing a rule of continence on the grandmother (both before and after the child is born) her attention is turned towards the infant, because its good health is believed to be in part the result of her own actions. When her attention is thus concentrated on the new child she is more ready to undertake seriously all her obligations as a grandmother. The rule is as follows: as soon as the daughter of a woman becomes pregnant she informs her mother, and from that time on until the child is able to walk the grandmother must not cohabit with her husband. When the child walks and the mother resumes cohabitation with her own husband she brings to her mother a garment and a dish of the child saying: 'I have brought these things.' The grandmother then knows she is free to live with her husband again . . . The rule for continence for grandmothers cannot be easily broken. Medicine does exist to avert evil consequences, but women are afraid to seek it for fear of ridicule. Moreover, if the rule is broken before the child is born, the grandmother cannot be present at the birth, a great deprivation to her. One way to avoid observance of the rule exists when the grandmother of the pregnant woman is alive. The pregnant woman may go to her at the time of birth and be under her care, not her mother's. Therefore a woman may avoid observing this rule for the first children of her eldest daughters, but as time passes and her various daughters continue to have children she will be debarred completely from cohabitation with her own husband, and her thoughts and services will be devoted to her successive grandchildren. This rule explains why elderly Hehe men continue to seek young wives.

ELIZABETH FISHER BROWN, 1935

---

from a letter to the Princess Royal of Denmark

Plashet House, Eleventh Month, 23rd 1822

Dear and respected Friend,

[. . .] I take up my pen to inform thee, that upon the first of this month, through the tender mercy of my God, I was safely delivered of a sweet boy, and to add to our cause of joy and thanksgiving, my dear daughter had also one born on the same day, so that twenty-four hours added a son and grandson to our already numerous family; we have, both of us, with our infants, been going on well . . .

ELIZABETH FRY

from Lark Rise

While the novelette readers, who represented the genteel section of the community, were enjoying their tea, there would be livelier gatherings at another of the cottages. The hostess, Caroline Arless, was at that time about forty-five, and a tall, fine, upstanding woman with flashing dark eyes, hair like crinkled black wire, and cheeks the colour of a ripe apricot. She was not a native of the hamlet, but had come there as a bride, and it was said that she had gipsy blood in her.

Although she was herself a grandmother, she still produced a child of her own every eighteen months or so, a proceeding regarded as bad form in the hamlet, for the saying ran, 'When the young 'uns begin, 'tis time for the old 'uns to finish.' But Mrs Arless recognized no rules, excepting those of Nature.

FLORA THOMPSON, 1939

Masters and Johnson found that many of the elderly . . . regarded sex as 'unsuitable for old people'. (1966)

Sexual activity is expected to decrease. In village gossip, it is legitimate to speculate on whether an old man is still potent. Sexual relations between old and young are regarded as blighting to the younger partner and tabooed. Even continued sexual relations between an old couple are regarded as abnormal. Often they no longer sleep together, and they may even occupy separate houses.

ELIZABETH COLSON AND THAYER SCUDDER,
'Old Age in Gwembe District', 1981

Honour widows that are widows indeed. But if any widows
have children or nephews let them learn first to shew piety at
home, and to requite their parents . . .

For she that is a widow indeed, and desolate, trusteth in
God, and continueth in supplications and prayers day and
night. But she that liveth in pleasure is dead while she lives.

I Timothy 5: 3–6

A young man may desire a woman old enough to be his mother
but not his grandmother. A woman of seventy is no longer
regarded by anyone as an erotic object.

SIMONE DE BEAUVOIR, *Old Age*, 1971

Biologically women's sexuality is less affected by old age than
men's. Brantôme bears this out in the chapter of his *Vie des
Femmes Galantes* that he dedicates to 'Certain Old Ladies who
take as much pleasure in love as the young ones'. Whereas a
man of a certain age is no longer capable of erection, a woman
'at no matter what age is endowed as it were with a furnace . . .
all fire and fuel within' . . . In other words a woman continues
in her state of erotic object right up to the end. Chastity is not
imposed on her by a physiological destiny but by her position
as a relative being . . . She has a delightful awareness of her
body as something desirable, and this awareness comes to her
through her partner's caresses and his gaze. If he goes on desir-
ing her she easily puts up with her body's aging. But at the first
sign of coldness she feels her ugliness in all its horror . . . This
lack of assurance strengthens her fear of other people's opinions: she knows how censorious they are towards old women

who do not play their role of serene and passion-free grand-mothers.

SIMONE DE BEAUVOIR, *Old Age*, 1971

Masturbation . . . If widowhood or some other reason leaves you without an available partner, it is a sensible way of keeping an essential part of yourself viable . . . If this has to be a major sexual outlet for you, make it dignified and important as well as private. Make the room comfortably warm, with soft music if you like that, and the telephone unplugged.

JOAN GOMEZ, *Sixty Something*, 1993

'Oh life isn't so bad,' she said. 'I can tell you a secret. Even old women like Mrs Maleboge are still quite happy. They still make love.' I was so startled by this that I burst out: 'You don't say!'

She put on the sweet and secret smile of a woman who knows much about this side of life.

'When you are old,' she said, 'that's the time when you make love, more than when you are young. You make love because you are no longer afraid of making babies. You make love with young boys. They all do it, but it is done very secretly. No one suspects, that's why they look so respectable in the daytime.'

BESSIE HEAD, 'The Special One', 1977

My grandmother was a Cherokee Indian. She got married for the fifth time when she was seventy-nine. She divorced her husband two years later because she refused to get up and milk the cows at five in the morning. She kept the names of all her husbands, so that at the end of her life, on her gravestone she had this great list of names.

Quoted in A. DICKSON, *Menopause: The Woman's View*, 1987

---

from Love's Work

Yvette was the most enthusiastic and inventive grandmother. She couldn't spend enough time with her grandchildren, and she was especially close to Miriam's two children, who lived downstairs in the main body of the spacious Victorian house that Yvette had bequeathed to her daughter. She frequently visited her favourite son and his wife in Southampton with their older children. Another son would visit from London with his Sephardi wife and their two children, and the remaining two sons lived in Israel and Australia.

Yvette was completely devoted to pleasure without guilt. This was what made her such an attentive and encouraging confidante. She would listen with rapt attention to my confessions of pain and rage, but invariably dismiss my scruples, overcoming the nihilism of the emotions by affirming the validity of every tortuous and torturing desire. Although I was thus tutored by her, I watched with squeamish propriety as Yvette playfully squeezed her three-year-old grandson's balls and penis. 'Aren't children meant to emerge to independence with a residue of resentment from the fact that it is the mother who accidentally arouses but explicitly forbids genital pleasure?' I ventured with theoretical pedantry in remembrance of Freud, and of the narrow border between child care and child abuse. Yvette positively relished my staid inhibitions, which she dismissed airily as contrary to the universal and sacred spirit of lust. A Grand Mother indeed.

In the far, dark corner of Yvette's main room there stood a heavy, veneered chest of drawers with a pride of family photographs jostling on top. The three bottom compartments of this tallboy were jammed full with pornographic material, which, one day, after I'd known her for quite a while, Yvette showed me. The photographs were almost entirely of women, clad in enough to titillate, and revealing proud genitals in various *contrapposto* positions. Yvette possessed very little male pornography, not because it is less available, but because it didn't interest her.

When I remarked one day, in a different context, that I couldn't reconcile her grandmotherly identity with her prodigious sexuality, she looked sadly and wisely at me as the one corrupted by unnatural practices, 'Have you forgotten the connection between sex and children?' She was, of course, partly right.

GILLIAN ROSE, 1997

———

Great Grandmother Rene Jackson had no thoughts of marriage when she hobbled through the arrival hall of a Cyprus airport on sticks for a holiday.

After 18 years of widowhood, romance was the last thing on her mind, but friendship with Emin Aslan, an artist young enough to be one of her many grandchildren, led to marriage. Now she is trying to persuade the British authorities to allow her new husband into the country.

Mrs Aslan, who lives in sheltered accommodation in Birkenhead, celebrates her 70th birthday today, but she insists her marriage to the 26-year-old Kurd . . . is not just a marriage of convenience. 'I know cynics say he is just using me to get into the country, but this is a love marriage and we have a very physical relationship. My love life is great.' [. . .]

'The age gap does not bother us,' she said yesterday. 'People think you should grow old gracefully, but I'm not just going to sit around and wait to die.'

Mrs Aslan said the relationship had been greeted coolly by her five children, 12 grandchildren and three great-grandchildren.

GEOFFREY GIBBS, *Guardian*, 20 May 1998

---

from Coast Salish Elders

Old age not only brought new responsibilities, it conferred freedom from certain restrictions. Among the Upper Skagit – and probably elsewhere, too – old age, when one's reproductive responsibilities were discharged, was the time for love affairs. People found the prospect of an alliance between beautiful youth and experienced old age romantic. Unlike contemporary Western culture, which accepts such a relationship between an older man and a younger woman but stigmatizes the reverse, Coast Salish people [of western Canada] found the old of either sex suitable lovers for the young.

PAMELA AMOSS, 1981

Lively Grandmothers

from My Grandmothers and I

I ran to the hall. Helen stood there, puffing as usual. Lengths of wire, with sharp prongs at each end, were wound round her neck, and bells on metal rings were hanging from her arms. In one hand she held a hammer and in the other a basket full of tins.

'The trip-wires first,' Grand said, briskly, 'bring a candle, dear.'

'Take a candle child to light your mother through the snow!' I giggled because Helen looked so funny. Grand stretched the wires across the room and hammered the sharp pegs into the floor between the Persian rugs. She made piles of tins here and there about the room.

'What is she doing, Helen?' I asked.

'Them's for trapping the thieves what come in the night,' she whispered. 'We don't want to be murdered in our beds now, do we?'

'I should think not!' I exclaimed, much startled. The old Monk at home was bad enough. 'There aren't any thieves in Bryanston Square – at least we don't set any traps,' I boasted loudly.

'The things there are all very well in their way,' Grand condescended, 'but they don't compare with the treasures here . . . Now for the bells.' She hooked them over the doors.

'You'd better fetch what you need from your box and say goodnight to Helen. Take care not to walk on the paint.'

There was a notice tacked to a tread: 'Edith H-H painted this staircase in 1905'. I picked my way with Edward and my nightgown under my arm, swinging my new check sponge-bag.

In Grand's bedroom the windows were open so that when we opened the door, the curtains billowed like sails. She lit the gas with a pop and said: 'You will sleep on the Chesterfield dear. Do as I do, we can both be modest.' Turning her back, she drew a huge white tent over her head.

I sat down and unlaced my boots. Grand was performing amazing contortions, writhing under her tent and kicking strange garments aside: a pair of stays shot across the room.

I managed to undo my dress and, shaking with cold, fingered the straps of my harness. It was buckled at the back. I saw some scissors on the table, and after a moment's reflection, with two quiet snips, cut through the canvas. I crumpled the contraption in a ball and hid it with Edward under my blanket. I felt wide awake and wicked. It was the slyest thing I'd ever done. I discarded my petticoats, lawn and flannel, my silk vest and my drawers until but for my socks I stood naked.

Grand turned round: 'My dear child! Where is your kimono? The one your father sent you last Christmas from the East?'

I had forgotten to fetch it from my hamper.

She picked up the paisley shawl and draped it round my body. She was still wearing her tent. 'Wait while I turn off the light but bring the candle.'

We climbed another flight of stairs. After much rattling of matches she again lit the gas and turned it very low. An elaborate illuminated notice was nailed over the bath: 'Edith H-H painted this bath with white enamel and varnished the mahogany surround in 1906. After use visitors are requested to clean gently with brush provided and polish with soft cloth hanging on the right. Kindly confirm that taps are not dripping.'

'Stand well back!' she ordered, approaching the geyser, 'just in case it explodes.' A sinister hiss was followed by a violent bang and a roar. 'Keep well away till the water runs. You never know.' She held up a warning finger.

I cowered in the doorway. A thin stream of boiling, rusty water cascaded into the bath, filling the room with steam. My hair clung round my neck in a damp, sweaty mass and my nose felt full.

She shouted out of the fog: 'Stay where you are! Shut your eyes! I'm going to get in when I've turned on the cold.'

I sank to the floor coughing. I couldn't see a thing but I could hear a dragon snorting and then a long agonized sigh, followed by sudden pandemonium: pipes thumping and banging and invisible water gurgling in torrents.

'Look alive!' she cried. 'Your turn next. The water isn't dirty; it's only lather from the Castile soap.'

In a daze I sponged my face and washed myself a little in the narrow bath.

'That's enough!' She pulled out the plug and, blinded by steam, flicked a huckaback towel in my eye. 'I'll scrub, you can polish. Here's the soft rag.'

I wiped with frenzied dabs but water appeared from nowhere; dripping from the ceiling and running down the walls. The faster I mopped the enamel, the wetter it became.

'That'll do! I think you must be tired?'

'I am rather,' I confessed. Pushing the hair off my forehead, I followed her down to the bedroom. She held the candle, which wobbled and threw our grotesque shadows on the walls.

I collapsed on the sofa and drew the scratchy blanket up to my chin. The harness was curled up in a nest by Edward.

'But what about your prayers?'

'God bless,' I said, lying where I was, 'God bless . . .' I mumbled the list of names, 'and help me to be a good girl. Amen.'

'My pet, you should be reverently on your knees, but perhaps this once . . .'

Although I was tired, I stayed awake, missing my smooth linen sheets, quilt and pillows. No wonder Fowler was reluctant to leave me in such a dangerous place, where hot baths devitalized and geysers exploded; and robbers came in the night to murder one in bed. Grandmother would think it quite unsuitable, possibly disastrous. At this moment, I was sure, at least forty thieves were lurking downstairs. No, not lurking, tumbling about over the wires, stubbing their toes and barking their shins on the sharp corners of Italian tables. Inflamed with rage they would seize weapons off the walls, which Grand had imprudently left at their disposal, and creep up the stairs and come in without knocking. Fowler knew she would never see me again; that was why she was crying. Surely we would have some warning. The bells would ring! Would the bells ring? Would we have time to hide in the cupboard?

I sat up. 'Grand?'

'Yes dear, what is it? Aren't you asleep?'

'When the bells ring, what shall we do?'

'I will tell you,' she said, in a confident tone. 'You will spring out of bed and twirl this large wooden rattle, round and round, out of the window, and I will blow several short sharp blasts on that whistle tied to the end of my bed.'

'Then what'll happen?' I asked, anxiously clutching at Edward.

'The good police will come to our rescue. The dear, brave men – what admirable patience they show with the smallest problem – telling foreigners their way about and what omnibus to take . . .'

'I don't think they'll get here in time to catch the thieves.' I was breathing deeply. The trip-wires were wrong and would only make the thieves angry. I could see their eyes smouldering with revenge as they reached for the daggers on the walls.

'It is to be hoped they'll sprain their ankles,' she said with a shrug. 'I assure you we can always rely on the police. I contribute to their funds.'

'Are you sure?' I persisted.

'Quite sure,' she said, reaching to snuff out the candle. She hadn't said her prayers.

DIANA HOLMAN HUNT, 1960

---

from My Place

It was towards the middle of that year that Nan and I had our first major row. I arrived home from school one day with the facts from a science lesson freshly imprinted in my brain, and proceeded to inform Nan that when it came to eradicating germs, onions were totally useless.

For years, she had been using freshly chopped onions to sterilise our house and it was the first time I'd ever openly criticised any of her theories concerning our health.

Nan was cross, she said high school had gone to my head and then she accused me of being as silly as my mother. I pointed out that none of my friends ever got sick and they lived without the stink of moulding onions. Nan retaliated by asserting that, one day, they'd probably all fall down dead and then they'd wish they'd known about onions.

That was the last straw. I walked into my room, flung back the curtains and collected up all the onion quarters that sat neatly along my bedroom window-sill. I hesitated at picking up two of them. They were slightly mouldy and they looked at me as if to say, remove us and you'll get a deadly disease, just like your Grandmother says! I grasped them courageously with my bare hands and flung them dramatically in the kitchen bin. 'No more onions,' I told Nan quietly, but firmly.

I was trying to be rational about the whole thing. After all, I was studying science. By the time Mum arrived home, we were at it again. Nan knew just how to provoke me. I must have been under the influence to throw away her onions, she said. Had I been sneaking her brandy? Didn't I realise that I was putting the lives of my brothers and sisters at risk? How else could we maintain a germ-free environment.

Mum just stood and watched us in amazement. Nan began to explain what it was all about. I stormed back into my room and screamed, 'I don't care what you say, Mum, no onions. Steph's room doesn't stink the way mine does.'

Mum came and stood in the doorway of my bedroom and eyed me sympathetically. Nan came up behind her and held up a fistful of freshly cut onions, just to annoy me. 'Here they come, Sally,' she growled. 'I'm bringing them in!'

'MUM!' I screamed.

'Well, perhaps you should leave it for now, Nan,' Mum suggested tactfully. 'Put those ones in the bathroom.'

For the next few days, my room remained onion-free. But then one day, as I lay on my bed, a strong oniony smell came wafting through. I checked my window-sill, nothing there.

Suddenly, out of the corner of my eye, I saw a small, curved, white object jutting over the top of my wardrobe. I grabbed the broom from the kitchen and knocked them down.

I ranted and raved at Nan over this latest intrusion, but she just chuckled and continued to puff on her cigarette.

The following week, she resorted to tucking the onions in the same drawer in which I kept my underpants. Even Mum thought that was funny. 'You wait until she tucks onions in your corsets,' I grumbled, 'then you won't be laughing.'

'Keep your voice down, Sally,' Mum said, horrified. 'She might hear you. Don't go giving her any more ideas!'

Our battle remained unresolved for the next few weeks, until Nan discovered a product called Medic, which had a very strong, hospital-type odour. It came in a small, blue spray can and was specifically for use with people suffering from colds and flu.

'What a marvellous clean smell that has, Glad,' Nan commented as Mum sprayed a small amount in the kitchen.

'I thought you might like it,' Mum smiled. 'That's why I bought it, you know what that smoker's cough of yours is like. This will help you breathe.'

'Aah, that's good, Glad,' said Nan as she inhaled deeply. 'I can feel it clearing my lungs.' Nan thumped her chest with her fist. 'By gee, I feel good now, that's a good medicine. Smells like it's got some of the old cures in it, it's not often you get a medicine like that these days.'

From then on, my room smelled of Medic. My clothes and my rugs smelled of Medic. Nan sprayed Medic down the toilet and in the bathroom. The whole house smelled of Medic. I disliked the smell, but I wouldn't have dared utter one word of criticism. Medic was better than onions.

SALLY MORGAN, 1987

from Running in the Family

Lalla's great claim to fame was that she was the first woman in Ceylon to have a mastectomy. It turned out to be unnecessary but she always claimed to support modern science, throwing herself into new causes. (Even in death her generosity exceeded the physically possible for she had donated her body to six hospitals.) The false breast would never be still for long. She was an energetic person. It would crawl over to join its twin on the right hand side or sometimes appear on her back, 'for dancing' she smirked. She called it her Wandering Jew and would yell at the grandchildren in the middle of a formal dinner to fetch her tit as she had forgotten to put it on. She kept losing the contraption to servants who were mystified by it as well as to the dog, Chandit, who would be found gnawing at the foam as if it were a tender chicken. She went through four breasts in her lifetime. One she left on a branch of a tree in Hakgalle Gardens to dry out after a rainstorm, one flew off when she was riding behind Vere on his motorbike, and the third she was very mysterious about, almost embarrassed though Lalla was never embarrassed. Most believed it had been forgotten after a romantic assignation in Trincomalee with a man who may or may not have been in the Cabinet.

MICHAEL ONDAATJE, 1983

------

from Taken Care Of

Both my grandmothers suffered from troubles of a hirsute nature. My grandmother Sitwell's was fraught with more danger, as it was impossible to guess where her hair would be found next. After my grandmother had taken a house in London, sometimes these two coils (one destined for the top of her head, the other for the back) would take refuge in Leckly's back pocket, and she, forgetting this, would go shopping in Oxford Street and Regent Street, whereupon her two charges would attempt to escape from their temporary home, arousing in the spectators (from the very nature and place from which they emerged) the conjecture that Leckly was an escapee from the Zoological Gardens.

Deprived of her crowning glories, my grandmother would be obliged to take to her bed until Leckly could remember where those adornments had been put – for she feared the all-seeing eye of her regiment of curates. I am *not* denigrating the ministers of the Low Church – earnest, self-sacrificing, infinitely helpful to their flocks, and sadly underpaid – but my grandmother adopted unfortunate examples, such as are found in every Church. These examples were at once particularly smooth, and particularly uncultured. They had, so to speak, a spiritual smell as of a winter garden full of mouldering cabbages, and were, for the most part, exactly of that colour.

[. . .] My grandmother Londesborough's hirsute troubles were less poignant that those of Lady Sitwell, as everybody was terrified of her, and nobody dared to giggle in her presence.

Lady Londesborough's footmen (who constituted as large a regiment as that of my grandmother Sitwell's curates) were forbidden to look at each other in her presence, or to speak excepting in their professional capacity. They might speak to Martin, the butler, but on no account were they to look at him. Otherwise, their silence was only broken at their extreme peril.

My grandmother Londesborough never spoke to any of the servants excepting the butler Martin and the old housekeeper, Mrs Selby, who had a face like a large red strawberry, covered with faint silvery hair . . .

One evening, at the beginning of November, my grandmother (who was then at Londesborough Lodge in Scarborough) went up to bed with her hair of the usual brown colour. Next morning when she came down, at eleven o'clock, to an enormous breakfast (eggs and bacon, cold grouse, ham, cold partridge, home-made buns and buttercup-coloured cream and butter, hothouse peaches and grapes), the autumnal hue of her hair had changed to the most snow-bound of winters. My aunts, not daring to appear conscious of this phenomenon, stared at their plates. My grandfather concentrated on the breast of a cold partridge. The footmen seemed to be bound, more than ever, in a spell of silence.

My grandmother's white wig – for such it was – appeared at the most opportune moment, for the date was the 5th of November, a day (I may remind my American readers) dedicated to the memory of Guy Fawkes, who had plotted to blow up the Houses of Parliament, and was then celebrated by children wheeling a perambulator containing a battered-looking dummy, and begging for 'a penny for the poor guy'.

After breakfast, on this auspicious occasion, my grandmother took up her usual place in a bathchair at the entrance of Londesborough Lodge gardens.

Seated against a background of a frieze of captive daughters and a melancholy-looking footman, she must have presented a remarkable appearance. So much so that a very small curate, who was accompanied by his wife and multitudinous children, seeing her and remembering the date and its implications, placed a penny in her lap saying, genially, 'Remember, remember, the fifth of November.'

EDITH SITWELL, 1965

That reminds me of my ex-step-grandmother-in-law (work that one out) who in her declining years had problems with what she called her waterworks. She could only go if she could hear running water. That was fine at home, but I once took her to the theatre, and escorting her to the lavatory in the interval was a nightmare that I continue to relive to this day.

You know how it works in theatres – two tiny loos and 100

frantic women queuing for them. We were roughly half-way along the line and my ex-step-grandmother-in-law said ominously that she did not know if she could hold out but at least, I thought, we'd be spared the running water scenario. Not a bit of it. 'It's no good, I can't go. You'll have to turn on the taps Susan,' she called from the cubicle. Apologising miserably to the waiting women, I turned on the cold tap. 'Susan, are you there? I can't hear a thing; put both taps on full,' commanded the voice from the cubicle. The twin jets spluttered, hit the enamel like pressurised fire hoses and sprayed the entire room. The women at the front sprang back to avoid being soaked.

'For God's sake, what's happening?' came the frightened, muffled voices of the unfortunates at the back who were being pressed against the walls and were in danger of suffocation. 'Are you there Susan? I can't hear the taps. Have you turned them on? There's so much noise going on, you'll just have to open the door or I'll be here all night.

I hesitated, but the matter was out of my hands. 'Open the door, for God's sake. Open the door or we'll all be here all night,' yelled 40 frantic, wet, cowering women in the powder room of the Haymarket theatre. At a stroke my ex-step-grand-mother-in-law, voluminous denture, pink winceyette knickers round her ankles, was revealed. 'That's better; now we're in business,' she said. I tell you the spontaneous applause that broke out when she finally stood up and pulled the chain would have gratified Dame Edith herself.

SUE ARNOLD, Independent Weekend Review, 10 July 1999

---

from Magnolias Grow in Dirt

One final group which participates in bawdry, however, is less bound on keeping up the image. I have to confess that many of the women who tell vile tales are gloriously and affirmatively old! They transcend the boundaries – not by their station and employment – but by aging beyond the strictures that censure would lay on the young. The South, like many traditional cultures, offers an increase in license to those who advance in age, and ladies I have known take the full advantage offered them in their tale-telling. They seem to delight in particular in presenting themselves as wicked old ladies. Once, when my grandmother stepped out of the bathtub, and my sister commented that the hair on her 'privates' was getting rather sparse, Granny retorted that 'grass don't grow on a race track.'

A number of stories I've heard concern old women's fancy for young men . . . As the Southern Black comedienne, Moms Mabley, used to say: 'Ain't nothin' no old man can do for me 'cept bring me a message from a young man.' I confess I look forward to old age if I can be as bad as Granny and Moms.

RAYNA GREEN, 1977

from The Harem Within

Yasmina, my maternal grandmother, lived on a beautiful farm with cows and sheep and endless fields of flowers, one hundred kilometers to the west of us, between Fez and the Ocean. We visited her once a year, and I would talk to her about frontiers and fears and differences, and the why of it all. Yasmina knew a lot about fear, all kinds of fear. 'I am an expert on fear, Fatima,' she would tell me, caressing my forehead as I played with her pearls and pink beads, 'And I will tell you things when you are older. I will teach you how to get over fears.'

Often, I could not sleep the first few nights on Yasmina's farm – the frontiers were not clear enough. There were no closed gates to be seen anywhere, only wide, flat, open fields where flowers grew and animals wandered peaceably about. But Yasmina explained to me that the farm was part of Allah's original earth, which had no frontiers, just vast, open fields without borders or boundaries, and that I should not be afraid. But how could I walk in an open field without being attacked? I kept asking. And then Yasmina created a game that I loved, to help put me to sleep, called *mshia-f-lekhla* (the walk in the open fields). She would hold me tight as I lay down, and I would clasp her beads with my two hands, close my eyes, and imagine myself walking through an endless field of flowers. 'Step lightly,' Yasmina would say, 'so you can hear the flowers' song. They are whispering, "*salam, salam*" (peace, peace).' I would repeat the flowers' refrain as fast as I could, all danger would disappear, and I would fall asleep. '*Salam, salam*,' murmured the flowers, Yasmina, and I. And the next thing I knew, it was morning and I was lying in Yasmina's big brass bed, with my hands full of pearls and pink beads. From outside came the mixed music of breezes touching the leaves and birds talking to one another, and no one was in sight but King Farouk, the peacock, and Thor, the fat white duck.

Actually, Thor was also the name of Yasmina's most hated co-wife, but I could only call the woman Thor when thinking about her silently to myself. When I said her name out loud, I had to call her Lalla Thor. *Lalla* is our title of respect for all important women, just as *Sidi* is our title of respect for all important men. As a child, I had to call all important grownups Lalla and Sidi, and kiss their hands at sunset, when the lights were turned on and we said *msakum* (good evening). Every evening, Samir and I would kiss everyone's hands as quickly as we could so we could return to our games without hearing the nasty remark, 'Tradition is being lost.' We got so good at it that we managed to rush through the ritual at an incredible speed, but sometimes, we were in such a hurry that we would trip over each other and collapse onto the laps of important people, or even fall down on the carpet. Then everyone would start laughing. Mother would laugh until there were tears in her eyes. 'Poor dears,' she would say, 'they already are tired of kissing hands, and it is only the beginning.'

But Lalla Thor on the farm, just like Lalla Mani in Fez, never laughed. She was always very serious, proper, and correct. As the first wife of Grandfather Tazi, she had a very important position in the family. She also had no housekeeping duties, and was very rich, two privileges that Yasmina could not abide. 'I could not care how rich this woman is,' she would say, 'she ought to be working like all the rest of us. Are we Muslims or not? If we are, everyone is equal. Allah said so. His prophet preached the same.' Yasmina said that I should never accept inequality, for it was not logical. That was why she named her fat white duck Lalla Thor.

FATIMA MERNISSI, 1995

---

from Public Servant, Private Woman

By far the most important of Granny's causes was Women's Suffrage. As early as 1880 she had seconded a resolution about it at a public meeting in Nottingham. 'She did it very nicely,' wrote Grandpa, 'her clear voice being heard distinctly in all parts of the hall.'

It is now often taken for granted that the *suffragettes* (the militants) alone won votes for women. But the *suffragists* (the constitutionalists) also contributed much to change the climate of opinion and many of them believed indeed that the militants did more harm than good. As well as my grandmother, Maudy and my uncles' wives – Nellie, Lena and Hilda – were all devoted workers.

Granny's diaries for these years are full of references to 'the Movement' and they show that often besides my aunts, one or other of the uncles joined the meetings and marches, though there were occasions when, as Granny writes, 'None of the he's cared to go.' Granny was in London to join the march of 1911. I am proud of this but I am quite proud of the fact that my father – who I am sure was out of sympathy with the cause and even more, no doubt, with this public expression of it – insisted nevertheless on marching along beside his mother-in-law as his code of behaviour would have required.

[. . .] However, as a child, I knew nothing of my grandparents' and aunts' involvement in public affairs. My grandmother appeared to us simply as the ever-loving Granny who always had time and thought for us and we loved her dearly in return. I have been happy to find between the pages of her diary for 1907 this letter for her birthday from Bimbi, then aged five – printed carefully in capitals on a tiny piece of paper: DEAR GRANNY I LOVE YOU. SO DOES BAY. BIMBI.

ALIX MEYNELL, 1988

from Wild Swans

My grandmother, now in her mid-fifties, kept more signs of her femininity than my mother. Although her jackets – still in the traditional style – all became the same color of pale gray, she took particular care of her long, thick black hair. According to Chinese tradition, which the Communists inherited, hair had to be well above the shoulder for women of middle age, meaning over thirty. My grandmother kept her hair tied up in a neat bun at the back of her head, but she always had flowers there, sometimes a pair of ivory-colored magnolias, and sometimes a white Cape jasmine cupped by two dark-green leaves, which set off her lustrous hair. She never used shampoo from the shops, which she thought would make her hair dull and dry, but would boil the fruit of the Chinese honey locust and use the liquid from that. She would rub the fruit to produce a perfumed lather, and slowly let her mass of black hair drop into the shiny, white, slithery liquid. She soaked her wooden combs in the juice of pomelo seeds, so that the comb ran smoothly through her hair, and gave it a faint aroma. She added a final touch by putting on a little water of osmanthus flowers which she made herself, as perfume had begun to disappear from the shops. I remember watching her combing her hair. It was the only thing over which she took her time. She did everything else very swiftly. She would also paint her eyebrows lightly with a black charcoal pencil and dab a little powder on her nose. Seeing her eyes smiling into the mirror with a particular kind of intense concentration, I think these must have been among her most pleasurable moments.

Watching her doing her face was strange, even though I had been watching her do it since I was a baby. The women in books and films who made themselves up now were invariably wicked characters, like concubines. I vaguely knew something about my beloved grandmother having been a concubine, but I was learning to live with contradictory thoughts and realities, and getting used to compartmentalizing them. When I went out shopping with my grandmother, I began to realize that she was different from other people, with her makeup, no matter how discreet, and the flowers in her hair. People noticed her. She walked proudly, her figure erect, with a restrained self-consciousness.

JUNG CHANG, 1991

from Grandma Isn't Playing

Grandma Krupek stood framed in the doorway with the new green of the backyard lawn behind her. Then she stepped into the kitchen.

They stared at her, the three of them. It is noteworthy that not one of them laughed. It was not only amazement that kept them from this; it was something in her face, a look of shyness, a look of courage, a look of resolve, a curious mixture of all three that blended to make an effect of nobility.

Then, 'Well, my God!' said Mae Krupek, and dropped a pan in the sink with a clatter and spatter.

Anna Krupek was dressed in slacks and shirt, the one blue, the other gray, and her hair was bound in a colored kerchief. On her feet were neat, serviceable, flat-heeled shoes, in her hand was a lunch box such as workmen carry.

'Hello,' said Grandma Krupek inadequately. She put down her lunch box, went to the sink, and retrieved the pan and its contents.

Between them Steve and Mae said all the things that people say in astonishment, disapproval, and minor panic: 'What does this mean!' 'Have you lost your mind!' 'You can't do a thing like this!' 'What will people say!' 'We'll put a stop to it.' 'You're making a fool of yourself and all of us.'

Only Gloria, between tears and laughter, kissed her grandmother and gave her a hearty smack behind and said, surveying the slim little figure in trousers and shirt, 'Sexagenarian is right!'

Anna Krupek stood her ground. Quietly, stubbornly, over and over again she said, 'I work in airplane factory. Is defense. Is fine. I like. I make plane for Mart. In a week only I learned so quick.'

'You can't do that kind of work. You're too old. You'll be sick.'

Anna's was a limited vocabulary, but she succeeded in making things reasonably plain.

'Say, in factory is a cinch. Easier as housework and cooking you betcha.' Then, fearful of having hurt them, 'I cook again and make everything nice in the house after we fight the war, like always. But now I make airplane for Mart.' She just glanced at Gloria. 'For Mart and other boys.'

Mae drew a long breath, as though she had come up after being under water. 'We'll see about that. Steve, you've got to speak to them. You have her fired. I won't stand for it.'

'My boss is Ben Chester. I don't get fired. Years and years I worked for his ma, cleaning and washing. Ben, he is crazy for me. I don't get fired. No, sir!'

Mae's lips were compressed. She was too angry for tears. 'The neighbours! And everybody laughing at us! At your age!'

Grandma Krupek wagged her head. 'Oh, is plenty old ladies working in airplanes.' She shot another lightning glance at Gloria. 'Old ladies and kids too. Next to me is old lady she is getting new false teeth for hundred and fifty dollar! And her hair marcel each week. I save my money, maybe I travel.'

'Travel!' echoed Mae, weakly.

But Gloria leaped the gap at last. 'Could I get a job there, do you think? Could I do it?'

'Sure thing. Two, three weeks you could travel – oh – New York or – uh – Seattle – or –' with elaborate carelessness. 'And back.'

Mae turned to Steve. 'Well, your mother won't stay here any longer, that's one sure thing. I won't have it.'

'O.K.,' said Anna Krupek, without rancor.

Steve spoke quietly. 'You're staying here, Ma. This is your home.'

Anna's face was placid but firm. 'On day shift I am through I am home five o'clock. I help you, Mae. You ain't such a bad cook; you got to learn only. I was afraid in factory first, but I learn. Like when I cross the ocean alone to come to this country. I was afraid. But I learn.'

She looked at her two hands as she had once before, almost as though they belonged to someone else. She looked at them and turned them as she looked, palms in and then palms out, curiously, as at some rare jewels whose every facet reflected a brilliant new light.

'What you think! I make airplane. I sit in chair, comfortable,

I put a little piece in a little hole it should fit nice, and for this I am pay fifty dollar a week.' She shook her head as though to rid it of a dream. 'Zyg, he won't believe it.'

EDNA FERBER, 1947

---

from Daughter Rails Over 'Absent' Granny

Goes out too much, spends too much time with her friends, is reluctant to help out with family chores: this mantra is familiar to every parent with difficult teenage children.

Only when Cherry MacAlister-Cotterill lists similar complaints she is referring not to a tiresome adolescent but to her 46-year-old mother. Frustrated by her mother's refusal to settle into the traditional role of dutiful grandmother, she has resorted to advertising for surrogate grandparents for her six small children.

A picture of Mrs MacAlister-Cotterill, aged 27, with her husband, Jamie, and children Liam, Kirsty, Garrie, Dale, Caeron, and Kellen all under 10 appeared in the local newspaper last week under the headline 'Wouldn't you like to be our grandparents?' Beneath the photograph, she explained that her own parents simply did not have the right grandparenting qualities. 'My Mum is just not a granny-type person. She is only 46, works and she would sooner go for a night out with the girls. Being a granny is just not her thing,' she said.

Commentators said yesterday that their predicament is one experienced by growing numbers of families as the traditional bond between grandparents and grandchildren begins to fray. Modern grandparents tend to be healthier and more energetic than their predecessors; often they are still working, or simply less inclined to devote large amounts of their time to childcare.

Mrs MacAlister-Cotterill hopes to find an older couple who

have more time on their hands and will conform to a more nostalgic vision of the role 'bake cakes, tell wonderful stories and take the children on summer outings'.

'My nanny used to tell me all about being a nurse in the war and it was fascinating. That's what I want for my children. My mum is likely to tell them about the swinging 60s which isn't quite the same thing,' she said.

AMELIA GENTLEMAN, *Guardian*, 24 March 1999

from Sarah Bernhardt, My Grandmother

We stopped seven days in Chicago. A large number of people crowded into the matinées and evening performances at the Auditorium Theatre. No more cars or caravans or cabins; we were steeping ourselves in cosmopolitan life once more. My grandmother gave luncheons and dinners . . . Sarah Bernhardt organized a charity matinée for the Art Union and, for the first and last time in my life, I was on the stage with her. I played the part of the French soldier in *Les Cathédrales*. I put on the infantryman's uniform which Sarah wore in *Au Champ d'Honneur*, and went on to the huge stage of the Auditorium Theatre. The curtain rose over what looked to me like a great black abyss. The only quality that I possessed in common with my illustrious grandmother was unconquerable stage-fright. I said my piece and, as I made the sweeping gesture introducing the Strasburg Cathedral (Sarah Bernhardt), the safety-pin which held up my sky-blue trousers gave way. What on earth was I to do now? I was completely at a loss; my grandmother prompted me with my words, but no sound issued from my lips. At last, in the sudden energy of despair, holding my trousers up with one hand and pointing with the other to the five Cathedrals lined up behind me, I roared out my words in a stentorian voice.

So that when Sarah Bernahrdt's voice followed mine it was like listening to sacred music after a jazz band. Deafening applause. I turned to the audience. Sarah bowed and whispered to me:

'Your trousers, Lysiane! Hold your trousers up!'

LYSIANE BERNHARDT, 1949

from Russia Through Women's Eyes

But her star was fated to shine once more on the Russian stage . . . In 1872 we moved to Moscow. That same year the Polytechnic Exhibition opened, and the People's Theatre, of which the best people in Russian society had dreamed for so long, was established. My grandmother received a letter from a provincial company written some time before it reached her. She was invited to join them at the new theatre. My grandmother was overcome with emotion.

'They remembered me! Goodness gracious! They didn't forget me . . . The darlings!' she said. There were tears in her eyes, and her voice trembled as she kissed the letter.

She thought it over for a whole day. She paced up and down the hall, and no one dared disturb her. 'I've decided, Mashenka,' she told my mother finally. 'I will act once more. It will be my swan song . . .'

My mother, my sister, and I were all excited . . . Only our father frowned.

'What's the matter?' my mother asked in astonishment. My sister and I were attending the Elizavetinsky Institute at the time. The headmistress, Countess Z——va, a haughty and narrow-minded woman, completely unsuited to educate young people, had welcomed us with open arms. She treated poor girls with open contempt. But we were rich girls from an old gentry family, we spoke excellent French, and we were well-mannered. She spoiled us, and we were counted among her favorites from the very first day. But our father knew human nature, and without suspecting that we children were listening to their conversation, he told Mother, 'They mustn't find out about this at the institute.'

'Why ever not?' our mother asked in surprise.

'Ask Anastasiia Nikitichna yourself. She acted under a different name to protect you when you were a girl. And she didn't even tell me, her future son-in-law, about her past . . . Surely you know artistes aren't considered respectable here in Russia?'

'What nonsense!' my mother retorted angrily. 'Those are old prejudices . . . Times have changed . . . Think of the reception Fedotova gets when she appears in *Old Kashir* [a popular melodrama]!'

'But I've heard that Countess Z——va . . .'

'Good Lord! There are lots of countesses, but only one Mochalova . . .'

[. . .] The play was a great success. So were the others that followed. The Grand Duke Konstantin Nikolaevich was delighted and personally thanked the artistes for the great pleasure they had given him. My family was there, in a box, to see Grandmother's triumph. But Grandmother strictly forbade us to talk about it when we returned to school.

One winter's day, the headmistress came into my classroom. Her face was blacker than a storm cloud, and she glared venomously at me. My heart missed a beat. And with good reason. The scene that followed was so horrible that even now I cannot speak of it calmly.

'Who is your grandmother?' the headmistress demanded haughtily. I stood up. I was told later that I was as white as a sheet. There was a painful silence.

'My grandmother is an *artiste*,' I whispered very softly.

'She is an *actress*,' the Countess interrupted me sharply. Her face was red with anger. 'A female actor . . . She prances about in public for money, like a clown.'

'That's a lie!' I screamed, unable to stop myself.

'Silence!' the headmistress hissed and stamped her foot. 'I'm talking . . . She prances about like a clown . . . And where does she do this? In the People's Theatre, for peasants, in front of trash, for the scum of society . . .'

I hid my face in my hands as though I had been slapped. The class groaned in unison.

'I've found out everything!' the headmistress raged. 'I could hardly believe my ears when I was told . . . The shame!'

But then something occurred that had never happened before in all the annals of the institute. I was told later that I lunged forward, my face pale and contorted.

'It's a lie, a lie!' I screamed furiously and shook my clenched fist over my head. 'Don't you dare say . . . *that* . . . about my grandmother . . . She's an honorable woman, yes she is!' I shouted, beside myself.

There was a terrible silence. Unable to believe her ears, the headmistress took a step back. Suddenly, I collapsed face down on my desk. And a hysterical scream ripped from my throat – it was the first and only fit of hysteria I've ever had in my life.

ANASTASIA VERBITSKAIA (1861–1928)

---

from The Gambler

At first Granny began looking about at the players. She began in a half whisper asking me abrupt, jerky questions. Who was that man and who was this woman? She was particularly delighted by a young man at the end of the table who was playing for very high stakes, putting down thousands, and had, as people whispered around, already won as much as forty thousand francs, which lay before him in heaps of gold and banknotes. He was pale; his eyes glittered and his hands were shaking; he was staking now without counting, by handfuls, and yet he kept on winning and winning, kept raking in the money . . .

Granny watched him for some minutes.

'Tell him,' Granny said suddenly, growing excited and giving me a poke, 'tell him to give it up, to take his money quickly and go away. He'll lose it all directly, he'll lose it all!' she urged, almost breathless with agitation. 'Where's Potapitch? Send Potapitch to him. Come, tell him, tell him,' she went on, poking me. 'Where is Potapitch? *Sortez! Sortez!*' – she began herself shouting to the young man.

I bent down to her and whispered resolutely that she must not shout like this here, that even talking aloud was forbidden, because it hindered counting and that we should be turned out directly.

'How vexatious! The man's lost! I suppose it's his own doing . . . I can't look at him, it quite upsets me. What a dolt!' and Granny made haste to turn in another direction.

[. . .] I explained as far as I could to Granny all the various points on which one could stake: *rouge et noir*, *pair et impair*, *manque et passe*, and finally the various subtleties in the system of the numbers. Granny listened attentively, remembered, asked questions, and began to master it. One could point to examples of every kind, so that she very quickly and readily picked up a great deal.

'But what about zéro? You see that croupier, the curly-headed one, the chief one, showed zéro just now? And why did he scoop up everything that was on the table? Such a heap, he took it all for himself. What is the meaning of it?'

'Zéro, Granny, means that the bank wins all. If the little ball falls on zéro, everything on the table goes to the bank. It is true you can stake your money so as to keep it, but the bank pays nothing.'

'You don't say so! And shall I get nothing!'

'No, Granny, if before this you had staked on zéro you would have got thirty-five times what you staked.'

'What! thirty-five times, and does it often turn up? Why don't they stake on it, the fools.'

'There are thirty-six chances against it, Granny.'

'What nonsense. Potapitch! Potapitch! Stay, I've money with me – here.' She took out of her pocket a tightly packed purse, and picked out of it a friedrich d'or. 'Stake it on the zéro at once.'

'Granny, zéro has only just turned up,' I said; 'so now it won't turn up for a long time. You will lose a great deal; wait a little, anyway.'

'Oh, nonsense; put it down!'

'As you please, but it may not turn up again till the evening. You may go on staking thousands; it has happened.'

'Oh, nonsense, nonsense. If you are afraid of the wolf you shouldn't go into the forest. What? Have I lost? Stake again!'

A second friedrich d'or was lost: she staked a third. Granny could scarcely sit still in her seat. She stared with feverish eyes at the little ball dancing on the spokes of the turning wheel. She lost a third, too. Granny was beside herself, she could not sit still, she even thumped on the table with her fist when the croupier announced 'trente-six' instead of the zéro she was expecting.

'There, look at it,' said Granny angrily; 'isn't that cursed little zéro coming soon? As sure as I'm alive, I'll sit here till it comes . . . Alexey Ivanovitch, stake two gold pieces at once! Staking as much as you do, even if zéro does come you'll get nothing by it.'

'Granny!'

'Stake, stake! it is not your money.'

I staked two friedrichs d'or. The ball flew about the wheel for a long time, at last it began dancing about the spokes, Granny was numb with excitement, and squeezed my fingers, and all at once—

'Zéro!' boomed the croupier.

'You see, you see!' – Granny turned to me quickly, beaming

and delighted. 'I told you so. The Lord Himself put it into my head to stake those two gold pieces! Well, how much do I get now? Why don't they give it to me? Potapitch, Marfa, where are they? Where have all our people got to? Potapitch, Potapitch!'

'Granny, afterwards,' I whispered; 'Potapitch is at the door, they won't let him in. Look, Granny, they are giving you the money, take it!' A heavy roll of printed blue notes, worth fifty friedrichs d'or, was thrust towards Granny and twenty friedrichs d'or were counted out to her. I scooped it all up in a shovel and handed it to Granny.

'Faites le jeu, messieurs! Faites le jeu, messieurs! Rien ne va plus!' called the croupier, inviting the public to stake, and preparing to turn the wheel.

'Heavens! we are too late. They're just going to turn it. Put it down, put it down!' Granny urged me in a flurry. 'Don't dawdle, make haste!' She was beside herself and poked me with all her might.

'What am I to stake it on, Granny?'

'On zéro, on zéro! On zéro again! Stake as much as possible! How much have we got altogether? Seventy friedrichs d'or. There's no need to spare it. Stake twenty friedrichs d'or at once.'

'Think what you are doing, Granny! Sometimes it does not turn up for two hundred times running! I assure you, you may go on staking your whole fortune.'

'Oh, nonsense, nonsense! Put it down! How your tongue does wag! I know what I'm about.' Granny was positively quivering with excitement.

'By the regulations it's not allowed to stake more than four thousand florins . . .'

'Why is it not allowed? Aren't you lying? Monsieur! Monsieur!' – she nudged the croupier, who was sitting near her on the left, and was about to set the wheel turning. *'Combien zéro? Douze? Douze?'*

I immediately interpreted the question in French.

'*Oui, madam,*' the croupier confirmed politely; 'as the winnings from no single stake must exceed four thousand florins by the regulations,' he added in explanation.

'Well, there's no help for it, stake twelve.'

'*Le jeu est fait,*' cried the croupier. The wheel rotated and thirty turned up. She had lost.

'Again, again, again! Stake again!' cried Granny. I no longer resisted, and, shrugging my shoulders, staked another twelve friedrichs d'or. The wheel turned a long time. Granny was simply quivering as she watched the wheel. 'Can she really imagine that zéro will win again?' I thought, looking at her with wonder. Her face was beaming with a firm conviction of winning, an unhesitating expectation that in another minute they would shout zéro. The ball jumped into the cage.

'Zéro!' cried the croupier.

'What!!!' Granny turned to me with intense triumph.

[. . .] Granny's winnings were counted out to her with particular attention and deference as she had won such a large sum. She received four hundred and twenty friedrichs d'or, that is, four thousand florins and seventy friedrichs d'or. She was given twenty friedrichs d'or in gold, and four thousand florins in banknotes.

This time Granny did not call Potapitch; she had other preoccupations. She did not even babble or quiver outwardly! She was, if one may so express it, quivering inwardly. She was entirely concentrated on something, absorbed in one aim.

'Alexey Ivanovitch, he said that one could only stake four thousand florins at once, didn't he? Come, take it, stake the whole four thousand on the red.' Granny commanded.

It was useless to protest; the wheel began rotating.

'*Rouge,*' the croupier proclaimed.

Again she had won four thousand florins, making eight in all.

'Give me four, and stake four again on red,' Granny commanded.

Again I staked four thousand.

'*Rouge,*' the croupier pronounced again.

'Twelve thousand altogether! Give it me all here. Pour the gold here into the purse and put away the notes. That's enough! Home! Wheel my chair out.'

FYODOR DOSTOYEVSKY, 1867, translated by Constance Garnett

---

from Grandma Rolled Her Own

Grandma had no patience with Prohibition . . .

[. . .] As Grandma's 'son' and escort I enjoyed beer foam, sarsaparilla, and root beer in some of the best speak-easies in Chicago, Cleveland, and New York. The 'son' subterfuge was for the benefit of snoopers and busy-bodies who might want to know who we were, and this would throw them off the track. It was just as well on Mother's account, too. If word had reached her that her boy was frequenting a Madison Street speak-easy, even under Grandma's protecting eye, she would have thrown several kinds of fits, and certainly would have put a stop to these delicious excursions.

One afternoon Grandma took me to Marshall Field's in Chicago to buy me a coat. I had admired her black-and-white checked coat with the velvet collar, so she decided it was only fair for me to have one like it. It took quite a lot of time and patience to find it, and when it was bought Grandma needed to have herself a glass of beer. A drop of sarsaparilla wouldn't hurt me, either, and it would put a nice finish on the afternoon.

We went to a very nice, respectable speak-easy in an old boarded-up saloon on Madison Street, between Dearborn and Clark, where Tom Moore, one of Grandma's roomers, was bartender. He was very handsome and ruddy-cheeked, and he knew us well, for we came there often. We knocked, and a mysterious eye looked us over through a peephole, something that always gave me a chill down my spine, even though I knew the welcome we would get was always hearty.

We had hardly got inside and sat down, in fact the foam was still hissing on Grandma's beer mug and I hadn't yet had time to lick off the top (my special treat), when there was a terrific crash and we saw the bright blade of an ax come through the peephole panel in the door. Before we could move, the room was full of policemen. A raid! Grandma whispered excitedly, 'My land, it's the Feds!' Tom Moore's harmless and delightful place was pinched.

A man in a tight-fitting, shiny suit, and wearing a derby that had seen better days, waved his arms and yelled, 'Keep your seats, ladies and gentlemen, please keep your seats.' He was talking to Grandma and me, because it was midafternoon and so far we were the only patrons. And his request came a little too late. Grandma and I had headed for the windows in the ladies' room and I had one leg on the way to freedom.

I was almost out of the window when one of the raiders looked into the ladies' room. 'Hey, Sarge!' he yelled, seizing me and hauling us both back into the outer room.

The sergeant stared at Grandma and at me. 'Madam,' he said sternly, 'what are you doing here?'

Grandma stared right back at him. She always did hate foolish questions. Couldn't he see the glass of untouched beer on the table?

'What's a lady doing breaking the law? And a little boy along, too!' he thundered.

His righteous air made no impression on Grandma. Dramatically she lowered her wonderful blue eyes, gave a great sigh, and remarked sadly, 'I've been looking all over for my husband. I don't know where he is, and he hasn't been home in three days. Tom Moore is an old friend of ours . . . I just stopped off to ask his advice about what I should do . . .' her words broke off and she gave a convincing sob. I was fascinated, and almost believed her myself.

The sergeant was impressed, too. He patted Grandma's shoulder in sympathy and led her to the front door. There now, ma'am, I hope you find your husband. I knew you weren't a lawbreaker.'

Grandma put one last fillip on the scene. 'Thank you, officer. You're *so* kind!' Then we scuttled off around the corner and peeked back to see Mr Moore and his helper go off in the wagon. My main regret was that we missed the ride in the wagon, which was just like the one in the Keystone Cops. Grandma was disgusted, too. She hadn't even got to drink her beer.

TED PECKHAM, 1954

———————

The answer if you ask me [to the Queen Mother's popularity] is that the Queen Mum has a reputation for liking her drop of gin. Everyone loves a granny, but a granny on the razzle is irresistible.

KEITH WATERHOUSE, *Independent* Weekend Review, 7 August 1999

———————

from The Bingo Palace

They say that [Lulu] was ready for the federal marshals when they drove up to the doors, though they were quiet, their tires hardly crunching snow [. . .]

They did not knock, they did not give her a chance to form an answer, just busted their way into her apartment and discovered her sitting there, ready. And she was prepared. All was in perfect order for their arrival. No possible doubt about it, none at all. For who else was attired in her full regalia at that hour, dressed traditional, decked out in black velvet with flowers from the woodlands beaded into the shining nap – red rose, yellow heart, white leaves, and winking petals – who else was dressed like Lulu? She carried her fan of pure white eagle tail-feathers. Four of them, upright, in her hand of a sexy grandmother. On the wrist of the other arm, there dangled her beaded carrying pouch, full of cosmetics and papers and identity proof. Of that, they disarmed her as with drawn guns they searched rudely through her precious things.

Let's say they found a knife, they found a weapon, they found something besides that machinery and bundled newspaper and Congressional material that she quoted as she took our money while playing cards. Let's say they found an Illinois matchbook, a pair of sawed-apart handcuffs, some direct proof her son had been to see her. Or let's say they didn't find a thing, but that motherhood itself was more than enough.

Whatever the reasoning, they questioned her. At this, we have to laugh.

[. . .] Maybe they thought Indians dressed that way all the time. Maybe they thought Indians dressed that way to go to bed at night. No one commented on or noticed Lulu's outfit, ceremonial and bold, as if she was ready to be honored. Her moccasins, she always called them works of art: smoked deerhide, expertly tanned. Little roses were beaded on the toes, white rabbit fur sewn inside, and meanwhile the rest of us wore house slippers, thin quilted robes. Listening at doorways, we called softly between ourselves, and shuddered with cold. Underneath her powwow dress, Lulu wore a pair of red long johns, we were sure. Winter is not gentle with us old ones and she anticipated drafts, who wouldn't, during the entry and seizure.

They were very smart, these federals. No doubt they were wise. They had seen a lot of hard cases, chased a lot of criminals, solved a great many crimes that would stump us ordinary Chippewas. And yet, the fact is, they had never encountered Lulu . . .] They spent hours, in which they should have been tracking down their wary escapee, asking Lulu one question, in many different ways, until she seemed to break down, shaking her hands and fanning herself with feigned distress.

'Yes, yes,' she whispered. 'Something happened.'

They got a story all right. One hour passed, then two, but then it's frustrating to question an old woman who is losing her memory [. . .]

Heads are spinning and just then, when their tongues are sticking in their cheeks and their brows are going up, she remembers perfectly.

'Of course, of course he was here. He came home.'

And at those words, of course, the ears perk and the recorders whir, but then the sense retreats, the poor old woman faints, slumps dead away, and must be revived with a strong fresh cup of coffee.

'Where else would he go?' she says when she wakes up, and hours later, it turns out that she has just returned from taking him up north across the border in her automobile. Where? That takes quite a while more to figure out [. . .]

Dreamy, she smiles, in her own time and place perhaps, but maybe they are onto her at last. Maybe they have lost their patience, it is true, or have finally understood that they are playing with a cat whose claws are plump and sheathed. They have dusted everything for fingerprints. They have examined every surface for nail clips and hair. They have looked into each drawer and sounded walls. Gone over each of her possessions, in turn, including the wanted poster, nicely framed.

We told her, we reminded her that she'd done wrong. We scolded Lulu Lamartine to read the warning, heed the label, pointed out that she harbored stolen government property upon her shelf. For that offense, they finally take her in, arrest her, cart her off but with a kind of ceremony that does not confuse a single one of us, for she has planned it. And all so perfectly! By this time, outside the door, in the hallway, so many popping lights of cameras, whining shutters. All of the North Dakota newspapers. By that time, the local tribal officials. The

Chippewa police. Jurisdiction issues? Sure, plenty of them right there to worry over.

There goes Lulu Lamartine, powwow perfect, chained at the wrists but still clutching the eagle-feather fan. Lulu Lamartine surrounded, walked off by muscle-bound agents, as if she would escape, and so frail! Removed from an old people's home! Lulu Lamartine luring dogs away, diverting attention, making such a big statewide fracas, and with her story, sending agents on a new goose chase. It is perfect, it is sinful, and any one of us could have told them they were getting into something like a mazy woods when talking to that woman.

LOUISE ERDRICH, 1994

---

from The Invention of Solitude

In the last paragraph of the last article about the case [in which Mrs Auster was acquitted of murdering her husband] the newspaper reports that 'Mrs Auster is now planning to take the children and leave for the east within a few days . . . It was said that Mrs Auster decided to take this action on the advice of her attorneys, who told her that she should go to some new home and start life without any one knowing the story of the trial.'

It was, I suppose, a happy ending. At least for the newspaper readers of Kenosha, the clever Attorney Baker, and, no doubt, for my grandmother. Nothing further is said, of course, about the fortunes of the Auster family. The public record ends with this announcement of their departure for the east.

Because my father rarely spoke to me about the past, I learned very little about what followed. But from the few things he did mention, I was able to form a fairly good idea of the climate in which the family lived.

[. . .] At the center of the clan was my grandmother, a

Jewish Mammy Yokum, a mother to end all mothers. Fierce, refractory, the boss. It was common loyalty to her that kept the brothers so close. Even as grown men, with wives and children of their own, they would faithfully go to her house every Friday night for dinner – without their families. This was the relationship that mattered, and it took precedence over everything else. There must have been something slightly comical about it: four big men, each one over six feet, waiting on a little old woman, more than a foot shorter than they were.

One of the few times they came with their wives, a neighbor happened to walk in and was surprised to find such a large gathering. Is this your family, Mrs Auster? he asked. Yes, she answered, with great smiles of pride. This is —. This is —. this is —. And this is Sam. The neighbor was a little taken aback. And these lovely ladies, he asked. Who are they? Oh, she answered with a casual wave of the hand. That's —'s. That's —'s. That's —'s. And that's Sam's.

The picture painted of her in the Kenosha newspaper was by no means inaccurate. She lived for her children. (Attorney Baker: Where could a woman with five children like these go? She clings to them and the court can see that they cling to her.) At the same time, she was a tyrant, given to screaming and hysterical fits. When she was angry, she would beat her sons over the head with a broom. She demanded allegiance, and she got it. [. . .]

My father lived with his mother until he was older than I am now. He was the last one to go off on his own, the one who had been left behind to take care of her. It would be wrong to say, however, that he was a mother's boy. He was too independent, had been too fully indoctrinated into the ways of manhood by his brothers. He was good to her, was dutiful and considerate, but not without a certain distance, even humor. After he was married, she called him often, haranguing him about this and that. My father would put the receiver down

on the table, walk to the other end of the room and busy himself with some chore for a few minutes, then return to the
phone, pick it up, say something innocuous to let her know he
was there (uh-huh, uh-huh, mmmmmm, that's right), and
then wander off again, back and forth, until she had talked
herself out.

The comical side of his obtuseness. And sometimes it served
him very well.

I remember a tiny, shriveled creature sitting in the front parlor
of a two-family house in the Weequahic section of Newark
reading the *Jewish Daily Forward*. Although I knew I would
have to do it whenever I saw her, it made me cringe to kiss her.
Her face was so wrinkled, her skin so inhumanly soft. Worse
than that was her smell – a smell I was much later able to identify as that of camphor, which she must have put in her bureau
drawers and which, over the years, had seeped into the fabric of
her clothes. This odor was inseparable in my mind from the
idea of 'grandma'.

As far as I can remember, she took virtually no interest in
me. The one time she gave me a present, it was a second- or
third-hand children's book, a biography of Benjamin
Franklin [. . .] The book had a blue cover and was illustrated
with silhouettes. I must have been seven or eight at the time.

After my father died, I discovered a trunk that had once
belonged to his mother in the cellar of his house. It was locked,
and I decided to force it open with a hammer and screwdriver,
thinking it might contain some buried secret, some long lost
treasure. As the hasp fell down and I raised the lid, there it
was, all over again – that smell, wafting up towards me, immediate, palpable, as if it had been my grandmother herself. I felt
as though I had just opened her coffin.

There was nothing of interest in it: a set of carving knives, a
heap of imitation jewelry. Also a hard plastic dress-up pocket-
book, a kind of octagonal box with a handle on it. I gave the

thing to Daniel, and he immediately started using it as a portable garage for his fleet of little trucks and cars.

PAUL AUSTER, 1989

---

from The Essential Kafir

In front of this motley crowd a witchdoctor was dancing; she was an ugly old withered hag, clad in a monkey-skin skirt, from which a dozen long tails were flying at a tangent. Round her waist was a belt of beadwork, and a couple of jangling bells were fastened to her skirt. Round her ankles were some dozen circular cocoon-like hollow balls filled with seeds, which rattled as she moved. On her head was perched a battered old straw hat of sailor type, and her face was rendered doubly hideous by the semi-drunken leer which disfigured it. In her hand she held a native battle-axe, which she brandished in the faces of the women and children. It might well have been one of the witches in *Macbeth* come to life and drugged with drink. She was the very picture of drunken devilry.

The dance was kept up at a furious pace, as she stamped about the open space in front of the drummers with a vigour that was surprising. She suddenly stopped dancing, placed her head on one side, as if listening for some voice beneath the ground, and then jumped about furiously and rushed at the drummers, or the women, as they increased their noise. Suddenly she pretended to be in a frenzy and *en rapport* with the ancestral spirits. She began to behave in an amazing fashion. Her body became seized with irregular jerking spasms; her head kept quite steady as she stamped at a tremendous rate with her feet; then the lower part of her body vibrated rapidly, as if the muscles were seized with a tremulous motion. After this she stood still while the upper part of her body was racked with the most tempestuous jerks, the outcome of nerve storms in her brain cells.

When one of the five drummers became slack in his work she darted over towards him and brandished her axe at him and he hastily started beating his drum with fury, as if he were intoxicated, laughing immoderately all the time. Meanwhile the witchdoctor and the people were yelling different tunes of their own, and clapping their hands in rhythmic sequence. When the women grew slack in their chanting or clapping, the old crone rushed at them with her axe and set them off singing at a brisk rate. Suddenly the witchdoctor ceased dancing and looked down at the earth, bent her ear to the ground, and made weird noises, which seemed to come from her stomach, listened again to the earth, made loud expostulations, and set off dancing again. In a moment every muscle in her whole body began to vibrate, jerk, twinge. She jumped up in the air, stamped upon the ground, ran furiously at the men, glided over to the women sideways, moving her feet so swiftly that her legs seemed rather to vibrate than to stamp, while she kept the upper part of her body perfectly steady and free from jerks. Then she moved back to the men in the same way, the vibrations of her legs being so rapid that one could scarcely see more motion than in the case of a bee's wing in flight. Finally, she gave a piercing yell, pulled a bangle off from her ankle with a furious jerk, and gave it to the third drummer boy . . .

DUDLEY KIDD, 1904

———————

Women preserve their youth much longer now than formerly and treat their children more as friends and contemporaries. A juvenile grandmother is no uncommon object, today, while daughters are scarcely younger, less developed, and less qualified to fill whatever position in life they may be called upon to occupy than their mothers.

When I first came out, it was a recognised fact among our family, friends and contemporaries, that when a woman reached the age of fifty years or thereabouts, or her daughters came out, she became, for all practical purposes, an old woman. At forty-five my mother who was still young and good-looking and sang beautifully, began to wear caps, and assumed the particular dress adopted by women who recognised that they had passed the age when they could any longer be called youthful. Nowadays mothers and daughters dress almost alike; and what is more common than the sight of a young and still beautiful mother dancing the evening away as merrily and as much sought after as her daughter.

LADY ST HELIER, *Memories of Fifty Years*, 1909

The woman who has small golden-haired grandchildren is not likely to have silver hair in a bun, serve lemonade on the porch, worry about slipping dentures and 'irregularity'. She would more realistically be portrayed as dressed in a jogging suit on her way to aerobic dancing, or in a suit coming home from work.

G. O. HAGESTEAD, 'Continuity and Connectedness', 1985

When Rachel [my granddaughter] was little, I used to walk about twenty blocks one way and twenty blocks back with my little girl. I used to walk by the U of C [University of Chicago], and there were some professors and they'd stand there. 'Wow, what a grandma, how do you do it?' I says, 'The older, the better, you know.'

BEATRICE POLLOCK in Sydelle Krammer and Jenny Masur (eds.),
Jewish Grandmothers, 1976

———————

[Lady Airlie's] gaiety never deserted her. On her ninetieth birthday her daughter Helen who went to call on her expecting to find her in tears over her changed fortune found her instead dancing an Irish jig to the music of a barrel organ playing under her window.

Let us take leave of her, as she would have wished, to the lilt of that jig, for she lived only a few weeks longer, and to her radiant faith there was no finality in death. 'The generations pass but the green shoots live,' she used to say.

MABELL AIRLIE, *Thatched with Gold*, 1962

———————

VI

POWERFUL OR HEROIC
GRANDMOTHERS

As the spider sits at the centre of her web, so, in the myths of the Navaho and Pueblo peoples, sits Spider Grandmother, the ultimate in powerful grandmothers, at the heart of an earth that, according to some of their creation myths, her weaving helped create. There's an echo of such powers in the tendency of traditional grannies to be busy at their knitting, like my grandmother knitting those pink-striped sweaters in scratchy wool. In an Israeli children's story called *Granny Knits*, the knitting granny knits an entire house for her grandchildren. More metaphorically, a matriarch like Ida Baker in Russell Baker's autobiographical memoir sits like a spider at the centre of her family web, making even her huge sons tremble, let alone their wives. Though I don't claim any such tyranny myself, I did sit at my sixtieth birthday party surrounded by my whole family, children and grandchildren, their friends and mine, thinking gleefully and proudly that but for me none of them would be here; in the case of my progeny and theirs but for me they wouldn't exist. If this is being a matriarch, I think I like it.

The point about matriarchs as grannies is of course that their bodies are no longer fertile. They cannot procreate. This makes them both safer and more dangerous. Safer because they are no longer temptresses, Delilahs, offering sexual threat. More dangerous because, the threat removed, their energy is freed for other activities, sometimes leading them into the world of men, and even replacing them, as my first extract, *Transcendence with Aging*, suggests. A recent television commercial neatly makes the point. For financial services claiming to be 'on the cutting edge', it shows a pert small grandson asking his obviously energetic grandmother if granddad is on 'the cutting edge'. 'I don't think so, dear,' she says, smiling at snoozing granddad. An equally apt illustration is that familiar figure, the recently retired man hanging disconsolately around the house, while his wife, despite no longer working herself, grows ever busier with voluntary work as well as with her grandchildren. Sometimes his response to his redundancy is to drop down dead. She, on the other hand, may live until she's ninety.

In patriarchal societies where women are especially restricted during their fertile years, the matriarch's influence over her sons becomes vital. On the Trucial Coast, for instance, the mother of the local sheikh gave her own audience, which was sometimes better attended – by men – than those of her menfolk. On a more domestic level, according to the Moroccan sociologist Fatima Mernissi, the Moroccan mother-in-law, although powerless outside the home and formerly, as a young wife, powerless within it, rules absolutely over her own compound. She ensures that her sons remain far closer to her than to their wives; her power over all of them and their children is symbolised by her sole possession of that ultimate phallic symbol, a large key. The key is to the food store. Granny is not just *a* provider, she is *the* provider here.

On a more psychic level, it is perhaps the very powerlessness of women in earlier years, in many societies and, till recently, in ours, that makes them so powerful as old women. Rage and frustration may be one component of it. I remember most vividly of all in my dying mother her sheer rage; rage at her fate, clearly, but rage too at all the things frustrated in her by her gender. A. S. Byatt once said the same thing of her mother, who, though she had a degree (unlike my mother), was never after marriage given the chance to use it. The power generated by that unused energy has to come out somewhere; if it does so as rage, it can in some cases turn to a kind of malice, both anger and malice far more potent than the often frail body which contains them. The labelling of old women as witches used to be one outcome.

An old doctor, a GP I knew at close quarters a few years back, had got further professionally than many women of her generation. But it did not prevent her gender constraining her profoundly in other respects. For the last three years of her life, after a stroke, she could barely speak. As she had never said any more than she had to, it did not change things much on some levels. But the nearer she got to her death, the more silent, the more physically disabled she became, her seeming meekness spilled over into a kind of atavistic mischief, of a kind which could not be described as malicious exactly but which seemed at times both morally indifferent and extraordinarily powerful, a life force in itself. How strong it was I became most fully aware of on a holiday week I spent with her in Spain eight months before she died, along with her carer, her daughter-in-law and a couple of her grandchildren; in the sparse holiday house she exerted such a gravitational force that the whole group of us, adults and children alike, revolved around her for the entire week.

The precise nature of that power became still clearer to me six months later, shortly before she died. I visited her one day around seven o'clock in the evening to find she had already gone to bed. Would I please go up and say good-night? her carer said. I'd experienced the old woman's lack of inhibition often enough by this time; she'd been known to answer the door stark naked, though not to me. So it wasn't so much the nudity of the figure I found crouched on a bed angled capriciously across the narrow, low-ceilinged room that startled me, or even the way she was grinning at me, quite aware of my discomfort. She'd always been a small, thin woman. She wasn't fat now, but enforced inaction had turned her chunky. She had no waist; her midriff was all belly. Her skin was brown as well as withered from long years of sun worship. The effect was so primal, so atavistic, that this long post-menopausal woman, this doomed granny, reminded me of nothing so much as one of those Neolithic fertility figures, crude, top-heavy, inanimate, yet representing an essence of female far more telling and strong than any emanating from a live young sex goddess or even from a heavily pregnant woman. Powerful granny indeed; terrifying in fact. And rather wonderful besides. I fled.

Heroic grandmothers are by no means always the same thing as powerful ones; though they may be. While sometimes the very heroism can make them not only seem powerful, but effectively be so, no matter how helpless in practical respects. The dignity of Maya Angelou's grandmother tormented by young white girls is one example. Of course, to emphasise the heroism of such women, as grandmothers, puts me in danger, I suppose, of falling into the same old trap of making their status as grandmothers distort, if not diminish, in some ways, their status as heroic women. The heroic Soviet grandmother is a gruesome example of just such overinflation.

Among beleaguered groups – like the black majority in southern American states, or those unfortunate enough to live on an English sink estate, or the Aboriginal minority in Australia – it is the older women who hold their society together inasmuch as it can be held, and most effectively fight its battles. Kevin Gilbert's women here are a good example of that. I can vouch for the significance of such women; years ago, in Australia, I interviewed several of them. One of the most depressing sights I saw there was a group of old women rolling drunk outside a store in the central township of Oodnadatta. To see the old men drunk is bad enough, but when you see that the old women have given up too, it's hard not to think that the group is almost lost. When it is not yet lost, the relative resilience of the old women over the old men is, of course, an extreme example of the way women's powers wax as men's wane. In such extreme cases, power – at least within the group – and heroism are pretty much one and the same thing.

It is grandmotherhood that turns some women into heroines. Poor women like the Russian slum dweller in one piece; like the South African township dustheap scavenger in another. All struggling, despite ageing and infirmity, to keep their families and their grandchildren together. This is not to mention the legions of AIDS grandmothers we met earlier, including the one who asserted wistfully her plans to travel after her retirement. 'But my grandchildren are my travel now.'

Grandparenthood also generated the heroism of the grandmothers of the Plaza Mayor, the Argentinian parents of disappeared children, turned heroic by tragedy in their attempts to rescue at least their grandchildren. As in the activities of the langur monkey Sol, retailed by Sarah Hrdy, there could be an evolutionary element in this: let my genes survive at all costs – and be seen to do so. But that's to trivialise a power far more profound and interesting, epitomised by the heroic efforts of such women.

Of course the Sikh heroine who let her grandsons be walled up rather than renounce her Sikh faith was acting way beyond the interests of genetic survival. On the contrary, she was surrendering it, not that she probably saw it in any such way. Whether the grandchildren in this instance appreciated her heroism is not recorded. Possibly not. Or just as possibly, they understood her actions far better than I can, finding my admiration for such heroism tinged with the utmost dismay and pity.

Indeed, much as I appreciate all the other examples of heroism here, I'm grateful that I don't have to emulate them. The kind of heroism I'd prefer for myself – achieving it is, I suspect, much harder than you might think – is that of simply having lived fully through the ages of women, like Ursula Le Guin's space grannies. Or better still, like Robert Coles's quite wonderful New Mexican woman, whose old husband said of her, 'She is old, all right, *vieja*, but I will dare say in front of her: she is *una anciana*; with that I declare my respect . . .'

---

from Transcendence with Aging

In America recent discussion of the middle years has given rise to a new concept of adulthood. The mature person today is one who keeps alive the energy and adaptability of youth while cultivating the wisdom of age. In similar fashion, the ideal adult also combines and blends both masculine and feminine traits – women becoming more assertive and independent, men tending toward greater nurturance, passivity, dependence, or contemplativeness [. . .]

David Gutmann (1977) has made the boldest and most far-reaching attempt to interpret the links between age and sex crossovers in midlife. In a series of anthropological and psychological studies undertaken in the Mayan highlands, among the Navaho, and in the Levant, Gutmann demonstrated a common tendency on the part of older males to abandon the vigorous assertive manner of their young adulthood and gradually take up more passive and contemplative roles. Women, on the other hand, are more likely to become increasingly powerful in domestic affairs as they grow older, abandoning the more dependent and passive ways of their youth. To Gutmann, these patterns seem the result of universal exigencies of human parenthood: Males must provide for and defend the domestic group during the early years of childbearing when women are more vulnerable and specialized in the nurture of the young. Later, as the parental generation ages and gradually gives over property and control to its successors, older males serve the interests of the group by relinquishing their grip on material things and concentrating on the spiritual order. Meanwhile women become the major managers of domestic affairs, often wielding power through their influence over younger men.

JANET ZOLLINGER GIELE, 1980

Spirited grannies are bad news for politicians. When President Clinton made his first visit as a new world leader to Moscow, he called in at a freshly privatised bread shop. Turning to the nearest *babushka* with his most winning smile, he projected his soundbite: 'Isn't it great to have so much choice these days? Which of these great breads should I take?' 'It depends,' said Gran, 'what kind of bread you like. The important thing is to hurry up because there's a queue behind you.'

East London produces its own brand of battling old lady, as Tony Blair discovered when faced with the unscripted interpolations of Miriam Lewis at the launch of the Government's annual report . . .

ANNE MCELROY, *Independent*, 28 July 1999

As Tony Blair held a question-and-answer session with patients and staff at Homerton Hospital, Hackney, Miriam Lewis, white-haired and carrying a stick, attacked. Mr Blair had explained how he had improved Government finances when she said: 'I get facts and figures from you, but appointments are still taking a long time. My husband has to wait months and months to see a consultant and has to wait longer and longer to get his test results.'

Mr Blair said that extra cash was going into the NHS. She

replied: 'I'm afraid we don't see it. All we see is that there are people who are worried there are going to be charges for dentists, prescriptions and home visits.'

Mr Blair, with Frank Dobson, the Health Secretary, listened as Mrs Lewis complained that many pensioners were so poor they were forced on to benefits, which they saw as charity. She told the Prime Minister: 'We feel that our pensions are nowhere near enough.'

Mrs Lewis, a local activist for pensioners and better health services, said that whenever she tackled local health chiefs they said the problems were due to a lack of resources, which was the Government's fault. Mr Blair said: 'You are right, you have come to the top, it's important that we have this dialogue. I think that the only way to answer it honestly is to say that I think we are making progress but there's a lot further to go.' Mrs Lewis interrupted: 'Well, hurry up!'

GEORGE JONES, *Electronic Telegraph*, 27 July 1999

––––––

from Grandmother Had No Name

My maternal grandmother had no name of her own. I never knew the significance of this until I returned again to China in 1982, my second visit since Liberation.

The fact is, I had learned years ago that grandmother had no name. During my early teens I came upon photos of her among old family documents. Two photos stood out in my memory. One was a three-by-five glossy black-and-white picture, showing her in a velvet turban with a piece of jewelry, probably jade, right in the center. Grandmother had a rather long face, unlike most moon-faced Chinese women of her generation, and her features looked distinctly Western – large double-lidded eyes, high-bridged nose, high cheek bones, and a wide mouth. I thought she looked at once exotic and beautiful. Only years later did I associate her Western features with her Muslim background. Another photo had her sitting in a rattan chair in the courtyard, with her children standing beside her, all five girls and one boy. She looked powerful but lonely in this picture, without Grandfather's presence [. . .]

With her reduced responsibilities at home, Grandmother spent a lot of time with me and my cousin Zhenli. Her bound feet limited her movements. She had to walk slowly and every step put a sharp pain through her entire body, so Zhenli and I would act as her substitute for a walking cane whenever we ventured outside together. She had developed a love for the waterpipe, a popular activity among ladies of the leisure class, and I was assigned the task of making long straws from yellow rice paper to light her pipe. After supper, we would all sit in the back-yard, watching the stars in the sky, listening to her story-telling, and the burbling of her waterpipe. I would often be lulled to sleep and carried back into the house. But, more often than not, after a long story, Grandmother would ask me to massage her back. 'I want those tiny fists pounding on my back, Rongrong,' she would say to me, and I would oblige her by using all my might to pound her backbones as hard as I could. Most of the time I thought of Grandmother as a hopeless and dependent old woman. I would be proved wrong soon enough.

The occasion was a visit from my paternal grandmother, Grandmother Pu. A native of Guangzhou province, she had big feet, spoke the hard-to-understand Cantonese, and, worst of all, was a pork-eater – a non-Muslim woman. Evidently Mother had broken with Muslim tradition by marrying a non-Muslim from another province, an event close to being open warfare with the parents in a Muslim family. Since Mother usually got what she wanted, she had gone ahead and married my father despite her family's opposition, and Grandmother Li had to become resigned to having a non-Muslim son-in-law. With this as a backdrop, the visit from Grandmother Pu was a critical one for Grandmother Li, who was determined to show utmost civility and hospitality. Having met Grandmother Pu before and having picked up some of the Cantonese dialect, I was the chosen family interpreter for the two grandmothers. The most immediate concern was food preparation, since Grandmother Pu loved her pork dishes and Grandmother Li forbade any pork products in the house. However, Grandmother Li hoped to convince Grandmother Pu that the healthy, delicate Muslim foods – Qingzheng cuisine – would be sufficient for her during her short stay with us. Grandmother Pu, on the other hand, had very little awareness of the importance of this issue and was soon asking for cooking utensils for herself so that she could cook in a separate section of the house. Eager to help and not recognizing the severity of the situation, I obtained the necessary cooking utensils for her. When the aroma of pork – the 'evil smell' – penetrated the thin walls of Grandmother Pu's room and escaped into the central courtyard, Grandmother Li became outraged. Along with my hapless Mother, I was summoned to grandmother Li's room. Sitting on top of her high rosewood bed, Grandmother sternly told me I had offended Allah's wishes and that I was a naughty, sinful girl. I stammered, 'But . . . Grandmother Pu can't have our kind of food,' but was stopped short by the cold stare, the only time I had faced real anger from Grandmother Li. Mother intervened at the appropriate moment and quickly ushered me out of Grandmother's room.

ALICE MURONG PU LIN, 1990

---

from American Plaid

Mrs N— was in her nineties, a spare thread of a woman, who ruled the four generations of her family and her set with matriarchal supremacy. Witty, worldly, with a gay sprightliness, we were drawn to her irresistibly, and became one with the group that lingered by her tea-table, her theatre seat, her chaise-longue, to hear her rapidly reeled-off recollections, her dry comments on current affairs, her wry prognostications of the future, with which, she 'thanked God', she would have no concern.

'I am the mother of two queens and the grandmother of three,' she informed me, and watched with amusement the bewilderment of the Britisher.

'A distinguished family indeed,' I murmured. 'You did say "queens" didn't you?'

'Yes,' she said with a pride she attempted to minimise by a slight grimace and a dismissive gesture of her small claws. 'Yes, Queens of the Mardi Gras.' [. . .]

At this moment a friend paused to ask after her health. 'I am as good as I ever was, except for a pain in my back,' she answered . . . 'My doctor talks about something called sacro-iliac, and I tell him he may be right, for it is certainly a sacré-hell-of-an-ache.' [. . .]

A little later I learned from admiring friends that Mrs N— had had a salon in Paris . . . that she was, possibly, the only woman who had got the best of an argument with Bernard Shaw, and, most impressive of all, that she had once snubbed Henry James while riding with him in a hansom cab.

CELILE DE BANKE, 1961

---

from Our Lives, Our Dreams, Soviet Women Speak

Oftobkhon Jabbarova is a mother-heroine. She is a stocky woman with long dark brown hair, pulled back on both sides. Her tweed blazer and briefcase made her look more like an attorney than a mother-heroine: it turned out she was both.

Jabbarova grew up without a father because he was killed [. . .] during the Revolution. Her mother was among the first women who took off their veils and she was killed, so Oftobkhon was brought up by her grandmother. As a girl she dreamed of becoming a lawyer. At the age of 15 she started to study at a training-school for day-care nurses . . . During the war she met a soldier, they went to the front together and they both came back. Her first child was born in 1945 and now she has 10 children from 16 to 41 years old and 18 grandchildren. Jabbarova said with pride that six of her children finished higher education . . . and that four of them went to Tashkent University, which is very selective . . . Jabbarova also realised her dream and graduated from the law school at the university. During the time she was studying for her law degree she had twins and she also graduated from a teacher training college. Jabbarova, her voice vibrating with emotion, said, 'All this education has become possible because of the concern of the state for families and there is aid to families with many children.'

HELENE BURGESS, 1988

Gwennie (later Lyon) went with her grandmother to the Gredos Mountains of Spain and experienced at first hand the adventure of tents, camps under the stars, donkey and horse rides, and the inevitable butterfly hunts. Members of the Nicholl family still recall with amused affection a letter from Gwennie describing her Spanish travels and recounting how Grandmama was received by the mayor and band of one remote Spanish village and conducted with great ceremony to the town hall. Minnie had been mistaken for Queen Victoria!

HILARY M. THOMAS, *Grandmother Extraordinary*, 1979

from Reclaimed Powers

The conventional wisdom in gerontology holds that the strongest bond of later life is between the aging mother and her daughters, excluding men. But this impression is based largely on parochial data from US subjects. The older wife in traditional societies, however, has a male ally: She moves to power in concert with the oldest son, with each party taking over allotted portions of the old father's social powers. Through marriage, the son attains adult status within the family, while his mother acquires a potential rival – and a potential servant – in the person of the daughter-in-law. If the mother can retain some emotional hold over the son even as his affections shift toward a wife, then she and the son may share dominion over the family, with the mother becoming a senior adviser, an éminence grise who works her will in the family via the son. The daughter-in-law then becomes something of a vassal to the mother-in-law, thereby enhancing the senior woman's scope and powers. In this scenario, the son's marriage is fundamental to his own as well as the aging mother's advancement within the family.

DAVID GUTMANN, 1988

---

from Mafia Women

One Palermo matriarch set up a family business dealing heroin on a large scale, employing three generations – down to the children who ran around the streets looking for buyers. Angela Russo was born in 1908, the daughter of a Palermo mafioso, a man of respect whom she admired and adored. Every son his wife bore him sickened and died, and Angela, the oldest of five girls, was the nearest thing he had to an heir. He took her hunting, and she learned to shoot at his side. She grew up commanding, as she herself says, respect and authority (later when she was accused of being a courier, she spurned the idea. Impossible, she said, *she* was the boss: 'I have always given the orders, why would I start running errands for others?')

During the winter months of 1981, police conducted an assiduous surveillance of several families who formed a network distributing heroin and cocaine across Italy. One of these was the Coniglio family, headed by Salvino Coniglio, who directed operations, drove a BMW and was constantly flying to Milan and Rome. His mother was Angela Russo, now 74. They lived in the centre of Palermo, four generations from great-grandmother Angela down. The house was the venue for meetings and appointments; there were phone calls day and night, with people leaving messages in code. The matriarch guaranteed her son, raised capital to buy the drugs, arranged deliveries.

If Salvino fitted the drug dealer stereotype, his mother and the other women in the household were above suspicion – with no previous convictions, they came and went as they pleased. The old lady often served as the courier, travelling by train to the mainland in her loud black and white checked coat with her battered suitcase – until investigators heard Salvino say on the telephone: 'I'm sending you my mother. Look after her, she's elderly – put her up in a nice hotel. She'll be wearing a black and white checked coat.'

'Sure enough,' says the carabiniere who arrested her, laughing until he nearly chokes on his cigar, 'we picked her up in that terrible checked coat, carrying a kilo of heroin from Palermo to Salerno.' Eight members of the family were arrested, including four women from three different generations. Grandma Heroin, as she became known during the trial, charged with trafficking in class A drugs, played the ignorant housewife. 'When we arrested her,' the carabiniere guffaws behind his huge desk, 'she said: "Cocaine, what's that? a detergent?"

'A detergent!'

Before the judge, Grandma Heroin exhibited sterling mafia characteristics. She refused to answer magistrates' questions; when her son Salvino, who appeared to be the brains, however scattered, of the family business, became a collaborator, she called him *infame*. 'Traitor, madman,' she screeched across the courtroom: 'Judas, good-for-nothing. Crazy, he's crazy. Your honour, he was struck down with meningitis at four years old, and the doctor warned me he would always be sick in the head.' When Salvino lost control, his mother threatened to kill him. In a typically mafioso formula, she invoked her right to do so: 'I made you and I can destroy you.'

CLARE LONGRIGG, 1997

---

from Roman History, Book LVII

Moreover, he bade his mother conduct herself in a similar manner, so far as it was fitting for her to do so, partly that she might imitate him and partly to prevent her from becoming over-proud. For she occupied a very exalted station, far above all women of former days, so that she could at any time receive the senate and such of the people as wished to greet her in her house; and this fact was entered in the public records. The letters of Tiberius bore for a time her name, also, and communications were addressed to both alike. Except that she never ventured to enter the senate-chamber or the camps or the public assemblies, she undertook to manage everything as if she were sole ruler. For in the time of Augustus she had possessed the greatest influence and she always declared that it was she who had made Tiberius emperor; consequently she was not satisfied to rule on equal terms with him, but wished to take precedence over him. As a result, various extraordinary measures were proposed, many persons expressing the opinion that she should be called Mother of her Country, and many that she should be called Parent. Still others proposed that Tiberius should be named after her, so that, just as the Greeks were called by their father's name, he should be called by that of his mother. All this vexed him, and he would neither sanction the honours voted her, with a very few exceptions, nor otherwise allow her any extravagance of conduct. For instance, she had once dedicated in her house an image to Augustus, and in honour of the event wished to give a banquet to the senate and the knights together with their wives, but he would not permit her to carry out any part of this programme until the senate had so voted, and not even then to receive the men at dinner; instead, he entertained the men and she the women. Finally he removed her entirely from public affairs, but allowed her to direct matters at home; then, as she was troublesome even in that capacity, he proceeded to absent himself from the city and to avoid her in every way possible; indeed, it was chiefly on her account that he removed to Capreae. Such are the reports that have been handed down about Livia.

DIO, c. AD 230

In the eighteen years between Grandfather George's death and my arrival in Morrisonville, Ida Rebecca established herself as the iron ruler of a sprawling family empire. Her multitude of sons, some of them graying and middle-aged, were celebrated for miles around as good boys who listened to their mother. If one of them kicked over the traces, there was hell to pay until he fell obediently back into line. In Morrisonville everybody said, 'It's her way or no way.'

Her sons' wives accepted the supremacy of mother-in-law rule as the price of peace and kept their resentments to themselves. When her boys married the women she approved, their wives were expected to surrender their swords in return for being allowed to keep their husbands for the spring planting.

RUSSELL BAKER, *Growing Up*, 1984

The older women achieve a status more closely resembling that of men. They have influence and authority over the daughters-in-law of the compound, as well as their own daughters still living at home. Mothers are greatly respected by their sons, and sons often have closer emotional ties to their mothers than their patriarchal fathers. *Grandmothers are respected as fathers*.

Quoted in DAVID GUTMANN, *Reclaimed Powers*, 1988

from The History of Rome, Book II

Then the matrons assemble in a body around Veturia, the other of Coriolanus, and his wife, Volumnia: whether that was the result of public counsel, or of the women's fear, I cannot ascertain. They certainly carried their point that Veturia, a lady advanced in years, and Volumnia, leading her two sons by Marcius, should go into the camp of the enemy, and that women should defend by entreaties and tears a city which men were unable to defend by arms. When they reached the camp, and it was announced to Coriolanus, that a great body of women were approaching, he, who had been moved neither by the majesty of the state in its ambassadors, nor by the sanctity of religion so strikingly addressed to his eyes and understanding in its priests, was much more obdurate against the women's tears. Then one of his acquaintances, who recognised Veturia, distinguished from all the others by her sadness, standing between her daughter-in-law and grand-children, says, 'Unless my eyes deceive me, your mother, children, and wife, are approaching.' When Coriolanus, almost like one bewildered, rushing in consternation from his seat, offered to embrace his mother as she met him, the lady, turning from entreaties to angry rebuke, says, 'Before I receive your embrace, let me know whether I have come to an enemy or to a son; whether I am in your camp a captive or a mother? Has length of life and a hapless old age reserved me for this – to behold you an exile, then an enemy? Could you lay waste this land, which gave you birth and nurtured you? Though you had come with an incensed and vengeful mind, did not your resentment subside when you entered its frontiers? When Rome came within view, did it not occur to you, within these walls my house and guardian gods are, my mother, wife, and children? So then, had I not been a mother, Rome would not be besieged: had I not a son, I might have died free in a free country. But I can now suffer nothing that is not more discreditable to you than distressing to me; nor however wretched I may be, shall I be so long. Look to these, whom, if you persist, either an untimely death or lengthened slavery awaits.' Then his wife and children embraced him: and the lamentation proceeding from the entire crowd of women, and their bemoaning themselves and their country, at length overcame the man; then, after embracing his family, he sends them away; he moved his camp farther back from the city.

LIVY, c. 27 BC

---

from The Real Queen Mother

Whatever [the Queen Mother's] impact on the monarchy over the past half century, there is no question that her influence on the next generation, in the shape of Prince Charles, has been immense. Members of her own family say that he is the son she never had. Clerics who know Charles intimately say that, given his frosty relationship with the Queen, Granny is the mother he feels he never had.

The Queen Mother is the only member of the Royal Family to whom he will talk about his personal problems, the only one who offers him the appreciation and encouragement he craves. Her perpetual optimism helps to dispel his inherent gloom. She always sees the doughnut while he sees only the hole.

His friends and aides believe that she, quite as much as Camilla, is his indispensable prop, that the extent of his psychological dependence on her is both bottomless and a touch unhealthy. His genuine passion for Scotland, his strong dynastic sense and his love of the countryside all, they say, came initially from her.

'I really fear for the Prince of Wales when she dies,' said one of his most ardent admirers. 'He will be devastated, there will be the most enormous depression. He still needs her terribly.'

Not only does Prince Charles adore his grandmother, he is also constantly in touch with her. 'He is absolutely besotted with her,' said one of those close to him. 'He has doted on her from an early age and still does. If only the Queen were like her, and he felt he could just pick up a phone and chat, as he does with the Queen Mother all the time.'

[. . .] Everyone has noticed how happy Charles is whenever he is with his grandmother. 'It's so lovely to see them together,' said one of her ladies-in-waiting. 'He'll arrive at a picnic at Balmoral and say to her: "Oh, your Majesty, I'm graciously honoured to see you," and she'll reply: "Would it please your Royal Highness to have a drink?" Then he'll kiss her all the way up her arms. If the Queen Mother asked him to swim the Channel, he'd do it.'

[. . .] It is significant for the future of the monarchy that Prince Charles has taken the Queen Mother's often extravagant lifestyle as a model for his own. 'His attitudes are very much like hers,' said a Palace insider. 'He mirrors her view of life. His mantras are the same as hers; he makes exactly the same noises about the decline of standards, that things are not what they used to be, and so on. In family gatherings, they stand very much together.'

Charles seems bent on proving that things can be just what they used to be. 'The Prince of Wales tries to emulate Granny in the grand life he leads,' said one of those who knows him well. 'The Queen and the rest of the Royal Family, who are altogether more frugal, think he is far too grand, but his grandmother has encouraged him to be like that, to indulge himself, to be really royal in the old style.'

He has certainly followed her lead. Like her, he has a fleet of cars, including two Aston Martins, a Bentley and two Vauxhall Omega estate cars, all for his own private use. Like her, he has a small regiment of servants – three butlers, four valets, three chauffeurs, four chefs and 10 gardeners. His annual arts weekend at Sandringham, according to one of those involved in the planning, must cost at least £20,000.

Those who have been guests there can quite see why. To them, he seems to be trying to out-granny Granny.

GRAHAM TURNER, 1999

---

from A Princess Remembers

My grandmother played a strong though less conspicuous part in the life of Baroda State. I can see her so plainly in the mornings, coping with her personal affairs – choosing saris, making up her mind about lengths of silk or cloth of gold that her maids held up, listening attentively to the cooks with menus for the day, giving orders to the tailor, asking about domestic details; in short, supervising the running of an enormous household – and still giving her alert attention to the grievances and complaints of any of her women subjects, whether it was the illness of a child or a dispute in a family about the inheritance of land.

This was all part of a maharani's duty, and so were the more ceremonial occasions, as when she presided over formal durbars in the women's apartments of the Baroda Palace. I especially remember the first one I saw, her birthday durbar. All the wives and womenfolk of the nobility and the great landowners were assembled in their richest clothes and jewellery to pay homage to my grandmother. She was seated on a *gaddi*, a cushioned throne, and wore a sari made of rose-pink cloth of gold, draped in the Maratha way with a pleated train between the legs.

Along with her dazzling sari, my grandmother wore all the traditional jewellery for this occasion, including heavy diamond anklets and a wealth of diamond rings on her fingers and toes. The noble ladies paid their respects to her with a formal folding of hands in a *namaskar* and offered her the traditional gold coin to signify their allegiance. At the end of the hall was a troupe of musicians and dancers from Tanjore in south India. Like many Indian princes, my grandfather maintained the troupe as palace retainers, and they always gave a performance of the classical south Indian dancing called *bharata natyam* at any important palace occasion. At such festive times, the family all ate off gold *thals*, while everyone else ate off silver. (This distinction always used to embarrass me.)

GAYATRI DEVI OF JAIPUR, 1984

When they are women of strong character, the senior women of ruling families can play an important part in affairs . . .

One remarkable woman of the Trucial Coast, Sheikah Hussah bint al-Murr, the mother of the present ruler of Dubai and wife of his predecessor, went far beyond this. [She] came so far out into open affairs as to hold her own *majlis* (public meeting), not for women but for men, sitting, receiving visitors as people said, like a sheikh, and when her husband was ruler it is said that more men visited her *majlis* than visited his.

P. A. LIENHARDT, 'Some Social Aspects of the Trucial States', 1972

Wise Old Cows

Elephants possess one of the most advanced and harmonious social organizations known amongst mammals. The basis of this is the matriarch: 'Wise old cows lead elephant herds' as one writer expressed it. William Bazé writing in 1950 of the Asian elephant in Vietnam stated: 'The wild herd, therefore, is ruled by a matriarchy. The oldest females . . . are usually the leaders of the herd.' Three quarters of all elephant groups examined in culling schemes in Kenya and Uganda included a matriarch ranging in age from 38 to 60 years with an average age of 49. These mothers or grandmothers are important in leadership and infant care and when a group is alarmed it always bunches on the matriarch, following her lead. Whether it is the African elephant or the Asian, it is the matriarch which always charges in case of danger and takes the rear position in flight.

C. A. Spinage, *Elephants*, 1994

Two Fat Ladies End Their Gang Patrols

Two grandmothers who weight 36 stone between them announced their 'retirement' yesterday after restoring order to the streets of a once lawless estate.

Residents were provoked, intimidated and robbed by hooligan gangs until Joyce Swift and Anne Jepson began patrolling Meadowbank in Rotherham, south Yorkshire, four years ago. Word spread after a teenager squared up to Mrs Swift and came off second best. A single blow from the 17.5-stone mother of four settled the issue.

Mrs Swift, 64, said last night that she and Mrs Jepson, 48, became frustrated by seeing teenagers causing trouble but fleeing before police arrived. She said: 'My mother-in-law, who is 93 now, was afraid to go out because of the glue-sniffers and other youngsters running wild. So we decided that where the police had failed through no fault of their own, two large, determined ladies might succeed.

'We patrolled in the day and into the evening looking out for people breaking into cars or property, or just making a nuisance of themselves. We carry some weight between us and we weren't afraid to use it. We have never been reported to the police for any incidents. We never started anything but we always finished it.'

She said: 'In any case there was no glory in it for the yobs if they complained that they had been bashed by a fat old grandmother. We became known as the two fat ladies and we built up a reputation, getting coverage in the local press, that helped us in what we were doing. Now we believe that our job is done and we are retiring our patrols.

'The street is a lot safer, some of the teenagers we chastised have since become parents themselves and they come round to talk to me, saying they have seen the error of their ways.'

A. J. MCILROY, Electronic Telegraph, 9 March 1998

from Because the White Man'll Never Do It

Aboriginal leadership is an amorphous thing. At the local level it still tends to be exercised by the older women, so continuing an old local tradition of Aboriginal life. I remember the influence exerted by my own Aboriginal grandmother at Condobolin some twenty years ago. What Ellen Naden-Murray said was well noted by all the Condobolin blacks and she used the weapon of Aboriginal 'shame' to devastating effect against whoever she felt needed it. Besides the authority of women like her, there was no discipline in the black community at all, except the discipline exerted by an external white force, the police. Within her community, Ellen's influence extended into everyday matters such as standards of daily conduct, the behaviour to be expected even of a drunk, the treatment and bringing up of children, the moral conduct of teenagers and so on. It even extended to adjudicating domestic disputes between husbands and wives. When necessary, she was in the habit of reinforcing her authority with a powerful left hook. She was six feet tall and weighed around 196 lbs.

KEVIN GILBERT, 1973

Mrs Mooney, a widow of 82, renowned for her belligerent language, formerly lived with a married daughter and family. 'My daughter's husband said to me, "You're nowt but an old nag." And I go up to him and says, "If I'm an old nag, it's thee has made me one with coming to look after thy wife and looking after thy children. You were fair to run to me when thy wife was ready to be confined. Put that in your pipe and smoke it." He said "It's time you went" and I gave him such a one across the chops and I says "Take that". I thought there'd be nowt left of me if I stopped with that lot' . . . Mrs Mooney is very infirm, is anaemic and incontinent and can scarcely walk. She had been living in a small house not only with her married daughter and son-in-law but with an unmarried daughter and five grandchildren . . . Her daughter was ill with a nervous complaint.

PETER TOWNSEND, *The Last Refuge*, 1962

---

from I Know Why the Caged Bird Sings

'Thou shall not be dirty' and 'Thou shall not be impudent' were the two commandments of Grandmother Henderson upon which hung our total salvation.

Each night in the bitterest winter we were forced to wash faces, arms, necks, legs and feet before going to bed. She used to add, with a smirk that unprofane people can't control when venturing into profanity, 'and wash as far as possible, then wash possible.'

We would go to the well and wash in the ice-cold clear water, grease our legs with the equally cold stiff Vaseline, then tiptoe into the house. We wiped the dust from our toes and settled down for schoolwork, cornbread, clabbered milk, prayers and bed, always in that order. Momma was famous for pulling the quilts off after we had fallen asleep to examine our feet. If they weren't clean enough for her, she took the switch (she kept one behind the bedroom door for emergencies) and woke up the offender with a few aptly placed burning reminders.

[. . .] The impudent child was detested by God and a shame to its parents and could bring destruction to its house and line. All adults had to be addressed as Mister, Missus, Miss, Auntie, Cousin, Unk, Uncle, Buhbah, Sister, Brother and a thousand other appellations indicating familial relationship and the lowliness of the addressor.

Everyone I knew respected these customary laws, except for the powhitetrash children.

[. . .] When I was around ten years old, those scruffy children caused me the most painful and confusing experience I had ever had with my grandmother.

One summer morning, after I had swept the dirt yard of leaves, spearmint-gum wrappers and Vienna-sausage labels, I raked the yellow-red dirt, and made half-moons carefully, so that the design stood out clearly and masklike. I put the rake behind the Store and came through the back of the house to find Grandmother on the front porch in her big, wide white apron. The apron was so stiff by virtue of the starch that it could have stood alone. Momma was admiring the yard, so I joined her. It truly looked like a flat redhead that had been raked with a big-toothed comb. Momma didn't say anything but I knew she liked it. She looked over toward the school principal's house and to the right at Mr McElroy's. She was hoping one of those community pillars would see the design before the day's business wiped it out. Then she looked upward to the school. My head had swung with hers, so at just about the same time we saw a troop of the powhitetrash kids marching over the hill and down by the side of the school.

I looked to Momma for direction. She did an excellent job of sagging from her waist down, but from the waist up she seemed to be pulling for the top of the oak tree across the road. Then she began to moan a hymn. Maybe not to moan, but the tune was so slow and the meter so strange that she could have been moaning. She didn't look at me again. When the children reached halfway down the hill, halfway to the Store, she said without turning, 'Sister, go on inside.'

I wanted to beg her, 'Momma, don't wait for them. Come on inside with me. If they come in the Store, you go to the bedroom and let me wait on them. They only frighten me if you're around. Alone I know how to handle them.' But of course I couldn't say anything, so I went in and stood behind the screen door.

Before the girls got to the porch I heard their laughter crackling and popping like pine logs in a cooking stove. I suppose my

lifelong paranoia was born in those cold, molasses-slow minutes. They came finally to stand on the ground in front of
Momma. At first they pretended seriousness. Then one of them
wrapped her right arm in the crook of her left, pushed out her
mouth and started to hum. I realized that she was aping my
grandmother. Another said, 'Naw, Helen, you ain't standing
like her. This here's it.' Then she lifted her chest, folded her
arms and mocked that strange carriage that was Annie
Henderson. Another laughed, 'Naw, you can't do it. Your
mouth ain't pooched out enough. It's like this.'

I thought about the rifle behind the door, but I knew I'd
never be able to hold it straight, and the .410, our sawed-off
shotgun, which stayed loaded and was fired every New Year's
night, was locked in the trunk and Uncle Willie had the key on
his chain. Through the fly-specked screen-door, I could see that
the arms of Momma's apron jiggled from the vibrations of her
humming. But her knees seemed to have locked as if they
would never bend again.

She sang on. No louder than before, but no softer either. No
slower or faster.

The dirt of the girls' cotton dresses continued on their legs, feet,
arms and faces to make them all of a piece. Their greasy uncol-
ored hair hung down, uncombed, with a grim finality. I knelt to
see them better, to remember them for all time. The tears that had
slipped down my dress left unsurprising dark spots, and made the
front yard blurry and even more unreal. The world had taken a
deep breath and was having doubts about continuing to revolve.

The girls had tired of mocking Momma and turned to other
means of agitation. One crossed her eyes, stuck her thumbs in
both sides of her mouth and said, 'Look here, Annie.'
Grandmother hummed on and the apron strings trembled. I
wanted to throw a handful of black pepper in their faces, to
throw lye on them, to scream that they were dirty, scummy
peckerwoods, but I knew I was as clearly imprisoned behind the
scene as the actors outside were confined to their roles.

[. . .] The tall one, who was almost a woman, said something very quietly, which I couldn't hear. They all moved backward from the porch, still watching Momma. For an awful second I thought they were going to throw a rock at Momma, who seemed (except for the apron strings) to have turned into stone herself. But the big girl turned her back, bent down and put her hands flat on the ground – she didn't pick up anything. She simply shifted her weight and did a hand stand.

Her dirty bare feet and long legs went straight for the sky. Her dress fell down around her shoulders, and she had on no drawers. The slick public hair made a brown triangle where her legs came together. She hung in the vacuum of that lifeless morning for only a few seconds, then wavered and tumbled. The other girls clapped her on the back and slapped their hands.

Momma changed her song to 'Bread of Heaven, bread of Heaven, feed me till I want no more.'

I found that I was praying too. How long could Momma hold out? What new indignity would they think of to subject her to? Would I be able to stay out of it? What would Momma really like me to do?

Then they were moving out of the yard, on their way to town. They bobbed their heads and shook their slack behinds and turned, one at a time:

''Bye, Annie.'

''Bye, Annie.'

''Bye, Annie.'

Momma never turned her head or unfolded her arms, but she stopped singing and said, ''Bye, Miz Helen, 'bye, Miz Ruth, 'bye, Miz Eloise.'

I burst. A firecracker July-the-Fourth burst. How could Momma call them Miz? The mean nasty things. Why couldn't she have come inside the sweet, cool store when we saw them breasting the hill? What did she prove? And then if they were dirty, mean and impudent, why did Momma have to call them Miz?

She stood another whole song through and then opened the screen door to look down on me crying in rage. She looked until I looked up. Her face was a brown moon that shone on me. She was beautiful. Something had happened out there, which I couldn't completely understand, but I could see that she was happy. Then she bent down and touched me as mothers of the church 'lay hands on the sick and afflicted' and I quieted.

'Go wash your face, Sister.' And she went behind the candy counter and hummed, 'Glory, glory, hallelujah, when I lay my burden down.'

I threw the well water on my face and used the weekday handkerchief to blow my nose. Whatever the contest had been out front, I knew Momma had won.

MAYA ANGELOU, 1971

---

from House Calls

Some time passes before I find house number 29. I need to find apartment 62. I have to go down dirty, slippery stairs to the basement. I walk down a dark corridor. I cannot see anything. It is dripping and damp, which would not be so bad on a hot day, but it smells of refuse and other kinds of rot. I extend my hand, so as not to bump into anything, and walk slowly. The janitor told me the door is at the end of the corridor. I feel something under my hand and push the door open. The room inside is half dark, the windows are small, and one of the windows looks out on the sidewalk. I look around. An old woman is lying on a kind of platform. She is all skin and bones. The pillow is dirty, and pieces of straw stick out of the holes in it. There is nothing else in the room.

I examine the old woman. She has a high temperature. She is weak and is coughing. Judging by these symptoms, I can tell she has influenza. I also notice that both her shoulders are red with dry, white blisters and callouses the size of a fist. I'm shocked: how could this decrepit old woman have been carrying such heavy loads on her shoulders? It seems she has been walking about two miles a day to the river Neva. 'They've been sending rafts of big logs fastened with crossbeams down the river. They sell the logs but chop up the beams and throw them on the riverbank. I don't know what they plan to do with them later, but if you give the workers some tobacco money, they let you take some of the wood.' The old woman has been going there daily, hauling half a dozen bundles of these beams on her shoulders. She was saving wood for the winter. Yesterday she could only bring two bundles, and today she can no longer even get up.

She is sixty years old. She recently buried her son, who died leaving her daughter-in-law with five children. The daughter-in-law works in a factory, and the old woman helps her out. She pleads with me to cure her. She's afraid her daughter-in-law will not be able to bring up the five grandchildren on her own. They are her beloved son's children.

I try to calm her. I tell her that there is nothing to worry about, that she only has a bad cold, and that she must stay in bed for a week. I give her some medicine with vodka, which I find in her cupboard, and cover her well. I give her some lime-leaf tea to brew instead of regular tea to make sure she takes more liquids. I tell her to send to my house tomorrow morning for medicine, which she is to drink, and give her some ointment for her callouses.

EKATERINA SLANSKAIA (b. 1853) in *Russia Through Women's Eyes*, 1996

from A Life of Mother Courage

[In the new South Africa,] I immediately thought of Cynthia Mthebe. It took about three weeks and a lot of searching, but a black colleague of mine, Victor Mathom, eventually tracked Cynthia down. She was still living in the camps in Tembisa, he said. And there were now two more children to feed, Thomas and Thandi, her grandchildren, who had been born since 1994.

And so on a southern summer morning six weeks ago I walked down a dusty track in Tembisa and shook hands with Cynthia Mthebe. She looked tired, and her clothes were covered in dust.

'So what's changed?' I asked. Cynthia pointed towards a shack of tin and wood and told me it was her new home. Jammed in on either side were the other squatter shacks and beyond them a huge, odoriferous rubbish dump. Squatterland is a place of bad smells – sweat, excrement, paraffin, wet clothes, stale beer, burning rubber, rubbish; of one small room where seven people sleep. The smell of the very poor.

Life had not really changed. The shack was better than the plastic sheet, but no mother would want to raise children there. In the summer the rains flooded the bedroom. In the winter the wind rattled through the holes in the corrugated sheeting. There was no sanitation, only a hole in the ground that Cynthia dug herself. Nor was there any electricity. Only 12 per cent of black South Africans have electricity. There was one big improvement. A water tap had been installed next to the shack.

Her life revolved around the children – five of her own and the two grandchildren. To feed her family she worked on the nearby rubbish dump. Every morning at 8am this 56-year-old climbed the hill to the dump to scavenge for tin cans. For every bag full of cans she received the equivalent of £3, and half of that went to the lorry that delivered them to the recycling depot.

It could take up to three days to fill a bag. Dirty, exhausting work for a woman who suffers from diabetes and high blood pressure. I went with her, several mornings in a row. There were perhaps 30 or 40 people 'working' the dump. As they tugged and probed, the flies rose in small clouds. 'It's dirty; I get sick. But what shall we do? We must work to put food on the table.'

FERGAL KEANE, *Independent*, 18 January 1999

Grandmothers of May Square

When in 1976, the Armed Forces seized control of the government of Argentina, they began to implement a systematic plan of destruction and of violation of the most fundamental human rights.

In this manner they caused 30,000 persons to disappear. Persons of all ages, from the most diverse social backgrounds. Among the disappeared there are hundreds of children who were kidnapped along with their parents or who were born in the clandestine detention centers where their pregnant mothers had been taken.

Many of the children were registered as children of members of the repressive forces; others were abandoned while others were left in institutions as children whose identity was unknown. In this way many children disappeared and their identity destroyed, depriving them of their rights, freedom and natural families.

In order to locate the disappeared children, the Grandmothers of May Square work on four different levels; denunciations before national and foreign governments, and before the judiciary, as well as advertisements in the press directed to the general public and personal investigations.

[. . .]

In order to help this work the Association has created a technical team made up of 18 professionals, including lawyers, doctors and psychologists.

Each one of the disappeared children has a case pending

before the judiciary, and when new information is received it is added to their files so that as time passes it will be able to determine the real identity of all the children and of those responsible for their kidnapping or illegal adoption.

[. . .]

Grandmothers of May Square is a civil non governmental organization which is not affiliated to any political party. Its aim is to locate the children who disappeared as a result of the political repressive methodology implemented by the military dictatorship and to restore them to their legitimate families, and to create the conditions which will guarantee that this terrible violation of the children's rights will never occur again, demanding punishment for all of those responsible for the repression.

We work for our children and for all of the children of future generations in the world, in order to preserve their identity, their roots and their history, the fundamental basis for human dignity.

As a result of the help from the Blood Center of New York and of the Association for the Advancement of Science (United States) it is now possible for us to prove that a child comes from a particular family with a certainty of up to 99.95% (Index of grandpaternity) based on very specialized blood tests of the grandparents, and if one of them has died, of the aunts and uncles of the child as well. These tests are now done at the Durand Hospital in Buenos Aires, a dependency of the Municipality of Buenos Aires.

The hematological tests consist of determining genetic markers as a result of the following tests:

(a) blood groups
(b) HLA or histocompatibility
(c) seric proteins
(d) blood cell enzymes

The results of these tests yield a conclusive proof both of the identity and affiliation of the child.

[. . .]

In 20 years of uninterrupted search we have been able to localize 58 disappeared children, out of which 8 had been assassinated. Of the rest, 31 are living with their true families and the others in close contact with their grandparents, in the process of adaptation, having been recovered their true identity and the true story of their lives. Some of these cases are still in process in the Justice Department.

In this work the Grandmothers draw upon the work of technical teams, integrated by proffessionals [sic] in the fields of justice, medicine, psychology and genetics.

Each and every one of the kids have an open case in the Justice Department, to which new denunciations are received constantly. These will constitute elements of proof that will determine the true identity of the kids as well as that of the people responsable [sic] for their kidnappings and illegal posession [sic].

In order to validate in time the blood analyses, we have installed a Bank of Genetic Data, created by law Nr. 23.511, where genetic maps of all the families of dissappeared children can be found.

ALL YOUNGSTERS WITH DOUBTS ABOUT THEIR TRUE
IDENTITY, COME TO US. WE WILL BE WAITING FOR YOU
WITH LOVE IN ORDER TO HELP YOU.

WE CONTINUE IN THE SEARCH FOR OUR
GRANDCHILDREN. IF YOU HAVE ANY INFORMATION
ABOUT WHERE WE CAN FIND THEM, WE WILL BE
HERE WAITING FOR YOUR CONTRIBUTION.

HELP US FIND THEM
GRANDMOTHERS OF MAY SQUARE, 1999

from The Woman That Never Evolved

A tale set in an unlikely scene: gray langur monkeys foraged peacefully along a shady lane leading to Abu's School for the Blind. The only sounds were the shuffling and crunching of monkeys eating dried plums, the cawing of Indian crows, and the tapping of white-tipped canes as two blind men clad in *dhotis* walked hand in hand up the tree-lined drive to the school.

In late July, at the monsoon's peak, the stately Bengal plums had provided all comers – birds, langurs, barefoot boys – with a sweet jamboree of burgundy-colored fruits. By September, only plums that had fallen to the ground remained. As usual, an aged female langur, whom I called Sol, fed on the periphery of the group, well apart from the other six adults, the five females, and the male that composed Hillside troop. Sol's black-gloved hands sifted nimbly through the leaf litter for remaindered jambol plums. When she found one, she turned her back on the others and privately gnawed at the husk with her worn teeth. Although she was the oldest female in the troop, Sol was subordinate to the others – nieces, daughters, and granddaughters – when it came to matters of food. If her feeding site caught the attention of others, some younger female would walk purposely toward Sol, mouth agape to expose pearly teeth – the universal vertebrate expression for 'move away', which Sol never contested.

Only the infants had eyes for a world beyond the leaf litter covering the plums, an enthusiasm for the ebullient society of other little monkeys. The four infants included one black new-born, two cream yearlings, and Scratch, so named for the transitional state of his fur when I first saw him – black with scratches of white. Langurs at birth are covered with feathery black hair. The pale skin beneath is nearly transparent and the blood visible under the skin tints the furless face, ears, and bottoms of the infant's feet flamingo pink. By the third month the naked face has turned completely black, like an adult's; the black fur starts to turn white, beginning with the hair on top of the head and then somewhat later, with a little white goatee. This gradual transformation from dark to cream color continues until some six months after birth, when the infant has turned white as a polar bear. At adolescence, the coat changes once again to the regulation silver-gray of a Hanuman langur. Scratch had just turned cream.

Two young langurs on the ground in late afternoon constitute a quorum for sport; four virtually guarantee handstands, tail-swinging, and mad tag. But on this afternoon no playfellow strayed from its mother. Scratch strained for less staid company, but each time he tried to leave, his mother hauled him back by one rear leg. The absence of play was the only discernible flaw in the Eden of that late afternoon.

For months the infants had been in jeopardy: on numerous occasions in the last few weeks the male I knew as Mug, the alpha male of Hillside troop, had stalked infants in his recently acquired harem. Twice in this period Scratch had been wounded as Mug's sharp canines grazed his skin. This was the other side of the coin: the dark side of a primate male's ability to remember particular consorts and to single out for special attention infants likely to be (or in this case, unlikely to be) his own. Scratch had been conceived in August of the previous year when another male (Shifty Leftless) had just taken over Hillside troop.

In the previous assaults, Mug's attack on Scratch had been thwarted by old Sol and a second defender, the three-legged female Pawless. These females had intervened, throwing themselves at the male and wrestling the infant from his grasp. But the odds lay in favor of Mug, who had the option to try, and try again, until he finally succeeded. So certain was Mug's eventual success that Scratch's mother had nearly ceased to resist – at least that is how I was tempted to interpret her lassitude.

Only days before, as the langurs fed in the swaying, flimsy

branches of a jacaranda, his mother (I called her Itch) had allowed Scratch to tumble from the tree, 12 feet to the grass. The male had been the first to reach the fallen infant. Sol and Pawless arrived second, Itch last, risking nothing as she hung back from the desperate tussle that ensued. It was left to the older females, one of them a grandmother past the age of reproduction, to rescue the infant.

[. . .] Few females in their breeding prime (such as Scratch's mother) could risk handicapping their own reproductive careers by helping another animal – even a close relative – in a dangerous fight. Self-sacrifice does occur, but it is exhibited by older female relatives approaching the end of their careers. For females such as old Sol, the reproductive cost of altruism in defense of her relatives would be very small, and the advantage would be real because their shared genes would be preserved by their act of defense. Younger females with more to lose must be more cautious.

SARAH BLAFFER HRDY, 1981

Near the Rover Sarsa, the two younger sons and their grandmother were captured by the Subhedar of Sirhind. The Subhedar tortured Mata Gujri to force her to accept the Islamic religion. But she was a brave woman and refused to succumb to any threats. One morning, in 1704, the Subhedar walled up her grandsons alive. As each brick was laid, she was offered Islam as an escape, but she continued to shout 'No, never!' That evening she was thrown from a high tower. With a smile she accepted her own death and that of her grandsons, for the cause of her community, religion and faith.

YASH KOLI (ed.), *The Women of Punjab*, 1983

from The Space Crone

If a space ship came by from the friendly natives of the fourth planet of Altair, and the polite captain of the space ship said, 'We have room for one passenger; will you spare us a single human being, so that we may converse at leisure during the long trip back to Altair and learn from an exemplary person the nature of the race?' – I suppose what most people would want to do is provide them with a fine, bright, brave young man, highly educated and in peak physical condition. A Russian cosmonaut would be ideal (American astronauts are mostly too old). There would surely be hundreds, thousands of volunteers, just such young men, all worthy. But I would not pick any of them. Nor would I pick any of the young women who would volunteer, some out of magnanimity and intellectual courage, others out of a profound conviction that Altair couldn't possibly be any worse for a woman than Earth is.

What I would do is go down to the local Woolworth's, or the local village marketplace, and pick an old woman, over sixty, from behind the costume jewelry counter or the betel-nut booth. Her hair would not be red or blonde or lustrous dark, her skin would not be dewy fresh, she would not have the secret of eternal youth. She might, however, show you a small snapshot of her grandson, who is working in Nairobi. She is a bit vague about where Nairobi is, but extremely proud of her grandson. She has worked hard at small, unimportant jobs all her life, jobs like cooking, cleaning, bringing up kids, selling little objects of adornment or pleasure to other people. She was a virgin once, a long time ago, and then a sexually potent fertile female, and then went through menopause. She has given birth several times and faced death several times – the same times. She is facing the final birth/death a little more nearly and clearly every day now. Sometimes her feet her something terrible. She never was educated to anything like her capacity, and that is a shameful waste and a crime against humanity, but so common a crime should not and cannot be hidden from Altair. And anyhow she's not dumb. She has a stock of sense, wit, patience, and experiential shrewdness, which the Altaireans might, or might not, perceive as wisdom. If they are wiser than we, then of course we don't know how they'd perceive it. But if they are wiser than we, they may know how to perceive that inmost mind and heart which we, working on mere guess and hope, proclaim to be humane. In any case, since they are curious and kindly, let's give them the best we have to give.

The trouble is, she will be very reluctant to volunteer. 'What would an old woman like me do on Altair?' she'll say. 'You ought to send one of those scientist men, they can talk to those funny-looking green people. Maybe Dr Kissinger should go. What about sending the Shaman?' It will be very hard to explain to her that we want her to go because only a person who has experienced, accepted, and acted the entire human condition – the essential quality of which is Change – can fairly represent humanity. 'Me?' she'll say, just a trifle slyly. 'But I never did anything.'

But it won't wash. She knows, though she won't admit it, that Dr Kissinger has not gone and will never go where she has gone, that the scientists and the shamans have not done what she has done. Into the space ship, Granny.

URSULA LE GUIN, 1976

———

'I am talking like my wife now! After all these years she sometimes falls into my silences and I carry on as she does. She is not just an old woman, you know. She wears old age like a bunch of fresh-cut flowers. She is old, advanced in years, *vieja*, but in Spanish we have another word for her, a word which tells you that she has grown with all these years. I think that is something one ought to hope for and work for and pray for all during life: to grow not only to become older but a bigger person. She is old, all right, *vieja*, but I will dare say in front of her: she is *una anciana*; with that I declare my respect and have to hurry back to the barn.'

ROBERT COLES, 'Una Anciana', 1970

VII

HELL'S GRANDMOTHERS

There's all kinds of different ways of being hellish. I start with a mythical grandmother overseeing hell itself, the Malayan Granny Long-breasts, and go on to ogress and witch grandmothers, those fantasies of female threat. Among them, the devouring lower lips – the vagina dentata – of the younger temptresses have turned into devouring upper lips and teeth drooling over the tender bodies of the young, in particular their grandchildren's. As a child I was haunted by an illustration in Perrault's version of the story of the Sleeping Beauty, showing the snake pit into which the prince's ogress mother orders her daughter-in-law and grandchildren to be thrown after finding herself tricked out of eating the two children. 'There are also wicked grandmothers, because there are wicked old women,' wrote the psychologist Helene Deutsch in 1945. 'Hence the term witch. These women do not want to be disturbed by their grandchildren, or . . . they want them for themselves, in burning envy of their daughters or daughters-in-law.'

'Wanting them for themselves' is another, metaphorical form of devouring the desired objects. I note, too, the conflation of the word 'wicked' with 'women who do not want to be disturbed by their grandchildren'. It is depressing to see a

woman psychologist, who made a career of describing the
female psyche, so judgemental of women who refuse to play
the role to which their age traditionally assigns them. But she
was very much of her time in doing so. Many writers before
1950 display a fundamental distrust if not hatred of women;
from Truby King with his strict injunctions against mothers
following their naturally loving instincts in rearing their
infants, to the author of the article I quote here, citing the
pernicious influence of the grandmother, who should be kept
away from the family at all costs. Such attitudes relate directly
to those that see women as virgins, earth mothers or sweet old
ladies, on the one hand, and as whores, harpies or witches, on
the other. On this reading, even a sweet, white-haired old
grandmother must be a destructive harridan underneath;
'Grandma Made Johnny Delinquent' – the title of another
such piece, unquoted here – sums it up.

It is not, of course, that there aren't plenty of hellish
grannies around in real life as well as fairy stories. Women
who've been hellish all their life aren't going to change the
moment they become grandmothers. Many 'sweet' old ladies,
like the endlessly, sweetly complaining one in Mary Lanvin's
story, can be a pain in the arse. Most research in this area
comes up with the obvious conclusion that women who've
warred with their children from the beginning and made their
lives hell are likely to find in their grandchildren yet more fuel
with which to wage the generation war, rendering family relationships more destructive than ever. (An only slightly less
obvious finding is that the influence of the grandmother is
more likely to be destructive where three generations live under
one roof – even if the grandmother does not hold more traditional views than the mother.)

That destructive mothers make destructive grandmothers
isn't invariable. My own children's paternal grandmother
played havoc in some ways with the psyches of her children,
yet turned into a grandmother who by sheer character and

individuality very much enriched her grandchildren's lives. And this without being an obviously useful grandmother in the traditional sense; willing childminder she wasn't. But 'she took us seriously', my daughter says. The old doctor I wrote of in the last section adored her grandchildren, but didn't know how to reach them. I never saw her read or sing to them; she barely touched, let alone cuddled them. The children responded by keeping a precise small physical distance from her, always. Yet she was a significant feature in their lives, of which the older ones talked matter-of-factly. This all goes to show that children tend to be far more tolerant than adults. For every grandchild who wishes their grandmother to hell or even to murder them as in the pieces with which I end this section, there are others who take seemingly undesirable, unaffectionate, hellish grandmothers exactly as they come; as one part of the background in which they grow up, and without which they'd be all the poorer. With them the grandmother may even not be hellish, however badly she may behave towards others. One factor in this could be precisely what we've seen earlier: that the grandmother is much less threatened by, certainly much less in competition with, children two generations away than she is with the one immediately below her. Her grandchildren bring out her best side in the way her own children never did, let alone her children-in-law, who grind their teeth at the very moment that their offspring shout for joy at the appearance of their 'hellish' yet, by them, beloved granny.

Even grandchildren of the same woman can see her quite differently. Grandchild A's granny from heaven can appear to Grandchild B as the granny from hell. My older boy cousins loved their grandmother – our grandmother. But I have a still older cousin, only seven years younger than my father, who claimed to have disliked her very much. The dislike stemmed partly, I suspect, from the fact that her father had been killed before she was born and the relationship between her mother and her grandmother had never been good. Yet my cousin was astonished by this; he assumed that everyone loved their grannies. Another example is the grandmother of a friend of mine who was in all respects hellish, a trial to everyone. But she loved my friend, her eldest granddaughter, spoiled her rotten, and gave her a sense of herself that nothing else did throughout her childhood.

Some women, of course, like some men, are just plain wicked; whether violent, abusive, self-centred, exploitative, or all of these things. In the category of wicked grandmothers, the one in the García Márquez story who prostitutes her granddaughter rates high. (Though not as high as Rose West, sexual abuser and murderer of her own daughter, among others. She was, is, a grandmother – and one who knits. It is another example of the added frisson words like 'murder' and 'rape' give to the word 'granny', whether the granny in question is the victim or the perpetrator, as in this case.)

But who says all women have to be good grandmothers, any more than all women have to be good mothers? Some women aren't any good at it, even if they'd like to be. Or at least they may be no good at being grandmother to the child in question; a grandchild and its grandmother can be incompatible, just like any two people, though it seldom leads to such cruelty as that inflicted on the Emperor Claudius by his grandmother Livia. The piece from John Cheever shows a grandmother and granddaughter with nothing to say to one another. In this case, it's a moot point whether the hell in a small way isn't the granny's as well as the child's.

In a small way, I said. For naturally this cannot compare with the hell of being murdered by your grandson, as in the extreme case of the eighteen-century grandmother with which the next section opens. Grandchildren can be from hell as surely as their grandmothers – even though reading between the lines of this account, it's easy to see the screwed-up boy gone to the bad and punished by remorse afterwards as well as by the gallows.

There are other kinds of hell for grandmothers; some of it related simply to being old: suffering from, or disabled by, one of the diseases of age, for instance. (An old woman I knew said mournfully at the accidental death of one of her friends, 'And she was the only one of us enjoying her old age.') There is the hell of being the grandmother of children in split families, where the daughter- or son-in-law denies her access, an increasingly common problem, leading to much grandparental depression. There is the hell of the immigrant Chinese grandmothers, finding themselves alone in a foreign culture, the language of which they don't understand, cut off from their children, let alone their grandchildren. Or, at the opposite end of things, the hell of those suffering from the exhaustion of never getting away from the grandchildren, as in the case of the AIDS grandmothers left raising their grandchildren, whom we met earlier, or the depressed grandmothers, cited by a letter printed in an Australian medical journal, overexploited by their daughters.

To be honoured, the old need to be few in relatively prosperous societies or in societies where their knowledge and skills are of value. In Korea, for instance, it was noted in 1951 that to reach the age of sixty 'puts one practically in the category of the immortals'; just so were the old treated. A Hopi Indian said that a long time ago people were taught to be good to the old, on the basis that their lives depended on them. But things change. Hopi women now are more likely to remark to their aged mothers, 'You are old, you can do nothing, you are not good for anything any more.' The wretchedness of the Xhosa grannies, a century ago, can still be seen many times over in many parts of the world. It always was and still is as typical of the treatment of old people as the respect accorded them in more sentimental accounts of the past.

In such circumstances, the only hope for the old is simply to have families who love and value them sufficiently to take good care of them when they are old and ill. This depends not only on their or their family's resources, but also, partly, on what kind of people they were to start with, and what kind of example they have set. There is a chilling – and telling – story from the Brothers Grimm where a small boy observing the way his parents treat his grandfather makes a wooden trough 'for them to eat out of when they are old'. In too many parts of the world, where the poor can scarcely feed themselves, there are few resources for those too old and sick to contribute anything. Organisations like Help the Aged and Adopt a Granny do what they can to fund projects for them in such communities. Undoubtedly some lives are transformed thereby. Far more are undoubtedly not. People reach into their pockets more willingly for children – noticing the old means being made aware of their own future disintegration. Perhaps those of us who find ourselves giving, do so as a wave to fortune as our own time slips on. 'Don't do this to me,' we cry – for what it's worth.

For we are aware, too, of horrific treatment of old people, particularly the demented, in homes for the old to be found in Western countries, despite the best efforts of their offspring to locate sympathetic environments for their aged parents. Even when they remain at home, old people can be abused. The reports of 'granny bashing' become more frequent; sometimes as exhausted carers of the demented old finally lose patience; sometimes out of more considered cruelty. Harry Graham's 'Ruthless Rhyme' about Hannah may be a joke, as indeed is his rhyme called 'Indifference'. Yet indifference is the commonest hell encountered by far too many of the old. No less than abuse, it is, in reality, very far from funny.

Grannies from Hell

Granny Long-breasts

After death, the Sakai say that 'Granny Lanyut' or 'Long-breasts', the Queen of Hell, washes their sin-blackened souls in hot water. All men's souls must be purified, and after death they proceed to Něraka (the Infernal Regions), where they come before the aforesaid personage, who is described as a giantess with pendulous breasts, which she throws over her shoulders . . . She makes the souls (after their purification) walk along the horizontal edge of a monstrous chopper, which hangs with point turned away from her over a big vessel, to the middle of which it nearly reaches. The water in this vessel is kept at boiling point, Granny Lanyut herself stoking the fire. A block of wood juts out from the opposite side of the copper so as nearly to meet the point of the blade, and the souls have to spring across the intervening gap. Bad souls fall in, good ones escape.

SKEAT AND BLAGDEN, *Races of the Malay Peninsula*, 1906

———

from The Sleeping Beauty in the Wood

Two whole years passed since the marriage of the prince and princess, and during that time they had two children. The first, a daughter, was called 'Dawn', while the second, a boy, was named 'Day', because he seemed even more beautiful than his sister.

Many a time the queen told her son that he ought to settle down in life. She tried in this way to make him confide in her, but he did not dare to trust her with his secret. Despite the affection which he bore her, he was afraid of his mother, for she came of a race of ogres, and the king had only married her for her wealth.

It was whispered at the Court that she had ogrish instincts, and that when little children were near her she had the greatest difficulty in the world to keep herself from pouncing on them.

No wonder the prince was reluctant to say a word.

But at the end of two years the king died, and the prince found himself on the throne. He then made public announcement of his marriage, and went in state to fetch his royal consort from her castle. With her two children beside her she made a triumphal entry into the capital of her husband's realm.

Some time afterwards the king declared war on his neighbour, the Emperor Cantalabutte. He appointed the queen-mother as regent in his absence, and entrusted his wife and children to her care.

He expected to be away at war for the whole of the summer, and as soon as he was gone the queen-mother sent her daughter-in-law and the two children to a country mansion in the forest. This she did that she might be able the more easily to gratify her horrible longings. A few days later she went there herself, and in the evening summoned the chief steward.

'For my dinner to-morrow,' she told him, 'I will eat little Dawn.'

'Oh, Madam!' exclaimed the steward.

'That is my will,' said the queen; and she spoke in the tones of an ogre who longs for raw meat.

'You will serve her with a piquant sauce,' she added.

The poor man, seeing plainly that it was useless to trifle with an ogress, took his big knife and went up to little Dawn's chamber. She was at that time four years old, and when she came running with a smile to greet him, flinging her arms round his neck and coaxing him to give her some sweets, he burst into tears, and let the knife fall from his hand.

Presently he went down to the yard behind the house, and slaughtered a young lamb. For this he made so delicious a sauce that his mistress declared she had never eaten anything so good.

At the same time the steward carried little Dawn to his wife, and bade the latter hide her in the quarters which they had below the yard.

Eight days later the wicked queen summoned her steward again.

'For my supper,' she announced, 'I will eat little Day.'

The steward made no answer, being determined to trick her as he had done previously. He went in search of little Day, whom he found with a tiny foil in his hand, making brave passes – though he was but three years old – at a big monkey. He carried him off to his wife, who stowed him away in hiding with little Dawn. To the ogress the steward served up, in place of Day, a young kid so tender that she found it surpassingly delicious.

So far, so good. But there came an evening when this evil queen again addressed the steward.

'I have a mind,' she said, 'to eat the queen with the same sauce as you served with her children.'

This time the poor steward despaired of being able to practise another deception. The young queen was twenty years old, without counting the hundred years she had been asleep. Her skin, though white and beautiful, had become a little tough, and what animal could he possibly find that would correspond to her? He made up his mind that if he would save his own life he must kill the queen, and went upstairs to her apartment determined to do the deed once and for all. Goading himself into a rage he drew his knife and entered the young queen's chamber, but a reluctance to give her no moment of grace made him repeat respectfully the command which he had received from the queen-mother.

'Do it! do it!' she cried, baring her neck to him; 'carry out the order you have been given! Then once more I shall see my children, my poor children that I loved so much!'

Nothing had been said to her when the children were stolen away, and she believed them to be dead.

The poor steward was overcome by compassion. 'No, no, Madam,' he declared; 'you shall not die, but you shall certainly see your children again. That will be in my quarters, where I have hidden them. I shall make the queen eat a young hind in place of you, and thus trick her once more.'

Without more ado he led her to his quarters, and leaving her there to embrace and weep over her children, proceeded to cook a hind with such art that the queen-mother ate it for her supper with as much appetite as if it had indeed been the young queen.

The queen-mother felt well satisfied with her cruel deeds, and planned to tell the king, on his return, that savage wolves had devoured his consort and his children. It was her habit, however, to prowl often about the courts and alleys of the mansion, in the hope of scenting raw meat, and one evening she heard the little boy Day crying in a basement cellar. The child was weeping because his mother had threatened to whip him for some naughtiness, and she heard at the same time the voice of Dawn begging forgiveness for her brother.

The ogress recognised the voices of the queen and her children, and was enraged to find she had been tricked. The next morning, in tones so affrighting that all trembled, she ordered a huge vat to be brought into the middle of the courtyard. This she filled with vipers and toads, with snakes and serpents of every kind, intending to cast into it the queen and her children, and the steward with his wife and serving-girl. By her command these were brought forward, with their hands tied behind their backs.

There they were, and her minions were making ready to cast them into the vat, when into the courtyard rode the king! Nobody had expected him so soon, but he had travelled post-haste. Filled with amazement, he demanded to know what this horrible spectacle meant. None dared tell him, and at that moment the ogress, enraged at what confronted her, threw herself head foremost into the vat, and was devoured on the instant by the hideous creatures she had placed in it.

The king could not but be sorry, for after all she was his mother; but it was not long before he found ample consolation in his beautiful wife and children.

CHARLES PERRAULT, 1697, translated by A. E. Johnson

The thing that interests me much in my life was when my great-grandmother who was very active in the act of witch-craft died. During her lifetime she disturbed children much in the family and it was herself who caused my brother and sister's death. When she died, her head was cut off by an active witch doctor who brought the head and placed it in front of his shrine so that it might no longer come back through a devil spirit to destroy the family as she did through her life-time. She was the only woman who caused a lot of destructions in my father's family and since she died there was peace in the family.

Quoted in IRIS ANDRESKI, Old Wives Tales, 1970

---

from Sun Chief

When I was four or five I was captured by the Spider Woman and nearly lost my life. One morning in May as I played in the plaza in my shirt my father said that he was going to his field. I wanted to go. But as he filled his water jar he said, 'You had better stay here, my jar does not hold enough for us both.' I began to cry. As he started down the south side of the mesa I followed along the narrow path between two great stones and came to the bottom of the foothill near the Spider Woman's shrine. My father had disappeared among the rocks. I happened to look to my left at a rock by the shrine where some clay dishes had been placed as offerings to the Spider Woman. There sat the old woman herself, leaning forward and resting her chin in her hands. Beside her was a square hole in the ground. She said, 'You are here at the right time. I have been waiting for you. Come into my house with me.' I had heard enough about the Spider Woman to know that no ordinary person ever sits by the shrine. I stood helpless, staring at her. 'Come into my house,' she repeated. 'You have been walking on my trail, and now I have a right to you as my grandson.'

My father had heard me crying as I followed him, so he asked a man whom he met coming up the mesa to take me back to the village. As this man came around the corner of a rock the old woman disappeared. She had been sitting close by the pile of firewood that the people had placed on the shrine for her as they passed up and down the mesa.

I thought I had not moved, but when the man saw me I was standing right under the rock and was being drawn into the hole. The Spider Woman has the power to do strange things. I had been caught in her web and could not step backward. When the man saw me he shouted, 'Boy, get out of the shrine! The Spider Woman may take you into her house!' I laughed in a silly manner but could not move. The man rushed up quickly and pulled me out of the shrine. As he took me up the mesa I felt sick and was unable to play any more that day.

During the night I had an awful dream. The Spider Woman came for me and said that now I belonged to her. I sat up and saw her heel as she disappeared through the door. Crying, I told my parents that the Spider Woman was after me. Every time I closed my eyes I could see the old woman coming again. My father, mother, and grandfather talked about what had happened at the shrine and took turns watching me. Once when I cried and said to my father, 'The Spider Woman will get me,' he put his hand on my head and replied, 'Well, my boy, you went too near her shrine. I fear you are hers now and that you will not live long.'

LEO SIMMONS (ed.), 1942

---

from Why Don't You Come Live with Me It's Time

Quickly Grandmother came to hug me, settled me into my chair as if I were a much smaller child sitting there at the kitchen table, my feet not touching the floor; and there was my special bowl, the bowl Grandmother kept for me, sparkling yellow with lambs running around the rim; yes, and my special spoon too, a beautiful silver spoon with the initial C engraved on it which Grandmother kept polished, so I understood I was safe, nothing could harm me; Grandmother would not let anything happen to me so long as I was there. She poured my oatmeal into my dish; she was saying, 'It's true we must all die one day, darling, but not just yet, you know, not tonight, you've just come to visit, haven't you, dear? and maybe you'll stay? maybe you won't ever leave? *now it's time?*'

The words *it's time* rang with a faint echo.

I can hear them now: *it's time: time.*

Grandmother's arms were shapely and attractive, her skin pale and smooth and delicately translucent as a candled egg, and I saw that she was wearing several rings, the wedding band that I knew but others, sparkling with light, and there so thin

were my arms beside hers, my hands that seemed so small;
sparrow-sized, and my wrists so bony, and it came over me, the
horror of it, that meat and bone should define my presence in
the universe; the point of entry in the universe that was *me* that
was *me* that was *me*, and no other, yet of a fragile materiality
that any fire could consume. 'Oh, Grandmother – I'm so
afraid!' I whimpered, seeing how I would be burnt to ash, and
Grandmother comforted me, and settled me more securely
into the chair, pressed my pretty little spoon between my fingers, and said, 'Darling, don't think of such things, just *eat*.
Grandmother made this for *you*.'

I was eating the hot oatmeal, which was a little too hot, but
creamy as I loved it; I was terribly hungry, eating like an infant
at the breast so blindly my head bowed and eyes nearly shut
brimming with tears and Grandmother asked, *Is it good? Is it
good?* – she'd spooned in some dark honey too – *Is it good?* and
I nodded mutely; I could taste grains of brown sugar that
hadn't melted into the oatmeal, stark as bits of glass, and I
realized they were in fact bits of glass, some of them large as
grape pits, and I didn't want to hurt Grandmother's feelings
but I was fearful of swallowing the glass so as I ate I managed
to sift the bits through the chewed oatmeal until I could
maneuver it into the side of my mouth into a little space
between my lower right gum and the inside of my cheek, and
Grandmother was watching, asking *Is it good?* and I said, 'Oh,
yes,' half choking and swallowing, 'oh, *yes*.'

A while later when neither Grandmother nor Harry was
watching I spat out the glass fragments into my hand but I
never knew absolutely, I don't know even now, if they were
glass and not for instance grains of sand or fragments of
eggshell or even bits of brown sugar crystalized into such a
form not even boiling oatmeal could dissolve it.

JOYCE CAROL OATES, 1992

The Grandmother: A Problem in Child-Rearing

A little episode which occurred in my consulting room a short time ago caused me to turn my thoughts on the influence which grandmothers exert in the lives of children. Out in my waiting room I heard the high-pitched voice of a woman haranguing someone incessantly in a sing-song, shrill baby talk which did violence to the ear. No child's tones were heard in answer. From this I assumed that here was a case of completely senseless motherhood expostulating with a small infant and venting her maternal satisfaction in this unnatural and disturbing manner. As a matter of fact, the woman who finally entered my office was almost 70 years old; furthermore, during the course of the consultation she showed herself to be an experienced and worldly-wise individual. She had in charge her 6-year-old granddaughter who had recently made an airplane journey from a foreign country unescorted, and who appeared to be a self-sufficient young lady. None the less, once the greetings were over, the child drew back apprehensively and burst into shrieks – this despite the fact that, as they were approaching the room, the grandmother kept assuring her insistently that 'Uncle Doctor' was exceedingly kind, and that he would hardly hurt her at all. Even to the untrained eye the girl was a picture of exuberant health; a thoroughgoing examination revealed no physical flaws. The grandmother, however, was extremely dissatisfied with everything about the child: her looks, the state of her nutrition, the quantity of food she ate and the amount of time she slept. Accepting the grandmother's complaints at their face value, one would have expected to encounter a seriously undernourished child in perilous physical condition. Whenever the grandmother found occasion to address her charge, she abandoned her natural manner of speech and fell promptly into the loud, artificial baby jargon which obviously perplexed the child and distressed her. My reassuring observations concerning the patient's physical condition and my diplomatically worded but authoritative advice concerning her upbringing fell upon unfriendly ears. Alluding to her own age and to the 4 children whom she had raised, the grandmother gave me to understand that neither her daughter-in-law – who, to be sure, was still only a child herself – nor I knew anything about the care and rearing of children. I was quite certain that her disappointment in me would lead her to consult my colleagues one after another until she found a more 'sympathetic' and more open ear.

It is not necessary to dwell overlong on this particular example. Every pediatrician who conceives that the proper upbringing of the children who are committed to his care is a part of his task, will have made this discovery: grandmothers exert an extraordinarily pernicious influence on their grandchildren. This is true whether the children are sent to live for longer or shorter periods of time under the care of the grandmother in her own domicile, or whether the grandmother merely resides in the home of the children's parents and, on the surface at least, plays a relatively unimportant role. My experience has persuaded me that this phenomenon represents the operation of a law; it is this conviction which emboldens me to call attention to the fact that the relationship between grandmother and grandchild constitutes a true pedagogic problem. Every pediatrician hears repeatedly the monotonous complaint that a child who was previously entirely docile has grown completely refractory since spending a summer with his grandmother. It is hard enough to look after a healthy infant with the grandmother about; when it comes to a sick child innumerable difficulties crop up if the grandmother is the nurse or even if she merely shares the responsibility of caring for the patient. Difficult as it may be to examine the occasional refractory child, this task becomes impossible when the grandmother enters upon the scene, and particularly when she is the only person in attendance.

[. . .] Certainly, that which has been referred to as a law cannot be explained on the basis of the unreasonableness of this or that grandmother. Some grandmothers, indeed, are marvellously reasonable – magnanimous, if you will; this does not keep them from exerting an unfortunate influence on their grandchildren from the moment they start to function in their official capacity. The difficulty, then, arises not so much from the personality of the individual as from something inherent in being a grandmother.

This something is neither the age nor the old-fashioned ideas of the grandmother. Now and then grandmothers are young; the young ones, however, must be classed with the rest. Sometimes mothers are elderly, but their age does not beget the same complications as those supplied by the grandmother. It does not solve our problem to generalize contemptuously concerning the outworn concepts of grandmothers; many of them have model views about raising children which they have tested and proved with their own families. This does not mean, however, that they are able to rear their children's children according to these principles. One must not forget that the grandmother's emotional attitude toward the child is apt to cause her to modify these principles in a very thoroughgoing manner in applying them to the grandchild; furthermore, she may fail to recognize the modification. The grandmother's peculiar attitude towards the child, not her age, constitutes the crux of the situation [. . .]

The objection can be advanced and sustained by example that these remarks are far from applicable to all grandmothers; indeed that some grandmothers are entirely unobjection-able [. . .] The ideal grandmother keeps to her proper place in her own circle as well as in that of her children and grandchildren. She does not overstep the limits of her position, she holds herself free of resentment and preserves a suitable aloofness in her relations with both child and grandchild. It is patent, however, that the ideal is seldom realized, whereas the tendency to succumb to human weakness is universal [. . .] These paragraphs have attempted to point out the possibilities of error and misdirection inherent in the relationship between grandmother and child, and to focus attention on the danger with which this relationship menaces the child. The practical conclusion is that the grandmother is not a suitable custodian of the care and rearing of her grandchild: she is a disturbing factor against which we are obligated to protect the child according to the best of our ability.

HERMANN VOLLMER MD, 1938

from Bodily Harm

One of the first things I can remember, says Rennie, is standing in my grandmother's bedroom. The light is coming in through the window, weak yellowish winter light, everything is very clean, and I'm cold. I know I've done something wrong, but I can't remember what. I'm crying, I'm holding my grandmother around both legs, but I didn't think of them as legs, I thought of her as one solid piece from the neck down to the bottom of her skirt. I feel as if I'm holding on to the edge of something, safety, if I let go I'll fall, I want forgiveness, but she's prying my hands away finger by finger. She's smiling; she was proud of the fact that she never lost her temper.

I know I will be shut in the cellar by myself. I'm afraid of that, I know what's down there, a single light bulb which at least they leave on, a cement floor which is always cold, cobwebs, the winter coats hanging on hooks beside the wooden stairs, the furnace. It's the only place in the house that isn't clean. When I was shut in the cellar I always sat on the top stair. Sometimes there were things down there, I could hear them moving around, small things that might get on you and run up your legs. I'm crying because I'm afraid, I can't stop, and even if I hadn't done anything wrong I'd still be put down there, for making a noise, for crying.

Laugh and the world laughs with you, said my grandmother. *Cry and you cry alone.* For a long time I hated the smell of damp mittens.

MARGARET ATWOOD, 1981

───────────

His grandmother, Augusta, always treated [Claudius] with the utmost contempt, spoke to him but rarely, and when she did admonish him on any occasion, it was in writing, very curt and sharp, or by messengers.

SUETONIUS (c. 70–c. 122), *Lives of the Twelve Caesars*

───────────

from I, Claudius

The day was chosen for our betrothal. I asked Germanicus about Urgulanilla, but he was as much in the dark as I was, and seemed a little ashamed of having consented to the marriage without making careful enquiries beforehand. He was very happy with Agrippina and wanted me to be happy too. Well, the day came, a 'lucky' one, and there I was again in my chaplet and clean gown again waiting at the family-altar for the bride to arrive. 'The third time's lucky,' said Germanicus. 'I am sure she's a beauty, really, and kind and sensible and just the sort for you.' But was she? Well, in my life I have had many cruel bad jokes played on me, but I think that this was the cruellest and worst. Urgulanilla was – well, in brief, she

lived up to her name, which is the Latin form of Herculanilla.
A young female Hercules she indeed was. Though only fifteen years old, she was over six foot three inches in height
and still growing, and broad and strong in proportion, with
the largest feet and hands I have ever seen on any human
being in my life with the single exception of the gigantic
Parthian hostage who walked in a certain triumphal procession many years later. Her features were regular but heavy
and she wore an almost perpetual scowl. She stooped. She
talked as slowly as my uncle Tiberius (whom, by the way, she
resembled closely – there was even talk of her being really his
daughter). She had no learning, wit, accomplishments, or
any endearing qualities [. . .] I am a pretty good actor, and
though the solemnity of the ceremony was broken by smirks,
whispered jokes and repressed titters from the company,
Urgulanilla had no cause to blame me for this indecorous-
ness. After it was over the two of us were summoned into the
presence of Livia and Urgulania. When the door was shut
and we stood there facing them – myself nervous and fidgety,
Urgulanilla massive and expressionless and clenching and
unclenching her great fists – the solemnity of these two evil
old grandmothers gave way, and they burst into uncontrolled
laughter. I had never heard either of them laugh like that
before and the effect was frightening. It was not decent
healthy laughter but a hellish sobbing and screeching, like
that of two old drunken prostitutes watching a torture or
crucifixion. 'Oh, you two beauties!' sobbed Livia at last,
wiping her eyes, 'What wouldn't I give to see you in bed
together on your wedding night! It would be the funniest
scene since Deucalion's Flood!'

'And what happened particularly funny on that famous
occasion, my dear?' asked Urgulania.

'Why, don't you know? God destroyed the whole word
with a flood, except Deucalion and his family, and a few animals that took refuge on the mountain tops. Haven't you

read Aristophanes's *Flood*? It's my favourite play of his. The scene is laid on Mount Parnassus. Various animals are assembled, unfortunately only one of each kind, and each thinks himself the sole survivor of his species. So in order to replenish the earth somehow with animals they have to mate with one another in spite of moral scruples and obvious difficulties. The Camel is betrothed by Deucalion to the She-Elephant.'

'Camel and Elephant! That's a fine one!' cackled Urgulania. 'Look at Tiberius Claudius's long neck and skinny body and long silly face. And my Urgulanilla's great feet and great flapping ears, and little pig-eyes! Ha, Ha, Ha, Ha! And what was their offspring? Giraffe? Ha, Ha, Ha, Ha!'

'The play doesn't get that far. Iris comes on the stage for the messenger speech and reports another refuge of animals on Mount Atlas. Iris breaks off the nuptials just in time.'

'Was the Camel disappointed?'

'Oh, most bitterly.'

'And the Elephant?'

'The Elephant just scowled.'

'Did they kiss on parting?'

'Aristophanes does not tell. But I'm sure they did. Come on, Beasts. Kiss!'

I smiled foolishly, Urgulanilla scowled.

'Kiss, I say,' Livia insisted in a voice that meant that we had to obey.

So we kissed, and started the old women on their hysterics again. When we were outside the room again I whispered to Urgulanilla: 'I'm sorry. It's not my fault.' But she did not answer except to scowl more deeply than before.

ROBERT GRAVES, 1936

from Four Women Living the Revolution

Mónica

Mami was very upset when Paco and I separated. She's retired from her job and now that she's old and has nothing to do, she leads a rather lonely, empty life. She wishes we'd go see her, talk with her, listen to her, but it isn't in us to understand the problems of her old age and help her bear them or even to sit and listen to her talk. She's sixty-five now, and it's only fair that in whatever time is left her, I should be considerate and remember to visit her. I really do make a conscious effort to act like a loving daughter because I've analysed all the things she did and now I understand why. I even kiss her when I arrive, but I can't bring myself to caress her. If she caresses me, it feels odd.

When she asks, 'Why didn't you phone me?' I start thinking up some excuse, 'Well, old lady, you see . . . ,' but with *mami* you can't say the slightest thing without having her complain that her children no longer respect her. Perhaps this is the moment when we should give her moral support, draw closer to her, try to understand her. But that's not the way it is; we haven't done any of that since we've married. My brother and sister have pulled away even more than I. *Mami* says that I'm the best of the lot, that none of us pays enough attention to her, and I think she's right. We've rejected her somewhat.

But she's a very difficult person to get along with. When you try to get close to her, her personality jars against you. She's frightfully domineering and still tries to rule our lives. I can't bear that. When she visits me on a Sunday, she tries to change my house around, and she interferes in important matters too, criticizing the woman who takes care of my children. *Mami* knows perfectly well that whether my children are at home or in an institution, whoever takes care of them is going to be human and have human defects. But she also knows that my children mean a lot to me and I'm not going to turn them over to just anybody. I say, 'Look, *mami*, whoever looks after my children is entitled to privileges in my home.' But that doesn't stop her. She nags and nags. 'None of you loves me anymore. I'm nothing but a burden to my daughters.' The best solution is to stay away from her. I've been more or less a good daughter, according to what was expected – one who studies, who marries a man of whom her parents approve, who devotes herself to her home and to providing her parents with grandchildren. Actually I don't think there is such a thing as a good daughter. We're simply individuals who respond to certain situations. I believe I responded pretty well, considering my temperament and environment.

OSCAR LEWIS ET AL., 1977

from Happiness

Certainly we knew that in spite of his lavish heart our grandfather had failed to provide our grandmother with enduring happiness. He had passed that job on to Mother. And Mother had not made too good a fist of it, even when Father was living and she had him – and later, us children – to help.

As for Father Hugh, he had given our grandmother up early in the game. 'God Almighty couldn't make that woman happy,' he said one day, seeing Mother's face, drawn and pale with fatigue, preparing for the nightly run over to her own mother's flat that would exhaust her utterly.

There were evenings after she came home from the library where she worked when we saw her stand with the car keys in her hand, trying to think which would be worse – to slog over

there on foot, or take out the car again. And yet the distance
was short. It was Mother's day that had been too long.

'Weren't you over to see her this morning?' Father Hugh
demanded.

'No matter!' said Mother. She was no doubt thinking of
the forlorn face our grandmother always put on when she was
leaving. ('Don't say good night, Vera,' Grandmother would
plead. 'It makes me feel too lonely. And you never can tell –
you might slip over again before you go to bed!')

'Do you know the time?' Bea would say impatiently, if she
happened to be with Mother. Not indeed that the lateness of
the hour counted for anything, because in all likelihood
Mother *would* go back, if only to pass by under the window
and see that the lights were out, or stand and listen and make
sure that as far as she could tell all was well.

'I wouldn't mind if she was happy,' Mother said.

'And how do you know she's not?' we'd ask.

'When people are happy, I can feel it. Can't you?'

We were not sure. Most people thought our grandmother
was a gay creature, a small birdy being who even at a great age
laughed like a girl, and – more remarkably – sang like one, as
she went about her day. But beak and claw were of steel. She'd
think nothing of sending Mother back to a shop three times if
her errands were not exactly right. 'Not sugar like that – that's
too fine; it's not castor sugar I want. But *not* as coarse as *that*,
either. I want an in-between kind.'

Provoked one day, my youngest sister, Linda, turned and gave
battle. 'You're mean!' she cried. 'You love ordering people about!'

Grandmother preened, as if Linda had acclaimed an attrib-
ute. 'I was always hard to please,' she said. 'As a girl, I used to
be called Miss Imperious.'

And Miss Imperious she remained as long as she lived, even
when she was a great age. Her orders were then given a wry
twist by the fact that as she advanced in age she took to calling
her daughter Mother, as we did.

There was one great phrase with which our grandmother opened every sentence: 'if only'. 'If only,' she'd say, when we came to visit her – 'if only you'd come earlier, before I was worn out expecting you!' Or if we were early, then if only it was later, after she'd had a rest and could enjoy us, be *able* for us. And if we brought her flowers, she'd sigh to think that if only we'd brought them the previous day she'd have had a visitor to appreciate them, or say it was a pity the stems weren't longer. If only we'd picked a few green leaves, or included some buds, because, she said disparagingly, the poor flowers we'd brought were already wilting. We might just as well not have brought them! As the years went on, Grandmother had a new bead to add to her rosary: if only her friends were not all dead! By their absence, they reduced to nil all *real* enjoyment in anything. Our own father – her son-in-law – was the one person who had ever gone close to pleasing her. But even here there had been a snag. 'If only he was my real son!' she used to say with a sigh.

MARY LAVIN, 1981

———

from The Provincial Lady in America

Sept 1st. Call upon aged neighbour, Mrs Blenkinsop, to meet married daughter, newly returned from India with baby . . . The baby [. . .] crawls about the floor and is said to be like his father. At this, however, old Mrs Blenkinsop suddenly rebels, and announces that dear Baby is the image of herself as a tiny, and demands the immediate production of her portrait at four years old to prove her words. Portrait is produced, turns out to be a silhouette, showing pitch-black little profile with ringlets and necklace on white background, and we all say yes, we quite see what she means.

Baby very soon afterwards begins to cry – can this be cause and effect? – and is taken away by Barbara.

Mrs B. tells us that it is a great joy to have them with her, she has given up the whole of the top floor to them and it means engaging an extra girl, and of course dear Baby's routine has to come before everything, so that her little house is upside-down – but that, after all, is nothing. She is old, her life is over, nothing now matters to her except the welfare and happiness of her loved ones.

Everyone rather dejected at these sentiments . . .

E. M. DELAFIELD, 1934

---

from The End of the Reign of Queen Helen
(1894–1985)

I remember first the mouth. Always open, mauve tongue cracked down the center from seven decades of use, disappearing into cavernous blackness beyond. Granny Gombar had a voice like a bull horn, ruined she said, from swallowing a fish bone at twenty-five. I suspected the Salems. I see one smoldering, caught in the bird's beak of a silver sculptured ashtray. I see her, through a haze of years and smoke, smoke and sun, slatting through blinds from the treeless yard. The affronted black eyes behind the butterfly glasses, the yellow skin, flat nose, white, tightly curled hair: the girth loosely encased in a flowered shift, the wide feet in cloth wedge sandals, and the wide mouth – always open.

'My son the doctor,' she bragged to her neighbors about my father who, in fact, was only a dentist.

That voice, screaming repartee at her powder blue parakeet Bootsie (1962–1965). 'You're late!' she'd bellow into the phone to my parents who used to drop my sister and me at her apartment for a few terrifying hours every few weeks. There, by the tea table, under the embroidered portrait of three cats in dresses jumping into a lily-pad pond, among the white ceramic figurines of shepherdesses and swans in eighteenth-century dress, Granny reigned.

She bought us coloring books, but wouldn't let us color. We sat idly by, watching her neatly fill in Bambi, Cinderella, or Lady and the Tramp. She never let us go near Bootsie. I wanted to take him/her/it, touch its pale blue feathers and squeeze it so its little purpley-black tongue would pop out. Bootsie was the last in line of her revered pets, the most notorious of which was a canine called Mitzi (1938–1947) who was fed scrap meat from a restaurant. 'That dog ate better than we did,' my father recalls bitterly.

'Eat! Eat! Eat!' she'd bellow at me. I was frozen with terror.

'You're not a Gombar!' she would shout at six-year-old me. 'You're like your mother's family. You've got those round cat eyes.'

'I was a beauty,' she would sometimes proclaim. Impossible to tell. Few photographs were taken in that family, as if there was nothing to celebrate. The earliest traceable picture of her is at sixty, her looks already obscured by glasses and garish fashions. The occasion: my father's college graduation (first in the family), where he stands pompadoured, but otherwise like a prisoner between his dour father and gloating mother.

'This is the year,' she would proclaim. 'I had a dream.' Hand over heart, upper arms billowing, bulk settled into the big easy chair. 'For my funeral I want a high mass and I want her (pointing to my older sister) to sing "Ave Maria".' Rosemary had the voice.

'She'll never die,' her sons would declare.

CHRISTINA GOMBAR, 1994

from Memoirs of Madame de La Tour du Pin

Meanwhile, the waters of Spa were shortening my poor mother's life. She was very unwilling to return to Hautefontaine, being quite sure that my grandmother would greet her, as she always did, with scenes and furious rages. She was not mistaken. But her health was worsening with every minute that passed and she began to long, as does everyone attacked by this cruel illness, for a change of air. She wanted to go to Italy and asked to return to Paris first. My grandmother consented, and it was only then that she began to realise the true state of her unfortunate daughter's health. At least, it was from that moment that she spoke of her state as hopeless, as indeed it was.

When we reached Paris, my grandmother gave up her own apartment to my mother as it was larger, and lavished on her every possible care. This was in such strong contrast with the outrageous manner in which I had seen her treat my mother only a few months before that I could not believe that she was sincere. Years later, when I was older and experienced, I realised that in a passionate nature, such sudden reverses of feeling are quite natural . . .

During her last days my mother was surrounded with care [. . .] But no one spoke of the Sacraments of or bringing a priest to her. There was no chaplain in that Archbishop's household. The maids, though some of them were undoubtedly devout, were too much in fear of my grandmother to dare to speak out. My mother herself did not realise that her last hours had come. She died of suffocation in my nurse's arms on the 7th of September 1782.

I was told the sad news the following morning by Madame Nagle, a good old friend of my mother's whom I found at my bedside when I awoke. She said that my grandmother had left the house, that I was to get up and go to her and beg her protection and care; she said that my future lay now in my grandmother's hands; that she was on very unfriendly terms with my father, who was in America, and that she would certainly disinherit me if she took a dislike to me, as seemed only too probable. My grieving young heart revolted against the deception which this good lady was imposing on me and she had the greatest difficulty in persuading me to allow myself to be taken to my grandmother. The memory of all the tears I had seen my mother shed, of the terrible scenes she had had to endure in my presence and the knowledge that such treatment had shortened her life, made it utterly repugnant to me to submit to my grandmother's dominion. But my old friend assured me that if I made the slightest difficulty, a strict convent would be my lot; that my father would certainly re-marry in order to beget a son, and would not want to take me to live with him; that I might be forced to take the veil and be sent to the same convent as my aunt, a nun in the Benedictine house at Montargis, who had not left the convent walls since she was seven.

[. . .] I therefore had to humour my grandmother who, on the slightest provocation, [also] threatened to send me into a convent. Her despotism ruled my entire life. Never had I seen anyone with such a strong need to dominate, to wield power. She began by separating me entirely from my childhood friends and she herself broke with all her daughter's friends. It is probable that in the correspondence she seized, she had found replies to well-grounded complaints which my mother had every right to make about the cruel state of dependence in which she had to live during the last years of her life, and also some very unflattering comments on my grandmother's iniquitous behaviour. My grandmother insisted that I should no longer see or communicate with the Mlles de Rochechouart, the Mlles de Chauvelin, or Mlle de Coigny. By a refinement of cruelty, my grandmother made the break with my young friends appear to come from me. I learned that I was accused of ingratitude, of fickleness and lack of feeling, and was not allowed to explain.

My good tutor, who knew my grandmother better than I did myself, was the only being to whom I could talk of my sorrows. But he pointed out to me most forcibly that it would be best to humour my grandmother, that my future life depended on her, that if I crossed her and she were to put me in a convent, she would still be clever enough to make it appear that the decision was my own; that, separated from my father, of whom I might at any moment be deprived by the fortunes of war, I would be entirely alone if my grandmother and my uncle should withdraw their protection. And so I had to resolve to endure the daily trials which were the inevitable consequence of the terrible nature of this woman on whom I was dependent. I can truthfully say that for five years, not one day passed without my shedding bitter tears.

1815, translated by Felice Harcourt

Give Me Daughters Any Day

In the old days, Ruth had been sent by her mother during the school holidays to be company for her widowed grandmother.

Every morning they went shopping locally in Mortlake, with Ruth carrying the zip-up vinyl bag, for half a pound of this and a quarter of that. On the way they might meet one of Vesta's neighbours, and there would be a formal five-minute exchange on the subject of physical deterioration, while Ruth stood to one side, staring at the pavement. The conversation over, she followed her grandmother off again with mortified canine obedience. Their main meal, at midday, of chops or offal or stew, was followed by Vesta's Rest.

Ruth sat on the rug in the sun and filled in her diary. *'Je suis avec ma grandmère,'* she wrote. *'Ce soir nous donnerons le poisson au chat de Mme Grayling, qui est au Minorca en vacances.*

Hier soir nous avons entendu Radio 2 depuis deux heures et joué aux cartes. Je suis absolument . . .' She paused and bit her biro. What was she, absolutely?

She gave up and started to read, alternating chapters of *Mansfield Park* with *Forever Amber*. At about four, she went back to the kitchen and laid the tea things. She was in a hot trance of reading and wanted never to speak again.

At ten past four her grandmother came downstairs.

'Always got your nose in some damn book,' she said. 'What are you reading *now*?'

'At Mansfield,' Ruth read aloud, 'no sounds of contention, no raised voice, no abrupt bursts, no tread of violence was ever heard; all proceeded in a regular course of cheerful orderliness.'

'How boring,' said Vesta. 'I like a bit of life. Why can't you put that down and be *company*.'

'I've got to revise,' said Ruth.

'Don't think exams will get you anywhere,' laughed Vesta. 'Look where they got your mother. Spending her time with drug addicts and sex maniacs and the scum of the earth. No wonder that rotten husband of hers upped and offed.'

'You mustn't talk like that about my father,' said Ruth.

'I'll say what I want in my own house,' huffed Vesta. 'He was a lazy, dirty good-for-nothing. It's no surprise *he* ended up in the gutter.'

'I won't listen!' shrieked Ruth.

'You're getting absolutely neurotic,' said Vesta with distaste.

From the top of the kitchen dresser she pulled down her own favourite book, *The Pageant of Life* by Dr Ethel Tensing, 1931.

'You listen to this and you'll learn a thing or two,' said Vesta, looking at Ruth severely over her reading glasses.

'Oh, no, please,' said Ruth.

'Don't be so ignorant,' said Vesta. 'Now this is her chapter on Adolescence.' She proceeded to read aloud the opinions of

half a century ago on subjects as various as menstruation and
the advisability of excess energy being channelled into a hobby.

'You could try stamp collecting,' chuckled Vesta.

'I don't need a hobby,' said Ruth. 'I've got reading. And as
far as I can see everything's just the same now I'm fifteen as
when I was seven. I still go to school. I still come here every
holiday.'

'Don't be so stupid,' said Vesta. 'You have your periods now,
don't you.'

'Shut up, shut up, shut up,' said Ruth.

'The young adult, or adolescent, is particularly susceptible
to unreasonable emotional swings,' Vesta read aloud.

'I'm going to be sick,' said Ruth, 'If you don't shut up. And
you can't pronounce menstruation or comparable.'

'When are you going to get a boyfriend,' said Vesta.

'When am I going to meet any boys,' said Ruth.

'It's not natural,' said Vesta. 'Maybe it's because of your
weight. But don't think you're going to help matters by trying
to wear lipstick. That cheap stuff you put on yesterday made
your lips look like two pieces of liver.'

'Shut up, shut up, shut up,' said Ruth, her voice higher this
time.

'Calming breathing exercises for adolescents,' read Vesta.
'Come on, now. Inhale deeply, filling the diaphragm with air.'

'You don't sound the "g",' snivelled Ruth.

HELEN SIMPSON, 1991

---

from Innocent Eréndira

'Iron all the clothes before you go to bed so you can sleep with
a clear conscience.'

'Yes, Grandmother.'

'Check the clothes closets carefully, because moths get hungrier on windy nights.'

'Yes, Grandmother.'

'With the time you have left, take the flowers out into the courtyard so they can get a breath of air.'

'Yes, Grandmother.'

'And feed the ostrich.'

She had fallen asleep but she was still giving orders, for it was from her that the granddaughter had inherited the ability to be alive still while sleeping. Eréndira left the room without making any noise and did the final chores of the night, still replying to the sleeping grandmother's orders.

'Give the graves some water.'

'Yes, Grandmother.'

'And if the Amadíses arrive, tell them not to come in,' the grandmother said, 'because Porfirio Galán's gang is waiting to kill them.'

Eréndira didn't answer her any more because she knew that the grandmother was getting lost in her delirium, but she didn't miss a single order. When she finished checking the window bolts and put out the last lights, she took a candlestick from the dining-room and lighted her way to her bedroom as the pauses in the wind were filled with the peaceful and enormous breathing of her sleeping grandmother.

Her room was also luxurious, but not so much as her grandmother's, and it was piled high with the rag dolls and wind-up animals of her recent childhood. Overcome by the barbarous chores of the day, Eréndira didn't have the strength to get undressed and she put the candlestick on the night table and fell on to the bed. A short while later the wind of her misfortune came into the bedroom like a pack of hounds and knocked the candle over against the curtain.

At dawn, when the wind finally stopped, a few thick and scattered drops of rain began to fall, putting out the last embers and hardening the smoking ashes of the mansion. The people in the village, Indians for the most part, tried to rescue the remains of the disaster: the charred corpse of the ostrich, the frame of the gilded piano, the torso of a statue. The grandmother was contemplating the residue of her fortune with an impenetrable depression. Eréndira, sitting between the two graves of the Amadíses, had stopped weeping. When the grandmother was convinced that very few things remained intact among the ruins, she looked at her granddaughter with sincere pity.

'My poor child,' she sighed. 'Life won't be long enough for you to pay me back for this mishap.'

She began to pay it back that very day, beneath the noise of the rain, when she was taken to the village storekeeper, a skinny and premature widower who was quite well known in the desert for the good price he paid for virginity. As the grandmother waited undauntedly, the widower examined Eréndira with scientific austerity: he considered the strength of her thighs, the size of her breasts, the diameter of her hips. He didn't say a word until he had some calculation of what she was worth.

'She's still quite immature,' he said then. 'She has the teats of a bitch.'

Then he had her get on a scale to prove his decision with figures. Eréndira weighed ninety pounds.

'She isn't worth more than a hundred pesos,' the widower said.

The grandmother was scandalized.

'A hundred pesos for a girl who's completely new!' she almost shouted. 'No, sir, that shows a great lack of respect for virtue on your part.'

'I'll make it a hundred and fifty,' the widower said.

'This girl caused me damages amounting to more than a million pesos,' the grandmother said. 'At this rate she'll need two hundred years to pay me back.'

'You're lucky that the only good feature she has is her age,' the widower said.

The storm threatened to knock the house down, and there were so many leaks in the roof that it was raining almost as much inside as out. The grandmother felt all alone in a world of disaster.

'Just raise it to three hundred,' she said.

'Two hundred and fifty.'

Finally they agreed on two hundred and twenty pesos in cash and some provisions. The grandmother then signalled Eréndira to go with the widower and he led her by the hand to the back room as if he were taking her to school.

'I'll wait for you here,' the grandmother said.

'Yes, Grandmother,' said Eréndira.

GABRIEL GARCÍA MÁRQUEZ, translated by Gregory Rabassa, 1981

---

from The Waves of the Wind

The elders sat on the stools, brandishing their large palm-leaf fans and chattering. The children darted to and fro, or crouched beneath the tallow trees playing pebbles. The women were bringing out bowls of salt vegetables and yellow rice, still hot and steaming. Small boats floated on the river, and if there had been a poet on board he might have said that the life of the peasants was a kind of heavenly bliss.

Such a comment, however, would have been irrelevant and untrue, because the poet would not have heard the remarks of Old Grandma Nine Ching. At that moment Old Grandma Nine Ching was in a rage. 'I have lived seventy-nine years', she said, striking the leg of her stool with a palm-leaf fan. 'I have lived enough. I would rather not have witnessed the degeneration of the young. I ought to die. There they are the supper all ready under their noses, and they keep on eating baked beans. That's the way to bring a family to destruction.'

Her great-granddaughter Six Ching, with her hands full of baked beans, approached the table. Hearing the old woman's words, she turned swiftly away and rushed to the river bank, where she hid behind a tallow tree. With infinite cunning the little girl stretched out her head, from which two round knots of braided hair fell along her cheeks, and she said loudly: 'You old witch, why don't you die?'

Old Grandma Nine Ching, though not in the least deaf, did not hear these words and kept muttering to herself: 'Every generation is more degraded than the last.'

In this village a peculiar habit prevailed. At birth every infant was weighed on a steelyard, and the actual number of *ching* which it weighed would form part of its name. Ever since her fiftieth birthday old Grandma Nine Ching had taken to grumbling. She would say that in her younger days the weather had never been so hot, nor the dried beans so hard. The world had changed for the worse. Six Ching was three *ching* less than her great-grandfather, and one *ching* less than her father. All this was indisputable. 'Every generation is worse than the former one', she would say emphatically.

Her granddaughter-in-law, who was Seven Ching's wife, came to the table with a basketful of rice in her arms. Throwing the ricebasket down on the table, she said resentfully: 'Always harping on the same subject, eh? But Six Ching at her birth actually weighed six *ching* and six and a half *liang*. That steelyard of yours is all wrong, and each *ching* on your steelyard is eighteen *liang* – not sixteen, as it should be. If we had used a standard steelyard, it would have been seven *ching*. And do you know, I believe the old steelyard which weighed grandpa only had fourteen *liang* . . .'

'Every generation is more debased than the former . . .'

LU HSUN, 1881–1935

from Peasants

Grannie stationed Sasha near her kitchen garden and told her to watch out for stray geese. It was a hot August day. The geese could have got into the garden from round the back, but now they were busily pecking at some oats near the inn, peacefully cackling to each other. Only the gander craned his neck, as though he were looking out for the old woman with her stick. The other geese might have come up from the slope, but they stayed far beyond the other side of the river and resembled a long white garland of flowers laid out over the meadow.

Sasha stood there for a few moments, after which she felt bored. When she saw that the geese weren't coming, off she went down the steep slope. There she spotted Motka (Marya's eldest daughter), standing motionless on a boulder, looking at the church. Marya had borne thirteen children, but only six survived, all of them girls – not a single boy among them; and the eldest was eight. Motka stood barefooted in her long smock, in the full glare of the sun which burned down on her head. But she did not notice it and seemed petrified. Sasha stood next to her and said as she looked at the church, 'God lives in churches. People have ikon lamps and candles, but God has little red, green and blue lamps that are just like tiny eyes. At night-time God goes walking round the church with the Holy Virgin and Saint Nikolay . . . tap-tap-tap. And the watchman is scared stiff!' Then she added, mimicking her mother, 'Now, dear, when the Day of Judgement comes, every church will be whirled off to heaven!'

'Wha-at, with their be-ells too?' Motka asked in a deep voice, dragging each syllable.

'Yes, bells and all. On the Day of Judgement, all good people will go to paradise, while the wicked ones will be burnt in everlasting fire, for ever and ever. And God will tell my mother and Marya, "You never harmed anyone, so you can take the path on the right that leads to paradise." But he'll say of Kiryak and Grannie, "You go to the left, into the fire. And all those who ate meat during Lent must go as well."'

She gazed up at the sky with wide-open eyes and said, 'If you look at the sky without blinking you can see the angels.'

Motka looked upwards and neither of them said a word for a minute or so.

'Can you see them?' Sasha asked.

'Can't see nothing,' Motka said in her deep voice.

'Well, I can. There's tiny angels flying through the sky, flapping their wings and going buzz-buzz like mosquitoes.'

Motka pondered for a moment as she looked down at the ground and then she asked, 'Will Grannie burn in the fire?'

'Yes, she will, dear.'

From the rock down to the bottom, the slope was gentle and smooth. It was covered with soft green grass which made one feel like touching it or lying on it. Sasha lay down and rolled to the bottom. Motka took a deep breath and, looking very solemn and deadly serious, she lay down too and rolled to the bottom; on the way down her smock rode up to her shoulders.

'That was great fun,' Sasha said rapturously.

They both went up to the top again for another roll, but just then they heard that familiar, piercing voice again. It was really terrifying! That toothless, bony, hunchbacked old woman, with her short grey hair fluttering in the wind, was driving the geese out of her kitchen garden with a long stick, shouting, 'So you had to tread all over my cabbages, blast you! May you be damned three times and rot in hell, you buggers!'

When she saw the girls, she threw the stick down, seized a whip made of twigs, gripped Sasha's neck with fingers as hard and dry as stale rolls, and started beating her. Sasha cried out in pain and fear, but at that moment the gander, waddling along and craning its neck, went up to the old woman and hissed at her. When it returned to the flock all the females cackled approvingly. Then the old woman started beating Motka and her smock rode up again. With loud sobs and in utter desperation, Sasha went to the hut to complain about it. She was followed by Motka, who was crying as well, but much more throatily and without bothering to wipe the tears away. Her face was so wet it seemed she had just drenched it with water.

'Good God!' Olga said in astonishment when they entered the hut. 'Holy Virgin!'

Sasha was just about to tell her what had happened when Grannie started shrieking and cursing. Fyokla became furious and the hut was filled with noise. Olga was pale and looked very upset as she stroked Sasha's head and said consolingly, 'It's all right, it's nothing. It's sinful to get angry with your grandmother. It's all right, my child.'

Nikolay, who by this time was exhausted by the never-ending shouting, by hunger, by the fumes from the stove and the terrible stench, who hated and despised poverty, and whose wife and daughter made him feel ashamed in front of his parents, sat over the stove with his legs dangling and turned to his mother in an irritable, plaintive voice: 'You can't beat her, you've no right at all!'

'You feeble little man, rotting away up there over the stove,' Fyokla shouted spitefully. 'What the hell's brought you lot here, you parasites!'

Both Sasha and Motka and all the little girls, who had taken refuge in the corner, over the stove, behind Nikolay's back, were terrified and listened without saying a word, their little hearts pounding away.

[. . .] When evening came and it was dark in the hut, they felt so depressed they could hardly speak. Angry Grannie sat dipping rye-crusts in a cup and sucking them for a whole hour. After Marya had milked the cow she brought a pail of milk and put it on a bench. Then Grannie poured it into some jugs, without hurrying, and she was visibly cheered by the thought that as it was the Feast of the Assumption (when milk was forbidden) no one would go near it. All she did was pour the tiniest little drop into a saucer for Fyokla's baby. As she was carrying the jugs with Marya down to the cellar, Motka suddenly started, slid down from the stove, went over to the bench where the wooden cup with the crusts was standing and splashed some milk from the saucer over them.

When Grannie came back and sat down to her crusts, Sasha and Motka sat watching her from the stove, and it gave them great pleasure to see that now she had eaten forbidden food during Lent and would surely go to hell for it. They took comfort in this thought and lay down to sleep. As Sasha dozed off she had visions of the Day of Judgement: she saw a blazing furnace, like a potter's kiln, and an evil spirit dressed all in black, with the horns of a cow, driving Grannie into the fire with a long stick, as *she* had driven the geese not so long ago.

ANTON CHEKHOV, 1897, translated by Ronald Wilks

---

from First Confession

'And what's a-trouble to you, Jackie?'

'Father,' I said, feeling I might as well get it over while I had him in good humour, 'I had it all arranged to kill my grandmother.'

He seemed a bit shaken by that, all right, because he said nothing for quite a while.

'My goodness,' he said at last, 'that'd be a shocking thing to do. What put that into your head?'

'Father,' I said, feeling very sorry for myself, 'she's an awful woman.'

'Is she?' he asked. 'What way is she awful?'

'She takes porter, father,' I said, knowing well from the way Mother talked of it that this was a mortal sin, and hoping it would make the priest take a more favourable view of my case.

'Oh, my!' he said, and I could see he was impressed.

'And snuff, father,' said I.

That's a bad case, sure enough, Jackie,' he said.

'And she goes round in her bare feet, father,' I went on in a rush of self-pity, 'and she know I don't like her, and she gives pennies to Nora and none to me, and my da sides with her and flakes me, and one night I was so heart-scalded I made up my mind I'd have to kill her.'

'And what would you do with the body?' he asked with great interest.

'I was thinking I could chop that up and carry it away in a barrow I have,' I said.

'Begor, Jackie,' he said, 'do you know you're a terrible child?'

'I know, father,' I said, for I was just thinking the same thing myself. 'I tried to kill Nora too with a bread-knife under the table, only I missed her.'

'Is that the little girl that was beating you just now?' he asked.

''Tis, father.'

'Someone will go for her with a bread-knife one day, and he won't miss her,' he said rather cryptically. 'You must have great courage. Between ourselves, there's a lot of people I'd like to do the same to but I'd never have the nerve. Hanging is an awful death.'

'Is it, father?' I asked with the deepest interest – I was always very keen on hanging. 'Did you ever see a fellow hanged?'

'Dozens of them,' he said solemnly. 'And they all died roaring.'

'Jay!' I said.

'Oh, a horrible death!' he said with great satisfaction. 'Lots of the fellows I saw killed their grandmothers too, but they all said 'twas never worth it.'

FRANK O'CONNOR, 1947

---

from The Common Day

When Carlotta was dressed, Agnes took her down to the living room. Mrs Garrison was waiting there. It was one of the rituals of that summer that she should spend an hour with Carlotta each afternoon. Left alone with her grandmother, the child sat stiffly in a chair. Mrs Garrison and the little girl bored one another.

Mrs Garrison had led an unusually comfortable life, so well sustained by friends and by all sorts of pleasures that she retained a striking buoyancy. She was impulsive, generous, and very kind. She was also restless. 'What shall we do, Carlotta?' she asked.

'I don't know,' the child said.

'Shall I make you a necklace of daisies, Carlotta?'

'Yes.'

'Well, you wait here, then. Don't touch the candy or the things on my desk, will you?'

Mrs Garrison went into the hall and got a basket and some shears. The lawn below the terrace ended abruptly in a field that was covered with white-and-yellow daisies. She filled her basket with them. When she returned to the living room, Carlotta was still sitting stiffly in her chair. Mrs Garrison did not trust the child and she inspected the desk before she settled herself on the sofa. She began to push a threaded needle through the hairy flowers. 'I'll make you a necklace and a bracelet and a crown,' she said.

'I don't want a daisy necklace,' Carlotta said.

'But you told me you wanted one.'

'I want a *real* necklace,' Carlotta said. 'I want a pearl necklace like Aunt Ellen has.'

'Oh, dear,' Mrs Garrison said. She put aside her needle and
the flowers. She remembered her first pearls. She had worn
them to a party in Baltimore. It had been a wonderful party
and the memory excited her for a moment. Then she felt old.

'You're not old enough to have pearls,' she told Carlotta.
'You're just a little girl.' . . . The day had got very hot. The heat
made Mrs Garrison sleepy and encouraged her to reminisce.
She thought about Philadelphia and Bermuda, and became
so absorbed in these memories that she was startled when
Carlotta spoke again.

'I'm not a little girl,' Carlotta said suddenly. 'I'm a big girl!'
Her voice broke and tears came to her eyes. 'I'm bigger than
Timmy and Ingrid and everybody!'

'You'll be big enough in time,' Mrs Garrison said. 'Stop
crying.'

'I want to be a big lady. I want to be a big lady like Aunt
Ellen and Mummy.'

'And when you're as big as your mother, you'll wish you
were a child again!' Mrs Garrison said angrily.

'I want to be a lady,' the child cried. 'I don't want to be
little. I don't want to be a little girl.'

'Stop it,' Mrs Garrison called, 'stop crying. It's too hot. You
don't know what you want. Look at me. I spend half my time
wishing I were young enough to dance. It's ridiculous, it's perfectly . . .' She noticed a shadow crossing the lowered awning at
the window. She went to the window and saw Nils Lund going
down the lane. He would have overheard everything. This
made her intensely uncomfortable. Carlotta was still crying.
She hated to hear the child cry. It seemed as if the meaning of
that hot afternoon, as if for a second her life, depended upon
the girl's happiness.

'Is there anything you'd like to do, Carlotta?'

'No.'

'Would you like a piece of candy?'

'No, thank you.'

Would you like to wear my pearls?'

'No, thank you.'

Mrs Garrison decided to cut the interview short and she rang for Agnes.

JOHN CHEEVER, 1980

Grannies in Hell

Richard Mosley was born at *Gothern-Hill* in the County of *Stafford*; His Father was a *Lock-Smith* in the same Town, who brought him up to his own Trade: But he often took oppetunity to neglect his Father's Business, spending his Time in Gaming, Playing, Drinking, and vain Company: . . . And to support and maintain his Extravagances, he came on *Monday* the *9th* of *October* last, to his Grand-Mother *Mary Payton* . . . to borrow Five Shillings in his Mother's Name, which she let him have; but she Supplied his Extravagancies but a short time: And tho' reduced to want, he . . . continued Stubborn and Relentless, Contriving how he might get Money to buy him Cloaths, and pay his Ale-Score . . . To this end he went again to his Grand-mother's house, the fourteenth of *October* following, after it was Dark, where she kindly received. And kept him all Night and the next Morning she chid him for his Idle Coursed Life: he missing his End of getting Money of her, left her the next Morning, and continued all the Day Lurking about the House; seeking an opportunity to get in and take the Money away, which was Seven Pound, that he supposed to be lodged in the House, but could not Effect his Purpose till after Sun-set, and then got in and lay Close till she was gone to Bed, and as he thought asleep: When he lighted a Candle and went into her Lodging-Chamber to look for the Money, upon which she saw and spoke to him, when to prevent her from discovering him he took up the Coal Hatchet and Knock'd her Brains out; and when he had done he cast the Bed-Cloaths over her and went away, and Lock'd the Door after him, carrying away the Key. The next day she was missed, and some neighbours coming about the House saw the Cow Unmilk'd and the Pig unserv'd, and called but no-Body answered, so that they sent two miles to her Daughters, who came with her Grand-children . . . who Breaking open the Door found her Dead being all Bloody: Two days after the Coroner Sat upon the Dead Body, and all present touch'd the Dead Body, according to Vulgar Custom, among which were her Daughter, *Richard Mosley*'s Mother, and his Brother's, and afterwards *Richard* himself; but no Signs of Guilt appeared from thence: However there were many circumstances that made it very probable that *Richard Mosley* was the Person . . . that Committed this Murther: . . . therefore it was concluded to have him apprehended, and strictly examined for the same, and well knowing that one *John Barrett*, had something to declare against him . . . he downright acused the said *John Barrett* of the Murther.

[. . .] the Jury acquitted *Barrett*. *Richard Mosley* hearing that *Barrett* had plainly quitted himself . . . declared with tears in his Eyes that he had falsely accused [him] . . . He then confessed all the circumstances by which he had done the Murther . . . with this addition, that while he was rummaging for the Money, his Grandmother rose up in the bed and said *Oh Rogue what dost thou here?* He to prevent being discovered took the Coal-Hatchet and struck her on the Forehead, that she fell down on the Pillow, and lest she should revive again, he gave her many more Blows, and cast the Cloaths over her: That as soon as it was done, he . . . was in such a Condition that he looked no further for the Money but hasted away, and thought he lock'd the Door after him . . . He said farther That he had nothing from his Grandmother but a pair of Gloves and Two-Pence or a Groat . . .

ANON., *The Whole Life . . . of Richard Mosley, aged about Sixteen Years old, [hanged] for the Murther of his own Grand-mother, Mary Payton*, 1707

Grandson Faked Kidnap in £10,000 Plot

A police sergeant's son faked his own kidnapping in an attempt to extort more than £10,000 from his grandmother.

Mark Bayliss, 20, who was sentenced to two and a half years in prison after admitting blackmail, had run up debts of thousands of pounds buying designer clothes, dining in expensive restaurants and taking drugs. He devised the scheme to steal from Judith Baker, 73, after losing his job as a trainee stockbroker in the City, St Albans Crown Court was told.

The court heard that on Sept 29 last year Mrs Baker received three photographs of her grandson supposedly showing him beaten, tied and gagged, with a letter demanding that Mrs Baker pay £10,400 into Bayliss's bank account.

But Mrs Baker, of Much Hadham, Herts, suspected a plot. She contacted her son-in-law, Michael Bayliss, then a sergeant with the Metropolitan Police, who called in detectives.

RYAN DUNLEAVY, *Electronic Telegraph*, 15 February 1999

---

from Roman History, Book LIX

Towards his mother, his sisters, and his grandmother Antonia he conducted himself at first in the most dutiful manner possible.

His grandmother he immediately saluted as Augusta, and appointed her to be priestess of Augustus, granting to her at once all the privileges of the Vestal Virgins. To his sisters he assigned these privileges of the Vestal Virgins . . . Yet, after doing all this, he showed himself the most impious of men toward both his grandmother and his sisters. For he forced the former to seek death by her own hand, because she had rebuked him for something . . .

DIO, c. AD 230, translated by Ernest Cary

Depression in Grandmothers

To the Editor: I have observed an increasing number of women who have presented with symptoms of anxiety or depression. The common causative factor is that they have been foisted with the care of their grandchildren while their daughters or daughters-in-law go out to work. All the patients feel obliged to help their children regardless of the cost to themselves – and all are frightened to relinquish their burden in case they offend their offspring.

I believe that this medical problem is a direct result of our economic climate and the unrealistic financial expectations of a modern society that necessitates a two-income family. Young persons have little thought for the misery and the burden that they are placing on their suffering mothers.

What finally prompted me to write this letter is my most recent such patient who was 'housebound' by the need to stay home from 6 a.m. to 6 p.m. – to look after her daughter's chihuahua!

MARK J. MACDERMOTT, MB BS, 1987

from Years of Childhood

Though I had myself already noticed a great change in grand-mother, my attention was especially called to it by a conversation between my parents, which I overheard while reading my book.

'What a change there is in your mother since your father's death!' my mother said. 'She seems to me even to have grown smaller; nothing really interests her; she has lost hold of every-thing. She speaks constantly of her loss; she pays little heed even to her daughter. When I say that Tatyana ought to be set-tled in life, and that a husband should be found for her, she won't hear of it: she only says, "As God pleases, so it will be."'

My father sighed and said, 'Oh yes, mother is quite changed; I don't think she will live long.'

I felt sorry for grandmother, and said, 'We ought to comfort grandmother and stop her from grieving.' My father was sur-prised by my sudden interposition; he smiled and said, 'Yes, you and your sister should go and see her oftener and try to cheer her up.' Accordingly, we began to go to her room several times a day. We usually found her sitting on her bed, with a spinning-wheel before her, and spinning goats' down, while a number of girls, belonging to the house or estate, were squat-ting round her and cleaning the hairs out of the tufts of down. Each girl, when she had cleaned her tuft, handed it to the old lady, who held it up to the light and, if she found no hairs in it, laid it in a basket near her; but, if the tuft was not properly cleaned, she handed it back and scolded the girl for her care-lessness. Grandmother's eyes were dull and leaden; often she grew drowsy over her work; sometimes she pushed the wheel suddenly away and said, 'What is the use of spinning to me? Time for me to go to Stepan Mihailovitch!' – and then she would begin to weep. At first, my sister and I did not know how to make advances to her: we only sat there for a little and then went away. But we learnt from our aunt how to please her.

In spite of her indifference to everything about her, she still kept her old liking for certain favourite dishes and dainties. Thus she was very fond of the berries of herb-paris, and of mushrooms fried in sour cream. Of the berries there were plenty in the kitchen garden; our aunt went there with us and showed us the place; and the three of us picked a whole basinful and took them in to grandmother. She seemed pleased. 'Splendid berries,' she said; 'so large and ripe,' and ate them with enjoyment; she wished to give us some, but we said we dared not eat them without mother's leave. Next, our aunt showed us the place where the mushrooms grew [. . .] Again helped by our aunt, we pulled out of the very ground a plateful of button-mushrooms and carried it in to grandmother. She was very much pleased, and ordered the cook to fry a whole panful for her. We had again to refuse her offer to treat us to mushrooms; she made an impatient gesture, and said, 'Dear! dear! how odd you are!' Having earned her favour in this way, we began to talk on different subjects to grandmother; and she was getting more friendly and taking more notice of us, when an unexpected incident occurred which cooled my feelings so much, that for a long time I only said 'Good morning' and 'Good-bye,' when I paid her a visit. We were talking cheerfully to her one day, when a red-haired village girl handed her a tuft of down which had already been rejected once; grandmother held it up to the light, and, seeing that there were hairs in it, with one hand caught the girl by the scalp, while with the other she pulled out a whip from under her pillows and began to lash the offender. I ran off. I was reminded of the National School, and felt no further wish to sit in grandmother's room, and watch her spinning at her wheel and the girls picking hairs out of the goats' down.

SERGEI AKSAKOV, 1791–1859, translated by J. Duff

from Cold Comfort Farm

Aunt Ada Doom sat in her room upstairs . . . alone.

There was something almost symbolic in her solitude. She was the core, the matrix, the focusing-point of the house . . . and she was, like all cores, utterly alone. You never heard of two cores to a thing, did you? Well, then. Yet all the wandering waves of desire, passion, jealousy, lust, that throbbed through the house converged, web-like, upon her core-solitude. She felt herself to be a core . . . and utterly, irrevocably alone.

The weakening winds of spring fawned against the old house. The old woman's thoughts cowered in the hot room where she sat in solitude . . . She would not see her niece . . . Keep her away . . .

Make some excuse. Shut her out. She had been here a month and you had not seen her. She thought it strange, did she? She dropped hints that she would like to see you. You did not want to see her. You felt . . . you felt some strange emotion at the thought of her. You would not see her. Your thoughts wound slowly round the room like beasts rubbing against the drowsy walls. And outside the walls the winds rubbed like drowsy beasts. Half-way between the inside and the outside walls, winds and thoughts were both drowsy. How enervating was the warm wind of the coming spring . . .

When you were very small – so small that the lightest puff of breeze blew your little crinoline skirt over your head – you had seen something nasty in the woodshed.

You'd never forgotten it.

You'd never spoken of it to Mamma – (you could smell, even to this day, the fresh betel-nut with which her shoes were always cleaned) – but you'd remembered all your life.

That was what had made you . . . different. That – what you had seen in the tool-shed – had made your marriage a prolonged nightmare to you.

Somehow you had never bothered about what it had been like for your husband . . .

That was why you had brought your children into the world with loathing. Even now, when you were seventy-nine, you could never see a bicycle go past your bedroom window without a sick plunge at the apex of your stomach . . . in the bicycle shed you'd seen it, something nasty, when you were very small.

That was why you stayed here in this room. You had been here for twenty years, ever since Judith had married and her husband had come to live at the farm. You had run away from the huge, terrifying world outside these four walls against which your thoughts rubbed themselves like drowsy yaks. Yes, that was what they were like. Yaks. Exactly like yaks.

Outside in the world there were potting-sheds where nasty things could happen. But nothing could happen here. You saw to that. None of your grandchildren might leave the farm. Judith might not leave. Amos might not leave. Caraway might not leave. Urk might not leave. Seth might not leave. Micah might not leave. Ezra might not leave. Mark and Luke might not leave. Harkaway might leave sometimes because he paid the proceeds of the farm into the bank at Beershorn every Saturday morning, but none of the others might leave.

None of them must go out into the great dirty world where there were cow-sheds in which nasty things could happen and be seen by little girls.

STELLA GIBBONS, 1932

---

from The Death of a Witch

The Bhils [of Rajasthan, India] also firmly believed in female witches; in fact they believed that every woman is likely to be inducted into the company of witches if she lives long enough.

Women who are suspected of practising witchcraft, bringing sickness upon their victims, are sometimes submitted to the ordeal of having their ankles tied with rope and then being swung, head down, from the branch of a tall tree in the hope that they will confess to having practised witchcraft and promise to desist. If this swinging does not have the desired effect, it is repeated after applying a paste of chopped red chillies to the unfortunate woman's vagina. This preoccupation with the demonic attributes of older women is the more remarkable because young Bhil men and women, including husbands and wives, appear to enjoy each other's company unashamedly, unconstrained by the Hindu taboo which prohibits any public display of affection between the sexes.

G. M. CARSTAIRS, 1983

from The Essential Kafir

The old women are scraggy, withered, and shrunken, their skin hanging on their bones. After a certain age they take but little interest in their personal appearance, and allow their hair to go unkempt and dishevelled. They are allowed to break many restrictions which are placed on younger women, being sometimes called men. They lose the grace of past days, and their bodies become bent and deformed. They are always horribly dirty. The natives are respectful to men in old age; but old women are excluded from such attention, so that their lot is sad indeed. A Kafir [an old name for the Xhosa people of South Africa] once said to me, 'They are cast-off things; their use is over.' Women have practically no rights, and their function is to work in the fields and bear children and generally administer to the pleasure of the men. If they cannot cook, or till the fields, or bear children, what can they do?

They are frequently left to starve or die of exposure and neglect, for they have to depend on the charity of the young and strong, and that is a precarious source of supply to rest upon in heathen kraals. The one weapon they have is their curse, which is a thing greatly dreaded by the people. But to be set off against this is the fact that they are frequently accused of being witches, and nothing is easier than to get a witch doctor to 'smell out' any old hag who makes herself objectionable. He must have a hard heart who does not feel a lump in his throat when he hears how these poor old creatures are slowly burnt to death because they will not give up the medicines which they are supposed to have used to cause sickness among the cattle. No wonder that old women sometimes make away with themselves to avoid the cruelty of their lot. Kafirs believe that any one who eats a certain tongue-shaped lobe of the liver of an animal (the *Lobus Spigelii*) is sure to forget their past. Only old women eat this, so that they may forget their sorrows – a fact that throws a lurid light on the sad lot of old women, and on the pleasurable nature of life in the case of the men, who have no wish to forget the past.

I shall never forget the picture presented by an old hag in Swazieland who managed to get a little girl to lead her out of her dark hut to beg from me. With great difficulty and after much shouting, she understood that a white man was at the kraal and that it was a good chance to beg for food. The old woman was literally bent double with age, the upper part of her body being parallel with the ground, so that she was like an inverted letter L, her body being supported by her hands, which clutched her thighs as if they were the angle-bits of a bracket. Her nose was eaten away with disease, and she was blind and deaf. I had never seen such a shrivelled, dried-up specimen of woe-begone humanity: her scraggy and pendent breasts were like empty bags of dirty skin and were hanging from a wrinkled, shrunken body. It was long since she had a tooth in her head, and handsful of skin could have been taken up at any part of her body, as if she had been a starved pug dog. She piteously begged for a little salt.

DUDLEY KIDD, 1904

The communists gave axes to the old ladies and said 'Go kill yourselves. You're useless.'

MAXINE HONG KINGSTON, *The Woman Warrior*, 1977

Indifference

When Grandmamma fell off the boat,
And couldn't swim (and wouldn't float),
Matilda just stood by and smiled.
I almost could have slapped the child.

HARRY GRAHAM, 1930

Chinese Grandmothers Speaking

Apart from Margaret Tan, director of another sheltered housing scheme, Cherish House, all the speakers are Hakka speakers, originally from Hong Kong, and now residents of Cannaught Gardens, a sheltered housing scheme for elderly Chinese, open ten years ago and run by Trident Housing Association in Birmingham.

Margaret Tan: The problem for the Chinese is that they are not seen. They don't make a fuss or demand anything. They are the hidden race. And when they get old, especially, access to public and social services is denied them because of their lack of English and their frailty. They can't get to the doctor, to the police. They can't ring 999 because they only speak Chinese. I wanted to get some information on one social service in Chinese but though they had the information in Bengali, Hindi, Urdu, they didn't have it in Chinese. I sent one of our residents to hospital once, and straightaway the hospital rang me and asked, 'Why did you send this person? What can we do? She only speaks Chinese.'

There's a problem with the Chinese old too that their children, the next generation Chinese, aren't interested in leisure the way the British are. They are just interested in money and status and cars. So they see the old people as a hindrance – they don't speak English, they are just the past, they are in the way. There are some cases of old people being dumped on the steps of churches, the way people used to dump unwanted children.

Mrs Lee 1, aged 76: I've nine grandsons and granddaughters. They very seldom come here. All of them are in England. I came here twenty-six years ago when I was fifty-one years old. I came from Hong Kong. My husband was working here already, so I followed with our sons and daughters. He was working in a Chinese takeaway, but I was busy looking after the children, so I did not work. I looked after the first grandchild too. I baby-sat and sometimes I cooked congee for him and the other babies. But I don't see him now. He never comes to see me. I played with him when he was little but now he has forgotten me. He's getting towards the end of school, I don't know exactly how old he is. The granddaughters don't come either. I don't know the ages of the youngest grandchildren – they do not live in Birmingham, they are in cities far away, I don't know the names of the cities. Though my eldest grandson speaks Chinese, many of the others don't. They still look like Chinese people, but their idea of Chinese culture is a Chinese takeaway. Recently one of my daughters came back to Birmingham – she has five children, she comes to see me sometimes but she doesn't bring the children. I seldom go to see her in her home. Sometimes she and my son-in-law take me to a Chinese restaurant.

Does it make me sad I see my grandchildren so little? What's the point of feeling happy or sad, I can't do anything about it. They all have their own lives, their own families. They are all working in the takeaway business like my husband.

When I was a child my grandmother lived in the same house as I did and my mother too. It's different now. Chinese families all used to live together, but not any more. It's better that old way. The grandmother can help take care of the grandchildren. No, I didn't teach them songs or anything. I don't know how to sing.

No, I wasn't surprised to see the British live so differently. That's no business of ours. But I think the British grandmother likes her grandchildren more than we like ours.

We were sitting in Mrs Lee's flat. At this point she got up and pulled out a letter and asked the care worker when her doctor's appointment was. She'd clearly had enough of this painful subject. Both care workers had previously found her cheerful and lively and had no idea of this family's neglect of the grandparents.

Mrs Lee 2, aged 67: I've been in England twenty-five years. My husband here first, I came later with my children. I have two daughters, each have two sons. I have three granddaughters from my two sons. My children were all born in Hong Kong. Their children all speak Chinese – they speak Cantonese, but because their parents speak Hakka they speak Hakka too.

My children come here to see me very frequently. They bring our grandsons and granddaughters to see my husband and me. A few years ago I used to help look after the children.

But they all go to school now. The eldest is seven years old, the youngest about three. These days I go shopping with them. I buy things for them. And when they come to my house I cook for them. I don't sing songs or tell stories, we don't do that.

I did not know my own grandmothers. They died when I was very young. My mother died early too. I had to bring up my own children. I see them and my grandchildren more than most people see their children and grandchildren. I'm lucky.

Mrs Wong: I have spent twenty-six years in England. I do speak a little English. I came by myself. My first husband was much older than me. It was a marriage made by a matchmaker. He came here nine years before me, but he was useless. He liked drinking, and gave me very little money. I even had to borrow money for the plane fare. I left my children in Hong Kong with my mother, and when I found work I went back to Hong Kong to fetch them. I arrived here with the children and baggage and no money. I had to work very hard to earn it all myself because my husband didn't. He died in 1987. My mother missed her grandchildren very much. I went back to Hong Kong every year to see her until she died, seven years ago. I haven't been back since.

I have only one grandchild from my eldest daughter but I haven't seen him for a couple of years. I always remember him. He is fourteen or fifteen years old now and disabled. I looked after him for seven years, I never closed my eyes looking after him while his mother was working. But then I hurt my back and I can't do it any more, and now my daughter won't speak to me. She is very bitter because when she left school I didn't have the money for her to go to university, she had to work in a takeaway like me. It's very difficult. The other children don't have children yet. But they did go to university. They are good to me. They love me because they know how hard I worked for them. But for my other three children I'd be crying all the time.

My second husband has five children, all born here. They're very western, they don't care about us. When they do come here their children, the grandchildren, are so innocent, the say 'bye-bye, grandma' and 'give us a kiss' in English, they don't speak any Chinese and they don't realise we can't understand. My husband can't speak to them at all, and not much to his children. His son does speak pidgin Hakka but it's not enough. Once I cooked a great meal for everyone and no one came because there was a confusion of dates, they hadn't understood each other.

Mrs Cheng, aged 87: I have three granddaughters and three grandsons. The eldest is twenty-six or twenty-seven. The youngest, eighteen. They visit me whenever they've got time. They can speak Hakka, but mostly they speak English. They don't usually eat meals at my house, but sometimes – once or twice a year – they take me to a restaurant. I've lived here since 1991. I didn't know anyone here before, but I have friends now.

I've been in England twenty-six years. I came when I was sixty, after my husband died. My son – he's sixty-one now and retired – he had a fish-and-chip shop, he brought me over. I lived alone then, over the fish-and-chip shop. He and his family lived elsewhere. It was lonely but what could I do about it? He only comes occasionally now. My friends' sons and daughters come to see them more often than he comes to see me.

We lived differently in Hong Kong. I was sent away from my family when I was a hundred days old to live with my husband's family – that had all been arranged. He was three years older than me and we were brought up together. We played together like brother and sister. Traditionally you got married at twenty and so we did. Things were all very formal at that time. He died when he was sixty. So of course I never knew my own grandmother. But my husband's grandmother brought me up. She loved me very much and treated me as a daughter.

Author's interview, November 1999

from Growing Old in Rural Taiwan

The senile, of course, as in all other societies, are the saddest of all. My landlady's 91-year-old adoptive mother was a case in point. On the one hand, this totally wacky crone was a source of amusement to all and sundry. Stories about her made the rounds of the village: once she woke up at 4 a.m. and claimed somebody had stolen all her raggedy hand towels; another time she came home a bit confused and accused her great-grandson of turning their house around while she was out. Everybody laughed, but there was a darker side to her senility that perhaps indicates more than anyone realizes the vulnerability and insecurity of the aged. Two or three times when the old woman was staying in our house, her adopted daughter, our landlady, went to the city and left her children to care for their grandmother. Each time, though they fed her and attended to her needs, the old woman accused her daughter of abandoning her or at least of locking the refrigerator so that she would have nothing to eat. In a way, it was as if this senile old woman was powerless to repress the kind of basic fears of old people that the clear-minded would never dare to mention: fears of desertion, starvation, or neglect in the absolute dependency of old age. Perhaps Chinese parents do indeed see filial obedience as being based on fear; and perhaps old people feel apprehension that once they become feeble and powerless there will be nothing left to make their sons and grandsons continue supporting them.

Probably to their credit, villagers neither tried to humor the old woman during these scenes nor even allowed her to get away with creating them. When she accused her daughter of locking the refrigerator or insisted that her towels had been stolen, everyone – including her own great-grandchildren and our octogenarian neighbor – argued with the ancient one, and argued quite vehemently. They seemed to be practicing some sort of 'reality therapy', trying somehow to show her that nobody, least of all her daughter, was out to get her. At the same time, since she was so unaware of her actual surroundings anyway, people made no pretense of being deferential or respectful. When she complained several nights in a row about how impossible it was to sleep in a bedroom she was temporarily sharing with two of her grandchildren, her daughter simply moved her to the corner of the kitchen. A day or two later, when I asked the younger woman how the old one was doing, she motioned mischievously to me to come peek; I followed her into the kitchen where we both snickered at the ridiculous heap snoring away on the cot in the corner.

STEVAN HARRELL, 1981

from Bodily Harm

After that my grandmother began to lose her sense of balance. She would climb up on chairs and stools to get things down, things that were too heavy for her, and then she would fall. She usually did this when my mother was out, and my mother would return to find her sprawled on the floor, surrounded by broken china.

Then her memory began to go. She would wander around the house at night, opening and shutting doors, trying to find her way back to her room. Sometimes she wouldn't remember who she was or who we were. Once she frightened me badly by coming into the kitchen, in broad daylight, as I was making myself a peanut-butter sandwich after school.

My hands, she said. I've left them somewhere and now I can't find them. She was holding her hands in the air, helplessly, as if she couldn't move them.

They're right there, I said. On the ends of your arms.

No, no, she said impatiently. Not those, those are no good

any more. My other hands, the ones I had before, the ones I
touch things with.

MARGARET ATWOOD, 1981

---

from Senile Patients Being Abused, Say Families

Relatives of people with dementia say sufferers are neglected
and mistreated by residential and nursing home staff, but families are afraid to complain in case it results in even more
abuse, says a report published today.

Old people are strapped to chairs, shut in their rooms,
turned into 'zombies' by drugs and left unwashed and
unshaven for days, sometimes with no change of clothes,
according to the Alzheimer's Disease Society. One in 10 of the
1,500 friends and relatives who responded to the society's
survey reported examples of neglect and mistreatment when
asked about standards of care.

But the society found that relatives were reluctant to complain about the abuse for fear that staff would 'take it out' on
the resident.

Places in care homes cost between £350 and £600 a week.
'Most of our members who responded said care was satisfac-
tory but 10 per cent said it was not. This was a much higher
figure than we expected,' said Harry Cayton, executive director
of the society.

'Friends and relations are frightened. We asked respondents
to the survey if they would speak to the media. No one was
prepared to come forward.'

The survey among members of the society found that 30 per
cent rated standards of personal care as poor or no better
than average. Sixty-nine per cent complained of a lack of
activities and occupational therapy for the residents.

Personal care and management of incontinence were also frequently criticised by family and friends. Nearly half said that support from their doctors was poor and that they were given little help in finding a home when they could no longer care for the patient at home.

One wrote: 'My mother was drugged and fastened in a chair. She was left isolated in her room. She was covered in huge, plate-like sores. Mum died screaming in agony. They said she was not in real pain, but that it was her dementia. If I had the sores she had, I'd be in pain.'

CELIA HALL, *Daily Telegraph*, 28 May 1997

Elder abuse is defined by Action on Elder Abuse as:

A single or repeated act or lack of appropriate action, occurring within any relationship where there is an expectation of trust, which causes harm or distress to an older person.

There are five main types of abuse:

- physical – for example, hitting, slapping, burning, pushing, restraining or giving too much medication or the wrong medication;
- psychological – for example, shouting, swearing, frightening, blaming, ignoring or humiliating a person;
- financial – for example, the illegal or unauthorised use of a person's property, money, pension book or other valuables;
- sexual – for example, forcing a person to take part in any sexual activity without his or her consent – this can occur in any relationship;
- neglect – for example, where a person is deprived of food, heat, clothing or comfort or essential medication.

An older person may either suffer from only one form of abuse, or different types of abuse at the same time.

1997

Inconsiderate Hannah

Naughty little Hannah said
She could make her Grandma whistle,
So that night, inside her bed,
Placed some nettles on a thistle.

The dear Grandma quite inform is,
Heartless Hannah watched her settle,
With her poor old epidermis
Resting up against a nettle.

Suddenly she reached the thistle!
My! You should have heard her
whistle.
A successful plan was Hannah's,
But I cannot praise her manners.

HARRY GRAHAM, 1909

VIII

OLD AGE AND DEATH

One hell for grandmothers, which I omitted mentioning in the last section, is that of losing young grandchildren. In the days of high infant mortality it must have been a common enough occurrence in the experience of those women who survived long enough to see their grandchildren. The seventeenth-century New England poet Anne Bradstreet wrote about the death of two of hers with a resigned eloquence not available to – or at least not recorded of – the aged Trojan queen Hecuba, mother of Hector, assuming she actually existed. The male playwright Euripides had to find words for Hecuba's grief as she held her slaughtered grandson in her arms. No matter; they are wonderful.

Other grandmothers, like the old woman in that curious poem by Tennyson, 'The Grandmother', live long enough to see their adult sons and daughters die before them. Though in her case it was a consequence of great age, it is not so where the sons are sent to war, as my two uncles were in 1914. My grandmother lost them both almost simultaneously with becoming a grandmother for the first time. The effect of her loss permeated my childhood, but undoubtedly permeated still more the childhood of that fatherless first grandchild, daughter of the eldest son, who failed to find in her a sympathetic granny.

Only eight when my grandmother died, I managed to squeeze out a tear or two, thinking that I ought to cry for a dead granny. But actually I didn't feel anything much. I had seen so little of her, and never known her as anything but old, unlike the grandchildren of much younger women, whose first experience of ageing and death, as Nathalie Angier points out, is almost always that of a grandparent. Having never watched a grandparent grow old, I wonder as I begin ageing myself how that affects my attitude to ageing. Unlike some of my friends, I've not yet met the related physical problems. But I know that, like most people, I fear death less than I fear that process of disintegration. As I fear reaching the stage when, as in the piece from Margaret Laurence's *The Stone Angel*, my young start to wonder what I'm still here for.

I doubt if I fear age more than anyone else. But maybe I'm less tolerant of it than some. I've quoted research suggesting that teenagers who are in contact with their grandparents are much less dismissive or prejudiced against the old than those who aren't. Whether these same teenagers will view their own old age differently is hard to tell. No doubt, like me, they will do their best to stave it off. Coming from a generation relatively aware of the issues, compared to past generations, and with that awareness backed up by information fed me by my younger sister, a nurse specialising in geriatrics, I am lucky perhaps to have some idea of how to protect myself from conditions against which it is possible to protect oneself. Statistics claiming that more than half of women over fifty are not capable of walking a mile have little to do with age. Except for those disabled by arthritis or other inescapable conditions, they are due far more to the effects of physical inertia. The middle-aged women I see working out in the gym are presumably, just like me, trying to subvert that statistic, particularly as they near the age of sixty-two and that even more dread statistic that from this time on they can expect to suffer from one physical problem or another.

Indeed many other physical and mental miseries of old age, ranging from incontinence to depression, all too often dismissed by doctors as 'inevitable in someone of your age, dear, you just have to put up with it', can, in my sister's experience, be cured or at least mitigated, with benefit not only to the aged themselves but also, in the long term, the finances of the health service. Our attempts to delay the inevitable are comic, I don't deny. But going gentle into that good night is one thing; for it is possible to be too lively, and we must in the end accept our own mortality – old age and death alike are matters to be reflected on quietly. Yet I'm damned if I'll assist biology in its determination to get me. Anything that will help me frustrate it, from the torture of the gym to the blessings of HRT, I welcome.

It won't work, of course, for ever. Besides, though physical fitness helps in old age, it is not the only means of surviving it. My geriatrician sister insists that many so-called characteristics of the old have nothing to do with being old. People don't change overnight into something called an 'old person' unrelated to their past persona. An old man's obstinacy, his inflexibility, aren't due to age but to the fact he always was obstinate, his thinking always was inflexible. And I've met many old women whose thinking and vocabulary shift to meet the age they live in, as I've also known those whose appetite for life remains despite the greatest physical infirmity. 'I make sure I've got treats lined up,' I was told by my first literary agent, a women especially dear to me, who became in the months before she died a kind of replacement for my dead mother. At the time she could hardly walk and was grief-struck from the death of a sister she'd lived alongside all her life. Yet she was better company than almost anyone else I've ever met, and remains the best example I know of how to face what's coming as the years move on, no matter what form it comes in.

That woman never married. She didn't have the comfort I

have, contemplating final dissolution, of knowing that through my grandchildren something of me and my mother and my grandmother remains and will go on. It seems to matter. Not to have descendants would be, we feel – and it was a childless friend I talked to who expressed his feeling precisely in this way – to find oneself the point where infinity turns finite. Thereby you lose a whole sector of the unit of human time that is the space between a grandparent's memory of their own childhood and the grandchild's memory and knowledge of those memories.

I know I have tended to conflate ageing and grandparent-hood throughout this book. In another context it would be interesting to separate the two, and to get the perspective of others who are ageing like ourselves but who have chosen not to have children. Do they regret that more late in life? Do we who are grandparents – or some of us, anyway – inflate the sense of ongoing that our grandchildren give us, mainly in order to forget through them what can't be avoided in the end: our inevitable physical extinction? Or do they really extend the meaning of our lives in some way? A bit of both, most likely. But either way, I can't be sure.

The existence of grandchildren is in all events a double-edged sword. Whether or not they extend our sense of ourselves in time, they most certainly remind us that we are ageing, point out the brevity of generations in general. They do so in part because, no matter how close we feel to those immediately above and below us, their experience and ours is weighted differently. Their very language is weighted differently; it is language, after all, that helps to shape experience. In these days of the millennium, for example, we know that the words and concepts 'century' and 'millennium' are wholly human constructs; yet human constructs or not, these words and concepts have developed meanings that we have lived with all our lives. The meanings they grow for our grandchildren will be different ones altogether.

Let me explain. In my case, given the age of my grandparents when my father was born, my human unit of time, between their memories of childhood and my knowledge of it, is especially long – and would be still longer if they'd stayed alive long enough to report to me.

Both my grandparents lived half their lives in the nineteenth century. My grandfather, for instance, went out with his father in the 1950s to see snipe in the marsh which, since the 1860s, has been the home of ambassadors and other lordlings, London's Belgrave Square. More than half my life, on the other hand, will have been lived in the century, the twentieth, that encompassed almost all my parents' lives, but which my grandchildren will scarcely see. Their lives are due to unfold in a new millennium. Yet how can I comprehend the fact that where to me and my generation the term 'twentieth century' has always denoted something new and modern, from this year on, and to our grandchildren for always, it will denote history, the past. This may not be such a common way of assessing the fact that one is, undeniably, ageing. But given that I am writing at the turn of both century and millennium, it's hard not to see it like that. The gulf between my grandchildren's view of it and mine is hard to bridge. Yet both the existence of and awareness of it is essential, I think, to who and what we are, and who and what they are, also.

My own children's first experience of death was that of their step-grandfather when they were six and eight. He'd been far more of a significant presence in their lives than any natural grandmother had been in mine, and they were both upset. Standing in the garden under their window, I was startled to hear one ask the other, giggling, 'Do you think the worms are eating Tiger?' Such physical matter-of-factness would have been their way of confronting, for the first time, the facts of mortality and the mutability of human lives and relationships. It seemed no more out of order than the graphic detail in extracts here of what happens to the bodies of some grandmothers before and after death. In the case of the stuffed granny in the poem by Susannah Buck I even find endearing, not to say comforting, its hint of communication between generations transcending death.

These days, of course, I only have to look in the mirror to see how much nearer my own dissolution I am than I was when I overheard my children discussing their grandfather's corpse. My face in the mirror was never something that pleased me. Now, the one comfort when I survey what time has done to my complexion is that it doesn't affect one jot the way my elder granddaughter sees me. I am what I am, part of her life; why should she care about the lines, the lurking wrinkles? Every last one of those other, prematurely dead grandmothers, too, would see them as a privilege, I guess, not to say luxury. It's a salutary reminder that, given my family doom, I am lucky to have lived long enough to see them.

———

from The Trojan Women

[*He goes out with his Soldiers, leaving the body of the Child in* HECUBA's *arms.*]

HECUBA.
Set the great orb of Hector's shield to lie
Here on the ground. 'Tis bitter that mine eye
Should see it . . . O ye Argives, was your spear
Keen, and your hearts so low and cold, to fear
This babe? 'Twas a strange murder for brave men!
For fear this babe some day might raise again
His fallen land! Had ye so little pride?
While Hector fought, and thousands at his side,

Ye smote us, and we perished; and now, now,
When all are dead and Ilion lieth low,
Ye dread this innocent! I deem it not
Wisdom, that rage of fear that hath no thought . . .
　Ah, what a death hath found thee, little one!
Hadst thou but fallen fighting, hadst thou known
Strong youth and love and all the majesty
Of godlike kings, then had we spoken of thee
As of one blessèd . . . could in any wise
These days know blessedness. But now thine eyes
Have seen, thy lips have tasted, but thy soul
No knowledge had nor usage of the whole
Rich life that lapt thee round . . . Poor little child!
Was it our ancient wall, the circuit piled
By loving Gods, so savagely hath rent
Thy curls, these little flowers innocent
That were thy mother's garden, where she laid
Her kisses; here, just where the bone-edge frayed
Grins white above – Ah heaven, I will not see!
　Ye tender arms, the same dear mould have ye
As his; how from the shoulder loose ye drop
And weak! And dear proud lips, so full of hope
And closed for ever! What false words ye said
At daybreak, when he crept into my bed,
Called me kind names, and promised: 'Grandmother,
When thou art dead, I will cut close my hair,
And lead out all the captains to ride by
Thy tomb.' Why didst thou cheat me so? 'Tis I,
Old, homeless, childless, that for thee must shed
Cold tears, so young, so miserably dead.
　Dear God, the pattering welcomes of thy feet,
The nursing in my lap; and Oh, the sweet
Falling asleep together! All is gone.
How should a poet carve the funeral stone
To tell thy story true? 'There lieth here

A babe whom the Greeks feared, and in their fear
Slew him.' Aye, Greece will bless the tale it tells!
   Child, they have left thee beggared of all else
In Hector's house; but one thing shalt thou keep,
This war-shield bronzen-barred, wherein to sleep.
Alas, thou guardian true of Hector's fair
Left arm, how art thou masterless! and there
I see his handgrip printed on thy hold;
And deep stains of the precious sweat that rolled
In battle from the brows and beard of him,
Drop after drop, are writ about thy rim.
   Go, bring them – such poor garments hazardous
As these days leave. God hath not granted us
Wherewith to make much pride. But all I can,
I give thee, Child of Troy – O vain is man,
Who glorieth in his joy and hath no fears:
While to and fro the chances of the years
Dance like an idiot in the wind! And none
By any strength hath his own fortune won.

[*During these lines several Women are seen
approaching with garlands and raiment in their
hands.*]

    EURIPIDES, 415 BC, translated by Gilbert Murray

———————

In Memory of My Dear Grandchild Elizabeth Bradstreet, Who Deceased August, 1665, Being a Year and Half Old

Farewell dear babe, my heart's too much content,
Farewell sweet babe, the pleasure of mine eye,
Farewell fair flower that for a space was lent,

Then ta'en away unto eternity.
Blest babe, why should I once bewail thy fate,
Or sigh thy days so soon were terminate,
Sith thou art settled in an everlasting state.

By nature trees do rot when they are grown,
And plums and apples thoroughly ripe do fall,
And corn and grass are in their season mown,
And time brings down what is both strong and tall.
But plants new set to be eradicate,
And buds new blown to have so short a date,
Is by His hand alone that guides nature and fate.

ANNE BRADSTREET, 1665

I had never seen my grandmother young and her ever having
been so seemed to me at most a matter of tradition.

JULIANA HORATIA GATTY, 'Mrs Overtheway's Remembrances',
1866

My grandson, Domingo, asked me a while ago what it is like
to be one hundred. He is ten. I told him to be one hundred is
to live ten of his life times. He seemed puzzled, so I knew I
had been thoughtless. I took him around. I put my hand
besides his and we compared skins. I said it is good to be
young and it is good to be old. He didn't need any more
explanations. He said when you're young you have lots of
years before you, but when you're old you have your children
and grandchildren and you love them and you're proud of
them. I took him around again and hugged him tightly, and in

a second he was out there with his father and his grandfather, looking at the cows.

ROBERT COLES, 'Una Anciana', 1970

———————

[Mrs Ruby Harm, aged 73:] It's funny when you think about being old, I don't really see myself as old and I don't think my grandchildren see me as old. I think they see an old lady as someone bent over with a stick and hardly able to walk. That's how I remember my granny – she was an old granny to me for as long as I knew her – nowadays people stay looking younger for much longer. I suppose it's because they keep interested in clothes and fashions and that. I think we all pay more attention to our appearances than we used to. I go to the hairdressers every fortnight now – and I shall do so while I can. I like to keep myself smart although I don't change my style of clothes to follow fashion. No, I don't think of myself as old and I don't think people see me as being old. I mean people know roughly what age I am but they don't seem to think of me as old, and that's nice really.

Quoted in JANET FORD AND RUTH SINCLAIR, *Sixty Years On*, 1987

———————

Alice George

1681, March 1st. This day I saw Alice George, a woman, as she said, of 108 years old at Allhallow-tide last: she lived in St Giles' parish, Oxford, and has lived in and about Oxford since she was a young woman; she was born at Saltwych, in Worcestershire; her father lived to eighty-three, her mother to ninety-six, and her mother's mother to 111. When she was young she was neither fat nor lean, but very slender in the waist; for her size she was to be reckoned rather amongst the tall than the short women; her condition was but mean, and her maintenance her labour. She said she was able to have reaped as much in a day as a man, and had as much wages; she was married at thirty, and had fifteen children, viz. ten sons and five daughters, besides five miscarriages; she has three sons still alive, her eldest, John, living next door to her, seventy-seven years old the 25th of this month. She goes upright with a staff in one hand, but I saw her stoop twice without resting upon anything, taking up once a pot, and at another time her glove from the ground. Her hearing is very good, and her smelling so quick, that as soon as she came near me, she said I smelt very sweet, I having a pair of new gloves on that were not strong scented. Her eyes she complains of as failing her since her last sickness, which was an ague that seized her about two years since, and held her about a year; and yet she made a shift to thread a needle before us, though she seemed not to see the end of the thread very perfectly. She has as comely a face as ever I saw any old woman have, and age has neither made her deformed nor decrepit. The greatest part of her food now is bread and cheese, or bread and butter, and ale. Sack revives her when she can get it; for flesh she cannot now eat, unless it be roasting pig, which she loves. She had, she said, in her years, a good stomach, and ate what came in her way, oftener wanting victuals than a stomach. Her memory and understanding perfectly good and quick. Amongst a great deal of discourse we had with her, and stories she told, she spoke not one idle or impertinent word. Before this last ague she used to go to church constantly, Sundays, Wednesdays, and Saturdays; since that she walks not beyond her little garden. She has been ever since her being married, troubled sometimes with vapours, and so is still, but never took any physic but once, about forty years since. She said she was sixteen in 1588, and went then to Worcester to see

Queen Elizabeth, but came an hour too late, which agrees with her account of her age.

JOHN LOCKE, Journal, 1681

The Duties of the Decline of Life

We come now to the period when gray hairs and augmenting infirmities forebode with louder and louder admonition the common termination of mortality. The spring and summer of life are past; autumn is far advanced; the frown of winter is already felt. Age has its privileges and its honours. It claims exemption from the more arduous offices of society, to which its strength is no longer equal; and immunity from some at least of the exertions, the fruit of which it cannot enjoy. Deprived of many active pleasures, it claims an equivalent of ease and repose. Forced to contract the sphere of its utility, it claims a grateful remembrance of former services. From the child and the near relation, it claims duty and love: from all, tenderness and respect. Its claims are just, acceptable, and sacred. Reason approves them; sympathy welcomes them; Revelation sanctions them. 'Let children requite their parents.' 'Despise not thy mother when she is old.' 'Intreat the elder women as mothers.' 'Ye younger, submit yourselves unto the elder.' 'Thou shalt rise up before the hoary head.' But if age would be regarded with affection and reverence, it must shew itself invested with the qualities by which those feelings are to be conciliated. It must be useful according to its ability, by example, if not by exertion. If unable to continue the full exercise of active virtues, it must display the excellence of those which are passive. It must resist the temptations by which it is beset, and guard itself against indulging faults on the plea of informity. In a word, if the 'hoary head' is to be 'a crown of glory', it must be 'found in the way of righteousness'.

ANON., 1796

To ——, in Her Seventieth Year

Such age how beautiful! O Lady bright,
Whose mortal lineaments seem all refined
By favouring Nature and a saintly Mind
To something purer and more exquisite
Than flesh and blood; whene'er thou meet'st my sight,
When I behold thy blanched unwithered cheek,
Thy temples fringed with locks of gleaming white,
And head that droops because the soul is meek,
Thee with the welcome Snowdrop I compare;
That child of winter, prompting thoughts that climb
From desolation toward the genial prime;
Or with the Moon conquering earth's misty air,
And filling more and more with crystal light
As pensive Evening deepens into night.

WILLIAM WORDSWORTH, 1824

Old people have a different sort of beauty. Like fruit in a still life or rocks and minerals in a museum. It's not designed to be sexy. It just shows we are part of nature. Children love the cuddliness of their grandparents – the wispy hair like ducklings' down, the speckly skin like thrushes' breasts, the ears that have acquired a teddy-bear quality. My daughter, who is twelve, has told me sternly that by the time I become her child's granny I must be white-haired and plump with appley cheeks. I fear this may require the services not of a cosmetic surgeon but a landscape gardener. But that of course is what nature is.

SUE LIMB, *Growing Pains*, 1998

---

from Emma

'. . . she can see amazingly well still, thank God! with the help of spectacles. It is such a blessing! . . . Jane often says, when she is here, "I am sure, grandmama, you must have had very strong eyes to see as you do, and so much fine work as you have done too! I only wish my eyes may last me as well."'

[. . .] Emma said something very civil about the excellence of Miss Fairfax's handwriting.

'You are extremely kind,' replied Miss Bates . . . 'I am sure there is nobody's praise that could give so much pleasure as Miss Woodhouse's. My mother does not hear; she is a little deaf, you know. Ma'am,' addressing her, 'do you hear what Miss Woodhouse is so obliging to say about Jane's handwriting?'

[Emma] had almost resolved on hurrying away directly, under some slight excuse, when Miss Bates turned to her again . . .

'My mother's deafness is very trifling, you see, just nothing at all. By only raising my voice, and saying anything two or three times, she is sure to hear; but then she is used to my voice. But it is very remarkable that she should always hear Jane better than she does me. Jane speaks so distinct! However, she will not find her grandmama at all deafer than she was two years ago; which is saying a great deal at my mother's time of life . . .'

JANE AUSTEN, 1816

from Family Web

The old lady picked up a sickle near the door and led us out of the house: she ignored the stranger and threaded her way through the neighbours who were still clustered at the doorway.

I put on my shoes outside.

'Who was the man answering some of our questions?' I asked.

'Who? Oh yes, that man. He's . . . he's the old man's grandson. He's the brother of Thayee. He's . . .' Her voice trailed off.

'Does he live in the house?'

'Oh no! He's only the son of the old man's daughter. And even now there are quarrels.'

'Quarrels?' I said, too sharply, for she suddenly seemed to check herself.

'There's always a quarrel in this house,' she said in a friendly way. 'See, the women keep fighting. I scold them and they shout at me in return, "You old hag, who do you think you were born of? Were you born to your father? Aren't you a bastard?" Yes, they say all that. And they fight over anything. But do you think I'll let them go without scolding if they haven't swept the floor, if they haven't washed the dishes, or if they don't come to the fields? See, I told one of them to bring some food to the fields, but did she come? She didn't come. And you think I'll let her go without scolding?'

The old lady walked stiffly down the street, her eyes moving sharply from side to side to see what was going on.

'See, nobody does any work. Does anyone take the cattle? Does anyone take out the sheep?'

Turning into the main street, she walked to the family's second house, opened the front door, and let out a flock of sheep.

'Ayee, Saroji! Saroji!' she shouted, brandishing a stick, till a small girl of six ran up the steps. 'Hey, child, why aren't you out in the fields? Take the sheep at once, and don't come back till evening.'

Without a word, the girl took the stick from her grand-mother and brandished it at the sheep, forcing them to move slowly out of the village. The old lady bent to the ground – I thought to pick up twigs till she moved towards my feet.

'No, no,' I said, stepping hastily back. 'You don't have to touch my feet.' Such self-abasement appalled me – I felt it was she who should receive my respect as the female head of her house who had given us hospitality.

She groped again for my feet. I took her arms gently and made her straighten up. Perhaps I had given insult by refusing to accept her obeisance and by touching her so intimately, but I knew I did not want to become part of any hierarchy for it meant the manipulation of power over those in a lesser role. I was not interested in power; I had no wish to change the family's lives.

The old lady grinned and told me to come back the follow-ing day. Then she turned and hurried after the sheep, her body hunched forward, her mouth working silently.

SARAH HOBSON, 1978

It made her sad to realize that a fortnight in the company of her maternal grandmother was no longer, to be honest, her idea of heaven. She had reluctantly come to the conclusion that Granny P could be a little stultifying. She was a pre-dictable and limited woman, whose persistently partisan indulgence towards Christina – and equally persistent coolness towards Pam – was an embarrassment rather than a triumph. Moreover, there was not the previous thrill to be got from shipping trips alone with Granny P, since the two of them no longer shared a passion for shiny shoes.

BARBARA TRAPIDO, *Juggling*, 1994

from Culture and Aging

Mrs Burbank lives with [her] granddaughter and her own daughter who is divorced and blind. 'I still love being a grand-mother,' she says, but she adds that she was happiest in this role only up until the girl turned twelve. 'I used to enjoy taking her places,' she says, 'and she was very companionable, but in high school she was very difficult.' Often – as in this case – when a relationship with a grandchild had been deeply felt, estrangement during the child's teen-age years can be experi-enced as a serious loss: 'My granddaughter was a very warm outgoing young child, but now she doesn't even know me. There was a time when I was home with my grandchild all day. We were very close, but her mother was jealous of me. Now, whenever she comes home on a weekend from college and I try to ask her how she's doing in school, sometimes she doesn't even bother answering me. I realize there is a large dif-ference between her age and mine, but I have gone through many things and I could help her in some of her problems, but I don't have the chance to do so. She seems more like a stranger than a grandchild.' During later interviews, Mrs Burbank's granddaughter had even ceased to drop by on weekends: 'She used to write once a month and now it's only holidays. She doesn't say much about herself.' Mrs Miller con-curs: 'As grandchildren grow older, they have other interests. They forget about you. They figure you're old.'

M. CLARK and B. ANDERSON, 1967

Grandmother Love Poem

Late in her life, when we fell in love,
I'd take her out from the nursing home

for a chaser and two bourbons. She'd crack
a joke sharp as a tin lid
hot from the teeth of the can-opener,
and cackle her crack-corn laugh. Next to her
wit, she prided herself on her hair,
snowy and abundant. She would fit it up
at the nape of the neck, there in the bar,
and under the white, under the salt-and-
pepper, she'd show me her true colour,
the colour it was when she was a bride:
like her sex in the smoky light she would show me
the pure black.

SHARON OLD, c. 1985

<hr />

Karin got a First, and Gram's delight in this was unbounded.
She collected all the letters of congratulation, and all the newspaper cuttings she could find, and did everything she could to
make Karin and every one else realize her glory to the full. Her
delight and sympathy lasted on through the following year,
the last of her grandchild's academic career.

RAY STRACHEY, *A Quaker Grandmother*, 1914

<hr />

'Red letter day' reads Granny's diary for 29th September, 1925.
'News in *The Times* of Bay's great success – an appointment in
the Civil Service! She is 12th in order of merit and one of only
two women ever admitted, out of 200 candidates! Oh how
excited we all were!'

[. . .] The odd thing is that I don't remember what I felt myself
in the midst of all the excitement. All I have is a flat, wholly

unemotional memory of getting the news, standing half-dressed
in my home-made calico knickers in the 'barrack room' at
Broughton, and of Granny in her four-poster bed sitting surrounded by newspapers and smiling all over her wrinkled face:
'None of my children has "set the Thames on fire"' she said as
she kissed me, 'but now one of my granddaughters has.'

ALIX MEYNELL, *Public Servant, Private Woman*, 1988

---

from Chronicle of My Mother

After dinner Mother usually sat for about two hours on a
cushion on the living room carpet, at times listening to the
family conversation and at other times drifting off into her
own world. Soon she became drowsy and nodded off, and
whenever she came to, she put her hands to her kimono collar
and looked slightly embarrassed.

As soon as Yoshiko became aware that Mother was sleepy
she got up quickly and took her hand, saying, 'Well, it's night-
night time.' If Mother refused to go, Yoshiko said,
'Naughty-naughty, now, it's night-night time,' and proceeded
to get Mother on her feet and half-carry her up the stairs leading to the bedrooms. It was Yoshiko's task to put Mother to
bed, and it was her special talent. If anyone else attempted it
there was great resistance, for in this matter mother was indulgent only toward Yoshiko – although during the day when
Mother was agitated she was more unkind to Yoshiko than to
any of us. I had never seen Yoshiko put Mother to bed, but at
times Yoshiko talked about it, saying that things went
smoothly one night or not so well another night.

'I do it very quickly. I help her take off her kimono, put on
her night kimono, get her under the covers, tuck her in, then
pat her on the shoulders. Then I get some tissues, her wallet,

and a flashlight, show them to her and tell her I have placed
these items by her, and set them down by her pillow. Then I pat
her on the shoulders again. She does not seem to settle down
unless I do this. Then I go out into the hall, switch off her light
so that only her room is dark, and stand there a while. If she
doesn't get up within two or three minutes, then she's fine.'
Yoshiko probably put Mother to bed in that manner every
night. I liked listening to Yoshiko talk about it. Her conversation captured the intimacy between that singular pair –
grandmother and granddaughter.

YASUSHI INOUE, translated by Jean Oda Moy, 1982

---

from Old Age in Gwembe District [southern Africa]

Siagondo was born in 1872. She had had an adventurous
youth, which had included capture and escape from Ndebele
raiders. In 1956 her husbands, of which there had been several,
were long dead. Her only surviving son had disappeared as a
labor migrant. Her two living daughters were elderly widows
whose own sons had also gone off to work and not
returned [. . .] Siagondo, however, had been induced to move to
the homestead of a wealthy lineage kinsman who had a sense
of responsibility for the old woman. At 84, she was alert and
active. Two years before she had decided that she no longer
would be bothered with a field, and she was cooked for by the
other women of the homestead. Her kinsman supplied her
with clothing and blankets – she was as well dressed as she
cared to be. She ate by herself because she regarded the small
children as unmannerly and did not wish to dip into the same
dish with them. But she was willing to keep an eye on the
babies, could chuckle over a joke, and when she was of a mind
to was quite prepared to walk as much as six or seven miles to

visit kin. Indeed, her memory made her the linchpin of her lineage, for its members were held together by her reminders of their common origin. Siagondo was also a mourner at most funerals in the neighborhood. After all, she had no other duties and could spend time at such occasions.

In 1962, at 90, Siagondo still lived with the same kinsman, who had had a new house built for her after the resettlement. On good days she was still a cheerful companion who was prepared to adventure on new experiences. Those who looked after her regarded her as an asset – they were sure nobody else in all of Gwembe could be as old, and they delighted in her wit. She in turn was somewhat contemptuous of the young, who were so ignorant of all she could remember. One day she said with great scorn, 'Why these youngsters don't even know where Panda-ma-tenka is!' And she sang a song about the place, which had a short-lived fame between about 1880 and 1888. By mid-1963, however, she kept more and more within her house, cried about her aches, and complained of neglect and the noise of the children. People in the village began to dwell on the trials of the old when they spoke of Siagondo.

She died in 1964, having seen her great great grandchildren.

ELIZABETH COLSON AND THAYER SCUDDER, 1981

---

from At the Bay

'My Australian Uncle William?' said Kezia. She had another.

'Yes, of course.'

'The one I never saw?'

'That was the one.'

'Well, what happened to him?' Kezia knew perfectly well, but she wanted to be told again.

'He went to the mines, and he got a sunstroke there and died,' said old Mrs Fairfield.

[. . .] 'But why?' asked Kezia. She lifted one bare arm and began to draw things in the air. 'Why did Uncle William have to die? He wasn't old.'

Mrs Fairfield began counting the stitches in threes. 'It just happened,' she said in an absorbed voice.

'Does everybody have to die?' asked Kezia.

'Everybody!'

'*Me?*' Kezia sounded fearfully incredulous.

'Some day, my darling.'

'But, grandma.' Kezia waved her left leg and waggled the toes. They felt sandy. 'What if I just won't?'

The old woman sighed again and drew a long thread from the ball.

'We're not asked, Kezia,' she said sadly. 'It happens to all of us sooner or later.'

Kezia lay still thinking this over. She didn't want to die. It meant she would have to leave here, leave everywhere, for ever, leave – leave her grandma. She rolled over quickly.

'Grandma,' she said in a startled voice.

'What, my pet!'

'*You're* not to die.' Kezia was very decided.

'Ah, Kezia' – her grandma looked up and smiled and shook her head – 'don't let's talk about it.'

'But you're not to. You couldn't leave me. You couldn't not be there.' This was awful. 'Promise me you won't ever do it, grandma,' pleaded Kezia.

The old woman went on knitting.

'Promise me! Say never!'

But still her grandma was silent.

Kezia rolled off the bed; she couldn't bear it any longer, and lightly she leapt on to her grandma's knees, clasped her hands round the old woman's throat and began kissing her, under the chin, behind the ear, and blowing down her neck.

'Say never . . . say never . . . say never –' She gasped between the kisses. And then she began, very softly and lightly, to tickle her grandma.

'Kezia!' the old woman dropped her knitting. She swung back in the rocker. She began to tickle Kezia. 'Say never, say never, say never,' gurgled Kezia, while they lay there laughing in each other's arms. 'Come, that's enough, my squirrel! That's enough, my wild pony!' said old Mrs Fairfield, setting her cap straight. 'Pick up my knitting.'

Both of them had forgotten what the 'never' was about.

KATHERINE MANSFIELD, 1922

---

from A Granddaughter's Fear

My grandmother is the first person I have watched grow old. I used to adore her; she still keeps loving poems and letters I wrote to her as a child. She was always a vivid, energetic woman, selling bonds for Israel, working long hours in charity thrift shops. She told stories about her past with the narrative panach of Isaac Bashevis Singer. Wherever she went, she made flocks of friends – a trait that I, a lonely and sullen girl, profoundly admired.

But then hard times began to pile up around her like layers of choking silt. Although she'd stoutly nursed three husbands through terminal illnesses, she became depressed when her siblings – all older than she – started to die. After she lost her last sister, in 1982, my grandmother just about lost her mind. She still had many friends, but she clamored for ever more attention from her children and grandchildren. She became an emotional hair-trigger; she had temper tantrums at parties, seders, my sister's wedding.

As my grandmother has worsened, so has my response to

her. My mother implores me to be decent and stay in touch, and I launch into all the reasons that I don't. But my excuses sound shallow and glib, even to me. The truth is that my grandmother terrifies me.

I have in my mind a pastel confection of the perfect old woman. She is wise and dignified, at peace with herself, and quietly proud of the life she has forged. She doesn't waste time seeking approval or cursing the galaxy. Instead, she works at her craft. She is Georgia O'Keeffe painting, Louise Nevelson sculpturing, Marianne Moore writing. Or she is a less celebrated woman, who reads, listens to Bach, and threads together the scattered days into a private whole.

Of course, there are many things my fantasy doyenne is not. She's not strapped for money. Her joints don't ache, and her breath doesn't rattle. She isn't losing her memory, her eyesight, her reason. Above all, she is not the old woman I know best.

I love my grandmother. She still has her good hours, when her mind is quick and clear. Inevitably, though, her mad despair bursts to the surface again. She discovers a new reason to weep, blame, and backstab, and I discover a new excuse for staying away.

I want to age magnificently, as O'Keeffe and Moore did. I want to be better in half a century than I am at thirty-one, but I doubt that I will be. When I look at my grandmother, fragile, frightened, unhappy, wanting to die but clinging desperately to life, I see myself – and I cannot stand the sight.

My grandmother died in September of 1991, a day before her eighty-third birthday. I still dream about her, more often now, in fact, than I did immediately after her death. In my dreams she is always much younger than she was when she died, and she is always completely sane and strong. She becomes herself again, my grandmother at her best, and I stare at her in wonderment and relief. My dreaming mind is a child's mind –

*sentimental, grandiose, rewriting stories so that their endings
can be born.*

NATALIE ANGIER, 1995

---

from The Right of the Old and Young

Thanks to the size of Momo's house, the young couple, Momo
and Martha, have been able to live apart from the old women:
they form two separate families; thus avoiding friction; the old
couple live on the ground floor, the husband and wife on the
first.

[. . .] They say it was the doctor's orders. 'It is unwise,' he
appears to have stated, 'to let two old women who are so
unwell live at close quarters with the children, in dining-room
and parlour.' These considerations of health have given rise to
the division of the household into two, the young – as we have
said – occupying the first floor, the old on the ground floor.
Each family does its own cooking. But sometimes the sound of
the children crying upstairs brings the old women hurrying to
the stairs; then, halfway up, they remember they have been
told not to go upstairs, so they turn back in silence, with
drooping heads.

At other times – very often, in fact – one of the children,
probably Mariuccia, will escape downstairs (she had grown so
used to it!) and take refuge in granny's lap, blind granny.

Martha the laborious, Martha the sharp-eyed, knows what
has happened. She goes after her child, catches her with her
granny. 'Come back at once!' says she peremptorily, beckoning
hard. The little girl sees, obeys, runs back to her; the grandmother, feeling her slip away, reaches out her trembling hands
for the golden head, the dear little head with the baby smell;
but it has gone. She dares not call her; her shaggy grey head

sinks down on her knees. Motionless she stays for hours on
end, brooding on the mysterious patterns woven by the darkness: such mysterious, such terrible pictures that the dead
eyeballs will start out of their sockets at times, and the feeble
mind reel. Then the nurses have to be sent for from the hospital, because one of her cruel attacks is coming on. Martha
goes so far as to say that her mother-in-law is mad, and that it
would be charitable to put her into an asylum for treatment.
But she is not mad; she has only lost the sight of those external eyes which see nothing but the things of this world; and
when infirmity closes the eyes to the light, others, mysterious
ones, are opened within, that see things horrible and tragic, so
that whoever looks on them becomes distraught.

Except when she is in the throes of an attack, the grandmother is quiet and contented. Steadily and slowly, her soft
slippers go padding up and down the rooms; one hand feels
along the wall, the other is outstretched and moves from side
to side with a regular, unchanging motion as if to clear away
the darkness that has been closing in on her for years and
years. She is trying to make a rift for the light to come through,
for sometimes the blackness is not quite so dense. In brilliant
sunshine, or when the oil lamp is high and bright, her eye can
catch just a glimmer. Ah, the light! 'Merciful Lord,' she prays,
'grant me light once more. Even the ants can see – let me see as
much as they!'

Apart from this, Momo's mother has nothing the matter
with her; and except when she is attacked by her fits of melan-
cholia she is mild and placid. She will ask about the hens in the
chicken run: how many eggs they are laying, what price they
are fetching. She wants to know if the washerwoman has
brought back all the washing; she dwells at length on the days
when she did the laundry herself at home: the good old days!
She remembers the old zest for work, that she has no longer.
Her lips tremble, as she mumbles to herself: oh, dear, the fur-
niture has not been properly dusted; and she flaps a duster

about the room. She lingers lovingly over the food in her bowl, the good, nourishing food that puts new life in her veins.

'You have to keep her in hand worse than a child,' says Martha, 'she'd gobble up a bowlful twice over if you gave her the chance.'

'An iron digestion,' remarks the doctor.

'She'd digest nails!' exclaims Martha.

'She'll live to bury us all yet,' says Momo.

'Yes, there's no telling how many more years she'll drag on,' the doctor says. 'Five, or maybe ten, there's no knowing.'

'And the amount of things she uses up!' says Martha. 'The lamp, for instance, half a litre of oil every evening. If she is supposed to be blind, why does she want a lamp at all?'

'The sensation of warmth is converted, in her case, into one of light,' explains the doctor.

Yes, when you come to think of it, this aged creature hovering about the place like a ghost, with that hand of hers trying to make a rift in the darkness, with those great blank eyeballs starting from their sockets, starved for light, – the sight of her, day after day – you can understand how sooner or later it gets on the nerves of those who have to live with her.

[. . .] Momo is driven to exasperation by the plaintive sound of [her] voice.

'Why can't she take herself off? She ought to have been dead long ago. She clings to life far more than I do myself.'

And his venomous tone really might make you think he's a bad man. But the fact is that not only Momo, but all of us, find it hard to know our own folk any longer when they have grown old and decrepit . . . The actual moment of the change is not recorded, but it is a fact that Mother or Aunt are Mother and Aunt no longer. Only the ghosts of what they were remain . . .

ALFREDO PANZINI, 1869–1939, translated 1930

from The Stone Angel

Later, when she and Mr Troy have gone, I have another visitor. At first, I can't place him, although he is so familiar in appearance. He grins and bends over me.

'Hi, Gran. Don't you know me? Steven.'

I'm flustered, pleased to see him, mortified at not having recognized him immediately.

'Steven. Well, well. Of course. How are you? I haven't seen you for quite some time. You're looking very smart.'

'New suit. Glad you like it. Have to look successful, you know.'

'You don't only look. You are. Aren't you?'

'I can't complain,' he says.

He's an architect, a very clever boy. Goodness knows where he gets his brains from. Not from either parent, I'd say. But Marvin and Doris certainly saved and did without to get that boy through university, I'll give them that.

'Did your mother tell you to come and see me?'

'Of course not,' he says. 'I just thought I'd drop in and see how you were.'

He sounds annoyed, so I know he's lying. What does it matter? But it would have been nice if it had been his own idea.

'Tina's getting married,' I say, conversationally.

I'm tired. I'm not feeling up to much. But I hope he'll stay for a few minutes all the same. I like to look at him. He's a fine-looking boy. Boy, indeed – he must be close to thirty.

'So I hear,' he says. 'About time, too. Mom wants her to be married here, but Tina says she can't spare the time and neither can Angus – that's the guy she's marrying. So Mom's going to fly down east for the wedding, she thinks.'

I never realized until this moment how cut off I am. I've always been so fond of Tina. Doris might have told me. It's the least she could have done.

'She didn't tell me. She didn't say a word.'

'Maybe I shouldn't have said—'

'It's a good job somebody tells me these things. She never bothers, your mother. It never occurs to her.'

'Well, maybe she forgot. She's been—'

'I'll bet she forgot. I'll just bet a cookie she did. When is she going, Steven?'

A long pause. My grandson reddens and gazes at my roses, his face averted from mine.

'I don't think it's quite settled yet,' he says finally.

Then all at once I understand, and know, too, why Doris never mentioned it. They have to wait and see what happens here. How inconvenient I am proving for them. *Will it be soon?* That's what they're asking themselves. I'm upsetting all their plans. That's what it is to them – an inconvenience.

Steven leans toward me again. 'Anything you want, Gran? Anything I could bring you?'

'No. Nothing. There's nothing I want.'

'Sure?'

'You might just leave me your packet of cigarettes, Steven. Would you?'

'Oh sure, of course. Here – have one now.'

'Thank you.'

He lights it for me, and places an ashtray, rather nervously, close by my wrist, as though certain I'm a fire hazard. Then he looks at me and smiles, and I'm struck again with the resemblance.

'You're very like your grandfather, Steven. Except that he wore a beard, you could almost be Brampton Shipley as a young man.'

'Oh?' He's only mildly interested. He searches for a comment. 'Should I be pleased?'

'He was a fine-looking man, your grandfather.'

'Mom always says I look like Uncle Ned.'

'What? Doris's brother? Nonsense. You don't take after him a scrap. You're a Shipley through and through.'

He laughs. 'You're a great old girl, you know that?'

His tone has affection in it, and I would be pleased if it weren't condescending as well, in the same way that gushing matrons will coo over a carriage – *What a cute baby, how adorable*.

'You needn't be impertinent, Steven. You know I don't care for it.'

'I didn't mean it like that. Never mind. You should be glad I appreciate you.'

'Do you?'

'Sure I do,' he says jovially. 'I always have. Don't you remember how you used to give me pennies to buy jaw-breakers, when I was a kid? Mom used to be livid, thinking of the dentist's bills.'

I'd forgotten. I have to smile, even as my mouth is filled once more with bile. That's what I am to him – a grandmother who gave him money for candy. What does he know of me? Not a blessed thing. I'm choked with it now, the incommunicable years, everything that happened and was spoken or not spoken. I want to tell him. Someone should know. This is what I think. *Someone really ought to know these things*.

MARGARET LAURENCE, 1964

————

from Mid-life

When I was born, she was forty-two. In those days, her hair was marcel-waved and her pink lipstick perfectly applied. One of my early memories is of walking with her in Rittenhouse Square, where there would always be a passerby who was convinced she was Paulette Goddard.

I cannot pinpoint precisely when she began to fade, but along the way were the usual signs: the afternoon naps, the sudden, inexplicable moments of rage, the quiver of a mouth once firmly set.

Long before, she had told me that forty to sixty were the best years in a woman's life. I wanted to believe her, though I had begun to wonder what happens after sixty, especially now that she was in decline and I was embellishing a medical vocabulary, which already included useful terms like menopause and osteoporosis, with the names of other, less familiar age-related diseases like senile dementia.

And I could not watch my grandmother grow old without perceiving her journey as a road map to my own future. For while I intended to be, at ninety, a spunky old lady who drove a red sports car and worked every day and flirted with sixty-year-old men, that was also the way I had envisioned old age for my grandmother. That it had not turned out that way extinguished my hopeful faith that aging is only for others. Finally I knew that if I lived long enough, what had happened to her on the far side of mid-life would happen to me.

ELIZABETH KATZ, 1997

---

from The Grandmother

I

And Willy, my eldest-born, is gone, you say, little Anne?
Ruddy and white, and strong on his legs, he looks like a man.
And Willy's wife has written: she never was over-wise,
Never the wife for Willy: he wouldn't take my advice.

II

For, Annie, you see, her father was not the man to save,
Hadn't a head to manage, and drank himself into his grave.
Pretty enough, very pretty! but I was against it for one.
Eh! – but he wouldn't hear me – and Willy, you say, is gone.

III

Willy, my beauty, my eldest-born, the flower of the flock;
Never a man could fling him; for Willy stood like a rock.
'Here's a leg for a babe of a week!' says doctor; and he
    would be bound,
There was not his like that year in twenty parishes round.

IV

Strong of his hands, and strong on his legs, but still of his
    tongue!
I ought to have gone before him: I wonder he went so young.
I cannot cry for him, Annie: I have not long to stay;
Perhaps I shall see him the sooner, for he lived far away.

V

Why do you look at me, Annie? you think I am hard and
    cold;
But all my children have gone before me, I am so old:
I cannot weep for Willie, nor can I weep for the rest;
Only at your age, Annie, I could have wept with the best.

ALFRED, LORD TENNYSON

---

from Una Anciana

But now, during the last moments of life, I think I have learned
a little wisdom. I can go for days without an upset. I think I
dislike our priest because he reminds me of myself. I have his
long forefinger, and I can clench my fist like him and pound
the table and pour vinegar on people with my remarks. It is no
good to be like that. A man is lucky; it is in his nature to fight
or preach. A woman should be peaceful. My mother used to
say all begins the day we are born: some are born on a clear,

warm day; some when it is cloudy and stormy. So, it is a consolation to find myself easy to live with these days. And I have found an answer to the few moods I still get. When I have come back from giving the horses each a cube or two of sugar, I give myself the same. I am an old horse who needs something sweet to give her more faith in life!

The other day I thought I was going to say good-bye to this world. I was hanging up some clothes to dry. I love to do that, then stand back and watch and listen to the wind go through the socks or the pants or the dress, and see the sun warm them and make them smell fresh. I had dropped a few clothespins, and was picking them up, when suddenly I could not catch my breath, and a sharp pain seized me over my chest. I tried hard to stand up, but I couldn't. I wanted to scream but I knew there was no one nearby to hear. My husband had gone to the store. I sat down on the ground and waited. It was strong, the pain; and there was no one to tell about it. I felt as if someone had lassoed me and was pulling the rope tighter and tighter. Well here you are, an old cow, being taken in by the good Lord; that is what I thought.

I looked at myself, sitting on the ground. For a second I was my old self again – worrying about how I must have appeared there, worrying about my dress, how dirty it would get to be. This is no place for an old lady, I thought – only for one of my little grandchildren, who love to play out here, build their castles of dirt, wetted down with water I give to them. Then more pain; I thought I had about a minute of life left. I said my prayers. I said goodbye to the house. I pictured my husband in my mind: fifty-seven years of marriage. Such a good man! I said to myself that I might not see him ever again; surely God would take him into Heaven, but as for me, I have no right to expect that outcome. Then I looked up at the sky and waited.

ROBERT COLES, 1970

Anyway, I don't think about getting older and not being able to get out and about. I don't think it will be like that. I think I will die quickly . . . If you think that you are ill, that you can't work, that you can't do this and that, then you will be ill. It's better not to think about it, but to keep going. That is why I like to have my grandchildren around me. They make me feel young. I like to have them in the house, I enjoy that, and they love me a lot. I don't like it quiet, I like the children to talk and laugh and to have friends to talk with me . . . I don't cry much unless it is because some people are ill or in trouble or they die. Then I cry, but not at anything else.

MRS PATEL, quoted in Janet Ford and Ruth Sinclair,
Sixty Years On, 1987

And there was no one else to care for you and guard you but a woman, the mother of your father, and she, by reason of her great age, herself stood in need of others to care for her.

DIONYSIUS OF HALICARNASSUS, c. 20 BC

I saw a kite on its string, tugging, bounding – as far away as my grandmother – dance against the blue from its tie of invisible delight.

In the caves of blue within the blue the grandmothers bound, on the brink of freedom.

ROBERT DUNCAN, *The Structure of Rime IV*, 1960

My grandmother died in the blue arms of a jacaranda tree.
She could read thunder.

> MICHAEL ONDAATJE, *Running in the Family*, 1983

Being . . . close to the horizon of dying, brings the grandmother full circle to understanding how the child sees it as
'new'.

> NOR HALL, *The Moon and the Virgin*, 1980

To witness a death is to endure an intimacy that binds you to
the most fundamental of collective experiences. In half-lit
rooms throughout the world, at every moment of the day
and night, sorrowing people seek to retain composure, while
keeping vigil over someone who will soon disappear for
ever . . .

> ELIZABETH KATZ, *Mid-life*, 1997

[Grandma] didn't seem very sick, but in a few days she was
dead. She and I spent a long afternoon, the day before she
died, discussing the possibilities in a string of hot-dog
stands.

> TED PECKHAM, *Grandma Rolled Her Own*, 1954

Elizabeth Fry

On Saturday morning, our mother awakened, suffering severely in her head. Gerard went to read to her at half-past seven o'clock, he soon returned and told me that he had read grandmamma the 27th psalm which she had asked for, but that she did not talk and he thought she was not well. Half an hour later Willie went to see her. She in no way referred to Gerard having been there before, and against asked Willie for the 27th Psalm. When he came back he said 'grandmamma seems quite heavy this morning.' Her dressing was very slowly accomplished, she leaned her head upon her hand and spoke very little . . . She did not ask for a child while she was dressing, the only morning she had omitted to do so, nor did she remark their absence.

Memories of Her Mother, by R.E.C., 1845

from The Year I Was Eight

One night long after my bedtime, I heard my grandmother come upstairs, and begin to run her bath. I slipped out of bed and went across the landing to talk to her. In a little while she sent me back to bed, and as I went she said, 'Goodbye, dearest.' I laughed at her. 'You don't mean goodbye, Granny, you mean goodnight,' I said, and she smiled, and said, 'Goodnight.'

After I had got back to bed, I heard a heavy thump, and then a lot of coming and going on the stairs as I drifted off to sleep.

The next morning they told me Granny was ill, too ill even for me to go and see her. Because my grandfather was a step-grandfather, the house was full of his family, who either didn't like me or were always very busy, so at once I felt very lonely. I couldn't believe my grandmother wouldn't like to see me, however ill she was, and the house was full of rushing around, and everyone frowned the minute they clapped eyes on me, and looked worried. I went out, and walked on the path to the beach. I saw a lizard basking on a rock, and I was frightened to go past it because I thought it was a snake and I took the markings on its back to be those of a viper. But I found a scruffy handful of flowers, mostly sea-pinks, and then I crept back into the house, going up the back stairs instead of the main ones, and slipped into my grandmother's room. It was empty. The bed was made, pulled flat and smooth, and tucked-in all round. A clean starched pillow-case upon the pillow showed not a single crease.

I crept out, holding my flowers. The more I thought about it, the more terrified I became. Every single person in the house had lied to me that morning. They had all said Granny was ill in bed. I began to remember that they were all step-relatives, and to think of stories about wicked servants and horrible stepmothers. My grandfather seemed to have gone out; I could have trusted him, but I didn't see him that day.

They put a lunch for me on the corner of the kitchen table, and told me that my mother was coming, that she would be here very soon. 'What have I done?' I asked them. 'Doesn't Granny want me any more?' 'Be good now, and *do* stop asking questions,' they said.

When my mother came in the evening, I flew to her, screaming, and flung myself at her; and then I saw that she was crying; floods of silent tears pouring down her face. 'Hasn't the child been told?' she said. Then, 'Granny's dead, dear,' she said to me, letting fresh tears fall; and all the other people looked stiff, and turned away.

JILL PATON WALSH, 1967

from A Trip to the Coast

The old woman put her hands up to her head and did not answer.

'What's the matter, lady, aren't you feeling well. You got a headache?'

'I feel all right.'

'How did you cure those people?' May said boldly, though her grandmother had always told her: don't let me catch you talking to strangers in the store.

The little man swung round attentively. 'Why I hypnotize them, young lady. I hypnotize them. Are you asking me to explain to you what hypnotism is?'

May who did not know what she was asking flushed red and had no idea what to say. She saw her grandmother looking straight at her. The old woman looked out of her head at May and the whole world as if they had caught fire and she could do nothing about it, she could not even communicate the fact to them.

'She don't know what she's talking about,' her grandmother said.

'Well it's very simple,' the man said directly to May, in a luxuriantly gentle voice he must think suitable for children. 'It's just like you put a person to sleep. Only they're not really asleep, do you follow me, honey? You can talk to them. And listen – listen to this – you can go way deep into their minds and find out things they wouldn't even remember when they were awake. Find out their hidden worries and anxieties that's causing them the trouble. Now isn't that an amazing thing?'

'You couldn't do that with me,' the old woman said. 'I would know what was going on. You couldn't do that with me.'

'I bet he could,' May said, and was so startled at herself her mouth stayed open. She did not know why she had said that.

Time and again she had watched her grandmother's encounters with the outside world, not with pride so much as a solid, fundamental conviction that the old woman would get the better of it. Now for the first time it seemed to her she saw the possibility of her grandmother's defeat; in her grandmother's face she saw it and not in the little man who must be crazy, she thought, and who made her want to laugh. The idea filled her with dismay and with a painful, irresistible excitement.

'Well you never can tell till you give it a try,' the man said, as if it were a joke. He looked at May. The old woman made up her mind. She said scornfully, 'It don't matter to me.' She put her elbows on the counter and held her head between her two hands, as if she were pressing something in. 'Pity to take your time,' she said.

'You really ought to lay down so you can relax better.'

'Sitting down—' she said, and seemed to lose her breath a moment – ' sitting down's good enough for me.'

Then the man took a bottle-opener off a card of knick-knacks they had in the store and he walked over to stand in front of the counter. He was not in any hurry. When he spoke it was in a natural voice but it had changed a little; it had grown mild and unconcerned. 'Now I know you're resisting this idea,' he said softly. 'I know you're resisting it and I know why. It's because you're afraid.' The old woman made a noise of protest or alarm and he held up his hand, but gently. 'You're afraid,' he said, 'and all I want to show you, all I mean to show you, is that there is nothing to be afraid of. Nothing to be afraid of. Nothing. Nothing to be afraid of, I just want you to keep your eyes on this shiny metal object I'm holding in my hand. That's right, just keep your eyes on this shiny metal object here in my hand. Just keep your eyes on it. Don't think. Don't worry. Just say to yourself, there's nothing to be afraid of, nothing to be afraid of, nothing to be afraid of—' His voice sank; May could not make out the words. She stayed pressed against the soft-drink cooler. She wanted to laugh, she could not help it, watching the somehow disreputable back of this man's head and his white, rounded, twitching shoulders. But she did not laugh because she had to wait to see what her grandmother would do. If her grandmother capitulated it would be as unsettling an event as an earthquake or a flood; it would crack the foundations of her life and set her terrifyingly free. The old woman stared with furious unblinking obedience at the bottle-opener in the man's hand.

'Now I just want you to tell me,' he said, 'if you can still see – if you can still see—' He bent forward to look into her face. 'I just want you to tell me if you can still see—' The old woman's face with its enormous cold eyes and its hard ferocious expression was on a level with his own. He stopped; he drew back.

'Hey what's the matter?' he said, not in his hypnotizing but his ordinary voice – in fact a sharper voice than ordinary, which made May jump. 'What's the matter, lady, come on, wake up. Wake up,' he said, and touched her shoulder to give her a little shake. The old woman with a look of intemperate scorn still on her face fell forwards across the counter with a loud noise, scattering several packages of Kleenex, bubble gum, and cake decorations over the floor. The man dropped the bottle-opener and giving May an outraged look and crying, 'I'm not responsible – it never happened before,' he ran out of the store to his car. May heard his car start and then she ran out after him, as if she wanted to call something, as if she wanted to call 'Help' or 'Stay.' But she did not call anything, she stood with her mouth open in the dust in front of the gas pumps, and he would not have heard her anyway; he gave one wildly negative wave out the window of his car and roared away to the north.

May stood outside the store and no other cars went by on the highway, no one came. The yards were empty in Black Horse. It had begun to rain a little while before and the drops of rain fell separately around her, sputtering in the dust.

Finally she went back and sat on the step of the store where the rain fell too. It was quite warm and she did not mind. She sat with her legs folded under her looking out at the road where she might walk now in any direction she liked, and the world which lay flat and accessible and full of silence in front of her. She sat and waited for that moment to come when she could not wait any longer, when she would have to get up and go into the store where it was darker than ever now on account of the rain and where her grandmother lay fallen across the counter dead, and what was more, victorious.

ALICE MUNRO, 1983

---

from The Grandmother

Grandmother knew she had not many days to live; therefore, like a good housewife, she set her house in order. First she made her peace with God, then she distributed her little property. Each one received a keepsake. For all who came to see her she had a kind word, and when they left, her eyes followed them till they were out of sight. Even the Princess, with the son of Hortense, came to see her, and when they were leaving, she looked long after them; for she knew she should never see them again. Even those dumb brutes, the cats and dogs, were not forgotten. She called them to her bed, caressed them and allowed Sultan to lick her hand. 'See to them,' she said to Adelka and the servants, 'for every creature is grateful for kindness.' But Vorsa she called to herself and said: 'When I die, Vorsilka, – I know my time is near at hand, for I dreamed last night that George came for me, – when I die do not forget to tell it to the bees, so that they shall not die out! The others might forget.' Grandmother knew that Vorsa would do it; for the others did not believe as she did and, therefore, might neglect to do it in time, even though they were willing to fulfill all her wishes.

Towards evening of the day following the children's return, Grandmother was quietly passing away. Barunka read to her the prayer of the dying, she repeating the words after her. Suddenly the lips ceased to move, the eye was fixed upon the crucifix hanging over the bed, the breathing stopped. The flame of life went out like a lamp in which the oil has been consumed.

Barunka closed her eyes. Christina opened the window 'so that the soul might have freedom to fly away'. Vorsa, not delaying among the weeping, hastened to the hive which the miller had set up for Grandmother some years before, and rapping upon it called three times: 'Bees, bees, our Grandmother is dead!' and then she sat down upon the bench under the lilacs and sobbed aloud. The miller went to Zernov, to have the bell tolled. He himself offered to do this service; he felt oppressed in the house; he wanted to go outside so that he could weep and ease his grief. 'I missed Victorka; how, then, can I forget Grandmother!' he said on the way. When the tolling of the bell was heard, announcing to the people that Grandmother was no more, the whole neighborhood wept.

BOZENA NEMEC, 1881

―――――

from Chronicle of My Mother

Towards evening, a young Buddhist from a village several miles away came for the ceremonial sutra readings prior to the placing of the body in the casket. At seven, Mitsu and my eldest daughter arrived from Tokyo, and after they had burned incense Mother was put in her casket. The female relatives swathed her arms and legs in white wrappings and placed a white covering on her head. Unlike the red head covering she had worn on her eighty-eighth birthday, the white one suited her well. She was the picture of one setting forth on a journey. Shikako placed a short dagger at Mother's breast; Soko, Mitsu, and the grandchildren surrounded her face with chrysanthemums.

That night a wake was held. Soko's daughter and son-in-law were there. This son-in-law was a young psychiatrist who had come to visit Mother in Izu from time to time during the past two years, and on each occasion he had examined her. I thought the relative tranquillity of her last years was largely the result of this young man's ministrations, and I thanked them both, my niece and her husband, on Mother's behalf.

This young doctor had last called about ten days before to examine Mother, and he said he had not at that time expected a drastic change in her condition. Then he told us the results of that particular examination.

'At the end,' he said laughingly, 'Granny really gave it to me. After I completed the examination and we were all drinking tea in Granny's room, Granny looked at me and asked my wife, who was seated beside me, who "that person" was. My wife told her I was the doctor who had just examined her, and Granny said softly, speaking to no one in particular, "There are all kinds of doctors." I was bowled over. She certainly took me down a peg.'

I thought that must have been a moment when, from within Mother's drastically withered body – which toward the end could almost be held in one hand – a final flicker of her old spirit suddenly flared.

Two days later, on the twenty-fourth, Mitsu, Soko, Shikako and her husband, and I rose at five. At six I stood in front of Mother's casket, then I stepped aside and watched from the sidelines as friends and relatives came forward and made their final farewells. Mother's face looked very young and very brave then. I used a stone to nail the coffin shut. The coffin was placed on the vehicle used as a hearse, and about twenty relatives and neighbors boarded it. The hearse went onto the Shimoda Highway, left the highway at Shuzen Temple, entered a road that ran along the Omi River, and traveled toward the crematorium through a small ravine heavily forested with maples. The scattered villages in the ravine appeared to be perpetually damp with dew, perhaps because of the shade of the surrounding maples.

When we arrived at the crematorium the priest read a sutra, after which the coffin was immediately placed in the cremation furnace. I followed one of the workers around to the back of the building, reentered through another door, and stood in front of the furnace opening. There, following his directions, I lit an oil-stained rag with a match. Instantaneously, red flames leaped on the other side of the furnace opening and the fire began to roar.

YASUSHI INOUE, translated by Jean Oda Moy, 1982

Many jars of considerable beauty had been lined up on the ruai . . . One, an exquisite T'ang, stood alone in a far corner. This, he told her, was reserved for a grandmother who had chosen it as her burial urn. 'But how will it fit inside?' she asked.

'She will,' he replied curtly.

'How?' He gazed at her. 'They will cut the top off, fold her up and stuff her in. They will drain a hole in the bottom for fluids and let them drain through the floor.'

C. S. GODSHALK, *Kalimantaan*, 1998

from Gods, Graves and Grandmothers

On Good Friday . . . grandmother died. I found her lying in bed in an unnatural position: she was curled up in an umbilical pose, one hand a little raised as though warding off attack, an expression of entreatment on her face. A thin stream of dried-up spittle clung to the side of her chin [. . .]

Lila came in to check up why grandmother was not up till so late. When she saw Ammi's body on the bed she went stiff with shock, and collapsed down on the floor . . . right where she had been standing. It was left to me to run out and inform Phoolwati and the Pandit.

They rushed to Ammi's room [. . .] Phoolwati slapped Lila tightly across her cheeks to revive her. They stood staring at grandmother's mortal remains. She looked small and pitiful, lying there on the cot. Phoolwati began weeping and the Pandit settled himself crosslegged in a corner of the room and went into a trance.

Her death quickly became a real tamasha. When he returned from his meditations Pandit Kailash Shastry sent me out of the room, insisting that my presence there was inappropriate. Phoolwati and I waited outside, looking round us at the suddenly unfamiliar temple.

Lila was not to be budged. Ultimately the Pandit had to relent to allow her to stay on [. . .] When they re-emerged, grandmother was no longer lying on the cot. She was seated on the ground in an improbable posture, with one hand still raised as if warding off the attack. I was too numbed to ask any questions, and in any case I knew very little of the rituals surrounding death. Perhaps all dead people were made to sit upright after death, perhaps it was part of the decorum.

The public who were by now thronging the temple precincts, were informed that my grandmother had not died, which was something mere mortals did. She had obtained maha-samadhi, by voluntarily relinquishing her consciousness to the larger universe.

There was a stampede. The police had to be called in to contain the mobs, who came, it seemed to me, not in curiosity but in genuine sorrow. Somewhere, somehow, my grandmother's incredible energy and power had touched and moved and changed them. They filed past the hastily executed cordons and barricades, to the courtyard where Ammi's body was propped up surrounded by lamps and camphor and incense. Their eyes seemed to be asking some questions, begging some hope, from grandmother's lopsided figure and raised arm.

The arm, Pandit Kailash Shastry informed them [. . .] was raised in blessing. Her samadhi was no ordinary samadhi, for even in death she remembered those she had left behind and gave them strength.

The mourners came with garlands and incense sticks and offerings, and soon the air was sticky and sweet and turgid with the smells of sweat and marigolds and incense [. . .] The day passed in crowds and confusion and fasting. No food was to be cooked for the next thirteen days, and my stomach was already churning with hunger. In desperation I ate a banana which somebody had offered to Hanumanji, and some mouldy sweetmeats I found in our room. Phoolwati got me tea from the tea-shop, and in all the activity and excitement I forgot that my grandmother was dead and I was absolutely alone in the world [. . .]

Since grandmother had obtained maha-samadhi, Pandit Kailash Shastry had decided she would be buried in the temple precinct, seated in the lotus position, as was usual in such cases. Phoolwati advocated cremation, she wanted a funeral procession with a band and balloons and rejoicing, as befitted one who had lived to over the age of ninety . . . No one consulted her next-of-kin on what was to be done and in any case I had no opinion on the matter.

My life had always possessed a haphazard and unreal quality, and now, when I contemplated my grandmother, contorted into an extraordinary death pose by the indefatigable Pandit, my last link with reality snapped. This was not my grandmother, in fact she had not been my grandmother for quite some time now. Yet whatever continuity and cohesion my life had ever contained had been gifted by her. What was to become of me?

On an impulse, I opened the old tin trunk which we had brought with us before Ryasuddin Rizvi had decamped with my mother [. . .] I rummaged and searched until I found what I was looking for, an amber chunni sequinned with silver, embroidered with gold [. . .] I carried it out and draped it around my grandmother's fragile shoulders, hugging and kissing her as I did so. She almost toppled over, but Phoolwati and [the] Pandit had gone to the tea-shop for a snack, and there was no one to restrain me.

Meanwhile the crowd surged on, hungry for miracles. As none had occurred, Pandit expeditiously decided to announce one. The chunni, he announced to a few close devotees, was a funerary gift from the Goddess Durga, Ma Shakti herself. It had mysteriously draped itself round the departed saint even as the mourners milled round her mortal remains. The chunni was saffron, the sacred colour – it was a sign, a blessing, a certain case of direct intervention from the cosmic powers.

The miracle created the expected stir [. . .] The crowds surged forward to witness the hand of God . . . The offerings of flowers and coconuts piled up and had to be continuously removed. They were taken back to Phoolwati's shop, from which she recycled them to the next batch of visitors. On Pandit Kailash Shastry's instructions, Phoolwati and I undressed grandmother and bathed her with Ganges water. After that we rubbed her body with ashes and sacred vibhuti. I averted my eyes from the sight of her nakedness, but Phoolwati seemed not in the least embarrassed. After this we wrapped her still-seated figure in two lengths of yellow cloth. Then the Pandit came in and ceremoniously placed a rosary of rudrashka beads around her neck.

A sort of bamboo basket suspended from a bamboo pole had been made ready for the occasion. Grandmother was perched on this and carried out back to the courtyard, where a circular grave, about five feet deep, had been dug for her.

The sound of castanets and temple bells and the tears and wails of her bhaktas echoed through the temple. Buckets of salt were poured into the pit, and then grandmother was lowered in, her legs still crossed in padmasana and her arm raised in benediction [. . .]

The ceremonies continued. Pandit Kailash Shastry filled up the hole with salt until it reached grandmother's neck, pressing it down until the head was immoveable.

Phoolwati put her arms around me and ushered me inside. The learned Brahmins picked up the coconuts from the pile in the basket which had been kept ready for the purpose, and systematically set about smashing Ammi's skull. Inside our room, deep in Phoolwati's sweaty embraces, I could hear the muffled sounds of coconuts breaking, somewhere in the course of which the prana spilled out of my grandmother's cephalus.

NAMITA GOKHALE, 1994

The Buck

When I was ten,
Grandmother told me
to get her stuffed when she died
like the buck head by the door
catching webs of evil
in his antlers.

She was to be seated
in the living room
on the sofa
(or chair, our choice),
facing the piano where I would play
Brahms, Liszt or Chopin.
Her eyes were to be open
(maybe a little touch of glass,
for sparkle) and looking upwards
(slightly to the right)
like St Teresa
or Sebastian pierced with arrows,
her hands – demurely covered
in white lace fingerless gloves –
propped holding the dome of heaven.
Her lips would be slightly open to show
slightly parted pearlized teeth,
our guardian angel, mother of God.

When we went shopping for perfume,
or oil to treat her skin,
or maybe a new pair of gloves
or a light-bulb for her ever-burning lamp,
she and her buck would wait for our
return.
Four times ten I was,
I still bang a keyboard all day;
dust floats up into my eyes, ears,
mouth, my nose and many pores –
shadow fingers reach
like antlers across my page.
She listens. I sing.

SUSANNA RICH, 1993

EPILOGUE

Late Song

I wrote this poem for my family and read it to them at the party:

It's a still morning, quiet and cloudy
the kind of grey day I like best;
they'll be here soon, the little kids first,
creeping up to try and frighten me,
then the tall young men, the slim boy
with the marvellous smile, the dark girl
subtle and secret; and the others,
the parents, my children, my friends –

and I think: these truly are my weather
my grey mornings and my rain at night,
my sparkling afternoons and my birdcall at daylight;
they are my game of hide and seek, my song
that flies from a high window. They are
my dragonflies dancing on silver water.

Without them I cannot move forward, I am
a broken signpost, a train fetched up on

a small siding, a dry voice buzzing in the
ears;
for they are also my blunders
and my forgiveness for blundering,
my road to the stars and my seagrass chair
in the sun. They fly where I cannot follow

and I – I am their branch, their tree.
My song is of the generations, it echoes
the old dialogue of the years; it is the tribal
chorus that no one may sing alone.

LAURIS EDMOND, 1998

AFTERWORD

S o; we reach the end, I think. This, the third of my autobiographical anthologies, is definitely the last. When I
started out, with the *Book of Twins and Doubles*, I did not
expect more books would follow. I had no idea even that it
would turn into an autobiographical exercise. Though perhaps
I should have guessed that what generated it – the need to
understand the nature of twinship after the death of my twin –
would tend to lead me that way. And so it did.

In the case of the book on sisters that followed *Twins*, the
idea was not even my own. But if I started in consequence
with marginally less enthusiasm, or certainly less sense of
involvement, it became clear early on that it would be a further
exercise in exploring family history; in particular in exploring
the grief brought on by the early death of many other women
in my family. Only when I was finishing it did we learn for sure
that there was a mutation on the BRCA1 gene on my mother's
side of the family, and that this was the cause of my mother's
death from breast cancer, of her sister's, of my twin's also. But
we hadn't needed to know the cause to encompass the grief.
We encompassed it all the more when, in the middle of my
research, my younger sister too fell prey to the disease; fortunately she, like me, has so far survived the experience.

In my introduction to this final book of the trilogy, on grandmothers, I have already explained the lack of them in my family. No more need be said here. But I would like to add that, as with the other books, the grief involved was only a small part of an otherwise immense and in some ways unexpected delight in exploring not only my own past, but that of my family, on both sides. Picking my father's brains endlessly and those of cousins and other relations – the only means to understanding our family history, given the lack of grandparents to tell the stories up till now – was pure pleasure. And that is to leave aside the pleasure I got from researching the material in which to embed these fragments of our family past.

In the case of this third book, of course it has not only been the past embedded there. I've also had to incorporate my consciousness of the fact that I as the grandmother will become increasingly an onlooker rather than a protagonist in our family drama. Imagining this future – which for a grandmother has to contain the prospect of dissolution – has, I'm aware, made for a somewhat different emphasis. In the previous books I was, autobiographically, trying to contain and understand the past in the light of our particular genetic heritage. Here, since I am still only in the early stages of grandmotherhood and of ageing, I am also using my family past, and that of my other contributors, not just as a means of illuminating what has been experienced but also as a means of mapping what is still to come.

The family story continues, of course. Medicine advances daily; but the mutation still lurks – may lurk – in the six women of the next generation down, and the four little girls in the generation after that. But their chances of surviving it get better all the time. In the young ones in particular, its effects may be counteracted by a simple pill. Let's hope. It is not possible to lay all the ghosts, of course; grief is a lifelong exercise of feelings, and even if there is the chance of much less grief to come, I – we – cannot help fearing sometimes that it may not have vanished altogether.

Perhaps, in the course of making these books, some small act of exorcism has been performed, for me at least. But my part is done now. The way my book of grandmothers has turned out makes it clear that it is time for me to sit back, to say farewell to this past on the one hand, and to relinquish the family future to the new generation on the other, while I move on into new projects of my own. And so I shall.

ACKNOWLEDGEMENTS

The editor and publishers wish to thank the following for permission to use copyright material: Abuelas de Plaza de Mayo for website material, 'Grandmothers of May Square' (1999); Age Concern for material from an Age Concern survey (1999); American Medical Women's Association for material from D. Joslin and R. Harrison, 'The "Hidden Patient": Older relatives raising children orphaned by AIDS', *JAMWA*, 53 (1998) pp. 65–71. Copyright © 1998 American Medical Women's Association, Inc.; Paul Bergne for material from Diana Holman-Hunt, *My Grandmothers and I*, Hamish Hamilton (1960) pp. 34–8, 81; Blackwell Publishers for material from Elizabeth Fisher Brown, 'Hehe Grandmothers', *Journal of Anthropological Institute of Great Britain and Ireland*, 65 (1935) pp. 92–5. Copyright © Royal Anthropological Institute; Marion Bull for material from 'The Cevennes', *Independent*, 3.10.98; Carcanet Press for material from Robert Graves, *I, Claudius* (1936) pp. 125–7; Constable Publishers for material from Mary Lavin, *Happiness* (1981) pp. 197–8; Shelagh Duckham Cox for original material written for this book; Curtis Brown on behalf of the authors for material from Angela Neustatter, *The Demon in the Eye*, Michael Joseph (1996) p. 262. Copyright © Angela Neustatter 1996; and Stella

29–30. English translation copyright © The Harvill Press 1969; John Hawkins & Associates, Inc. on behalf of the author for material from Joyce Carol Oates, 'Why Don't You Come Live With Me It's Time' from *Heat*, Plume, Penguin Books Inc. (1992) pp. 370–1. Copyright © 1992 by The Ontario Review, Inc.; David Higham Associates on behalf of the author for material from Jill Paton Walsh, 'The Year I Was Eight' included in *Allsorts 4*, Ann Thwaite, Macmillan (1967) p. 68; and on behalf of the Estate of the author for Edith Sitwell, *Taken Care Of*, Hutchinson (1964) pp. 62–5; Independent Newspapers (UK) Ltd for material from Rachel Sylvester, 'Grannies given a role in schools', *Independent on Sunday*, 1.11.98; Sue Arnold, 'A chain reaction in the ladies' lavatory', *Independent*, 10.7.99; Fergal Keane, 'A life of mother courage', *Independent*, 18.1.99; and Anne McElvoy, 'The times when granny knows more than the prime minister', *Independent*, 28.7.99; The Jerusalem Review for Ruth Fainlight, 'A Mother's Eyes', *The Jerusalem Review* (1999); H. Karnac (Books) Ltd for material from Phyllis Grosskurth, *Melanie Klein: Her Life and Works*, Maresfield Library (1986) Chap. 5; Alfred A. Knopf, a division of Random House, Inc., for Sharon Olds, 'Grandmother Love Poem' from *The Dead and the Living* by Sharon Olds (1983) p. 21. Copyright © 1983 by Sharon Olds; Kodansha International Ltd for material from Yasushi Inoue, *Chronicle of my Mother*, trs. Jean Oda Moy (1982), pp. 120–1, 162–3; Ellen Levine Literary Agency, Inc. on behalf of the author for material from Michael Ondaatje, *Running in the Family*, Victor Gollancz (1983) pp. 123–4. Copyright © 1982 by Michael Ondaatje; Lutyens & Rubinstein Literary Agency on behalf of the author for material from Peter Gordon, 'Stone Soup and Seaweed', *Food Illustrated* (1997). Copyright © 1997 Peter Gordon and Michael McGrath; Macmillan Publishers for material from Imogen Lycett Green, *Grandmother's Footsteps* (1994) pp. 19–22, 29–30; Ewan MacNaughton Associates for material from Celia Hall, 'Senile patients being abused, say families', *Electronic Telegraph*, 28.5.97; Robert Shrimsley, 'State could pay grannies to mind baby', *Electronic Telegraph*, 8.1.99; George Jones, 'Tony Blair, question and answer session', *Electronic Telegraph*, 27.7.99; A. J. McIlroy, 'Two fat ladies end their gang patrols', *Electronic Telegraph*, 9.3.98; and Graham Turner, 'Influential grandmother', *Electronic Telegraph*, 7.7.99; Ruth P. MacPherson for material from Esther Clark Wright, *Grandmother's Child*, (1959) pp. 28–9; The Orion Publishing Group for material from Alix Meynall, *Public Servant, Private Woman*, Victor Gollancz (1988), pp. 24, 25; Jared Diamond, *Why is Sex Fun?*, Phoenix (1997) pp. 157–9, 163–4; and Jane Goodall, *Through a Window*, Weidenfeld and Nicholson (1992) pp. 143; Orient Paperbacks for material from Nergis Dalal, *The Sisters* (1973) pp. 48–53; Oxford University Press for material from Flora Thompson, *Lark Rise to Candleford* (1945); Peter Owen Publishers for material from Alice Lin, *Grandmother Had No Name* (1990) pp. 13–4, 19–20; Patten Press for Grace Goldin, 'Persimmons and Hermit Crabs' in *Winter Rise* (1981) p. 51; Penguin Australia Ltd for material from Diane Bell, *Generations: Grandmothers, Mothers and Daughters* (1987); Penguin UK for material from Maxim Gorky, *My Childhood*, trs. Ronald Wilks, Penguin Classics (1966) pp. 64–6, 162–3. Copyright © Ronald Wilks 1966; Anton Chekhov, 'Peasants' from *The Kiss and Other Stories* by Anton Chekhov, trs. Ronald Wilks, Penguin Classics (1982) pp. 58–62. Copyright © Ronald Wilks 1982; and Margaret Forster, *Hidden Lives*: *A Family Memoir*, Viking (1995) pp. 266–7. Copyright © Margaret Forster 1995; Perseus Book Publishers, a member of Perseus Books, LLC, for material from Fatima Mernissi, *Dreams of Trespass: Tales of a Harem Girlhood*, pp. 24–6, 42. Copyright © 1994 by Fatima Mernissi; Peters, Fraser & Dunlop on behalf of the Estate of the author for material from Ivy Compton-Burnett, *Parents and Children*, Penguin Books (1941) pp. 13–5. Copyright © Estate of Ivy Compton-

Burnett 1941; and on behalf of the authors for material from Helen Simpson, 'Give Me Daughters Any Day' from *Four Bare Legs in a Bed* by Helen Simpson, Minerva (1991) pp. 37–40; and Frank O'Connor, 'First Confession' from *The Stories of Frank O'Connor*, Macmillan (1953) pp. 59–60; Random House UK for material from Gillian Rose, *Love's Work*, Chatto & Windus (1997) pp. 24–5; R. K. Narayan, *The Grandmother's Tale*, William Heinemann (1993) pp. 3–4; Gabriel Garcia Marquez, *Innocent Erendira*, trs. Gregory Ramassa, Jonathan Cape (1981) pp. 10–1; Marcel Proust, *Swann's Way*, trs. Scott Moncrieff and Terence Kilmartin, Chatto & Windus (1996) pp. 10–2; Margaret Atwood, *Bodily Harm*, Jonathan Cape (1982) pp. 53, 56–7; Clare Longrigg, *Mafia*, Chatto & Windus (1997) pp. 137–8; Celile de Banke, *American Plaid*, Hutchinson (1961) pp. 142–3; and Katherine Anne Porter, 'The Old Order' from *Collected Stories* by Katherine Anne Porter, Jonathan Cape (1964) pp. 26, 27–8; Rogers, Coleridge & White Ltd on behalf of the author for material from Frances Partridge, *Hanging On: Diaries Dec. '60–Aug. '63*, HarperCollins (1990) pp. 179–80; Routledge for material from Madeleine Kerr, *The People of Ship Street*, (1958) pp. 48–50; and with the Bertrand Russell Peace Foundation for Bertrand Russell, *The Autobiography of Bertrand Russell* (1961) pp. 20–2, 122; Sheil Land Associates on behalf of the author for material from Alan Sillitoe, *Raw Material* (1978) pp. 76–80; The Shoe String Press for material from Charlotte Ikeb, *Aging and Adaption* (1983) pp. 167, 173; The Society of Authors as Literary Trustees of the author for Walter de la Mare, 'The Cupboard' from *The Complete Poems of Walter de la Mare* (1969); South African Medical Journal for material from a letter by Barbara D. Richardson, *South African Medical Journal* 15.11.75; South Coast Poetry Journal for Susanna Rich, 'The Buck', *South Coast Poetry Journal*, 13 (1993); Stanford University Press for material from Henry Sharp, 'Old Age Among the Chipewyan', pp. 106–8, Pamela

the author for material from John Cheever, *The Common Day*, Ballantine Books (1980) pp. 30–2. Copyright © 1980 by John Cheever; Yale University Press for material from Leo Simmons, *Sun Chief: Autobiography of a Hopi Indian* (1942) pp. 47–8; and Toby W. Clyman and J. Vowles, *Russia Through Women's Eyes* (1996) pp. 349–52.

Every effort has been made to trace copyright holders and to obtain their permission for the use of copyright material. The authors and publishers will gladly receive any information enabling them to rectify any error or omission in subsequent editions.

REFERENCES

AGE CONCERN survey. *Across the Generations*, September 1998.

AIRLIE Mabell. *Thatched with Gold. The Memoirs of Mabell Countess of Airlie*, ed. Jennifer Ellis, Hutchinson 1962.

AKSAKOV S. T. (Sergei Timofeevich) (1791–1859). *Years of Childhood*, trs J. Duff, E. Arnold 1916.

AMOSS Pamela T. 'Coast Salish Elders' in *Other Ways of Growing Old*, ed. P. Amoss and S. Harrell, Stanford University Press 1981, p. 231.

ALCOTT Louisa M. *Little Men*, 1871.

ANDRESKI Iris. *Old Wives Tales*, Stock, New York 1970.

ANGELOU Maya. *I Know Why the Caged Bird Sings*, Virago 1984, pp. 26–32.

ANGIER Natalie. 'A Granddaughter's Fear' in *The Beauty of the Beastly*, Little, Brown 1995.

ANON. *The Jottings of an Old Woman of Eighty*, London 1853 (1794).

ANON. 'Autobiography of an Indian Fox Woman' in *40th Annual Report of the Bureau of American Ethnology to the Secretary of the Smithsonian Institute Washington 1918*, Washington GPO 1919.

ANON. *The Whole Life, Conversation, Birth, Parentage, and Education of Richard Mosley, aged about Sixteen Years old, for the Murther of his own Grand-mother, Mary Payton . . .* London, 1707.

ANON. *The Duties of the Decline of Life*, 1796.

ARNOLD Sue. *Independent* Weekend Review, 10 July 1999.

ATWOOD Margaret. *Bodily Harm*, Cape 1981, pp. 53, 56–7.

AUSTEN Jane. *Emma*, 1816.

AUSTER Paul. *The Invention of Solitude*, Faber and Faber 1989, pp. 41–52.

BABEL Isaac. 'Karl-Yankel', trs. Walter Morison in *The Collected Stories*, Penguin 1961.

BAILLIE Lady. *The Book of Noble Englishwomen*, Edinburgh 1875.

BALFOUR Jessie. *Tales of a Grandmother*, privately printed 1923.

BAKER Russell. *Growing Up*, Sidgwick and Jackson 1984, pp. 32–4.

BANKE Cecile de. *American Plaid*, Hutchinson 1961, pp. 142–3.

BANKS Melissa. Interview by Simon Hattenstone, *Guardian*, 19 July 1999.

BEAUVOIR Simone de. *Old Age*, trs. Patrick O'Brien, André Deutsch and Weidenfield and Nicolson 1971, p. 347.

BELL Diane. *Generations. Grandmothers, Mothers, Daughters*, McPhee Gribble, Penguin 1987.

BELL Vanessa. Letter to Angelica Garnett, quoted in Frances Spalding, *Vanessa Bell*, Ticknor and Fields 1983, p. 341.

BELL Vanessa. *Selected Letters*, ed. Regina Miller, Bloomsbury 1993.

BERNHARDT Lysiane. *Sarah Bernhardt, My Grandmother*, Hurst and Blackett 1949.

BIESELE Megan and Nancy Howell. 'The Old People Give You Life' in *Other Ways of Growing Old*, ed. P. Amoss and S. Harrell, Stanford University Press 1981, pp. 77–8.

BRADSTREET Anne. *The Works of Anne Bradstreet*, ed. Jeannine Hensley, Belknap Press, Cambridge, Mass. 1967, pp. 235–7.

BRUBAKER Timothy H. *Family Relationships in Later Life*, Sage Publications, Beverly Hills, CA 1983.

BULL Marion. 'The Cevennes', *Independent*, 3 October 1998.

BUNYAN John. *The Pilgrim's Progress*, ed. Roger Sharrock, Penguin 1970.

BURGESS Ernest ed. *Ageing in Western Societies*, University of Chicago Press 1960, pp. 286, 439.

BURGESS Helene. *Our Lives, Our Dreams, Soviet Women Speak*, Progress Publisher, Moscow 1988, pp. 777–8.

CARSTAIRS G. M. *The Death of a Witch*, Hutchinson 1983, p. 19.

CATHER Willa. 'Old Mrs Harris' in *Obscure Destinies*, Cassell, Australia 1932, pp. 94–9, 132–4.

CHADWICK Douglas. *The Fate of the Elephant*, Viking 1992, p. 38.

CHEEVER John. 'The Common Day' in *The Stories of John Cheever*, Ballantine Books, New York 1980, pp. 30–2.

CHEKHOV Anton. 'Peasants' in *The Kiss*, trs. Ronald Wilks, Penguin 1982, pp. 58–62.

CHERNIN Kim. *In My Mother's House*, Virago 1985, pp. 300, 305.

CLARK M. and B. Anderson. *Culture and Aging*, Charles C. Thomas, Springfield, Illinois 1967, pp. 292–3.

COLE Thomas. *The Journey of Life*, Cambridge University Press 1992, p. 53.

COLES Robert. 'Una Anciana' in *The Old People of New Mexico*, University of New Mexico Press 1970.

COLSON Elizabeth and Thayer Scudder. 'Old Age in Gwembe District' in *Other Ways of Growing Old*, ed. P. Amoss and S. Harrell, Stanford University Press 1981, pp. 149–50.

COMPTON-BURNETT, Ivy. *Parents and Children*, Cambridge University Press 1947.

CORDER Susanna. *Life of Elizabeth Fry*, London 1853, p. 330.

COX Shelagh Duckham. Original material written for this book.

CUNNINGHAM-BURLEY Sarah. 'Becoming a Grandmother', *Aging and Society*, 1987, p. 467.

DALAL Nergis. *The Sisters*, Hind Pocket Books, Delhi 1973.

DAVIES-ADETUGBO Anita A. 'Breastfeeding in Rural Yoruba Communities', *Social Science and Medicine*, vol. 45, No. 1, 1997, pp. 118–19.

DELAFIELD E. M. *The Provincial Lady in America*, Virago 1984.

DE LA MARE Walter. 'The Cupboard' in *Peacock Pie*, Constable and Co. 1904, p. 42.

DEVI Gayatri. *A Princess Remembers*, Century Publishing 1984.

DIAMOND Jared. *Why Is Sex Fun?*, Phoenix 1998, pp. 154–65.

DICKSON A. *Menopause: The Woman's View*, Grapevine 1987.

DIO. *Roman History*, trs. Ernest Cary, Loeb Classical Library, Heinemann 1924.

DOBRÉE 'Louisa Emily'. In *The Housewife*, vol. IV, 1889.

DOUDNEY Sarah. *The Girl's Own Paper*, 22 December 1883.

DOSTOYEVSKY Fyodor. *The Gambler*, trs. Constance Garnett, Heinemann 1949, pp. 65–9.

DUNCAN Robert. *The Structure of Rime IV. Opening of the Field*, Grove Press, New York 1960.

DUNLEAVY Ryan L. 'Grandson Faked Kidnap in £10,000 Plot', *Electronic Telegraph*, 15 February 1999.

EDMOND Lauris. Interview; 'Late Song', Auckland University Press 1998; original material written for this book.

ELLISON Dorothy. *Tales of a Grandmother*, privately printed c. 1930s.

ERDRICH Louise. *The Bingo Palace*, Flamingo 1994, pp. 261–5.

ERIKSON E. and J. Kivnick. *Vital Involvement in Old Age*, W. W. Norton 1986.

EURIPIDES. *The Trojan Women*, trs. Gilbert Murray, London 1905.

FAINLIGHT Ruth. 'A Mother's Eyes', *Jerusalem Review*, 1999.

FERBER Edna. 'Grandma Isn't Playing' in *One Basket*, Simon and Schuster, New York 1947, pp. 157–61.

FINE Anne. *The Granny Project*, Penguin 1983.

FIRTH Raymond. *We the Tikopia*, George Allen and Unwin 1930.

FISHER BROWN Elizabeth. 'Hehe Grandmothers', *Journal of Anthropological Institute of Great Britain and Ireland*, vol. 65, 1935, pp. 91–2.

FORSTER Margaret. *Hidden Lives*, Penguin 1996, pp. 266–7.

FORD Janet and Ruth Sinclair. *Sixty Years On*, Women's Press 1987.

FRY Elizabeth. *Memories of Her Mother, by R.E.C.* (for private circulation), 1845, p. 26.

FULFORD Roger ed. *Darling Child. Correspondence of Queen Victoria and the Crown Princess of Prussia*, Evans Brothers 1976.

GARCÍA MÁRQUEZ Gabriel. 'Innocent Eréndira' in *Innocent Eréndira*, trs. Gregory Rabassa, Picador 1981.

GATTY Juliana Horatia. 'Mrs Overtheway's Remembrances', 1866.

GENTLEMAN Amelia. 'Daughter Rails Over "Absent" Granny', *Guardian*, 24 March 1999.

GIBBONS Stella. *Cold Comfort Farm*, Penguin 1932.

GIBBS Geoffrey. *Guardian*, 20 May 1998, p. 7.

GIELE Janet Zollinger. 'Adulthood as Transcendence of Age and Sex' in *Themes of Work and Love in Adulthood*, ed. N. Smelser, E. Erikson, Grant McIntyre 1980, p. 166.

GILBERT Kevin. *Because the White Man'll Never Do It*, Angus and Robertson (Australia) 1973, p. 136.

GLYN Elinor. *Reflections of Ambrosine*, Duckworth 1903, pp. 5–6.

GLYN Elinor. *The Sayings of Grandmothers and Others*, Duckworth 1908.

GODSHALK C. S. *Kalimantaan*, Little, Brown 1998.

GOKHALE Namita. *Gods, Graves and Grandmothers*, Rupa and Co., New Delhi 1994.

GOLDIN Grace. 'Persimmons and Hermit Crabs' in *Winter Rise*, Patten Press, Richmond, Surrey 1981.

GOLDSMITH Annabel. 'At Last I Am a Grandmother', *Electronic Telegraph*, 9 May 1998.

GOMBAR Christina. 'The End of the Reign of Queen Helen' in *For She Is the Tree of Life*, Conari Press, Emeryville, CA 1994.

GOMEZ Joan. *Sixty Something. A Positive Handbook to the Third Age of Life*, Thorson 1993.

GOODALL Jane. *Through a Window*, Weidenfeld and Nicolson 1992.

GORDON Peter. 'Stone Soup and Seaweed', originally printed in an airline magazine, 1997.

GORKY Maxim. *My Childhood*, trs. Ronald Wilks, Penguin 1966, pp. 60–3, 64–7, 162–4.

GRAHAM Harry. 'Indifference' in *More Ruthless Rhymes*, E. Arnold 1930.

GRAHAM Harry. 'Inconsiderate Hannah' in *Ruthless Rhymes for Heartless Homes*, E. Arnold 1909.

GRANDMOTHERS OF MAY SQUARE (Internet).

GRAVES Robert. *I, Claudius*, Arthur Baker 1936, pp. 124–7.

GREEN Rayna. from 'The Bawdy Lore of Southern Women', *Southern Exposure*, Institute for Southern Studies 1977, pp. 30–1.

GREER Germaine. *The Change*, Hamish Hamilton, London 1991.

GROSSKURTH Phyllis. *Melanie Klein*, Maresfield Library 1987.

Guardian, 'The Gran Canyon', December 1996.

Guardian, 20 March 1998.

GUTMANN David. *Reclaimed Powers*, Hutchinson 1988, pp. 161–2.

HADER Marvin. 'Importance of Grandparents in Family Life', in *Family Process*, vol. 4, 1965, p. 236.

HAGESTEAD Gunhild O. 'Women and Grandparents as Kin-keepers' in *Our Aging Society*, ed. A. Pifer and L. Bronte, Norton, New York 1986, p. 148.

HAGESTEAD Gunhild O. 'Continuity and Connectedness' in *Grandparent-hood*, ed. R. Bengston, Sage 1985.

HALL Celia. *Daily Telegraph*, 28 May 1997.

HALL Nor. *The Moon and the Virgin*, Women's Press 1980.

HALLE E. et al. 'The Role of Grandmothers in Transsexualism', *American Journal of Psychiatry*, April 1980, p. 497.

HARDY Thomas. 'In Childbed' in *Collected Poems*, Macmillan 1962.

HARRELL Stevan. 'Growing Old in Rural Taiwan' in *Other Ways of Growing Old*, ed. P. Amoss and S. Harrell, Stanford University Press 1981, pp. 207–9.

HARRISON Joslin. 'The Hidden Patient', *Journal of the American Medical Women's Association*, Spring 1998, pp. 47–8.

HEAD Bessie. 'The Special One', 1977.

HERON Liz. In *Truth, Dare or Promise*, Virago 1985.

HOBSON Sarah. *Family Web*, John Murray 1978.

HOLMBURG Allan R. 'Cultural Differences and the Concept of Time' in *Aging and Leisure*, ed. R. W. Kleemeier, Oxford University Press, New York 1961, pp. 88–9, 93.

HOLMES Oliver Wendell. *Over the Teacups*, Boston 1891.

HRDY Sarah Blaffer. *The Woman That Never Evolved*, Harvard University Press 1981, pp. 76–8, 93.

HUDSON Mark. *Our Grandmothers' Drums*, Secker and Warburg 1989, p. 127.

HUGHES Shirley. Interview.

HUNT Diana Holman. *My Grandmothers and I*, Hamish Hamilton 1960.

IKEB Charlotte. *Aging and Adaption*, Archon Books, Hamdon, CT 1983, p. 175.

Independent, 2 April 1997, 2 December 1997.

Independent, Pandora column, April 1999.

INOUE Yasushi. *Chronicle of My Mother*, trs. Jean Oda Moy, Kodansha International, Tokyo, Harper & Row, New York 1982.

ITO Susan. 'Obasan in Suburbia' in *For She Is the Tree of Life*, Conari Press, Emeryville, CA 1994.

JOSLIN D. and R. Harrison. 'The "Hidden Patient": Older Relatives Raising Children Orphaned by AIDS', *Journal of the American Medical Women's Association*, Spring 1998, 53(2), pp. 65–71, 76.

JONES George. *Electronic Telegraph*, 27 July 1999.

JUNG Chang. *Wild Swans*, HarperCollins 1991, pp. 264–5.

KATZ Elizabeth. *Mid-life*, Fourth Estate 1997.

KAY Margarita and Marianne Yoder. 'Hot and Cold in Women's Therapeutics', *Social Science and Medicine*, vol. 25, No. 4, 1987, pp. 350–1.

KEANE Fergal. 'A Life of Mother Courage', *Independent*, 18 January 1999.

KERR Madeline. *The People of Ship Street*, Routledge and Kegan Paul 1958, pp. 48–50.

KIDD Dudley. *The Essential Kafir*, A. & C. Black 1925.

KINGSTON Maxine Hong. *The Woman Warrior*, Allen Lane 1977.

KITZINGER Sheila. *Becoming a Grandmother*, Simon & Schuster 1997.

KOBIAKOVA Alexsandra. In *Russia Through Women's Eyes*, ed. T. W. Clyman and J. Vowles, Yale University Press 1996.

KOLI Yash ed. *The Women of Punjab*, Chic Publications 1983.

KORNHABER A. and K. Woodward. *Grandparents, Grandchildren, the Vital Connection*, Doubleday 1981, p. 1.

KRAMMER Sydelle and Jenny Masur eds. *Jewish Grandmothers*, Beacon Press, Boston 1976, p. 148.

LA TOUR DU PIN Madame de. *Memoirs*, trs. Felice Harcourt, Harvill 1969, pp. 24–30.

LAURENCE Margaret. *The Stone Angel*, Macmillan 1964, pp. 252–4.

LAVIN Mary. 'Happiness' in *Selected Stories*, Penguin 1981, pp. 197–8.

LAW Phyllida. Author's interview.

LE GUIN Ursula. 'The Space Crone' in *Dancing at the Edge of the World*, Grove Atlantic 1989, Paladin 1992.

LEWIS Oscar et al. *Four Women Living the Revolution*, University of Illinois Press 1977.

LIENHARDT P. A. 'Some Social Aspects of the Trucial States' in *The Arabian Peninsula*, ed. D. Hopwood, George Allen and Unwin 1972.

LIMB Sue. *Growing Pains*, Radio Four, 31 October 1998.

LIVY. *The History of Rome*, trs. D. Spillen, George Bell and Co. 1896, Book II, Chapter 40.

LOCKE John. Journal (1681) in *Life and Letters of John Locke*.

LONGRIGG Clare. 'Grandma Heroin' in *Mafia Women*, Chatto & Windus 1997.

LORENZ Gordon. 'There's No One Quite Like Grandma', EMI Music Publishing 1980.

LU Hsun. 'The Waves of the Wind' in *Chinese Short Stories*, ed. and trs. Yuan Chia Hua and Robert Paine, Transatlantic Arts 1946.

LYCETT GREEN Imogen. *Grandmother's Footsteps*, Macmillan 1994.

MACDERMOTT Mark J. 'Depression in Grandmothers', *Medical Journal of Australia*, 6 April 1987.

MANSFIELD Katherine. 'At the Bay' in *Collected Stories*, Book Club Associates 1973, pp. 226–7.

MANSFIELD Katherine. 'The Voyage' in *Collected Stories*, Book Club Associates 1973, pp. 325–7.

MCELROY Anne. *Independent*, 28 July 1999.

MCILROE. *Electronic Telegraph*, 9 March 1998.

MEAD Margaret. *Blackberry Winter*, Angus and Robertson 1973, pp. 274–7, 283–4

MERNISSI Fatima. *The Harem Within*, Bantam 1995, pp. 24–6, 42.

MEYNELL Alix. *What Grandmother Said*, Colt, Cambridge 1998.

MINKLER Meredith et al. 'Raising Crack Cocaine Grandchildren', *American Journal of Psychiatry* 64(1), January 1994, pp. 20–9.

MOLESWORTH Mrs. *Grandmother Dear*, London 1878.

MOORE Susanna. *The Whiteness of Bones*, Chatto & Windus 1981.

MORGAN Sally. *My Place*, Fremantle Arts Centre Press 1987, pp. 97–100.

MUNRO Alice. 'A Trip to the Coast' in *Dance of the Happy Shades*, Penguin 1983, pp. 186–9.

NARAYAN R. K. *The Grandmother's Tale*, Heinemann 1993, pp. 3–4.

NEMEC Bozena. *The Grandmother*, trs. Frances Gregor, Chicago 1881.

NEUSTATTER Angela. *Look the Demon in the Eye*, Michael Joseph 1996.

NOY Dov ed. *Folk Tales of Israel*, Routledge and Kegan Paul 1963, pp. 25–7.

O'CONNOR Frank. 'First Confession' in *The Stories of Frank O'Connor*, Hamish Hamilton 1953, pp. 59–60.

OATES Joyce Carol. 'Why Don't You Come Live with Me It's Time' in *Heat*, Penguin, USA 1992, pp. 368–9.

OLD Sharon. 'Grandmother Love Poem' in *The Sign of Saturn. Poems 1980–87*, Secker and Warburg 1992, p. 21.

ONDAATJE Michael. *Running in the Family*, Gollancz 1983, pp. 122–4.

OZ Amos. 'How to Cure a Fanatic' from the BBC lecture series, 'Sounding the Century' 1999.

PANZINI Alfredo. 'The Right of the Old and Young' in *Great Italian Short Stories*, ed. Decio Pettoello, Ernest Benn 1930.

PAISH C. H. In *Work and Leisure*, February 1893.

PARCA Gabriella ed. *Italian Women Confess*, George Allen and Unwin 1963, p. 178.

PARTRIDGE Frances. *Hanging On. Diaries Dec 1960–Aug 1963*, Flamingo, pp. 178–80.

PECKHAM Ted. *Grandma Rolled Her Own*, Coward McCann, New York 1954.

PERRAULT Charles (1628–1703). 'The Sleeping Beauty in the Wood', trs. A. E. Johnson, Constable 1921.

PLOSS H. and M. Butels. *Das Weib* in Helene Deutsch, *The Psychology of Women*, Grune and Stratton, New York 1945, p. 486.

PORTER Katherine Anne. 'The Old Order' in *Collected Stories*, Jonathan Cape 1964, pp. 89–91.

PROUST Marcel. *Swann's Way*, trs. C. K. Scott Moncrieff and Terence Kilmartin, revised Dennis Enright, Vintage 1996, pp. 10–12.

PU LIN Alice Murong. *Grandmother Had No Name*, Peter Owen 1990, pp. 13, 19–20.

RICH Susanna. 'The Buck', *South Coast Poetry Journal*, No. 13, June 1993, State University of California, Fullerton, CA.

RICHARDSON Barbara D. 'Lactation in Grandmothers', letter to the *South African Medical Journal*, 15 Nov 1975, p. 2028.

ROSE Gillian. *Love's Work*, Vintage 1997, pp. 24–5.

ROTH H. Ling. *The Natives of Sarawak and British North Borneo*, Truslove and Hanson 1896.

ROY Manisha. *Bengali Women*, University of Chicago Press 1975.

RUSSELL Bertrand. *Autobiography*, George Allen and Unwin 1961, pp. 20–22, 122.

SAND George. *Flaubert–Sand. The Correspondence*, trs. F. Steegmuller and B. Bray, Harvill 1993, p. 57.

SARTRE Jean-Paul. *The Words*, Fawcett World Library, New York 1977, p. 14.

SENIOR Olive. 'Guinea Hen' in *Common . . . Places*, Commonwealth Institute poetry website.

SHARP Henry S. 'Old Age Among the Chipewyan' in *Other Ways of Growing Old*, ed. P. Amoss and S. Harrell, Stanford University Press 1981, pp. 106–8.

SHOSTAK Marjorie. *Nisa. The Life and Words of a !Kung Woman*, Harvard University Press 1981.

SHRIMSLEY Robert. 'State Could Pay Grannies to Mind Baby', *Electronic Telegraph*, 8 January 1999.

SIBBALD Susan. *Memoirs*, ed. Francis Pager Hett, John Lane 1926.

SILLITOE Alan. *Raw Material*, Star Books 1978, pp. 76–80.

SIMMONS Leo. *Role of the Aged in Primitive Societies*, Yale University Press 1945, p. 86.

SIMMONS Leo ed. *Sun Chief*, Yale University Press 1942, pp. 47–50.

SIMPSON Helen. 'Give Me Daughters Any Day' in *Four Bare Legs in a Bed*, Minerva 1991, pp. 42–4.

SINGH Renuka. *The Oppression of Women by Women*, Data Centre, New Delhi 1980, p. 28.

SITWELL Edith. *Taken Care Of*, Atheneum, New York 1965.

SKEAT and Blagden. 'Granny Long-breasts' in *Races of the Malay Peninsula*, Macmillan 1906.

SLANSKAIA Ekaterina. In *Russia Through Women's Eyes*, ed. T. W. Clyman and J. Vowles, Yale University Press 1996.

SMITH Hannah Whitall. *A Quaker Grandmother* (written and ed. Ray Strachey), N. Y. Fleming, H. Revel and Co., London and Edinburgh 1914, pp. 12–13, 25–6, 35–6.

SMITH Mary F. *Baha of Karo*, Faber 1954, pp. 143–6.

SMITH Pauline. 'Desolation' in *The Little Karoo*, Travellers Library 1950.

SONUGA-BARKE E. J. et al. 'The Mental Health of Muslim Mothers', *British Journal of Clinical Psychology*, November 1998, p. 399.

SPALDING Frances. *Vanessa Bell*, Ticknor and Fields 1983.

SPENCER J. 'Shawnee Folk Lore', *Journal of American Folklore* 22, pp. 319–26.

SPINAGE C. A. *Elephants*, T. & A. D. Poyser 1994, pp. 128–9.

SPRING-RICE Margery (d. 1971). *Working Class Wives*, Virago 1981, p. 53.

ST HELIER Lady. *Memories of Fifty Years*, 1909.

STRACHEY Ray. See Smith, Hannah Whitall.

SUETONIUS (c. 70–c. 122). *Lives of the Twelve Caesars*, trs. H. M. Bird, Argus Books, USA 1930.

SYLVESTER Rachel. 'Grannies Given a Role in Schools', *Independent*, 2 November 1998.

TENNYSON Alfred Lord. 'The Grandmother' in *Poetical Works*, Collins Clear Type Press.

THOMAS Hilary M. *Grandmother Extraordinary*, Stewart Williams 1979, pp. 185–8.

THOMPSON Flora. *Lark Rise to Candleford*, Penguin 1973, pp. 94–6, 112–13.

THOMPSON Paul, Catherine Itzi and Michelle Abendstern. *I Don't Feel Old*, Oxford University Press 1990, pp. 187, 248.

TOWNSEND Peter. *The Family Life of Old People*, Routledge and Kegan Paul 1959, pp. 90–1.

TRAPIDO Barbara. *Juggling*, Hamish Hamilton 1994, pp. 96–7.

TURNER Graham. 'The Real Queen Mother', *Electronic Telegraph*, 7 July 1999.

VALENTINE Tim. 'Great-Grandma's Swing'. Internet 1997.

VERBITSKAIA Anastasia. In *Russia Through Women's Eyes,* ed. T. W. Clyman and J. Vowles, Yale University Press 1996.

VICTORIA Queen. *Dearest Child. Letters between Queen Victoria and the Princess Royal*, ed. Roger Fulford, Evans Brothers 1964, pp. 159, 160–1.

VOLLMER Hermann. 'The Grandmother. A Problem in Child-Rearing', *American Journal of Orthopsychiatry*, 1938, pp. 378–82.

WAKESCHLAG et al. 'Not Just Ghosts in the Nursery', *Child Development* 1996, p. 2141.

WALKERDINE Valerie. In *Truth, Dare or Promise*, Virago 1985.

WALSH Jill Paton. 'The Year I Was Eight' in *Allsorts* 4, Macmillan 1967.

WARNER Sylvia Townsend. 'The Children's Grandmother' in *Winter in the Air*, Chatto & Windus 1955, pp. 35–7.

WATERHOUSE Keith. from the *Independent* Weekend Review, 7 August 1999.

WEBB Mary. *The House in Dormer Forest*.

WELTY Eudora. *One Writer's Beginnings*, Faber & Faber 1985.

WHITE Isobel, Diane Barwick and Betty Meehan. *Fighters and Singers*, George Allen and Unwin, Sydney 1985.

WILLIAMS Cayte. 'Why Grandmother, What Big Heels You've Got' from 'Real People', *Independent on Sunday*, 1 August 1999.

WILLIAMS Mary Hope. *The Nine Lives of Minnie Winder or I Did What I Could*, Minerva 1997, p. 207.

WOOD V. and J. F. Robertson. 'The Significance of Grandparenthood' in *Time, Roles and Self in Old Age*, ed. J. F. Gubrium, Human Sciences Press, New York 1976, pp. 286–7.

WORDSWORTH William. 'To ——, in Her Seventieth Year' (1824) in *Collected Poems*, Oxford University Press 1904.

WRIGHT Esther Clark. *Grandmother's Child*, privately published, Nova Scotia, Wolfville, Canada 1959.